Professors and Their Politics

Professors and Their Politics

Edited by
NEIL GROSS and SOLON SIMMONS

Johns Hopkins University Press
Baltimore

© 2014 Johns Hopkins University Press
All rights reserved. Published 2014
Printed in the United States of America on acid-free paper

2 4 6 8 9 7 5 3 1

Johns Hopkins University Press
2715 North Charles Street
Baltimore, Maryland 21218-4363
www.press.jhu.edu

Library of Congress Cataloging-in-Publication Data

Professors and their politics / edited by Neil Gross and Solon Simmons.
   pages cm
   Includes bibliographical references and index.
   ISBN-13: 978-1-4214-1334-1 (pbk. : alk. paper)
   ISBN-13: 978-1-4214-1335-8 (electronic)
   ISBN-10: 1-4214-1334-5 (pbk. : alk. paper)
   ISBN-10: 1-4214-1335-3 (electronic)
   1. College teachers—United States—Political activity.   2. College teachers—
United States—Attitudes.   I. Gross, Neil, 1971–.   II. Simmons, Solon.
   LB2331.72.P77 2014
   378.1'2—dc23   2013035780

A catalog record for this book is available from the British Library.

*Special discounts are available for bulk purchases of this book. For more information,
please contact Special Sales at 410-516-6936 or specialsales@press.jhu.edu.*

Johns Hopkins University Press uses environmentally friendly book materials,
including recycled text paper that is composed of at least 30 percent
post-consumer waste, whenever possible.

CONTENTS

Professors and Their Politics

Introduction

If journalists, op-ed writers, and reformers are to be believed, American higher education is in crisis. True, college and university enrollments are at an all-time high. But amid skyrocketing tuition costs, reports that undergraduates are studying—and learning—less than in decades past, moral scandals around college athletics and executive pay, rising international competition, and the appearance of online learning technologies that call into question the traditional faculty role, critics have been busy suggesting that the system has reached a breaking point (e.g., Arum and Roksa 2011; Delbanaco 2012; Hacker and Driefus 2010; Taylor 2010). Public confidence in higher education is down, as measured by opinion polls, and it is in this context that a variety of proposals for reform have been floated. These range from plans to overhaul the curriculum to calls for more seamless transfer arrangements between community colleges and four-year institutions, efforts at increasing transparency around college pricing and postgraduation job placement, and manifestos for a "revolution in global online higher education" (Friedman 2013).

Politics is a subtext in many of these discussions. Critics and reformers on the left argue that the root cause of higher education's malaise is that colleges and universities have been remade by the forces of neoliberalism (Kleinman, Feinstein, and Downey 2013; Kleinman and Vallas 2001; Newfield 2011; Rhoten and Calhoun 2011). Having adapted all too well to the market sensibilities that came to pervade other social spheres beginning in the 1970s, institutions of higher education are now said to suffer from a withdrawal of state support—which has required the offloading of operating costs onto students—from the embrace of low-road employment strategies, from too much willingness to bend to the whims of corporate donors, and from practices of "academic capitalism" involving the forging of new and unsavory relationships between universities, science, and the knowledge economy (Slaughter and Rhoads 2009). But it is not just the institutions that suffer. So, too, according to this line of thought, do their personnel and students—and through them, democracy, as American higher education, catering increasingly to the affluent, retreats from its historic twentieth-century role as a leveler of social inequality and provider of public culture. Conservative business elites, politicians, and wealthy alumni are sometimes portrayed as hidden hands behind these developments.

On the other side, conservative intellectuals and commentators do nothing to hide their deep dissatisfaction with American colleges, which they see as bastions of liberal or even radical politics. If the system is in need of reform, conservatives argue, it is because the professoriate, one of the most left-leaning occupational groups, has watered down educational standards to make room for pedagogy that borders on indoctrination, has resisted accountability standards, and has placed its own preferences—for esoteric research and low teaching loads—above those of students (e.g., California Association of Scholars 2012; Riley 2011).

This book, a collection of original studies on the politics of the university by sociologists, historians, and a scholar of international relations, does not directly weigh in on these debates. Setting aside both sweeping political-economic interpretation and partisan polemic, it addresses in social scientific terms questions to do with the relationship between higher education and politics—with a special focus on the faculty—as politics is conventionally understood: contestation over the power of the state. What in fact are the political views of American academicians today? What policies and parties do they favor? What accounts for their views and for the views of students? Do professors' political commitments carry over into their research and teaching and, if so, to what effect? And what kinds of reactions outside the university are generated by professorial or student politics, real or perceived? In exploring questions like these, the book marks a turn in the sociological study of colleges and universities, signaling a recognition—once common but now too often ignored—that institutions of higher education may be as important for their interchange with the political arena as for their other societal effects. At the same time, although the book does not take a stance in current policy discussions, by virtue of its close examination of academics and their politics it sheds light on an important part of the terrain over which higher education reformers struggle—and thus, we hope, will be of as much interest to the higher education policy community as to social scientists.

The American college and university sector is enormous. It consists of more than four thousand institutions of higher education, which together enroll more than twenty million students. A third of young American adults earn bachelor's degrees, and higher education—through the training it provides, the technology spillovers it produces, and the employment opportunities it offers—has become a major driver of economic growth in an otherwise sluggish economy.

A small subfield, the sociology of higher education is replete with rich studies of this sector. The bulk of the scholarship in the area explores the relationship between higher education and social inequality, treating the main product of colleges and universities as educational credentials of varying value on the labor market and examining the extent to which the status characteristics of young people, such as their class background, race, or gender, advantage or disadvantage them in the scramble for credentials. Other important strands of work consider the social experiences of students, look at institutions of higher education through an organizational lens, and document the shifting fate of the academic profession (for a review, see Stevens, Armstrong, and Arum 2008).

Only rarely have sociologists of higher education turned their attention to politics. Instead, study of the higher education–politics nexus has generally been left to scholars working under the banner of the sociology of intellectuals, to a small number of higher education researchers with links to political science, and to historians.

The sociology of intellectuals, for its part, is a venerable tradition of inquiry dating back to the founding of the discipline. Canonical figures in sociology such as Karl Marx, Emile Durkheim, and Max Weber wrote extensively about intellectuals—not simply about academics, whose social significance, though on the rise in mid- to late-nineteenth-century Europe, was not what it is today, but about all manner of knowledge producers, from priests and prophets who penned religious texts to journalists who formed part of the revolutionary vanguard. For Marx and Weber, at least, and for the Hungarian-born sociologist Karl Mannheim, who in the 1920s and 1930s sought to parlay general social-theoretical interest in intellectuals into a coherent research program, no question was more important than the relationship between intellectuals' politics and their class situation. Are intellectuals merely spokespersons for their class interests—in their personal convictions, their advocacy for one ideology or another, or their embrace of an intellectual system with political implications—with the nature of those interests depending on the backgrounds from which thinkers hail in a given historical situation? Or can other factors—educational experiences, generational dynamics, religious commitments, cross-class alliances—sometimes intervene to push intellectuals' politics and ideas in unexpected directions, with consequences for social power?

As the intellectual role, which had already transformed between Marx's day and Mannheim's, was remade once again in the mid twentieth century, the sociology of intellectuals changed with it. Educational expansion, driven partly by an increase in white-collar work, broadened the intellectual stratum in both the capitalist West and the state-socialist Eastern bloc. In this context, to whom precisely should the label "intellectual" be applied, sociologists asked. In addition, the sciences, natural and social, seemed poised, because of their rapid growth, to displace more traditional sources of cultural authority, and sociologists of intellectual life attended to the battles they believed would follow—to skirmishes between what Edward Shils (1972) memorably called "the intellectuals and the powers." In the 1960s and 1970s, campus protests raised new questions and concerns.

And yet class was never far below the surface in the writings of sociologists of intellectuals during this time. In *The Future of Intellectuals and the Rise of the New Class* (1979), for instance, firebrand sociologist Alvin Gouldner took up the idea that the postwar intelligentsia, encompassing academics, writers, journalists, research scientists, computer programmers, and others, might be starting to form a class of its own. Having as one of its hallmarks the embrace of what Gouldner called a "culture of critical discourse," this "New Class" would sometimes act in its own interests—to secure positional advantage for its members—but was also capable, Gouldner asserted, of acting in the service of universal interests and might thus fundamentally alter democratic politics. For Seymour Martin Lipset, who wrote extensively about faculty and student politics in the New Left era, the primary goal was to understand the roots and limits of campus radicalism, which he himself had been swept up in as a student in the 1930s and 1940s before coming under moderating influences. But Lipset made as much as did Mannheim of the failure of traditional theories of class politics to explain the liberal political sympathies of the professoriate—a privileged, high-status group that might be thought inclined toward conservatism (Ladd and Lipset 1976). When French sociologist Pierre Bourdieu (1988 [1984]) set his analytic sights on the May 1968 student uprising in Paris, using it as an occasion to develop a sociological theory of French academic life, class was again a major concern. To be sure, Bourdieu elaborated an account of the "academic field" that had as an aim to discredit the hypothesis that ideas could be understood as a simple reflection of thinkers' relationship to the means of production. But another way of reading Bourdieu is to see him as developing a more sophisticated theory of class, and this theory—which borrows from Weber in recognizing the multidimensionality of social stratification—ends up being deployed, in books like *Dis-*

tinction (1979) and *Homo Academicus* (1988 [1984]), to explain not simply the left tendencies of intellectuals overall but also the variation in political belief across segments of the intellectual community.

Over the past two decades, the sociology of intellectuals has remained a vibrant enterprise, changing substantively but never straying too much from its original interests. Attending to new world-historical realities, it has explored the role of intellectuals in the collapse of Eastern European communism, student uprisings in China, prodemocracy movements in the Middle East, and the promotion of market liberalization in Latin America and the United States—with the class circumstances of the intelligentsia factoring in each of these accounts. Under the influence of feminist, Foucauldian, and postcolonial theorizing, the sociology of intellectuals has also broadened its understanding of politics, moving beyond both Weberian, state-centered concerns and Marxian interest in the establishment of a political-economic order to examine the effect of intellectual work on legitimizing a range of power relations across a panoply of historical settings, from social Darwinist apologia for racism and colonialism in turn-of-the-century social science to the gendered presuppositions of the contemporary life sciences. Still other work has taken up the participation of intellectuals in new movements for social change, such as the environmental movement, or has sought to establish better relations with the cognate subfields of the sociology of knowledge and the sociology of science, which, under diverse influences, have been moving away from the study of ideology. (For reviews, see Eyal and Buchholz 2010; Frickel and Moore 2006; Kurzman and Owens 2002.)

By any measure, the sociology of intellectuals has been a worthwhile pursuit. When the subfield has turned its attention to the politics of the university, however, it has run up against certain limits. First, because sociologists of intellectuals have typically looked at a whole host of knowledge producers in a given setting in order to grasp their collective role in furthering social change, they have not usually developed fine-grained individual-level models of political belief formation or practice geared toward the distinctive institutional circumstances faced by academics. Yet the training, recruitment, employment, and social experiences of professors differ greatly from those of journalists, fiction writers, and private sector economists, say, and they vary over time, across national systems of higher education, and by disciplinary and institutional location. No plausible explanation of academics' politics can ignore this complexity, for one lesson of contemporary political sociology is that while one may be able to identify some general sociodemographic correlates of political belief and behavior, politics is ultimately tied to people's experience in highly specific settings of group interaction, especially those, such as the university, that tend to be all-encompassing (see Fine 2012). The quotidian reality of academic life matters, for politics and for knowledge production generally (Camic, Gross, and Lamont 2011), and though sociologists of intellectuals have had important things to say about changes in the economics of the university environment (e.g., Berman 2011), how such changes affect the daily lives of professors and would-be professors in ways that might impact their political commitments has been undertheorized.[1]

Second, with the exception of Lipset (who employed a range of methodologies) and a few others, the sociology of intellectuals has long been the purview of scholars who are wedded to comparative-historical methods and have steered clear of quantitative research involving the analysis of data from social surveys, even when studying recent periods. Historical scholarship on intellectuals and politics has been vital; as many of the chapters of this volume show, it is impossible to understand the politics of the contemporary American university, for example, without knowing the history of the institution (a point to which we return below.) But there are many important questions—not least, questions about the precise contribution made by this or that factor in accounting for academics' political beliefs—that cannot be answered satisfactorily absent the analysis of large-scale survey data. Although survey data are insufficient in themselves for explanation, they are a privileged source for isolating patterns of covariation in social life. Third, in the sociology of intellectuals, the long-standing focus on class has sometimes kept alternative hypotheses about the sources of political commitments from coming into view and inhibited the forging of connections to other intellectual traditions with less of a critical-theoretical slant, including the sociology of organizations, the sociology of culture, and the sociology of higher education itself. Fourth and finally, the sociology of intellectuals has tended to focus on contentious rather than more mundane party politics, its ultimate explanandum being large-scale sociopolitical transformation rather than routine political life in a (more or less) stable democracy. Other scholarship—by researchers examining the effects of higher education on students' political attitudes, for example, or in a different vein, by historians writing of the McCarthy era or the tumult of the 1960s or debates about objectivity—has gone some way toward filling the gap (e.g., Hanson et al. 2012; Novick 1988; Schrecker 1986), bringing the study of higher education into dialogue with political science and the history of politics. But this work has been piecemeal and, by sociological standards, much of it has been atheoretical.[2]

This volume attempts a fresh start. Informed by the sociology of higher education—by its attention to organizational architecture and educational trajectories and its concern with the quantitative evaluation of causal claims—but also by the insights of the sociology of intellectuals and other approaches, its chapters seek to understand the politics of the university, and the politics of the professoriate in particular, as outcomes of complex social processes that may be inflected by class but are not reducible to it and that, in turn, factor as inputs into still other processes that may ramify across society. No single intellectual paradigm binds the chapters together, but all are characterized by theoretical pluralism and syncretism, by stringent evidentiary standards, and by the shared belief of their authors that colleges and universities and the people who spend time in them—whether for four years or a career—are, among many other things, important actors on the political stage.

Whatever the limitations of the sociology of intellectuals, social scientists have certainly known for some time that American academics tend to be more left- than right-leaning, where political orientation is understood as a matter of attitudes toward redistribution and market regulation and toward equal rights and recognition for minority groups. As Lipset noted in his 1976 book with Everett Carll Ladd Jr., *The Divided Academy*, intellectuals in the United States, including leading social and natural scientists, can be found involved with left causes dating back to the dawn of the twentieth century, if not before. Progressive academics railed against monopolies and the dangers of big business, championed the cause of labor, helped to staff settlement houses for immigrants, and protested abuses in the criminal justice system. On social issues such as women's rights or race, a significant number of professors held views that would place them more in the conservative than the liberal camp, according to the logic of today's political classifications, while the visibility of Progressive activists in the academy may lead us, in retrospect, to overstate their numbers. Still, the historical evidence suggests liberal tendencies, just as many French and British professors at the time threw their support behind left political movements in their countries, intermingled though this often was with a discordant nationalism. During the Great Depression, American academics ventured even further into the political fray, many aligning themselves with New Deal policies and ideals—and in fact serving as advisors to the New Deal coalition of government, business, and labor.

It was not until the middle of the twentieth century, however, that scholars were able to use survey data to quantify the extent of academe's commitment to

liberalism. In a groundbreaking study from 1955, Paul Lazarsfeld surveyed social scientists (Lazarsfeld and Thielens 1958). The main goal was to assess the
impact of McCarthyism, but Lazarsfeld also queried his respondents about social and political issues. He found social scientists to be well to the left of the
general electorate and more liberal than others in their communities—which
made them especially vulnerable to attack by McCarthy and his allies.

Following in Lazarsfeld's footsteps, Ladd and Lipset analyzed data from a
nationally representative survey of American academics conducted in 1969,
covering professors in all fields and across the full spectrum of institutions.
Their analysis confirmed that social scientists were especially likely to be liberals and progressives, but it also showed that the academic profession as a whole
was a center of liberal political belief. Forty-six percent of professors in their
study could be classified as left or liberal, compared with 20 percent of the U.S.
population. In recent national elections, Democratic candidates had won the professorial vote by margins of 20 percent or more. Much of Ladd and Lipset's book
was devoted to describing the political terrain of the academy, highlighting disciplinary cleavages—between liberally inclined arts and sciences fields and
more conservative applied programs—as well as divides between professors of
different generations. Yet the book also laid out a theory of academics' politics,
which traced professorial liberalism back to the very nature of the intellectual
role.

In the 1980s and 1990s, new surveys of American academe were fielded.
Some, such as follow-up studies to the 1969 Ladd and Lipset survey or those
done by the Higher Education Research Institute at the University of California,
Los Angeles, asked after professors' political views, although not in as much
depth as had the authors of *The Divided Academy*. Others, undertaken by social
scientists interested primarily in showcasing the leftward drift of the university
since the 1960s, suffered from a variety of methodological problems (as described
in chapter 1 of this volume).

What, then, do the politics of American academe look like in our day, when
higher education is in flux and when previously excluded social groups—
women, racial and ethnic minorities, gays and lesbians—have been making
major inroads? To answer this question, in 2006 we conducted our own nationally representative survey of the social and political attitudes of American college and university professors, the results of which we summarize in chapter 1.
While the survey shows that the academic profession is indeed liberally oriented and a Democratic Party stronghold, it also reveals a sizable center-left bloc
in higher education and provides some evidence—now possibly called into

question by more recent surveys conducted in the wake of the Occupy Wall Street movement (see Jaschik 2012)—that commitments to political radicalism may be in decline among the youngest generation of professors.

But what explains the liberal tilt of the professoriate? This is the question addressed by the chapters in part II. In chapter 2, Ethan Fosse, Jeremy Freese, and Neil Gross consider several competing theories of professorial liberalism. Following on the heels of a paper by Fosse and Gross that used data from the General Social Survey (GSS) to evaluate some of these theories, comparing the several hundred GSS respondents over the years who were professors with the more than forty thousand who were not, and looking to see which factors accounted statistically for the political differences between the two groups, Fosse, Freese, and Gross use data from the National Longitudinal Study of Adolescent Health to examine the predictors of graduate school attendance. Young Americans who identify as political liberals, they find, are significantly more likely than their conservative peers to attend PhD programs. Is this because liberals and conservatives differ in their social class backgrounds, with liberals more apt to come from New Class families? Is it because liberals and conservatives have different values, with conservatives prioritizing monetary success and early family formation, neither of which is congruent with a professorial lifestyle? Do cognitive or personality differences between liberals and conservatives, of the sort flagged in recent research in political psychology, explain differential rates of graduate school attendance? Or might other processes be at work—processes to do with "political typing," to which the sociology of intellectuals has historically devoted little attention?

In chapter 3, Clem Brooks takes up several of these same issues but with the valuable addition of cross-national data from the International Social Survey Program. Like Fosse, Freese, and Gross, Brooks considers the possibility that professorial liberalism might result from self-selection—from the greater tendency of liberals to *want* to become professors, given the prevailing political climate on many campuses. Informed by the work of scholars who have debated the New Class thesis, however, Brooks also explores the role of group composition in explaining the phenomenon. In different countries in different periods, different social groups have entered the professoriate and the professional stratum as a whole. How much of the liberal political orientation of academics results from the makeup of these groups and the political leanings of their members, owing to economic interests, education, and other factors as these take shape in the light of the structuring of national political economies? Brooks provides some answers, while also layering descriptive richness onto the findings from chapter

1: American professors may be more liberal than the general population in some respects, but compared with professors elsewhere they are considerably less supportive of the welfare state.

Chapter 4 moves on to examine yet another hypothesis sometimes put forth to explain the liberal leanings of academics: that liberal professors discriminate against conservatives in the recruitment of graduate students, in the hiring of colleagues, and in tenure and promotion. To this end, Fosse and Gross, writing with Joseph Ma, analyze data from a field experiment testing for political bias in the graduate admissions process. Finding much less evidence of bias than one would expect if the discrimination hypothesis explained the bulk of professorial liberalism, the authors conclude that their data bolster the argument for self-selection. They also suggest that whatever professors' personal political sympathies, most feel bound by professional norms proscribing the evaluation of academic personnel on political grounds.

The chapters in part III turn to the student experience. Kyle Dodson, in chapter 5, reexamines the finding from higher education research and political science that attending college or university results in more liberal social and political attitudes and higher levels of political participation. Noting that this finding has recently been called into question by studies showing that many of the political differences between the college-educated and the non-college-educated stem not from the experience of college-going but from background factors that also predict educational attainment, Dodson argues that the debate could be usefully reframed by focusing on different possible mechanisms of political growth and change—in particular those associated with academic versus social experiences—and the distribution of exposure to these mechanisms across types of students.

Continuing with the theme of differentiated effects, in chapter 6, Amy Binder and Kate Wood draw from their interview-based study of conservative collegians at two schools: a flagship public university in the West and an elite private research university in the East. On both campuses, they find, conservative students perceive themselves to be in a minority position vis-à-vis a liberal professoriate and a liberal student body. But Binder and Wood show that conservatives at the two institutions adopt divergent styles of political engagement in response to this predicament, one provocative and confrontational, the other restrained and intellectual. Looking skeptically on the argument that this is a function of the kind of student selected to attend the two schools, Binder and Wood attribute the difference to group learning processes, with student political organizations linked to different branches of the national conservative movement serving as the main sites for cultural transmission and identity formation.

Part IV shifts gears. Here, contributors examine two critical eras in the history of the modern American university. In chapter 7, Andrew Jewett rereads the intellectual history of the immediate postwar period. Did social scientists at the time (and other scholars), producing innovative work on such topics as democratic politics, community, and the American national character, assume the virtues of objectivity, aping to some extent the epistemological stance of the natural sciences? Generally yes, finds Jewett, echoing Carl Schorske (1997), who has described this as a time of "new rigorism" in the American academy. But in practice, Jewett claims, this often meant that scholars surreptitiously brought center-left political commitments into their work, "naturalizing" them by treating departures from liberal ideals, whether by individuals or by whole societies, as regrettable forms of deviancy. Not surprisingly, this behavior infuriated conservatives (as well as radicals on the left) and helped spur some of the critiques of the academy we see today.

In chapter 8, Julie Reuben moves the historical clock forward to the contentious 1960s. These were indeed dramatic years for higher education. But, she concludes, student unrest and the subsequent entry into academe of scholars who had taken part in political protest and cultural rebellion did not change the university as much as some have claimed. New opportunities were carved out for women and people of color, and academic fields were born or reshaped to address their experiences. And some political radicals brought their ideas into the curriculum. Yet these changes were generally constrained, Reuben argues, by norms of political moderation, dating back to the founding of the research university, that lent support to the idea of "institutional neutrality"—an idea that was transformed through its confrontation with student and faculty radicalism, but not abandoned. The 1960s were thus more of a symbolic watershed than anything else, as some of the more impertinent challenges to the academic status quo were drained of energy, and the usual business of the university— training and credentialing students for careers and generating research that could be used to enhance local and national governance and be put to commercial use—continued on.

This idea of containment resurfaces in part V, where contributors address the dynamics of institutional transformation. In chapter 9, Fabio Rojas trains the lens of organizational sociology on the rise of ethnic studies programs in the 1960s and 1970s. The liberal climate on many campuses and in the country as a whole allowed such programs to gain a foothold, but Rojas also describes the organizational challenges faced by ethnic studies entrepreneurs owing to their radical political commitments, the interdisciplinary nature of the fields they sought to develop, and the marginalized constituencies they served. Eventually, ethnic studies did become institutionalized, once practitioners resigned themselves to a more academic agenda. This leads Rojas to conclude that while institutions of higher education can be remade by activism, this is so only within limits, as colleges and universities are ultimately hide-bound places constrained by academic tradition.

The weight of the past also figures heavily in Patrick Thaddeus Jackson's chapter. Jackson seeks to account historically for the political inclinations of his field, international relations. Against the view that a conservative, realist position currently dominates the international relations community, Jackson describes his peers as a mostly liberal bunch (primarily in the philosophical sense), committed normatively to values of democracy, pluralism, and human rights but focused intellectually on understanding geopolitics in scientific terms. Jackson's historical narrative highlights the resistances encountered by scholars who sought to import European-style realism into the United States in the mid twentieth century. In a setting where academic legitimacy flowed to those who got on board the bandwagon of objectivity—even if a somewhat illusory objectivity, as in Jewett's account—realists found themselves having to "translate" their claims into the language of political-scientific behavioralism, which inevitably muted their political and philosophical thrust. In this way the realist threat to liberal hegemony in the field was reduced, though, in the end, neoconservatism was able to establish a beachhead.

Where Rojas and Jackson stress change amid continuity and constraint, Thomas Medvetz, in chapter 11, tells a story of more significant institutional reconfiguration. Throughout the 1950s and 1960s, conservative intellectuals were frustrated by their inability to use higher education as a staging ground for the development of their ideas. Perceiving themselves as locked out of the social sciences and humanities, they sought alternative institutional venues from which to advance the conservative cause. Medvetz shows how one such venue, the conservative think tank, emerged as an institutional form that coevolved with liberal academe, its organizational structures and knowledge-making practices taking shape partly in reaction to those found in higher education. This reaction was not a complete rejection. In fact, argues Medvetz, conservative think tanks operated at the edges of the academy and were energized by their academic marginality. With financial support from business elites and conservative philanthropies, they flourished and became major influences on American life.

Finally, in our brief conclusion, we situate the volume's findings more directly against the backdrop of current policy debates, offer some thoughts on the likely future of disputes over the professoriate, and issue a call for a new political sociology of higher education (the phrase is an adaptation of Scott Frickel and Kelly Moore's [2006] appeal for a "new political sociology of science") that would have at its core some of the matters taken up by our contributors.

But can something be said now, in anticipation of the chapters, about what they add up to? With the caveat that they represent, not a comprehensive look at the politics of the American university, but efforts at investigating a multifaceted phenomenon from several interesting angles, it does seem possible to identify some recurrent themes that hint at broader insights.

The first is that, in the context of the United States—a relatively conservative, antistatist nation in terms of its political culture—colleges and universities *are* politically unusual places. Faculty members may not experience this on a day-to-day basis. After all, many of the leading centers of American academic life are located in regions of the country or cities or towns where a plurality of voters feel an affinity with the Democratic Party and with progressive ideals, such that no one in Cambridge, Massachusetts, is going to see Harvard as a redoubt of blue in a community of red. Nationally, however, institutions of higher education stick out for the number of personnel they employ who are committed to the values of the left and for the fact that students—though often not political—are more likely to be left/liberal than conservative (though student liberalism has declined dramatically since the late 1960s and early 1970s). This has not gone unnoticed by social scientists, as the work of sociologists of intellectuals and others attests. But the significance of the fact that American colleges and universities are in some sense political aberrations—"exceptions to American exceptionalism," as Frederic Jaher (2002, 29) puts it in another context—has yet to be fully appraised. Are the social dynamics that are responsible for this the same as or different from those that account for other instances of political concentration across the institutional and occupational space of American society, from the progressive commitments of social workers to the conservative views of many business executives and members of the clergy? Have the size and stature of the American university and the symbolic power of its endorsements contributed to the success of the left in recent decades in progress on social equality? Or has this very size lent strength to the right, as it has girded itself to do battle with a powerful foe? How and in what ways have the distinctive political leanings of the professoriate affected academics' work of knowledge production and dissemination, coloring the content of academic fields, shaping pedagogical practices, and influencing professorial engagement in the public sphere? And, to return to a point made earlier, how, precisely, are heated debates about the financing of higher education, collective bargaining rights for faculty, standardized learning outcome measures, and federal support for academic research undergirded by policymakers' attitudes toward professors and their politics? These questions have not been addressed in great depth in previous research. Although this volume nuances the claim that professors tend to be liberal, the data it reviews suggest that stereotypes of the liberal professor are not without some grounding, warranting a range of inquiries into consequences.

Second, the chapters make clear that explaining the political predilections of faculty and students is no easy thing. This is a topic on which it is possible to spin out endless hypotheses. Some of these reflect the rhetoric of partisan bickering, with professors said by liberals to be naturally on the left because of their higher intelligence, or said by conservatives to be unnaturally so because of undemocratic efforts to silence conservative voices. Other hypotheses have roots in social-theoretical frameworks removed from popular discourse. One lesson of this volume is that all such hypotheses must be treated as hypotheses and carefully evaluated on theoretical and empirical grounds before being accorded truth-value. The political attitudes and orientations of those in the higher education sector are complicated social effects, reflecting the influence of multiple, interacting, and contextually variable causal processes to which theory might alert us but which are impossible to pin down without painstaking empirical research. Research of this sort is still in its infancy, however, hindered by the general lack of interest in politics in the sociology of higher education, by the monocausal assumptions of many theoreticians, by the decline of interest among political scientists in processes of political socialization, and by a paucity of data. In the light of continued expansion of higher education, we will need more research on the causes of faculties' and students' political attitudes in the years to come if we are to gain a better understanding of key American political dynamics. The chapters in this volume illuminate a path forward by calling certain simplistic hypotheses into question, identifying others that seem more promising, and raising the methodological bar.

Third and finally, the chapters suggest how deeply rooted in history the politics of the university are. How tempting it is, in a time of high political drama, to imagine that campuses look as they do politically because of the social forces and the actions of individuals and groups—whether praiseworthy or blameful—that are buffeting higher education at this very moment. And yet we are reminded—whether by Fosse, Freese, and Gross's mention of the historical origins of political typing, by Brooks's chapter showing how the politics of national professoriates reflect the historical development of their country's welfare regime, by Jewett's and Reuben's chapters etching the connections between present-day controversies and campus political disputes from previous eras, or by the chapters by Rojas, Jackson, and Medvetz, each in its own way—that higher education politics owe as much to the past as to the present.

One might see these historical legacies as limiting the current possibilities for change and reform. What hope is there for bringing greater ideological diversity to the academy, conservatives might ask, when it has been a site of liberal politics for so long? Or, leftists may wonder, is it realistic to think that academic disciplines already retrofitted to accommodate the concerns of feminists and multiculturalists could be further reengineered to reflect new phases of diversification of the American polity, new exigencies, and the corresponding need for new forms of knowledge? But this is to see the glass as half empty. The fact is that in the university, as elsewhere in society, social change does occur, constantly, against the press of inertia. Social change is commonly stochastic in nature, unpredictable and occurring for reasons identifiable only in hindsight. But when change is made—by actors working together in a concerted fashion—this is often because the agents of change, far from being deterred by history, are inspired and informed by it, crafting their strategies as best they can with an eye toward the longue durée and alert to meaningful structural and symbolic openings. Our goal in assembling this volume was neither to facilitate nor impede change. But we hope that its contents, not least around historical matters, prove informative as various parties urgently discuss recasting, reforming, and preserving America's unique and—in our view—quite special system of higher education.

As a last point, we note that several of the chapters in the volume—chapters 1, 2, and 4—had previous lives as working papers released on the Web. Findings from the studies reported in these chapters are also discussed in Gross's book *Why Are Professors Liberal and Why Do Conservatives Care?* (2013), although not in nearly as much detail as is presented here. We have included these pieces in the volume, modified from their working-paper versions, so that they can be preserved as part of the scholarly record.

NOTES

This volume would not have been possible without grants from the Richard Lounsbery Foundation. We are grateful to the foundation for its support, and in particular to Jesse Ausubel and Maxmillian Angerholzer.
    1. But see Brym (1980), who focuses on the intellectual stratum more broadly.
    2. An exception is the work of Loss (2011), who approaches higher education from the standpoint of American political development.

PART ONE

THE LAY OF THE LAND

CHAPTER ONE

The Social and Political Views of American College and University Professors

NEIL GROSS AND SOLON SIMMONS

In 1955, sociologist Paul Lazarsfeld set out to study how American social scientists were faring in the era of McCarthyism. Lazarsfeld employed interviewers from the National Opinion Research Center and Elmo Roper and Associates to speak with 2,451 social scientists at 182 American colleges and universities. A significant number of those interviewed reported feeling that their intellectual freedom was being jeopardized—although not as many as some scholars at the time predicted (Lazarsfeld and Thielens 1958). Lazarsfeld also asked his respondents about their politics. Analyzing the survey data on this score with Wagner Thielens in their 1958 book *The Academic Mind*, Lazarsfeld observed that liberalism and Democratic Party affiliation were more common among social scientists than within the general U.S. population and that social scientists at research universities were more liberal than their peers at teaching-oriented institutions.

Although *The Academic Mind* was published too late to be of any help in the fight against McCarthy (Garfinkel 1987), it opened up a new and exciting area of sociological research: study of the political views of academicians. Sociologists of intellectual life had long been interested in the political sympathies of intellectuals (Kurzman and Owens 2002), but most previous work had been historical. In the wake of *The Academic Mind*, however, several studies appeared that aimed to chart the distribution of political beliefs among college and university professors, to do so using surveys, and to leverage from the effort not simply a better understanding of the academic intelligentsia but also broader insights into political processes. Such studies were given special urgency by the contentious politics of the 1960s, which often centered on college and university campuses and raised the question of the allegiances of professors. Everett Carll Ladd Jr., and Seymour Martin Lipset's book *The Divided Academy* (1976), based largely on a nationally representative survey of the American faculty carried out in 1969, was the most prominent of these investigations. But as Michael Faia noted in a 1974 article, some half a dozen others were published during the same period. While Faia himself charged that Lipset, in work published prior to *The Divided Academy*, had overestimated the liberalism of professors, these studies generally confirmed Lazarsfeld and Thielens's finding that professors are more liberal than members of other occupational groups and concluded that insofar as this was so, professors "represent a negative case to the traditional equation of high socioeconomic status and political conservatism" (Finkelstein 1984, 169).

This was important research into an occupation of growing significance in the post–World War II period, given the expansion of higher education during this time (Schofer and Meyer 2005) and the associated transformation of college-going from an "elite" to a "mass" phenomenon (Trow 1973). Much of the research was carried out with methodological savvy and theoretical sophistication, and although some of the researchers clearly hoped that the findings could make their way into policy debates, the core agenda was the advancement of social science.

In the 1990s, a few sociologists continued to produce high-quality work on the topic (e.g., Hamilton and Hargens 1993; Nakhaie and Brym 1999). But an unfortunate tendency became evident: increasingly, those social scientists who turned their attention to professors and politics and employed the tools of survey research had as their goal simply to *highlight* the liberalism of the professoriate in order to provide support for conservatives urging the political reform of American colleges and universities. The past twenty years or so have witnessed a concerted mobilization on the part of conservative activists, think tanks, foundations, and professors aimed at challenging so-called liberal hegemony in higher education (see Doumani 2006; Messer-Davidow 1993; Slaughter 1988; Wilson 1995), and much recent research on faculty political views has been beholden to this program.

With this chapter we take a step toward moving the study of professorial politics back into the domain of mainstream sociological inquiry. We report on a survey of American college and university professors and their social and political attitudes that we carried out in 2006. Our purposes here are basic: to introduce the study and its methodology and lay out its findings. Where other recent studies have characterized the faculty as not simply extremely liberal but nearly uniformly so (Klein and Western 2004–5; Rothman, Lichter, and Nevitte 2005; Tobin and Weinberg 2006), we show that while conservatives and Republicans are rare within the faculty ranks, on many issues there are as many professors who hold center-left views as those who cleave to more progressive positions. At the same time, the age distribution indicates that in their overall political orientation, young professors post-September 11 may have been somewhat more moderate and less radical than their older colleagues—a trend that appears to have reversed more recently in the wake of the Occupy Wall Street movement and growing concerns about inequality and the failings of Republican governance.

Methods

Research on the politics of the American professoriate of late has been problematic, not because it is politically motivated per se, but for methodological reasons that might be traceable to a desire to score political points. Klein and Western (2004–5), for example, sought to estimate the political leanings of American professors by counting the number of registered Democrats and Republicans teaching at the University of California, Berkeley, and Stanford, unconcerned that these schools are not representative of higher education as a whole. Rothman, Lichter, and Nevitte (2005) reported the results of a survey of American and Canadian professors conducted in 1999, trumpeting the fact that their data showed a sharp turn to the left in the American sample when compared with a 1984 study, with 72 percent of professors identifying as left or liberal—but failing to take into account that the earlier study had included community college professors, who are typically more conservative, and their study had not. In a similar vein, Tobin and Weinberg (2006) surveyed the professoriate and claimed it was an exceedingly liberal occupation, but they achieved only a 24 percent response rate and did nothing to assess response bias. All three studies also employed ad hoc, nonstandard question wordings that raise flags about construct validity and render difficult systematic comparisons with the general population.

The nationally representative survey of the faculty that we undertook, the Politics of the American Professoriate survey (PAP), sought to avoid these problems. The study focused on professors working in fields in which undergraduates can take classes. Given the large number of such fields and our desire to have enough cases in each to make meaningful comparisons, we drew two-thirds of our sample from the twenty largest disciplinary fields, as measured by the number of bachelor's degrees awarded in 2004, with the remaining third drawn randomly from all fields. We decided to pay special attention to these twenty fields because they represent the main disciplinary venues in which undergraduate instruction is being carried out and hence are the fields where the politics of professors should matter most for the undergraduate experience. To construct our sample, we first randomly sampled from the National Center for Education

Statistics' (NCES) dataset on degree completions, locating a college or university where either bachelor's or associate's degrees in the relevant field were awarded. All colleges and universities report information on degree completion to the NCES, so the dataset is presumably comprehensive. We stratified the sample by institution type, focusing on community colleges, four-year colleges and universities, non-elite PhD-granting institutions, and elite doctoral universities (those in the top fifty in the most recent *U.S. News and World Report* ranking). Three graduate student research assistants were then employed to identify the department or program at each school most closely associated with the relevant degree. Next, we obtained, through an examination of websites or by phone calls if necessary, a list of full-time faculty teaching in that department or program and randomly selected one faculty member to include in the study. It is certainly possible that the faculty lists from which we sampled were not in all cases comprehensive or up to date; institutions and departments vary in how often they update their publicly available faculty rosters. But the procedure we employed was far more efficient and economical than attempting to obtain a printed roster from every school, and the chances that the omission of a few names here or there would produce a systematically biased sampling frame seemed low.

On the basis of this procedure, precontact and invitation letters were sent to 2,958 professors. Professors were offered a chance to win a gift certificate as an incentive to participate in the study. The precontact letters were written by David Cutler, then dean of the Social Sciences at Harvard, where one of the authors of this chapter (Gross) was teaching. Invitation letters were sent on behalf of Gross by the Center for Survey Research at Indiana University, which administered the survey on our behalf. Participants logged into a special password-protected website and filled out a questionnaire online. The questionnaire contained about a hundred items exploring a wide range of social and political attitudes and views of the university, as well as sociodemographic questions. A unique feature of the questionnaire is that most of the items were taken verbatim from well-established surveys of the general population—in particular, the General Social Survey (GSS), the National Election Studies (NES), and the Pew Values survey. Care was taken to minimize question order effects, and randomization of question and response category ordering was implemented where feasible.

In seventy-six cases, invitation letters turned out to have been sent to bad addresses or to people who were not on the faculty. The study closed eight weeks after the initial invitation letters were sent. After four follow-up contacts, one by postcard and three by email, we achieved a final response rate of 51 percent, with 1,471 valid cases. Focusing on professors with full-time appointments, as we do in this chapter, brings the sample size down to 1,416.[1] Whereas other samples of the American faculty employ a cluster design and contain many professors who teach at the same school, potentially compromising case independence, our sampling strategy yielded a sample in which 580 institutions are represented with only a single case, and no institution is represented with more than six cases. In a logistic regression model, type of institution was not a statistically significant predictor of response to our survey.

To better assess response bias, we conducted short phone interviews with a sample of one hundred nonresponders. Nonresponders were slightly more conservative than responders in terms of overall political orientation, with a mean score of 3.5 on a 7-point liberalism-conservatism scale, compared with a mean value on this question of 3.1 for responders. The difference between nonresponders and responders on a simple political party affiliation question was also relatively small and in the same direction. Nonresponders were 4 percentage points more Republican than responders, and 4.5 percentage points less Democratic. When asked, in an open-ended question format, why they did not respond, the majority of nonresponders—54 percent—said they had not had time to do so, 7 percent said they objected to some feature of the questionnaire design, and 7 percent said they were uncomfortable answering political questions, with the rest citing other factors. Although the differences between responders and nonresponders are small, it is probably the case that the figures we report in this chapter slightly underestimate the extent of conservative sentiment in the American academy. We are not sure why conservative academicians would be less inclined to participate in the study. It could be that they perceive their views to be academically marginalized and, despite assurances of anonymity, worried that revealing their political sentiments on a survey might harm them professionally. Alternatively, it could be that the study's affiliation with Harvard, treated in conservative discourse as a bastion of liberalism, or the authors' disciplinary affiliation with sociology, widely known as a liberal field, made nonresponders suspicious of the project. One finding we report below is that, on average, conservative academics are less politically active than liberal ones. Liberal professors might have participated at a slightly higher rate if they saw doing so as a form of political involvement, a chance to express their views about the direction in which the country is heading.

Once collected, the data were weighted to even out the effects of oversampling certain fields and institutions. They also received a post-stratification weighting based on NCES data to correct for the effects of having slightly un-dersampled women and African Americans.

One aspect of the study did not go as planned. Although our primary focus was full-time faculty members, we initially set out to also conduct a smaller, com-plementary survey of part-time faculty. We thought that doing so was especially important in the light of the casualization of academic labor in recent years: more than half of faculty members in American higher education can be classi-fied as contingent workers (though some of these work full-time on short-term contracts). Following a procedure similar to the one outlined above, except for relying more heavily on phone calls to departments to obtain lists of part-timers, we sent questionnaires to 475 part-time faculty. Due to logistical delays, this phase of the survey was not initiated until late in the spring 2006 semester, a grading crunch time for many part-time faculty members who have high teach-ing loads. Perhaps because of busy schedules, we wound up with a relatively low, 32 percent response rate for the part-time sample. Our budget did not allow us to conduct follow-up phone interviews with nonresponders in this group, so we cannot meaningfully assess response bias. Thus, we restrict the analyses that follow to respondents from the full-time sample, leaving for elsewhere the task of comparing the two samples.

Results
Political Orientation

Because much prior research on the political opinions of faculty has revolved around questions of political orientation, we begin by considering the distribu-tion of self-identified liberals and conservatives in academe. Our survey included an NES question that asked respondents, "When it comes to politics, do you usually think of yourself as extremely liberal, liberal, slightly liberal, moderate or middle of the road, slightly conservative, conservative, or very conservative?" Table 1.1 gives the percentages for the weighted sample.[2]

Several things about the findings immediately stand out. The first is that re-spondents on the left outnumber considerably those on the right. Only 20 percent of respondents identify themselves as any shade of conservative, compared with 62 percent who identify as any shade of liberal. By contrast, in the most recent it-eration of the NES survey before the PAP study, 31 percent of respondents in the general population identified as any shade of conservative, while 17 percent identified as any shade of liberal. Second, a high percentage of our respondents are located between the center and the center-left of the distribution. Collapsing the seven-point scale into a three-point one by recoding the slightly liberal as

TABLE 1.1
Political Self-Identification of Professors

Political orientation	%
Extremely liberal	9
Liberal	35
Slightly liberal	18
Middle of the road	17
Slightly conservative	11
Conservative	8
Very conservative	1

liberal and the slightly conservative as conservative, as some previous researchers have done, would thus minimize the significance of faculty respondents who do not feel comfortable locating themselves at the extremes of the political spectrum. To avoid this problem in our analyses below, we code those who identify as "slightly liberal" or "slightly conservative" as faculty moderates, alongside those who identify as "middle of the road." We would not be justified in doing so if it turned out that the "slightlys" were, in terms of their substantive attitudes, no different than their more liberal or conservative counterparts. But evidence indicates that they are different. We consider below a large number of attitudes items, but simply note for now that one set of items was taken from the Pew Values survey and asked about respondents' views on a variety of policy matters ranging from environmental regulation to censorship and the fight against terrorism. To assess whether there were differences between the slightlys and their colleagues further toward the extremes, we averaged scores on all twelve of the Pew items. In this exercise, a score of 1 would indicate the most liberal response possible on all of the items, a score of 3 would indicate an intermediary position, and a score of 5 would indicate the most conservative response possible. The score of those who stated their political orientation as extremely liberal or liberal was 1.4, while the score of those who identified themselves as conservative or extremely conservative was 3.7. (The moderation on the right here is interesting in itself.) The scores of those respondents closer to the center of the distribution were different: the slightly liberal scored 1.7, middle of the roaders 2.2, and the slightly conservative 2.8. Although the differences between the slightly conservative and their more conservative colleagues are greater than the differences between the slightly liberal and their more liberal colleagues, that there are differences at all provides further reason to think that the slightlys should not be treated as belonging to the extremes.

Collapsing the data accordingly, we find that 44 percent of respondents can be classified as liberals, 46 percent as moderates, and 9 percent as conservatives.

Such a recoding thus reveals a moderate faculty bloc that, while consisting of moderates who are considerably more left than right leaning (such that they are moderate only in the context of academia), is nevertheless equal in size to the liberal bloc.

In table 1.2 we use this same coding scheme to examine how professors in different broad disciplinary groupings score on our political orientation question. The physical and biological sciences look the most like the sample overall, with about equal percentages of liberals and moderates. Consistent with previous research going back to Ladd and Lipset, we find that the social sciences and humanities contain the highest proportion of liberals, at 58 and 52 percent, respectively. The biggest concentration of conservatives is to be found in business, with the next biggest concentration in the health sciences—which in our sample means mostly professors of nursing, as we did not purposively sample medical school faculty. Computer science and engineering are notable for their high percentage of moderates.

Table 1.3 shows the distribution of liberals, moderates, and conservatives across the different types of institutions of higher education represented in our sample. For the purposes of this analysis, we have disaggregated four-year, BA-granting schools into liberal arts and non–liberal arts colleges. Doing so reveals that a slightly higher proportion of liberals is to be found on the faculties of liberal arts colleges than on the faculties of elite, PhD-granting schools, while liberal arts colleges and non-elite PhD-granting schools also contain the fewest conservative faculty members. Community colleges house the most conservatives, at 19 percent, and the fewest liberals. In every type of institution except liberal arts colleges and elite, PhD-granting schools, moderates somewhat outnumber liberals.

TABLE 1.2
Political Self-Identification of Professors across Areas of Study

Area	Percentage		
	Liberal	Moderate	Conservative
Physical/biological sciences	45	47	8
Social sciences	58	37	5
Humanities	52	44	4
Computer science / engineering	11	78	11
Health sciences	21	59	21
Other	53	36	11
Business	21	54	25
Total	44	47	9

We conclude our examination of the political orientation variable—of limited analytic use by itself—by looking at the breakdown by age and gender. Table 1.4 shows that the youngest age cohort—professors aged 26–35—contains the highest percentage of moderates and the lowest percentage of liberals. Self-described liberals are most common among professors aged 50–64, who were teenagers or young adults in the 1960s, while the largest number of conservatives is to be found among professors aged 65 and older. These findings on age suggest a moderating trend, although, as noted earlier, a more recent survey conducted in 2010–11 by the Higher Education Research Institute at UCLA, containing only one question about politics, showed an apparent swing back to the left, with assistant and associate professors more apt than their full professor colleagues to describe themselves as "far left" (see Jaschik 2012).

As for gender, an examination of the sample as a whole reveals few differences between male and female professors in their tendency to describe themselves as liberals, moderates, or conservatives. Further analysis, however, shows gender differences *within* fields, as table 1.5 indicates. In the physical/biological sciences, more men than women are liberals, and more women than men are moderates. In the social sciences, more women than men are liberals. There are

TABLE 1.3
Political Self-Identification of Professors across Types of Institutions

	Percentage		
Institution type	Liberal	Moderate	Conservative
Community college	37	43	19
BA, non–liberal arts	39	48	13
Liberal arts	61	35	4
Non-elite, PhD	44	52	4
Elite, PhD	57	33	10
Total	44	47	9

TABLE 1.4
Political Self-Identification of Professors by Age

	Percentage		
Age	Liberal	Moderate	Conservative
26–35	33	60	7
36–49	42	50	9
50–64	50	42	8
65+	37	52	11
Total	45	47	8

TABLE 1.5
Political Self-Identification of Professors by Area of Study and Gender

Area/gender	Percentage		
	Liberal	Moderate	Conservative
Physical/biological sciences			
Female	25	75	0
Male	54	35	11
Social sciences			
Female	73	25	2
Male	51	42	6
Humanities			
Female	52	46	2
Male	53	41	6
Computer science / engineering			
Female	21	59	20
Male	10	81	9
Health sciences			
Female	22	57	21
Male	14	66	20
Business			
Female	20	37	43
Male	22	65	13
Other			
Female	53	37	10
Male	53	35	11

few significant gender differences between liberals and moderates in the humanities, but more men are conservative. In computer science and engineering, twice as many women as men are at either extreme of the distribution, while in business, there are more conservative women than conservative men.

Political Party Affiliation and Voting

Looking at overall political orientation gives us a first cut into professorial attitudes toward politics, but how exactly are professors positioned vis-à-vis the major U.S. political parties? To assess political party affiliation, we asked our respondents a series of questions drawn from the NES. We first asked, "Generally speaking, do you usually think of yourself as a Republican, a Democrat, or an Independent?" Those who chose one of the two parties were then asked whether they would call themselves a "strong" or "not very strong" affiliate of the party. Independents were asked to which of the parties they considered themselves closest. These questions yielded a seven-category party affiliation variable. We report the percentage distributions in table 1.6.

TABLE 1.6
Party Affiliation of Professors

Party affiliation	%
Strong Democrat	32
Weak Democrat	19
Independent-Democrat	20
Independent	9
Independent-Republican	7
Weak Republican	9
Strong Republican	5

TABLE 1.7
Party Affiliation of Professors by Area of Study

	Percentage		
Area	Democrat	Independent	Republican
Physical/biological sciences	53	32	14
Social sciences	56	37	7
Humanities	55	35	11
Computer science / engineering	28	48	23
Health sciences	33	43	24
Business	39	37	24
Other	59	30	11
Total	50	36	14

Collapsing this to a three-point scale, we see that 51 percent of professors are Democrats, 36 percent are Independents (with the Democratic-leaning greatly outnumbering the Republican-leaning), and 14 percent are Republicans.[3] In 2006, according to Gallup polls, 34 percent of Americans identified themselves as Democrats, 34 percent as Independents, and 30 percent as Republicans. By 2007, according to polls done by Pew, the percentage of Republicans had dropped to 25, while the percentage of Democrats remained nearly steady at 33. Our survey thus indicates that Democrats are doing better inside than outside academe by a margin of about 16 percentage points.

As table 1.7 shows, Democrats, Independents, and Republicans are distributed in about the same way in the physical/biological sciences, the social sciences, and the humanities. Consistent with the earlier observation that more conservatives are to be found in business and the health science fields, we find more Republicans teaching in these areas. Computer scientists and engineers also show a greater tendency to be Republican.

Further traction on this issue can be gained by examining the distribution of Democrats, Independents, and Republicans in the top twenty bachelor's-granting

TABLE 1.8
Party Affiliation of Professors by Disciplinary Field

	Percentage		
Discipline	Democrat	Independent	Republican
Accounting	33	18	49
Art	37	44	19
Biology	51	42	7
Business administration	53	32	15
Communications	49	39	12
Computer science	32	59	10
Criminal justice	40	41	19
Economics	34	38	28
Electrical engineering	14	55	31
Elementary education	41	21	39
English	52	47	2
Finance	26	39	35
History	78	17	4
Management information	33	46	20
Marketing	19	66	14
Mechanical engineering	28	64	7
Nursing	60	17	23
Political science	51	44	5
Psychology	77	15	8
Sociology	49	46	5

fields (table 1.8). The preponderance of Democrats over Republicans is particularly extreme in history and psychology; in these fields, nearly 80 percent of professors are Democrats. Independents comprise more than half of all professors in marketing (66%), mechanical engineering (64%), and computer science (59%). In five of the largest BA-granting fields—elementary education, electrical engineering, economics, accounting, and finance—more than a quarter of professors are Republicans.

One of the problems with relying on either party affiliation or political orientation questions to gauge the politics of faculty members—or anyone else—is that there may, in principle, be relatively liberal Republicans and relatively conservative Democrats, even though a consistent finding in prior research on professors' political views is that they exhibit more of what Converse (2006 [1964]) called ideological "constraint" than do other groups. As Ladd and Lipset (1976) put it, "professors' opinions should be more highly structured and interrelated than those of most groups outside the university" (39). So what is the relationship between political orientation and party affiliation in our sample? We answer this question in table 1.9, which shows the percentage of liberals, moderates, and conservatives within each party. About two-thirds of Democrats are liberals, and about one-third are moderates. These numbers are reversed for Independents. Among Republicans, about half consider themselves moderates, and the rest conservatives.

So much for party affiliation. Moving on, we ask: how do professors vote? Tobin and Weinberg (2006) reported that 72 percent of professors voted for John Kerry in the 2004 presidential elections, and 25 percent for George Bush. Our study shows a more uneven vote than that. Of our respondents who reported voting in the election (96%), 77 percent said they voted for Kerry, 21 percent for Bush, 0.5 percent for Ralph Nader, and 1.5 percent for other third-party candidates.

In table 1.10 we show the breakdown of Democratic, Republican, and other votes in the 2004 presidential election across broad disciplinary fields. Averaging the figures for the social sciences and humanities generates a ratio of Democratic to Republican voters of about 8:1. It is in the business and health science fields that Bush fared better, though even in business, Kerry did better than Bush by a margin of more than 2:1.

In table 1.11 we give the voting histories of our respondents in presidential elections since 1984, restricting the sample for each year to those who were old enough to vote at the time. These retrospective data are not as reliable as data

TABLE 1.9
Political Self-Identification of Professors by Party Affiliation

Party	Percentage		
	Liberal	Moderate	Conservative
Democrat	65	33	1
Independent	33	61	6
Republican	0	51	49
Total	45	46	9

TABLE 1.10
Voting among Professors in the 2004 Presidential Election across Areas of Study

Area	Percentage			
	Kerry	Bush	Nader	Other
Physical/biological sciences	78	21	1	1
Social sciences	88	6	1	5
Humanities	84	15	0	1
Computer science / engineering	62	33	0	5
Health sciences	48	52	0	0
Business	65	32	3	1
Other	82	18	0	0
Total	77	21	0	2

TABLE 1.11
Voting Histories of Professors in Presidential Elections since 1984

Party of presidential candidate	Percentage				
	2000	1996	1992	1988	1984
Republican	24	15	18	32	32
Democratic	67	75	76	64	63
Other	10	9	6	4	5

collected closer to the time of the elections, and we cannot know whether Democratic- or Republican-voting professors may have aged out of the study population in unequal numbers, skewing our results. Nevertheless, it is worth noting that while the percentage of professors voting Republican has declined by about 11 percentage points since 1984, the percentage voting Republican in 2004, according to our data, was actually higher than the percentage voting Republican in 1992 and 1996—which calls into question the claims of some conservative critics that the professoriate is growing more Democratic by the year.

On the basis of these retrospective data, we were also able to calculate the percentage of professors voting for one of the major parties in the 2004 presidential elections who, in a previous election, had voted for the opposing party. For Democratic-voting professors in 2004, the figure is 14 percent; for Republican-voting professors, 32 percent. Party switching when it comes to voting is thus fairly rare in academe, though by no means unheard of.

We conclude our discussion of professorial voting by considering how involved professors were in the 2004 campaign. To this end, we analyze a series of NES questions about political activities. Overall we find that professors who voted for Kerry or some other non-Republican candidate were more active in the campaign than were Bush voters. This may be evidence of a high level of political mobilization against the Bush administration or of the fact that conservative academics have historically been less active politically than their more progressive counterparts. Sixty-four percent of academic non-Bush voters said they talked to people about the candidates before the election and tried to convince them to vote one way or another, compared with 34 percent of Bush voters. Thirty percent of non-Bush voters said they attended political meetings, rallies, speeches, or dinners during the campaign, compared with 12 percent of Bush voters. Thirty-nine percent of non-Bush voters said they wore a campaign button or put a bumper sticker on their car or a sign in front of their house, compared with 12 percent of Bush voters. Forty-seven percent of non-Bush voters reported giving money to a political party or candidate during the 2004 election cycle, compared with 24 percent of Bush voters. Finally, non-Bush voters were more likely than Bush voters to report that they mentioned in class the candidate they would be voting for—8 and 3 percent, respectively. However, 93 percent of all professors said they did *not* mention in class which candidate they would be voting for.

Other Measures of Political Identity

Before moving on to consider the substantive attitudes items, we consider three other political identities professors may hold that would indicate something about their political views: whether they think of themselves as radicals, political activists, and Marxists. We queried respondents on these matters by presenting them with a series of labels—including "radical," "political activist," and "Marxist"—and asking them to indicate how well, on a seven-point scale ranging from "not at all" to "extremely well," the labels described them. Although the terms *radical* and *political activist* are typically associated with the left, some respondents who did not see themselves as having left sympathies identified as radicals or political activists. Table 1.12 shows the percentage of respondents in each broad disciplinary grouping who said these terms described them at least moderately well (with a score of 4 or higher); for radical and political activist, we count only those who also considered themselves liberals.

The table indicates that self-identified Marxists are rare in academe. The highest proportion of Marxist academics can be found in the social sciences, where they comprise 18 percent of all professors. (Among the social science fields for which we can issue discipline-specific estimates, sociology contains the most Marxists, at 27%—but it is important to add that among both social scientists and humanists, identification as a Marxist may signal theoretical orientation as

TABLE 1.12
Professors Identifying as Radical, Activist, or Marxist by Area of Study

Area	Percentage		
	Radical	Activist	Marxist
Physical/biological sciences	8	4	3
Social sciences	25	23	18
Humanities	20	27	5
Computer science / engineering	14	1	6
Health sciences	0	2	1
Business	4	5	2
Other	9	12	5
Total	13	15	6

much as political commitment.) In the humanities and social sciences, about a quarter of professors consider themselves radicals, and about a quarter activists. Consistent with our earlier claim that the number of moderates in academe appears to have been on the upswing in 2006, we find that self-described radicalism is more common among professors who came of age in the 1960s than among younger ones, suggesting generational change. For example, 18 percent of professors aged 50–64 consider themselves liberal radicals, compared with just 4 percent of professors aged 26–35. Similarly, whereas 19 percent of professors aged 50–64 consider themselves liberal activists, this is true of only 3 percent of professors in the youngest age cohort. Contrary to expectations of a continuous institutional status gradient in professorial radicalism, we find that community colleges and liberal arts schools house the highest percentage of radicals (15% and 20%, respectively) and activists (26% and 21%, respectively), while it is liberal arts colleges that are home to the highest proportion of Marxists (17%, compared with 3% in community colleges, 4% in other BA-granting schools, 4% at non-elite, PhD-granting institutions, and just 3% in elite, PhD-granting schools).

Social and Political Attitudes

Knowing what proportion of professors consider themselves liberals, moderates, or conservatives and what their party affiliations and voting tendencies are is certainly helpful in assessing their orientation toward the political field. Also helpful, however, is to understand their attitudes and views on the policy and value issues at the heart of American political contestation. Our survey contained a large number of attitudes questions. Rather than report responses to all of these items here, we focus on six broad attitude domains: views of socioeconomic issues, sex and gender, race and ethnicity, military force, the Middle East, and attachment to and identification with American culture. Obviously these are not the only topics on which professors (or others) have political views. Yet they are among the key concerns over which campus culture wars are being fought, so they merit special attention. For each domain, we have selected a handful of relevant attitudes questions from the survey.

SOCIOECONOMIC ISSUES

Here we analyze five questions. Two are from the Pew Values survey; these ask respondents whether they think government should do more to help the poor and whether businesses make too much profit. The other three are from the GSS and ask whether government should do more to reduce income differences between the rich and the poor, "perhaps by raising taxes on wealthy families or giving income assistance"; whether the government should see to it that everyone has a job and a "decent standard of living"; and whether the government wastes money that it collects through taxes.

Table 1.13 shows the percentage distributions for responses to the Pew items and the GSS question about wasting money on taxes. The other two items asked respondents to locate themselves on a scale from 1 to 7, and we have recoded responses into a three-category scheme. As the table shows, on the whole, professors favor efforts to reduce income disparities. Sixty percent agree that government should do more to help needy Americans (the comparable figure in the general population in 2007 was 54%), and 46 percent favor government action to reduce inequality. This does not mean, however, that professors generally favor making it the responsibility of government to ensure that everyone has a good job: only 21 percent of professors take this position. On views of corporate America, professors are about evenly split. Forty-seven percent say that business corporations make too much profit (compared with 65% of Americans in 2007 polls), with more than a third feeling strongly this way, while 44 percent say that business corporations make a fair and reasonable profit (compared with 30% in the general population). Finally, despite their support for government intervention to reduce inequality, on the whole, professors do not have much faith in government efficiency. A majority believes there is "a lot" of government waste.

SEX AND GENDER

For this domain we consider five questions. Four are taken from the GSS. These ask about respondents' views of homosexuality, the gender division of labor in the household, whether preschool children are likely to suffer if their mothers are in the workforce, and abortion. A fifth question asked respondents whether they thought the underrepresentation of women in the math, science, and engineering fields was mostly because of discrimination, mostly because of differences of ability, or mostly because of differences of interest. We report the responses to these items, along with the specific question wordings, in table 1.14.

As the table shows, professors have very liberal attitudes toward sex and gender. About 70 percent think that homosexuality is not wrong at all, about 75 percent are firmly prochoice, and nearly 60 percent strongly disagree with a "traditional" gender division of labor. There is more variation on the question of whether the preschool-age children of working mothers suffer: many more professors disagree with this statement than agree, but weak disagreement is more

TABLE 1.13
Professors' Views on Select Socioeconomic Issues

Survey question	Percentage				
	Strongly agree	Agree	Neither agree nor disagree	Disagree	Strongly disagree
The government should do more to help needy Americans, even if it means going deeper into debt.[a]	41	19	12	16	12
Business corporations make too much profit.	36	11	9	24	20
Do you think that people in government waste a lot of money we pay in taxes, waste some of it, or don't waste very much of it?	A lot — 55	Some — 42	Not very much — 3		
Some people think that the government in Washington ought to reduce the income differences between the rich and the poor, perhaps by raising the taxes of wealthy families or by giving income assistance to the poor. Others think that the government should not concern itself with reducing this income difference between the rich and the poor. Where would you place yourself in this debate?	Reduce inequality — 46	Neither — 39	Don't reduce inequality — 15		
Some people feel the government in Washington should see to it that every person has a job and a good standard of living. Others think the government should just let each person get ahead on her or his own. Which is closer to the way you feel?	Guarantee job — 21	Neither — 60	Don't guarantee job — 19		

[a]One of the unique and attractive features of the Pew Values items is that respondents are asked to select which of two oppositely valenced statements comes closest to their views and are then asked whether they feel strongly about the issue or not. This minimizes acquiescence bias and permits responses to be recoded in a continuous fashion. For this item, the oppositely valenced statement reads: "The government today can't afford to do much more to help the needy." In this table and tables 1.14 through 1.17, we report only the liberally valenced statements.

TABLE 1.14
Professors' Views on Select Sex and Gender Issues

Survey question/statement	Percentage			
	Always wrong	Almost always wrong	Wrong only sometimes	Not wrong at all
What do you think of sexual relations between two adults of the same sex?	17	3	11	69
	Strongly agree	Agree	Disagree	Strongly disagree
It is much better for everyone involved if the man is the achiever outside the home and the woman takes care of the home and the family.	4	9	31	56
A preschool child is likely to suffer if his or her mother works.	3	23	47	27
	Yes	No		
Should it be possible for a pregnant woman to obtain a legal abortion if the woman wants it for any reason?	75	25		
	Discrimination	Differences in ability	Differences of interest	
In many math, science, and engineering fields, there are more male professors than female professors. Do you think this difference is mainly because of discrimination, because of differences in ability between men and women, or because of differences of interest between men and women?	25	1	75	

common than strong disagreement. A further indication of how progressive the professoriate is on sex and gender was that, in response to another GSS question, 56 percent of professors in our sample described themselves as feminists: 63 percent of women and 51 percent of men. By contrast, the last time this question was asked on the GSS, in 1996, 27 percent of women and 12 percent of men described themselves as feminists (Schnittker, Freese, and Powell 2003, 611). As shown in table 1.14, on the question of the reason for the underrepresentation of women in math, science, and engineering, only about 1 percent of respondents support the "differences in ability" hypothesis. About a quarter blame discrimination, with the rest citing differences of interest. Cross-tabulations show that women are about twice as likely as men to blame discrimination (34% vs. 17%).

RACE AND ETHNICITY

Here we consider three items from our survey, all concerned with steps that might be taken in the educational realm to reduce racial disparities. The first, which we constructed based on a GSS question, asked professors whether they favored affirmative action in college admissions for African Americans and members of other racial/ethnic minority groups. The second, drawn directly from the GSS, asked whether lack of educational opportunity is a cause of disparities in jobs, income, and housing between blacks and whites. The third asked professors whether they agreed that the racial and ethnic diversity of the country should be more strongly reflected in the college curriculum. What do we find in response to these items?

Although the majority of professors favored affirmative action in college admissions, it is not an overwhelming majority. Excluding those who said they had no opinion on the matter, we find that 11 percent of our respondents strongly favored affirmative action in college admissions, and 47 percent favored it. Thirty-three percent opposed affirmative action, and 10 percent strongly opposed it.

On whether lack of educational opportunities is a cause of disparities between blacks and whites, we find much less variation: 85 percent of professors agreed that it is, reflecting the high value that professors obviously place on education. Two other survey questions are also worth mentioning here: 54 percent of professors cited ongoing discrimination as a cause of racial inequality, while just 18 percent agreed that there are racial differences in income because "most African Americans just don't have the motivation or will power to pull themselves up out of poverty."

On the curricular diversity question—again excluding those who said they didn't know—we find strong but not overwhelming support. Twenty-eight percent of professors strongly agreed that the racial and ethnic diversity of the country should be better represented in the undergraduate curriculum, 44 percent agreed, 21 percent disagreed, and 7 percent strongly disagreed.

MILITARY FORCE AND THE MIDDLE EAST

The attitude domains considered thus far concern domestic issues. Now consider views on military force and foreign policy. Here we examine responses to three Pew items: one that asks about the advisability of diplomacy versus military strength as strategies for achieving peace; one about the wisdom of using "overwhelming military force" to defeat terrorism; and a third that asks respondents' views on whether "we should all be willing to fight for our country, whether it is right or wrong."

On these items, there is wide agreement among professors. Eighty percent preferred diplomacy over military strength as a way to secure peace, with 64 percent feeling strongly about the matter (in 2007, the comparable figures in the general population were 49% and 18%). Professors are even more dovish in their views of using military force to defeat terrorism. Eighty-seven percent agreed that "relying too much on military force to defeat terrorism creates hatred that leads to more terrorism," with 75 percent feeling strongly about it. (When Pew asked this question of the general population in 2005, 51% of Americans said that relying too much on military force is problematic.) On the fight-for-country item, 79 percent of professors said that "it's acceptable to refuse to fight in a war you believe is morally wrong," with 68 percent feeling strongly this way. (In 2007, 45% of Americans said refusing to fight was acceptable.)

These questions concern military force in general. To probe foreign policy views more deeply, we turn next to questions about the Middle East and the war in Iraq. Table 1.15 shows responses to two questions about the war, and one about the Israeli-Palestinian conflict. The table clearly shows the professoriate's high level of opposition to the Iraq War. Eighty percent of professors in 2006 believed that President Bush lied about the reasons to go to war, and 66 percent advocated drawing down troop levels. Among those who thought that President Bush lied, those who felt strongly about the matter outnumbered those who did not by a ratio of nearly 15:1. At the same time, flying in the face of charges that many professors express a pro-Palestinian, anti-Israeli bias, only about 11 percent of professors in our sample say their sympathies lie more with the Palestinians in the Middle East conflict. Almost double that number side with the Israelis, while the largest group of professors—51 percent—say they sympathize with both sides.

TABLE 1.15
Professors' Views on Select Foreign Policy Issues

Survey question/statement	Strongly agree	Agree	Don't know	Disagree	Strongly disagree
President Bush misled the American people about the reasons to go to war in Iraq.	75	5	4	4	12
The current course cannot bring stability and we need to start reducing the number of U.S. troops in Iraq.	56	10	6	8	19

	Israelis	Palestinians	Both	Neither
In the Middle East situation, are your sympathies more with the Israelis or more with the Palestinians?	21	11	51	17

COSMOPOLITANISM

Finally, we consider evidence for whether American professors are "locals" or "cosmopolitans." This is an issue of long-standing importance in the sociology of intellectual life. On the one hand, theorists such as Alvin Gouldner (1965) have argued that, beginning with the philosophers of Ancient Greece, intellectuals in the West have tended to be cosmopolitans, identifying more with abstract ideals like reason and truth—and with the broad community of others who are committed to those same ideals—than with the polities of which they are members, a notion also implicit in Robert K. Merton's idea that the "ethos of science" is universalistic. On the other hand, observers of late-twentieth-century American intellectual life have noted that cosmopolitanism *qua* rejection of American identity was particularly characteristic of academicians in the United States in the post-1960s era (Kazin and McCartin 2006)—a fact sometimes said to be linked to the inability of the academic New Left to achieve a mass following (Rorty 1998). We approach this issue empirically by considering four items: one that asks whether professors agree that the growing number of newcomers from other countries threatens traditional American customs and values; one that asks how proud respondents are to be Americans; one that asks whether Western civilization and culture should be the foundation of the undergraduate curriculum; and one, taken from the World Values Survey, that asks professors whether they identify more with their locality or town, their state or region, the United States as a whole, or the world as a whole.

The responses can be quickly summarized. Does the growing number of newcomers threaten traditional American culture? Only 17 percent of professors think that it does. Are professors proud to be Americans? Excluding those who are not American, we find that 45 percent of professors are very proud of their national identity, and 33 percent are somewhat proud. Eighteen percent are not very proud, and 4 percent say they are not proud at all. Do professors think Western civilization and culture should be the foundation of the undergraduate curriculum? About 44 percent say that it should. Finally, with which geographic group do professors most identify? Twelve percent say the locality or town where they live, 19 percent say the state or region of the country where they live, 32 percent say the United States as a whole, and 38 percent say the world as a whole.[4]

Attitudes toward the Role of Politics in Teaching and Research

Although conservative critics of American higher education worry about the overrepresentation of liberals on the faculty, of greater concern to them is how this overrepresentation may be affecting teaching and research, especially in the social sciences and humanities. More important for us, this is also an interesting issue for the sociology of knowledge and the sociology of higher education. First, there is historical evidence to suggest that political commitments and identities among academicians, particularly in the social sciences and humanities (e.g., Novick 1988; Rojas 2007) but also in the natural sciences (e.g., Frickel 2004), may help spur the creation of new intellectual movements or fields (Frickel and Gross 2005), influence topic selection and affiliation with intellectual traditions and theoretical approaches (Gross 2002), and exert a significant effect on choice of methodology. Second, as discussed in chapter 5 of this volume, a large research literature suggests that students undergo a "liberalization" of "sociopolitical, religious, and gender role attitudes" as they proceed through college (Alwin, Cohen, and Newcomb 1991; Pascarella and Terenzini 1991, 559). While the size of this liberalization effect and its underlying mechanisms are subject to debate, one mechanism that might be thought operative is that students become more liberal through exposure to liberal professors who open them up to new ways of thinking or through exposure to a liberal campus culture to which professors and administrators lend their support. From the perspective of either knowledge production or a concern with higher education and its inputs to the political system, then, it becomes important to understand not just what professors' politics are but the social practices they enact that mediate the relationship between their politics, teaching, and research. Do professors inhabit disciplinary or institutional "epistemic cultures" (Knorr Cetina 1999) that stress the importance of objectivity and/or political neutrality? Or are they immersed in social environments where political engagement through their work is seen as a moral obligation? Such questions are best addressed through qualitative research that allows the nuances, complexities, and ambiguities of meaning at the core of epistemic cultures to be captured, and professors' actual behavior to be observed, but some preliminary sense of how professors think about the issues involved can be gleaned from an analysis of a few survey items.

To assess respondents' views, we presented them with a series of statements and asked them to tell us how much they agreed or disagreed with each. Table 1.16 shows their responses to three of these statements. The table indicates that when it comes to views of politics and teaching, the professorial community is about evenly split, with half of professors believing that a teacher's politics have no place in the classroom, and the other half more open to pedagogical styles in which teachers feel free to express their own positions. About 55 percent of respondents express agreement with the statement that when politically controversial issues arise in class, professors should keep their personal opinions to themselves. Similarly, about 40 percent of respondents in 2006 said that professors should not be allowed to voice their anti–Iraq War views in the classroom. In terms of research, the majority of respondents—71 percent—endorse the view that it is acceptable for professors to be guided by their political or religious values in their choice of research topic.

To probe the teaching side of things more, we constructed a variable to measure whether a respondent is fervent in the belief that one's personal politics should play no role in teaching. We coded respondents as fervent advocates of neutrality if they strongly disagreed with the statement about speaking out on the Iraq War *and* strongly agreed with the statement about keeping one's personal opinion to oneself in the classroom. About 10 percent of respondents fit these criteria. In our sample, fervent neutrality is most common among professors teaching at elite, PhD-granting schools (16%) and least common among professors teaching at liberal arts colleges (4%). Looking at broad disciplinary groupings, we see that the insistence on neutrality is about four times more common among professors in the physical and biological sciences, computer science and engineering, health sciences, and business (between 15% and 21%) than among professors of the social sciences (4%) and humanities (6%). There are also differences by political orientation. Perhaps reflecting support for the

TABLE 1.16
Professors' Views on the Role of Personal Politics and Religion in Teaching and Research

Survey question/statement	Percentage			
	Strongly agree	Somewhat agree	Somewhat disagree	Strongly disagree
Professors who oppose the war in Iraq should be allowed to express their antiwar views in the classroom.	23	37	20	20
When politically controversial issues arise in the classroom, college or university professors should keep their personal opinions to themselves.	17	38	37	8
It is acceptable for college or university professors to be guided by their political or religious beliefs in the selection of research topics.	26	45	16	13

Iraq War in 2006 and disdain for those who would criticize it in the classroom, 22 percent of conservative professors are ardent advocates of neutrality, compared with 12 percent of moderates and 5 percent of liberals. Not surprisingly, fewer self-identified faculty radicals (2%) than nonradicals (11%) fall into this category.

Views of Tenure

One theme in conservative critique of American higher education is that politicized faculty members too often hide behind the institution of tenure once they have been promoted, trading in their commitments to pursue original research and offer diligent instruction for partisan activity. In the eyes of critics, tenure means a guaranteed job for life, which equates with a lack of accountability to students, university administrators, trustees, and the public and is rife with potential for abuse. While conservative politicians, particularly at the state level, have sometimes echoed these criticisms, so far they have not found great resonance with the public. Other survey research we have done suggests that only about half of Americans have heard of tenure (Gross and Simmons 2006). For survey respondents who have not, when presented with a neutral explanation of tenure, most express support for the institution in principle, recognizing that it is important in order to protect academic freedom. But the majority of Americans do not believe that tenure should protect professors who hold what are seen as extreme political views. What is more, the public's attitudes toward tenure are tied to politics, just as they are among cultural and political elites who comment on higher education: conservatives and Republicans are less supportive of the institution and hold more restrictive views of academic freedom than liberals and Democrats. For reasons having little to do with public opinion, recent decades have witnessed a steady erosion of tenure as an institution. This has occurred as universities, under pressure to save money, have come to rely more heavily on contingent faculty and as college and university trustees at some schools—often business people who view tenure as a kind of protection afforded no other American worker—have worked behind the scenes to eliminate it (for a discussion, see Chait 2002).

How do professors feel about tenure, and how do their views vary depending on their tenure status, institutional location, and politics? These are questions that have been addressed in other surveys of the professoriate (e.g., Sanderson, Phua, and Herda 2000), but we thought it important to take them up in our study as well. Accordingly, we asked respondents to tell us how much they agreed or disagreed with a series of statements about tenure. The results are shown in table 1.17.

On the whole, these responses suggest that full-time faculty are strongly supportive of the institution of tenure but aware of its potential for abuse. On the one side, there is overwhelming support for tenure as a reward for a job well done, whatever this may mean at different institutions, and for the notion that tenure provides key academic freedom protections. On the other side, nearly all respondents know of at least some cases where tenure has protected incompetent faculty, and more than a third of respondents express agreement with the sentiment that tenure disincentivizes hard work. Perhaps reflecting these concerns, when asked to indicate which statement best described their attitudes toward tenure, 55 percent of respondents said the tenure system should be modified but not eliminated, 38 percent said it should remain as it is, and 7 percent said it should be phased out.

Some sense of how views about tenure are distributed in the professorial population can be had by looking at how different groups come down on the question of whether the tenure system should remain as is, be modified, or be phased out. Not surprisingly, professors who already have tenure are much more supportive of keeping the tenure system as it currently is than are those who do not have tenure. Forty-nine percent of tenured professors say the tenure system should remain as it is, compared with 21 percent of those who do not have tenure. This difference takes on greater meaning when we compare professors who

TABLE 1.17
Professors' Views on Tenure

Survey statement	Percentage			
	Strongly agree	Somewhat agree	Somewhat disagree	Strongly disagree
Tenure is a good way to reward accomplished professors.	35	48	12	5
Tenure is essential so that professors can teach, research, and write without having to worry about being fired if some people disagree with their conclusions.	49	34	12	5
Tenure sometimes protects incompetent faculty.	41	53	4	2
Giving professors tenure takes away their incentive to work hard.	5	32	31	32

are either tenured or in tenure-track jobs with those who are not. Forty-four percent of professors in the former group want the tenure system to remain as it is, compared with 14 percent in the latter group. While the tenured and those on the tenure track want to protect a key asset, those for whom tenure is not a possibility may feel that the system is unfair and would like to see it modified. Whether the preferred modification would involve simply expanding it to cover those not currently eligible we cannot say. What we can say is that, whether they are speaking from experience or from the standpoint of sour grapes, professors who are neither tenured nor on the tenure track are twice as likely to feel that tenure disincentivizes hard work: 60 percent of the former agree that this is so, compared with 30 percent of tenured or tenure-track professors.

Returning to the question of what should be done with the tenure system, we find differences on this variable across types of institutions. The greatest support for keeping the tenure system as is can be found in elite, PhD-granting schools, where professors earn the highest salaries and have the greatest economic incentive to preserve the institutional status quo. At such schools, 59 percent of respondents favor keeping the tenure system as it is. By contrast, only 21 percent of community college professors favor keeping the tenure system as is. At the same time, and possibly reflecting greater confidence in their ability to prosper and thrive no matter the institutional conditions, more advocates of eliminating tenure can also be found at elite, PhD-granting schools: about 11 percent, compared with about 6 percent at other types of institutions.

We find no significant differences on this question across political orienta-tion. On several of the other tenure items, however, conservative professors do differ from their liberal colleagues, though we caution that here (as elsewhere) observed differences across political position may actually reflect differences in institutional location. Twenty-two percent of conservatives, compared with 15 percent of liberals, disagree that tenure is a good way to reward accomplished professors. More significantly, 39 percent of conservative professors, compared with 15 percent of liberals, disagree that tenure is essential to protect academic freedom. And whereas 28 percent of liberals agree that tenure takes away profes-sors' incentives to work hard, half of conservative professors—49 percent—feel this way. This is the first hint of the phenomenon we explore below: conservative professors' expression of grievance with the current academic environment.

Perceptions of the University Environment

Given that conservatives are a rare breed in academia, and given the potential for the political commitments of faculty to shape research agendas, teaching, and campus culture, it is hardly surprising—independent of broader conservative campaigns—to find outspoken conservative professors voicing complaints about the direction in which the university is heading and the extent and conse-quences of "liberal bias" in academe. Such professors are very much in evidence in the public sphere. Some, like Emory's Mark Bauerlein, regularly voice their complaints in editorials in the *Chronicle of Higher Education* and other venues. But how widely shared are their sentiments? Our survey shows that conser-vative professors, whether outspoken or not, register high levels of dissatisfac-tion with the current university environment. More surprisingly, perhaps, a high proportion of moderates do so as well, at least in certain respects.

Our survey contained about a dozen questions on views of the university en-vironment. For most, we asked respondents about their level of agreement or disagreement with various statements we constructed. Rather than run through all the findings here, we focus on a select number of questions, collapsing the four-point agreement/disagreement scale to two points and noting the differ-ences between liberals, moderates, and conservatives.

One straightforward question we asked concerning the university environ-ment was whether respondents agreed that colleges and universities tend to favor professors who hold liberal social and political views. Overall, 43 percent of pro-fessors agreed with the statement, and 57 percent disagreed. Conservatives were much more likely than liberals to agree: 81 percent versus 30 percent. Nearly half of moderates, however—49 percent—also agreed that liberals are favored. (The question did not ask respondents to give their opinion on whether the situation was in any way unfair or what "favored" meant to them in this context.)

In the light of conservative complaints that liberal orthodoxy has such a stranglehold on the university that certain issues—such as possible gender differences in scientific or mathematical aptitude—cannot be discussed or debated, another question we asked was whether respondents agreed that professors are as curious and open-minded today as they have ever been. Overall, 80 percent said that professors are open-minded and curious. Forty-six percent of conservatives, however, said that professors are no longer as open-minded and curious, compared with 17 percent of liberals and about the same percentage of moderates. Thus, half of conservatives see a problem where liberals and moderates do not. Along similar lines, we asked respondents whether most professors are respectful when students voice opinions that differ from their own. The vast majority—88 percent—said that they are, but conservatives were nearly four times more likely than liberals and moderates to disagree that most professors are respectful.

What about views of political correctness on campus? We asked respondents to indicate their level of agreement with the statement "The adoption of attitudes often labeled 'politically correct' has made America a more civilized society than it was thirty years ago." Overall, 40 percent of respondents agreed. Whereas liberals expressed modestly high levels of agreement—60 percent, a figure that should give pause to those who assume that academic liberalism necessarily means subscription to the canons of political correctness—only 24 percent of moderates and 24 percent of conservatives said they agreed. Likewise, we asked respondents if, in their opinion, too many professors these days are distracted by disputes over issues like sexual harassment or the politics of ethnic groups, major concerns of the academic left. Only 18 percent of liberals said yes, too many professors are so distracted, but 42 percent of moderates did so, along with 64 percent of conservatives.

Together, these findings suggest that conservative professors are quite unhappy with the current campus environment, at least with regard to politics, and that some moderate professors share some of their complaints. Whether faculty moderates—who, as we have argued, comprise a sizable bloc—will ever feel so moved by these complaints that they throw their support behind conservative proposals for reform remains to be seen. Given that most moderates in academe fall in the center-left of the political spectrum, this may seem unlikely. On the other hand, it is interesting to note that most professors say they *would* welcome a greater diversity of political views on campus. Sixty-nine percent of respondents agreed with the statement "The goal of campus diversity should include fostering diversity of political views among faculty members." This question did not specify any particular kind of political diversity and said nothing about concrete steps that might be taken to achieve it, but the high level of agreement suggests that internal campaigns to promote political diversity within the professoriate have at least some mobilization potential.

Conclusion

Our aim in this chapter was to summarize the results of our 2006 survey of the American professoriate. Whereas early studies on the topic, carried out by sociologists like Lazarsfeld and Lipset, sought to measure political belief among professors and the distribution of such belief across fields and institutions—and to provide social-scientific explanations for observed patterns—more recent research, beholden to a political agenda, has had as its major goal to simply highlight the liberalism of the faculty. We show that there is more heterogeneity of political opinion among the professoriate than recent studies have recognized. Although we would not contest the claim that professors are one of the most liberal occupational groups in American society or that the professoriate is a Democratic stronghold, we show that there is a sizable and often ignored center/center-left contingent within the faculty; that in several important attitude domains—and in terms of overall political orientation—moderatism appears to have been on the upswing in 2006; that it is liberal arts colleges, not elite, PhD-granting institutions, that house the most progressive faculty; and that there is much disagreement among professors about the role that politics should play in teaching and research.

NOTES

1. In an earlier description of this work, we reported that there were 1,417 cases. Subsequent examination turned up a duplicate case in the dataset. Also, here we consistently code "don't know" responses as missing and use finalized versions of our weights.

2. Here and throughout the chapter, because of rounding, row and column percentages may not add to 100.

3. Pew surveys from 2007 showed that in the general population, 11 percent of Independents leaned Republican, and 17 percent leaned Democratic.

4. When this question was asked on the World Values Survey in the United States in 1999, with slightly different response options, 32 percent of Americans identified with their locality, 11 percent with their region, 35 percent with their country, 3 percent with

their continent, and 20 percent with the world as a whole. Identification with the world as a whole was slightly lower (15%) among those who had completed BA degrees or higher, a better comparison group for the professorial population. Our survey thus provides evidence that American professors have a more cosmopolitan, global identity than college-educated Americans in general.

PART TWO

EXPLAINING PROFESSORIAL LIBERALISM

CHAPTER TWO

Political Liberalism and Graduate School Attendance

A Longitudinal Analysis

ETHAN FOSSE, JEREMY FREESE, AND NEIL GROSS

Graduate and professional education—the training and certification of students beyond the baccalaureate level—is a crucial part of the American higher education enterprise. As of 2010, more than 1.8 million people were enrolled in graduate or professional degree programs in the United States. The number of graduate and professional degree students grew at a rate of about 4 percent per year over the preceding decade (N. Bell 2010), and data from the General Social Survey (GSS) show that by 2008, the percentage of American adults with advanced degrees had more than doubled since the 1970s, reaching just over 9 percent. These increases have probably been driven by several factors, including declining relative returns to the upper middle class of a bachelor's degree alone, changes in the life course and the temporal structuring of careers, and the continued lure of the United States for foreign students. But they also reflect the coming to maturity of a knowledge economy (Powell and Snellman 2004) and are tied to the proliferation of occupational roles requiring advanced technical knowledge and expertise.

While graduate education is sociologically significant in several respects, in this chapter we examine it from the standpoint of an interest in occupational politics, or the question of why workers in different occupations have the political views and allegiances they do. Although some occupations that require advanced degrees tend to be conservative, such as the medical profession, overall there is a strong association between the political liberalism of a field and the proportion of its workers who have undergone graduate or professional training. For example, GSS data show that of the ten most liberal major occupations in the United States from 1996 to 2008, five required advanced degrees of most workers, and two that did not—authors/journalists and creative artists—nevertheless had rates of advanced degree holding twice that of the general population. These aggregate patterns reflect the fact that liberal self-identification, Democratic Party affiliation and voting, and more progressive social and economic attitudes are correlated with advanced degree holding at the individual level.

Sociologists have long been aware of such associations, invoking them to help account for the liberalism of "New Class" occupations and the emergence of political cleavages around science and education (Brint 1984, 1985; Gerteis 1998; Manza and Brooks 1997; Manza, Hout, and Brooks 1995; Meyer et al. 2007). But the underlying explanations have remained unclear. Is there an intrinsic link between liberalism and intelligence, such that the more liberal views of those with advanced degrees reflect liberals' greater academic potential (Deary, Batty, and Gale 2008; Kanazawa 2010)? Do workers with advanced education tend to be more liberal because further cognitive development occurs with additional years of schooling, leading the intelligentsia to find fault with what they come to see as simplistic conservative ideologies? Does the liberalism of the highly educated reflect a collective effort at differentiation from both the middle-class and business elites (Bourdieu 1988 [1984]; Lamont 1987, 1992)? Or have those with liberal views come to so completely dominate the knowledge work fields that they refuse to hire colleagues with dissenting opinions (Klein and Stern 2009; Rothman, Lichter, and Nevitte 2005)?

To make headway with these questions, we examine the connection between advanced education and liberalism in one important occupation: the American professoriate. As chapter 1 of this volume shows, professors and instructors in higher education, who comprise about 1 percent of the U.S. workforce but exercise social influence disproportionate to their numbers, tend to have political views to the left of other Americans. Although scholars have advanced numerous theories to explain the politics of professors, a recent study by Fosse and Gross (2012), using GSS data, demonstrated that the main factor accounting for professors' politics is simply that most have doctoral or other advanced degrees. This study also proposed a theory to account for the connection between graduate school attendance and liberal political identification among professors: the theory that over the course of the twentieth century, the professoriate acquired a reputation as a liberal occupation, and young liberals today, acting on the basis of this reputation and seeking careers that accord with their political identities, are more likely than conservatives to aspire to become academics and get the education necessary to do so. This theory, highlighting political self-selection into academe, is at odds with most established sociological accounts of professorial liberalism, which focus on class interests or educational socialization. However, neither Fosse and Gross's self-selection theory nor competing hypotheses about the relationship between advanced education and liberalism could be directly tested with the cross-sectional data on which they relied.

Here we use a different data source to assess key claims of their theory. The National Longitudinal Study of Adolescent Health (Add Health), a study that began in 1994–95 with a nationally representative sample of students in grades 7–12, has 534 respondents who, by the fourth wave of data collection in 2007–8, had either completed PhDs or entered graduate school with the intention of earning a doctorate. We leverage this fact to evaluate three arguments essential to Fosse and Gross's account: first, that young people who are liberal are more likely to self-select into graduate school; second, that this self-selection is not spurious, resulting from the different values held by liberals and conservatives or from cognitive or personality differences between them; and third, that the liberalism of those with advanced degrees does not result primarily from their experiences of graduate education. We find empirical support for all of these claims except the one about personality differences; on this point our findings are more ambiguous. We conclude by discussing the implications of our analysis.

Previous Research
Education and Political Liberalism

A consistent finding by social scientists in the post–World War II era was that education is associated with more liberal social and political attitudes. Much early work on the topic was concerned with macro-level outcomes, arguing that the growth of schooling and literacy in the West over the nineteenth and twentieth centuries eroded traditional social orientations, in so doing laying the groundwork for modern industrial society (e.g., Inkeles 1974; Parsons and Platt 1973). Yet other scholars were interested in the link between educational experiences and attitudes in its own right. Although some studies reported a linear relationship between years of schooling and political liberalism, the bulk of this research focused on educational experiences occurring during what dominant psychological theories of the day portrayed as an essential stage of identity formation in the life course: late adolescence and early adulthood. Newcomb's (1943) longitudinal research at then all-female Bennington College was foundational here, showing that many students arrived on campus with conservative views, shifted positions, and remained more progressive from there on out, supporting throughout their lives those policies and politicians they saw as in line with the values they had adopted as "Bennington Women." Stouffer's (1955) study of political tolerance was similarly influential. Among other things, it reported that Americans who had been to college tended to be less authoritarian, in the sense of not supporting the political repression of dissidents, than those who had not. The more liberal tendencies of college graduates were also reported in Campbell and colleagues' classic contribution to political science, *The American Voter* (1960). Still other work showed that people with college degrees tended to be less religious, had more coherent political views, exhibited higher levels of political knowledge and sophistication, and participated more in the political process (see Feldman and Newcomb 1969; Pascarella and Terenzini 1991, 2005). A variety of mechanisms were posited to account for these findings, including socialization into an Enlightenment culture said to be institutionalized in colleges and universities, the consequent acquisition by college students of more sophisticated cognitive styles, and sustained exposure to diverse peers, thought to call into question people's otherwise taken-for-granted and parental-derived views of the social and political world. On the basis of these key works and other studies, by 1970 it was seen as "almost axiomatic that students become more liberal during their college years" (Chickering 1970, 599).

The focus of this research was undergraduate education. But in the 1970s, some sociologists began looking at the political consequences of graduate and professional training as well. The context was interest in the emerging postindustrial economy. As the ranks of knowledge workers within and outside the service sector swelled, sociologists took up the question of with which social groups and classes these workers would align and, hence, what structural shifts in the economy meant for the future of class relations and politics (D. Bell 1976; Bruce-Briggs 1979; Gouldner 1979; Konrád and Szelényi 1979). Quantitative and historical evidence showed that workers in certain knowledge work fields, such as academia, journalism, and the arts, tended to take liberal stances, favoring redistributionist economic policies and a stronger welfare state, protection for minority rights, and expansive civil liberties protections (Brint 1984; Ladd and Lipset 1976). Scholars debated how radical these stances were, whether they extended to knowledge workers in larger occupations such as engineering or computer programming, and the social origins of the politics of intellectuals, broadly defined. Where some, such as Gouldner (1979), viewed knowledge workers as potentially comprising a distinct class with common interests in the valorization of educational status over economic standing, others, such as Daniel Bell (1976), thought the intellectual stratum too fractured to engage in collective action. Yet both sides in the debate over the "New Class" saw graduate and professional training, which had expanded dramatically in the 1960s, as helping to account for intellectuals' distinctive worldviews. For Gouldner, post-baccalaureate education provided knowledge workers with their unique endowments of cultural capital, whereas for critics of the New Class thesis such as Bell and later Brint (1984, 1985), the liberalism of intellectuals and of American professionals generally in the post-1960s period reflected, in part, expanding educational requirements and opportunities—which translated into future workers spending more time as young adults in the classroom, where the liberalizing effects of higher education would accumulate beyond what was possible in four years of college.

The Politics of Professors

As we have already indicated, professors figured centrally in these discussions, since both historical and survey data showed the professoriate to be a left-leaning occupational group. Indeed, by the 1950s, it had become clear to many observers, not least conservative critics like William F. Buckley Jr. (1951), that professors stood to the left of the U.S. population.

Scholars such as Ladd and Lipset (1976) were intrigued by these findings, as they were by comparable findings on the liberalism of other knowledge work fields, since they seemed to suggest a problem with traditional theories of class politics: such theories would predict conservatism, not liberalism, among workers in high-status occupations. In the case of professors, Ladd and Lipset sought to make sense of the anomaly by arguing that professors' politics were determined not by class interests but by the centering of much academic work around "intellectualism" and creativity, which they saw as naturally at odds with many strains of conservative ideology. Ladd and Lipset argued that this was not principally a matter of professors' typical personality structures but reflected the academic role professors were called on to enact. They assumed that future professors learn much of that role in graduate school.

Ladd and Lipset's intellectualism hypothesis, however, is not the only theory of why professors tend to be liberal. As noted earlier, many sociologists who have taken up the topic highlight class dynamics, if different dynamics than those posited by traditional class politics accounts. The dominant approach here has been to follow Bourdieu (1988 [1984]) in focusing specifically on the disparity between professors' high levels of cultural capital and their moderate levels of economic capital, which is said to—among other things—generate resentment toward the business classes and the conservative economic policies such classes often favor. Other scholars claim that demographic differences between professors and other Americans, such as the tendency of professors to reside in cities and have fewer children, help account for their liberal politics (Wilson 2008). Still others observe that professors tend to be less religious than average and note that religiosity is associated with greater political conservatism (for a discussion, see Gross and Simmons 2009). Finally, some social scientists argue that future academics are less materialistic than those individuals who take private sector jobs and are more concerned that their jobs provide them with a sense of meaning. Greater materialism, these authors argue, is tied to support for conservative ideology and the Republican Party (Lamont 1987, 1992; Summers 2007). All of these hypotheses are plausible.

Yet, until recently, few studies had systematically evaluated competing claims by using nationally representative data. The paper by Fosse and Gross (2012) did precisely that. In addition to the theories mentioned above, it examined Ladd and Lipset's intellectualism hypothesis, both directly—using proxy measures for embrace of the intellectual role—and indirectly, by considering, equally in line with the work of Gouldner, Bell, and Brint, to what extent high levels of advanced degree holding among academics explain their liberal views. The data source, again, was the GSS. Fosse and Gross proceeded by asking how much of the politics gap between the 326 professors included in the sample between 1974 and 2008 and other Americans could be accounted for by variables associated with different hypotheses. They found that a model inclusive of variables from all their hypotheses accounted for about 43 percent of the politics gap. Advanced degree holding accounted for about 20 percent of the gap. Other significant factors included relatively high levels of religious disbelief among professors, intellectualism measured as a willingness to give a hearing to controversial ideas, and the disparity between professors' cultural and economic capital.

In puzzling through these findings, Fosse and Gross initially believed they provided support for the idea that professorial liberalism is a function of professors' educational experiences. Having gone to graduate school—during which future academics' cognitive capacities are honed as they learn the culture and practices of their fields—professors might wind up rejecting conservative beliefs, which, some have argued, have a relatively simplistic logical structure and which, around issues like climate change, are inconsistent with established science. To the extent that religious disbelief might also result from prolonged exposure to the educational system, graduate training could offer an additional pathway toward liberalization. Finally, graduate students might learn from their professors that progressive politics are expected of those who enter the academic profession (Menand 2010) and adjust their beliefs accordingly.

On further reflection, however, Fosse and Gross became wary of this interpretation. First, while research by political psychologists demonstrates an association between cognitive sophistication and more liberal politics, the magnitude of this association is not particularly large. What is more, the history of the right shows that conservatism's success has been dependent on its ability to creatively and intelligently reinvent itself time and again to adjust to changing political circumstances (for a review, see Gross, Medvetz, and Russell 2011). Some rank-and-file conservatives may be dogmatic and small-minded (just as some liberals may be), but there is little historical basis for the assumption that most movement elites have had these cognitive characteristics and hence no reason to see something inherent in conservative ideology that repulses smart, educated people. Second, there have been several historical contexts in which much of the professoriate, including its most sophisticated, elite sectors, has embraced conservative and even fascistic views, as was the case in Germany in the early twentieth century. Third, although it is generally true, as Ladd and Lipset noted, that the higher one looks in the academic hierarchy, the greater the liberalism—a fact suggestive of a possible relationship between intellectualism and liberal politics—there is one academic discipline in the United States whose members are hardly intellectual slouches and whose patterns of party affiliation, at least, come closer to mirroring that of the American electorate: economists. One could certainly construct an account of economics as an outlier case, given its connections to the field of power (see Fourcade 2010), or argue that economists are technicians rather than "true" intellectuals, but at the very least, the politics of economists call into question the simple equation of intellectual sophistication with left-wing views.

But there was an even more significant reason Fosse and Gross came to doubt that exposure to many years of higher education is the main cause of professorial liberalism: the received wisdom that higher education produces more liberal attitudes has recently been challenged. To be sure, questions have been raised around the edges of the finding for some time, with some scholars asking whether the amount and nature of liberalization might depend on highly variable features of the campus environment, others pointing out that while Americans with college degrees tend to have more liberal social views, they often have more conservative economic attitudes, and still others questioning whether observed political shifts in the undergraduate years translate into lifelong political commitments (see Pascarella and Terenzini 2005). Yet the past few years have seen more profound challenges: using matching techniques on longitudinal datasets that include respondents who go to college as well as those who do not, researchers have discovered that some—not all—of the long-observed liberalization effect of college attendance is a function of the fact that more tolerant, open-minded adolescents are more likely to pursue and complete bachelor's degrees (Jennings and Stoker 2008; Kam and Palmer 2008; see also the discussion in chapter 5 of this volume.) Although the issue is not settled empirically, these studies led Fosse and Gross to reconsider the claim that the liberalism of the highly educated results primarily from their graduate school experiences, which take place during what is, for most people, a less formative stage of the life course.

A New Theory of Professorial Liberalism

On the basis of these considerations, Fosse and Gross developed an alternative interpretation of their findings. They theorized that for committed liberal or conservative students, certain occupations fall within the bounds of normative acceptability—understood specifically in terms of identity fit—while other occupations fall outside those bounds, and that students are likely to give little serious thought to pursuing occupations seen as politically inappropriate. Fosse and Gross's argument drew from theoretical and empirical work on occupational sex segregation, which finds that cultural stereotypes associated with different lines of work, such as the view that engineering is an inherently masculine occupation, shape men's and women's educational and career aspirations (Correll 2001, 2004; Marini and Brinton 1984; Marini and Greenberger 1978; Marini et al. 1996). Just as sociologists of gender maintain that jobs can be "sex typed," so Fosse and Gross argued that jobs can be "politically typed." To the extent that the professoriate has developed a reputation for liberalism over the years, through historical processes flagged by Fosse and Gross, conservatives might shy away out of a desire to have a career that they and others would see as fitting, while liberals would be drawn in. According to Fosse and Gross, such a process of self-selection made sense of their finding that possession of an advanced degree is the most important factor accounting for the liberalism of the professoriate: liberals are more likely to go to graduate school with the intention of becoming professors. Since the professoriate might also be "religiously typed," viewed as an occupation poorly suited to fervent religious believers, a parallel process could explain the overrepresentation of religious skeptics among professors, with independent effects on faculty politics. Finally, Fosse and Gross speculated that self-selection processes could explain some portion of the politics gap not accounted for by their statistical models.

Fosse and Gross were not the first scholars to develop a self-selection account of professorial liberalism. One of the earliest exponents of such a theory was Friedrich Hayek (1949). Although, as we have noted, Ladd and Lipset's intellectualism hypothesis emphasized professional socialization, self-selection also figured in their account, in two ways. First, they argued that people with an intellectual disposition, who were more inclined to be liberal, were more likely to become professors, taking up the academic role. Second, Ladd and Lipset noted that members of one religious-ethnic group—Jews—were overrepresented in American academe in the mid twentieth century. The reason for this, they argued, was that intellectualism is prized in Jewish culture, while the American university, despite a history of anti-Semitism, was one of the first high-status institutional domains to become open to Jews. The result was that Jews were more likely than non-Jews to aspire to an academic career, which, given the long-standing commitment to leftist causes in many Jewish families, contributed to professorial liberalism. More recently, Woessner and Kelly-Woessner (2009) argued that the professoriate tilts left because liberals are more likely than conservatives to go to graduate school—a function, in their view, of the tendency of conservative undergraduates to be "simultaneously more family oriented, less interested in writing original works, more focused on financial success, less interested in developing a meaningful philosophy of life, and less interested in making a theoretical contribution to science" (51). Summers's (2007) argument that academia, as an occupation in the nonprofit sector, selects for workers who are less oriented toward profit making and the market, and hence are less likely to be conservative, is a version of the same theory (for an application of this hypothesis to the teaching profession, see Saint-Paul 2009).

Some of the specific claims made by these alternative self-selection theories are called into question by Fosse and Gross's empirical findings. For example, they found that the overrepresentation of Jews in academe contributes little to its liberalism. As for the idea that professors are more liberal because those who aspire to academic careers care more about meaning than about making money, Fosse and Gross found that variables measuring these job values accounted for little of the politics gap between professors and other Americans. More generally, however, the key difference between Fosse and Gross's theory of self-selection and other theories is this: Fosse and Gross maintain that selection into graduate school and an academic career track occurs *directly* on the basis of politics, through the reputation of the occupation and its perceived fit with political self-identity, and not indirectly through the association of liberalism with other characteristics such as a reduced focus on money making that form the real basis for self-selection.

To be sure, in Fosse and Gross's account, it is not that people decide to go to graduate school and become academics solely or even mostly *because* they are liberal. Future professors invariably have deep interests in their fields and aspire to become microbiologists or chemists or historians because they find those fields fascinating and hope to spend their careers engaged with them (however much some may also hope that their work will contribute to the social good, as they understand it). Instead, Fosse and Gross's argument was that political identity channels and constrains these interests. First, in general, liberal undergraduates should be more likely than conservatives to bundle their intellectual interests in a field with the aspiration to become professors. Second, in addition to the professoriate as a whole having a political reputation, individual disciplines also have reputations, and the proportion of liberals to conservatives who develop interests in given fields should mirror the reputations of those fields.

Whatever its possible theoretical appeal, Fosse and Gross's account, though emergent from their empirical findings, could not—to repeat—be directly tested with their data. They were able to point to a range of findings by others that lent indirect support. For example, Woessner and Kelly-Woessner (2009), analyzing data from a nationally representative survey of undergraduates, found that self-identified liberals were twice as likely as conservatives to say they intended to pursue a doctorate. Likewise, Gross and Cheng (2011), examining qualitative data from interviews with sixty-six American professors in six fields, found that most liberal academics recall that their political views were formed before they started graduate school. On the question of the professoriate's political reputation, Gross and Simmons (2006), looking at public opinion data, found that 68 percent of Americans agree that colleges and universities favor professors with liberal views and found that conservatives assign considerably less social status to professors than do liberals.

Some relevant older data also exist. Among many other questions, the 1969 Carnegie Commission survey of the professoriate asked respondents to recall their political views as college seniors. Ladd and Lipset (1976) noted a moderately high correlation between views held in college and professors' current political beliefs. Even more telling are findings from the Carnegie Commission's parallel survey of graduate students. Reported briefly in *The Divided Academy* and in greater detail in a technical report (Fay and Weintraub 1973), this survey showed the distribution of political belief among graduate students to be nearly identical to that of the professoriate. Where 46 percent of professors at the time held left/liberal views, so did 40 percent of graduate students. Where 28 percent of professors were some shade of conservative, so were 30 percent of graduate students (Ladd and Lipset 1976, 26). This amounts to prima facie evidence for self-selection.

Nevertheless, especially as applied to the contemporary professoriate, Fosse and Gross's claims remain untested. We provide such a test here. While our data do not permit us to scrutinize all the elements of Fosse and Gross's theory—in particular, their core argument that liberals are drawn into academe and conservatives pushed away because of the political reputation of the occupation—we are able to examine three interrelated claims, mentioned earlier, that would have to be true for their theory to be correct. First, liberalism during the college years should be a strong, statistically significant predictor of going to graduate school (although we would not expect it to be nearly as strong a predictor as, say, academic achievement). Second, the effects of prior liberalism on graduate school attendance should be robust and not explained away by variables exogenous to Fosse and Gross's theory. And third, the liberalism of graduate students should not result primarily from the graduate school experience itself. The truth of these three claims would not necessarily mean that Fosse and Gross's theory is right; alternative theories, including those focused on political discrimination or perceptions of bias in the graduate school admissions process and beyond, are equally consistent. But if any of these claims were false, Fosse and Gross's account would be called into question.

Data and Methods

Fosse and Gross could not test their theory directly because their self-selection account hinges on processes occurring over time that are best examined with longitudinal data. Yet none of the existing longitudinal studies examining graduate school attendance, such as the Department of Education's Baccalaureate and Beyond survey, include questions on political orientation. Recently, however, the three authors of this chapter realized that the Add Health dataset could be used to gain some traction on the empirical issues at hand. Add Health originally focused on the health behaviors of adolescents. The study began in 1994–95 with an in-school survey of more than ninety thousand adolescents in grades 7–12, drawn from a stratified random sample of 132 junior high and high schools across the country. About twenty-one thousand of these original respondents were selected for in-home interviews, where their parents or other caregivers were also surveyed; a second wave of in-home interviews, involving about fifteen thousand young people, took place in 1996. Wave 3 of data collection was conducted in 2001–2, when respondents were aged 18–26, and wave 4 in 2007–8, when respondents were aged 24–32. About 80 percent of wave 3 respondents are included in the wave 4 sample. In wave 4, 534 respondents stated that they were currently enrolled in a master's- or doctorate-granting program—not a professional degree program—and intended to complete a doctorate (or in a relatively small number of cases had already done so.) Although politics is not a central concern of Add Health, in waves 3 and 4, respondents were asked to place themselves on a commonly used liberalism-conservatism scale. Accordingly, we use the data to examine whether political orientation in wave 3 is an important predictor of graduate school attendance in wave 4 and what variables may moderate such an effect.

Given the goals of our study, we restrict the sample in several ways. First, we exclude all respondents who, by wave 4, had not completed a bachelor's degree. We do so because our interest is in the choice to go or not go to graduate school, and graduate school presumes a bachelor's degree. Second, by necessity we include only those respondents who were interviewed in both waves 3 and 4. It is possible that sample attrition has biased our results, but we doubt this bias is significant since attrition is low across the two waves. Moreover, survey researchers have documented that attrition tends to be lowest among well-educated respondents. Third, we exclude the very small number of respondents who were already enrolled in graduate school in wave 3. Finally, to ensure that no one in wave 3 is older than the youngest respondent in wave 4, which would complicate our analysis, we exclude respondents who in wave 3 were older than 24 years.

Our modeling strategy is straightforward: we fit a series of logistic regressions that add different hypothesized predictors of graduate school attendance. All analyses are weighted to adjust for the longitudinal structure of the data as well as the oversampling of certain groups that is a feature of the Add Health design. We deal with the problem of missing data by using listwise deletion. We also ran analyses using multiple imputation, but the findings remained substantively the same.

In our regression models, the categorical outcome variable is wave 4 enrollment in a nonprofessional master's- or doctorate-granting program or having already completed a PhD. As noted above, we imposed the restriction that respondents could score positively on the outcome variable only if, among those without a doctorate, they stated their intention to complete one, as measured in a wave 4 question on educational aspirations. Our reason for this restriction is to distinguish between respondents who would in principle be eligible for academic careers (outside community colleges) and those who plan to go no further than a master's. For purposes of analytic clarity, our models compare doctorate-bound/intended students with respondents with a bachelor's degree only. (Because of missing data, our regression models compare 286 doctorate seekers with 1,777 respondents who stopped at a bachelor's.)

Our main predictor variable is political self-identification, measured in wave 3. The Add Health question asks respondents, "In terms of politics, do you consider yourself conservative, liberal, or middle-of-the-road?" Responses are coded on a five-point Likert scale ranging from "very conservative" to "very liberal." Research in political science and political sociology shows that self-identification along a liberal-conservative continuum is associated with a wide variety of social and economic attitudes measures, as well as party affiliation and voting, especially among educated Americans—who make up the entirety of our sample (Baldassari and Gelman 2008; Jost 2006; Jost, Kay, and Thorisdottir 2009; Malka and Lelkes 2010). While it would have been useful to confirm that our findings hold true across other measures of politics, the only other politics question asked in wave 3 (aside from questions on political participation) is a party affiliation question that asks whether respondents are Democrats, Republicans, or Independents, or belong to some other party, with no measure of the strength of their affiliation. We prefer the self-identification variable because it can be modeled as a continuous or ordinal rather than nominal variable, is more theoretically connected to attitudes, has lower levels of missingness in the Add Health dataset, and is measured in both waves 3 and 4, allowing us to assess change over time. We do note that among respondents with a bachelor's degree or higher who answered both the self-identification and party affiliation question, 85 percent of conservatives described themselves as Republican, and 88 percent of liberals as Democrats.

We use several variables to determine whether political self-identification, as a predictor of graduate school attendance, is robust to controlling for other factors. To begin, our models control for gender, age at wave 3, and race. Class background is another obvious candidate for predicting graduate school attendance. Work in the sociology of education has shown that children of well-educated parents and those in professional occupations are more likely to attend graduate school (Mullen, Goyette, and Soares 2003). Research has also demonstrated that levels of liberalism tend to be higher in well-educated, professional class households (Gerteis 1998). Accordingly, we control for parental education and professional status to assess the possible impact on the liberalism–graduate school connection. Parental education is measured as a variable with five response categories in wave 2, separately for each parent. Professional status is measured by a wave 2 question asking respondents about the type of work their parents did at the time. We coded respondents as having professional parents if they reported their parents as having worked in one of two categories of "professional work," as a "manager," or as a higher-status "technical" worker, such as "computer specialist" or "radiologist."

Given research by political psychologists on the relationship between liberalism and intelligence, we also consider whether liberals might be more likely to go to graduate school because, on average, they have higher levels of general intelligence than conservatives. Waves 2 and 3 of Add Health include a picture-based vocabulary test, the results of which have been shown to correlate highly with other measures of cognitive ability (Zagar and Mead 1983). We standardize the wave 3 scores for this variable around their mean and include the z-score as an input in the models. The Add Health study also includes a measure of respondents' overall high school GPAs, taken from their transcripts. Although respondents might have higher or lower GPAs in college than in high school, with college grades being those that matter for graduate school admissions, high school grades are a relatively robust measure of academic preparation and motivation, qualities that should carry through to the college years.

Our models also include several other control variables measured during or after wave 3, when our political self-identification variable was measured. To explore the role of materialism in moderating our findings, we use a wave 3 question asking how important respondents think money is to a successful marriage or relationship. We would have preferred a question asking about job values, but no such question is asked in Add Health. Nevertheless, the variable we use is a reasonable, if rough, measure of how much importance people place on monetary success. Scholars have also theorized that conservatives may avoid graduate school because they prefer to start their families earlier (Woessner and Kelly-Woessner 2009), which would require that they work full-time after college or stay home to raise children. We evaluate this claim using a wave 3 variable measuring whether or not respondents have ever been married. In addition, Fosse and Gross argued that those who are religious are less likely to aspire to become professors, so we include a measure of religiosity in our models. Religiosity is measured with a wave 3 question asking respondents how important their religious faith is to them.

Finally, our models include several measures of personality characteristics, thought by political psychologists to be important predictors of liberalism. In particular, political psychologists have argued that "openness to new experience" is associated with liberalism, while "conscientiousness" is associated with conservatism (Jost and Hunyadi 2005). A key component of openness is "interest in abstract ideas," and it is plausible, as well as consistent with revisionist work on college education and politics highlighting prior selection processes, that this predicts not only liberalism but also the pursuit of an advanced education. It is equally conceivable that low conscientiousness could predict graduate school attendance, since the relatively unstructured nature of graduate school life might not appeal to those who are highly organized. Although our strong preference would have been to measure personality characteristics prior to graduate school attendance, in Add Health, questions designed to measure the "Big Five" personality traits are asked only in wave 4. We include the four-item conscientiousness scale in our models but, for reasons we describe below, disaggregate "openness to new experience" into two two-item subscales: "interest in abstract ideas" and "imagination."

Four caveats must be made about our data and methods. First, although we would have liked to do so, our models do not control for what discipline or type of field the doctorate seekers are in. There is no measure of this in wave 4, and in any event, with a limited number of doctorate-seeking respondents, the cell sizes in individual disciplines would have been too small to generate meaningful comparisons. In wave 3, Add Health did ask respondents who had completed undergraduate degrees what their college major/minor was. Since there is no necessary connection between undergraduate major/minor and graduate school program, we do not use this variable in our main analysis. However, aggregating to broad, multidisciplinary categories such as social sciences/humanities and science/technology/engineering/mathematics (STEM) to deal with the cell size issue, we do make use of undergraduate major/minor in supplementary analyses we discuss below. Second, while the Add Health data are well-suited to our purposes, they include only respondents who spent their adolescence in the United States. But nearly 30 percent of doctoral degree recipients in American universities, and about 15 percent of U.S. professors, were born overseas. Our data do not speak to the politics of this group. Third, while most people begin graduate school in their early twenties, a small number spend considerable time after college in the labor force or engaged in other pursuits before undertaking graduate work. People who fit this profile may be included in our sample, but depending on the timing of their educational experiences, they might show up as non–graduate school attendees. Finally, our outcome variable captures only those respondents who already had PhDs or were enrolled in graduate programs and stated their interest in completing a doctorate at the time of the wave 4 survey. Yet it is possible that some respondents began graduate school with the intention to complete a doctorate but dropped out or set their sights on a terminal master's or some other degree prior to the wave 4 survey. If politics systematically influenced this decision—for example, if conservative respondents were more likely to exit doctoral programs, perceiving the cards to be stacked against them in academe—this could have affected our results. Although we are not aware of any survey data demonstrating such a tendency, it is not outside the bounds of possibility, so additional caution is in order when interpreting our findings.

Results

Before discussing the results of our models, we review the differences in political identification by educational level among the young adults in our sample. Table 2.1 shows the distribution of political self-identification among those with a bachelor's degree only and among graduate students seeking (or already holding) a doctorate in waves 3 and 4 of the Add Health survey. In the fourth wave, among respondents with a bachelor's degree only, 35 percent identified as either liberal or very liberal, 41 percent as moderate, and 23 percent as conservative. In contrast, about 49 percent of doctoral degree seekers considered themselves either liberal or very liberal, 33 percent moderate, and 18 percent either conservative or very conservative.

Two things stand out about these descriptive findings. First, although the Add Health five-point political self-identification scale differs from that used in recent surveys of the professoriate, making comparisons tricky, the proportion of graduate school attendees who are liberal is about the same as the proportion of young professors who are liberal (although conservatives are underrepresented in the academic ranks, and moderates overrepresented, relative to their presence among graduate students). For example, data from Gross and Simmons's 2006 survey show that among professors who hold doctorates and are aged 40 or younger, 45 percent could be classified as liberal, 51 percent as moderate, and 4 percent as conservative. These numbers strongly suggest that professorial liberalism is highly related to who goes to graduate school: filling job openings in academe with a random draw from the pool of graduate students would produce a distinctly left-leaning occupation. Second, the findings are consistent with the line of research discussed earlier on college attendance and liberalism, which

TABLE 2.1
Distribution of Political Views in Waves 3 and 4 by Education, as Percentages

	BA only		Doctoral degree seekers	
Political views	Wave 3	Wave 4	Wave 3	Wave 4
Very conservative	3.2	4.3	2.1	2.7
Conservative	21.5	19.1	16.4	15.1
Moderate	49.2	41.3	46.0	33.3
Liberal	23.5	27.8	30.5	33.1
Very liberal	2.6	7.6	5.1	15.9
N	2,503	2,980	455	531

Source. National Longitudinal Study of Adolescent Health, Waves 3 and 4.
    Note. Columns may not add to 100 because of rounding. Analysis excludes respondents who were older than 24 in wave 3. Data are weighted.

demonstrates not simply that those with college degrees tend to have more liberal views at any age but also that *recent* college graduates comprise an especially liberal group (perhaps because most have not yet had the life-course experiences that, as research has shown, would moderate their liberalism, such as purchasing a home or investing in the stock market; see Conley and Gifford 2006; Davis and Cotton 2007). This means, as Woessner and Kelly-Woessner (2009) have also noted, that the pool of potential graduate students (i.e., young adults with a four-year college degree) is already tilted significantly left, so that some amount of the liberalism of graduate students (and professors) is a result of upstream processes related to the politics of college students. Nevertheless, in wave 3, future doctoral degree seekers are more liberal by 9 percentage points than those who will wind up with only a bachelor's degree.

Compared with the fourth wave, doctoral students in the third wave are less liberal and more moderate. A possible interpretation of this difference is that graduate school attendance causes a significant leftward shift in political identification among young adults. This conclusion cannot be supported by table 2.1 alone, however, since the results are not adjusted for confounders such as gender, race, or class background that might affect both political identification and educational attainment. Moreover, the data are aggregated, making it impossible to assess individual-level effects. Finally, the parallel leftward shift among respondents with a bachelor's degree suggests that the differences between the two waves may be due to factors unrelated to attending graduate school.

To address more directly the question of whether graduate school attendance moves people to the left politically, table 2.2 shows the percentage of respondents in both the graduate school and bachelor's-only groups who became more liberal between the two waves, showed no change, or became more conservative (restricting the analysis to those who were not at the extremes of the distribution in wave 3 and so could change in only one direction). About 42 percent of doctorate seekers showed no change in their politics between waves 3 and 4, 36 percent became more liberal, and 23 percent became more conservative. In contrast, about 52 percent of respondents with only a bachelor's degree showed no change, 29 percent became more liberal, and 19 percent became more conservative. While these numbers are consistent with the possibility of a modest graduate school liberalization effect, more striking is the significant liberalization in both groups. Perhaps this reflects a period effect: between waves 3 and 4 of the study, there was increasing dissatisfaction among young Americans with President Bush and the war in Iraq, as well as growing support for Barack Obama. The difference in liberalization between respondents in the graduate school and bachelor's-only group is

TABLE 2.2
*Percentage of Respondents Who Changed Political
Views between Waves 3 and 4 by Education*

Change	BA only	Doctoral degree seekers
More conservative	19.0	22.7
No change	51.9	41.5
More liberal	29.1	35.8
N	2,116	389

Source. National Longitudinal Study of Adolescent Health, Waves 3 and 4.
Note. Analysis excludes respondents who identified as "very conservative" or "very liberal" in wave 3, as well as those who were older than 24 in wave 3. Data are weighted.

7 percentage points—much smaller than the amount of liberalization experienced by the cohort overall—and is offset by more movement to the right among graduate school attendees.[1] Could this relatively small number be a result of the inclusion in our sample of doctorate seekers in all fields, such that a dramatic graduate school liberalization among students in the social sciences and humanities, say, is being offset by less movement among scientists and engineers? Again, we have no measure of field of study in graduate school, but when we recalculated the numbers for table 2.2, restricting the sample to students who had majored or minored as undergraduates in the social sciences or humanities, we found that the proportion who became more liberal was unchanged (35%), the proportion whose political views stayed the same was higher (47%), and the proportion who became more conservative was slightly smaller (18%).

We turn next to our logistic regression analyses, shown in table 2.3. What evidence is there beyond the descriptive statistics that young adults who identify as liberal are more likely to self-select into graduate school? The first four models in the table address this question. In the first model we include no controls. Liberal self-identification in wave 3 increases the log-odds of attending graduate school in wave 4 by 0.258 and is statistically significant. Since log-odds ratios are difficult to interpret, we restate this in terms of predicted probabilities. Given the distribution of the outcome variable, the coefficient for political self-identification in model 1 indicates that, for a case that is average on other characteristics in our data, a unit increase in political liberalism corresponds to about a 2.2 percentage point increase in the probability of attending graduate school versus receiving only a bachelor's degree, or about an 8.8 percentage point increase between someone who is very liberal versus very conservative. Fosse and Gross's claim that being a liberal increases the odds of attending graduate school thus finds empirical support.

TABLE 2.3
Predictors of Doctoral Degree Seeking in Wave 4

Variable	Model 1	2	3	4	5	6	7	8
Wave 3 liberalism	0.258** (2.61)	0.243* (0.101)	0.222* (0.099)	0.204* (0.102)	0.204* (0.103)	0.230* (0.104)	0.228* (0.106)	0.168 (0.106)
Female		0.340† (0.175)	0.403* (0.180)	0.359† (0.189)	0.358† (0.190)	0.327† (0.192)	0.328† (0.192)	0.414* (0.189)
Age		0.023 (0.051)	0.023 (0.051)	0.040 (0.053)	0.040 (0.054)	0.024 (0.055)	0.024 (0.056)	0.038 (0.057)
Black		0.542** (0.198)	0.719*** (0.207)	0.996*** (0.224)	0.994*** (0.237)	0.994*** (0.236)	0.997*** (0.244)	0.985*** (0.247)
Hispanic		-0.252 (0.325)	0.046 (0.337)	0.237 (0.356)	0.237 (0.356)	0.213 (0.351)	0.214 (0.349)	0.139 (0.349)
Native American		-0.463 (0.605)	-0.486 (0.634)	-0.475 (0.659)	-0.475 (0.659)	-0.513 (0.667)	-0.512 (0.666)	-0.485 (0.677)
Asian American		-0.591 (0.364)	-0.523 (0.371)	-0.446 (0.372)	-0.448 (0.377)	-0.452 (0.379)	-0.452 (0.379)	-0.451 (0.386)
Mother's education			0.117 (0.098)	0.099 (0.100)	0.099 (0.100)	0.102 (0.100)	0.102 (0.100)	0.117 (0.098)
Father's education			0.233* (0.094)	0.217* (0.097)	0.217* (0.097)	0.221* (0.096)	0.221* (0.096)	0.183† (0.100)
Mother professional			0.280 (0.198)	0.282 (0.200)	0.282 (0.200)	0.289 (0.200)	0.289 (0.200)	0.280 (0.201)

(continued)

TABLE 2.3 (continued)

Variable					Model			
	1	2	3	4	5	6	7	8
Father professional			-0.012 (0.195)	-0.052 (0.199)	-0.052 (0.199)	-0.048 (0.200)	-0.048 (0.200)	-0.066 (0.206)
GPA				0.593** (0.181)	0.593*** (0.180)	0.598*** (0.176)	0.599*** (0.176)	0.581*** (0.176)
Vocabulary (z)				0.187† (0.104)	0.188† (0.103)	0.189† (0.104)	0.188† (0.104)	0.061 (0.118)
Materialism					0.002 (0.036)	0.003 (0.036)	0.003 (0.036)	0.019 (0.037)
Ever married						0.442 (0.328)	0.445 (0.335)	0.453 (0.330)
Faith							-0.006 (0.109)	-0.011 (0.108)
Conscientiousness								-0.042 (0.048)
Abstract ideas								0.355*** (0.076)
Imagination								-0.052 (0.061)
Constant	-2.623*** (-8.15)	-3.270** (1.162)	-4.606*** (1.238)	-6.891*** (1.471)	-6.898*** (1.448)	-6.717*** (1.466)	-6.703*** (1.493)	-8.712*** (1.626)

Source. National Longitudinal Study of Adolescent Health.
Note. Weighted logistic regression models. N = 2,063. Analysis excludes respondents older than 24 in wave 3 and those who had not completed a bachelor's degree by wave 4. Standard errors in parentheses.
†$p < 0.10$, *$p < 0.05$, **$p < 0.01$, ***$p < 0.001$

In model 2 we control for basic demographic characteristics: gender, race, and age. In an era when the American academy is becoming increasing female, being a woman increases the odds of graduate school attendance. Consistent with Bowen and Bok's (2000) finding that African Americans who receive bachelor's degrees from highly selective schools are likely to enter professional degree programs, we find that being black increases the odds of graduate school attendance contingent on completion of a bachelor's.[2] Since women and African Americans tend to hold more liberal views, these variables moderate the liberalism effect, though only slightly.

Is the finding on political self-selection robust to additional controls? Perhaps politically liberal young adults tend to be raised in households that are better educated or of higher occupational status, and this accounts for their self-selection into graduate school. With model 3, we control for parental education and occupational status, both measured prior to political identification. The log-odds of graduate school attendance for a unit difference in political self-identification are now 0.222, corresponding with a 1.9 percentage point positive difference in the probability of attending graduate school. Father's education appears to be doing most of the statistical work here. Even with this moderation, however, the liberalism effect remains large in relative terms and statistically significant.

With model 4 we include other background variables: high school GPA (as a proxy for academic orientation and preparation) and vocabulary (as a proxy for cognitive ability). Both are statistically significant, positive predictors of graduate school attendance. While including them in the model further attenuates the liberalism effect, the attenuation is not large, reducing the effect to a 1.7 percentage point per unit positive difference in the probability of attending graduate school, which still translates into a 6.8 percentage point positive difference in the likelihood of graduate school attendance between someone who is very liberal versus very conservative.

The next four models control for variables measured at the same time as or after measurement of the political self-identification variable. Model 5 considers the effect of materialist values. At least operationalized as we have done here, materialism is a small, statistically not significant predictor of graduate school attendance, and including it in the model does not alter the liberalism coefficient. Model 6 includes as an input having been married in wave 3, which has a log-odds coefficient of 0.442. Early marriage corresponds with an unexpected 3.7 percentage point *increase* in the likelihood of pursuing a doctorate, although this effect does not meet classical standards of statistical significance. Relative to model 5, the liberalism coefficient is now inflated, but only slightly. This inflation makes sense, given that political liberalism and early marriage are negatively associated.

In model 7 we examine the effects of religiosity. Contrary to expectations, we find that the importance of religious faith in a respondent's life has no effect on her or his propensity to attend graduate school. Again, the liberalism coefficient remains largely unchanged.

Model 8 incorporates the personality variables as inputs. Although the coefficient for conscientiousness is negative, as research in political psychology might lead one to expect, it is not statistically significant. As for openness to new experience, in previous versions of the model not shown here, we found that openness—measured in Add Health with an index that combines four items (two measuring "interest in abstract ideas" and two measuring "having an active imagination")—is a large, positive, and statistically significant predictor of graduate school attendance. In our subsequent analysis, however, we discovered that "interest in abstract ideas" was responsible for the entirety of this effect. Accordingly, in model 8 we show the results with the two subcomponents of the openness index disaggregated. Not only does interest in abstract ideas strongly predict pursuing a doctorate, but it is also the only variable in our models that substantially reduces the size of the political identification effect, rendering it statistically nonsignificant by conventional criteria. In model 8 the coefficient for political self-identification is now 0.168, with a unit difference now corresponding to a 1.4 percentage point increase in the likelihood of attending graduate school.

Discussion

What do the findings tell us about the Fosse and Gross theory of professorial liberalism? They are clearly consistent with Fosse and Gross's main self-selection hypothesis. Both the cross-tabulations and the logistic regression models indicate that students who are liberal as young adults are more likely to pursue doctorates than their moderate or conservative counterparts, even after we control for various background variables such as gender and race. Moreover, several alternative self-selection theories receive little support from our data. For example, we find no evidence that liberals are more likely to pursue doctorates because they are less materialistic or less prone than conservatives to early marriage. As well, we find that little of the difference between liberals and conservatives in rates of graduate school attendance stems from differences in parental education levels.

Yet there is one prominent alternative theory of self-selection that we cannot rule out: that liberals self-select into graduate school because of psychological differences between them and conservatives. The findings here are mixed. We find no evidence that the liberalism effect is explained away by an association between conscientiousness or having a fertile imagination and attending graduate school. Cognitive ability and academic preparation do moderate the effect, but only modestly. Regarding an interest in abstract ideas, however, our results show that this aspect of personality is a major predictor of graduate school attendance and one that greatly reduces the political self-identification effect.

Do these findings mean that political-psychological theories of self-selection are correct and that the Fosse and Gross theory, built around the idea of occupational reputation, is wrong? While we do not doubt that cognitive and personality factors have some role to play in explaining professorial liberalism, four arguments counsel against this interpretation of our regression results. First, once again, the effects of cognitive ability and academic preparation on the liberalism coefficient are small. Second, concerning personality, if the finding on abstract ideas were a function of robust personality differences, why would a trait as fundamental to the construct of openness as degree of imagination fail to have any effect?

Third, as mentioned previously, our measure of abstract ideas comes from wave 4 of the survey and was thus taken after our measure of politics. It is therefore possible that political identification *leads* to greater interest in abstract ideas, in turn leading to a higher probability of attending graduate school. For example, we know from other research that liberals are more likely than conservatives to major in liberal arts fields (Porter and Umbach 2006), and it is certainly possible that majoring in liberal arts as opposed to a more applied field could stoke an interest in abstract ideas. Political differences in choice of major could be driven by personality, but there are other explanations.

Finally, while interest in abstract ideas reduced the liberalism coefficient to statistical nonsignificance, the reduction in the size of the coefficient itself is not overwhelming. Specifically, comparing model 7 with model 8, we find that the increased probability of attending graduate school associated with a unit increase in liberalism changes from 1.9 to 1.4. This is to say that while the coefficient for liberalism in model 8 no longer meets classical standards of statistical significance, political self-identification continues to predict graduate school attendance after our two-item measure of interest in abstract ideas is controlled for (although we cannot rule out the possibility that we would have been able to reduce the coefficient to zero had Add Health contained more extensive and reliable personality measures).

In the light of these considerations, we think that an equally or more plausible interpretation of the abstract ideas finding is that part of the normative social practice of contemporary American liberalism among the educated is to express some interest in abstract ideas (to profess appreciation for conceptual art, for example, or have a copy of *Discipline and Punish* on one's bookshelf), whereas it is part of the normative social practice of conservatism to downplay certain forms of intellectualism and abstraction in favor of an orientation toward more concrete ideas (such that a comparable book display might include more biographies and histories). To the extent that this is so, the finding on abstract ideas would be consistent with the occupational reputation thesis, for it would simply mean that, on average, liberals are more likely to conceive of themselves as intellectually minded—whether they are or not, in some objective sense (on the importance of self-representations of personality in helping to anchor its stability over the life course, see McAdams and Olson 2010). And it would mean that liberals pursue doctorates at higher rates because they perceive that (1) academe is a natural home for those of an intellectual bent, and (2) the intellectually minded, a group widely understood as having more liberal social and political attitudes, fit in well politically in the university.

There has been relatively little research by sociologists and political scientists into mainstream liberalism or conservatism as social practices—a glaring lacuna—but some studies lend credibility to this interpretation. For example, a consistent finding from American and European surveys is that conservatives report higher levels of happiness than liberals (Brooks 2008; Di Tella and MacCulloch 2005; Leone and Chirumbolo 2007; Napier and Jost 2008). Much of this difference is a function of income, religiosity, and marriage, but political psychologists have suggested that some of it is grounded in personality differences. Specifically, some psychologists contend that it is affectively more rewarding to support the status quo than to challenge it. Yet in one of the few pieces of ethnographic research on the topic, Wilkins (2008), studying an evangelical Christian group, found that the group defined itself in part around the happiness of its members—seen by them as a function of their religious commitments—and that group members were under strong normative pressures to engage in "happiness talk" and present themselves to others as content. Insofar as this finding is generalizable to other social settings, the social practices of conservatism, rather than psychological characteristics, could be responsible for the finding of greater happiness among conservatives—just as the finding from political psychology that the greater conscientiousness of conservatives manifests itself in the neatness of their home and office environments (Carney et al. 2008) could well be a product of different norms of housekeeping in liberal and conservative settings that might or might not have their origin in in-born psychological differences. In the same way, the greater "intellectualism" of liberals might be a function, not of psychology, but of how liberalism and conservatism, as practice-laden social identities, have come to be defined in the contemporary American context.

Although we thus interpret our findings as largely consistent with Fosse and Gross's theory, there is one finding that seems to be in tension: that pertaining to religion. Again, Fosse and Gross found that the lesser religiosity of professors compared with other Americans helped to explain their liberalism and theorized that relatively few people who are religiously devout—who also tend to be more politically conservative—form the aspiration to become professors, given the professoriate's reputation for secularism. Yet our data here show that religiosity does not affect the likelihood of pursuing a doctorate.

There are a number of possible explanations for this disparity. One is that whereas religiosity inhibited doctorate seeking in the past, it no longer does so today—whether because American colleges and universities are recognizing the need to accommodate the faithful (Cherry, DeBerg, and Porterfield 2001) or because certain highly religious groups, such as evangelical and fundamentalist Protestants, have experienced upward mobility in recent decades and are now in a position to support the advanced education of their young people (Greely and Hout 2006). Fosse and Gross's data, which reach back into the early 1970s, may not be recent enough to capture this change. Another possibility is that self-selection out of higher education on the basis of religiosity occurs at the undergraduate stage and is a result not of the irreligious reputation of the professoriate per se but rather of lingering perceptions that the climate on many college campuses is hostile to religious believers. A third possibility is that the religiously devout attend graduate school but tend not to enter the academic profession. The disparity could also result from different ways of measuring religiosity. Whichever of these possibilities is correct, our data do not provide evidence that, in general, people self-select out of graduate school because of their religious beliefs.[3]

Conclusion

We have shown, using longitudinal data, that Americans who are liberal during the typical college years are more likely to attend graduate school than are their moderate or conservative peers. We also demonstrate that this tendency does not arise because of the most commonly supposed factors and that attending graduate school results in only a modest shift farther to the left in terms of political self-identification. Despite the limitations of our data, which were not collected with the aim of identifying the predictors, political or otherwise, of graduate school attendance, we regard these findings as providing evidence that liberal politics constitutes an important basis for self-selection into doctoral education and the academic profession.

While our findings are consistent with Fosse and Gross's theory of self-selection based on institutionalized political reputation, we wish to reemphasize that several other theories are also compatible. For example, it is possible that in our models, youthful liberalism functions as a proxy for a more bohemian cultural disposition that, notwithstanding our efforts to control for class background and materialism, is best understood from the vantage point of an approach to class analysis, like Bourdieu's, that takes seriously status group dynamics and processes of cultural distinction. Alternatively, that liberalism predicts graduate school attendance could reflect discrimination against conservative students in the admissions process or a calculation on their part that they would face a hostile climate in academe. Our data do not allow us to arbitrate between these competing interpretations.

With that said, our findings do lead us to doubt—especially given the data reported in chapter 4 of this volume—that discrimination against conservatives in the academic labor market is the major cause of professorial liberalism. Some discrimination may occur and might help account for the underrepresentation of conservatives in the academic ranks relative to their presence in the graduate student population, as well as their particular underrepresentation at certain kinds of schools, such as elite research institutions. Yet the fact that just under half of graduate students are liberal seems a much more likely proximate cause of the phenomenon of professorial liberalism overall.

What are the broader sociological implications of our analysis? First, the absence of evidence that doctoral degree–granting programs lead people to become substantially more liberal suggests that the growth of such programs in recent decades has probably not done anything to directly push American society to the left, at odds with what New Class theorists of the 1970s would have forecast. (And in any event, while some attitudinal liberalization occurred during this time among members of the public—for example, around same-sex marriage—there has obviously been no major left realignment for which the expansion of graduate programs could serve as an explanation.) At the same time, while we have not examined here the political dynamics surrounding other, larger categories of graduate education, such as terminal master's or professional degree programs—because Add Health does not contain measures that would allow us to distinguish cleanly among them—we suspect, given our findings on self-selection, that the expansion of graduate education has had a significant *indirect* effect on the American political system. It has led to an increasing consolidation of liberalism among the highly educated, in occupations requiring advanced degrees, and in cities, states, and regions where such occupations flourish. GSS data show that in the period 2000–2008, nearly 15 percent of self-identified American liberals held advanced degrees of some kind, compared with about 7 percent in the 1970s. Although the percentage of moderates and conservatives with advanced degrees has also doubled, those numbers remain today about what they were for liberals in the earlier period. This means that more than ever before, the highly educated comprise a key constituency for American liberalism and the Democratic Party, one that may have surpassed a crucial threshold size, generating tensions with the working-class base around such issues as religion and the American use of force overseas and rendering the American left recurrently vulnerable to charges of elitism. This situation and the electoral dynamics that follow from it would be different were there no political self-selection into advanced education and had the growth of graduate education been equally distributed across ideological camps.

Second, our findings suggest the need for scholars of class politics to begin attending more systematically to processes of self-selection. Much of the effort that has gone into research on class politics in recent years has been concerned to show that class, variously defined, remains an important predictor of political attitudes and behavior (see Evans 1999; Manza, Hout, and Brooks 1995). In most of these analyses, class is presumed to have its political effects through the objective or subjective interests that workers' or families' class positions establish for them—interests that would be best achieved by voting for one candidate or party rather than another. Yet if, as we have shown, there is self-selection on the basis of politics into one occupation—the professoriate—then it becomes plausible to think that political self-selection may also be operating for other occupations. To the extent that this is so, interest-based models of class politics should be rethought, for more complex processes of political affiliation are probably at play for people in such fields. One important strand of class-analytic work that makes theoretical space for occupational self-selection—political and otherwise—is Grusky's neo-Durkheimian theory of class (see Grusky and Sorensen 1998; Weeden and Grusky 2005). But the fact of political self-selection does not seem to us to necessarily point in Grusky's direction so much as toward the need for a general reconstruction of class-political models with an eye toward dynamic life-course processes of the sort studied by scholars of political socialization (see Shapiro 2004) and, separately, of "vocational choice" (Holland 1984). Such a reconstruction would be all the more important if evidence were found of occupational self-selection by politics across national and historical contexts.[4]

Third, building off this last point, our findings on self-selection suggest the need for American sociologists to begin considering individuals' political orientations not just as outcomes to be explained, whether by reference to class or other factors, but also as predictors of other outcomes. We have shown that political liberalism affects the odds of pursuing a doctoral degree. Does political orientation influence other behaviors of interest to sociology as well, such as volunteerism and civic engagement, consumption, patterns of intergroup contact and travel, or childbearing or parenting styles? If the answer is yes, sociologists would profit by building politics into their explanatory models. In so doing, they might also help shed light on how liberalism and conservatism have become, in contemporary American society, not simply labels referring to clusters of political attitudes but highly meaningful social identities designating distinctive and increasingly irreconcilable worldviews and styles of life—of which the liberal taste for graduate education is merely one sign.

NOTES

For their helpful comments on earlier drafts of this chapter, we thank Amy Binder, Clem Brooks, Natalie Cotton, Andrew Gelman, Ann Mullen, Paul Quirk, Chris Winship, and participants in seminars at the University of British Columbia and the University of Victoria. The chapter uses data from the Add Health project, a study directed by Kathleen Mullan Harris, designed by J. Richard Udry, Peter S. Bearman, and Kathleen Mullan Harris at the University of North Carolina at Chapel Hill, and funded by grant P01-HD31921 from the Eunice Kennedy Shriver National Institute of Child Health and Human Development, with cooperative funding from twenty-three other federal agencies and foundations. Ronald R. Rindfuss and Barbara Entwisle assisted with the original design of the Add Health study. Information on how to obtain the Add Health data files is available at www.cpc.unc.edu/addhealth. No direct support for this analysis was received from grant P01-HD31921. We thank J. Alex Kevern and Rebecca Dickson for research assistance.

1. Since some respondents were still enrolled in college between waves 3 and 4, a possible objection to the period effect interpretation is that some of the aggregate change in both groups is a result of the liberalizing effects of higher education in general. Among Add Health respondents who had not received a bachelor's degree by wave 4, however, there was also a substantial increase in the percentage identifying as liberal or very liberal between the two waves.

2. NCES data show that African Americans now receive about 10 percent of bachelor's degrees (http://nces.ed.gov/programs/digest/d09/tables/dt09_285.asp), while data from the Council of Graduate Schools show that about 14 percent of graduate students who are U.S. citizens are African American (N. Bell 2010, 40).

3. Once again, however, we note that our data are not discipline specific. Although we think it sociologically unproductive to postulate an inherent tension between science and religious belief, we would not be surprised to find that people do select out of the physical and biological sciences, and perhaps some of the social sciences as well, on the basis of religiosity. Indeed, when we reran our models focusing solely on respondents who had majored or minored in STEM fields, we found that religiosity was strongly and negatively associated with graduate school attendance.

4. Scholars of class politics have not ignored self-selection entirely. For example, Inglehart (1990) posited that "postmaterialist" values influence occupational choice—a claim responded to by Müller (1999, 174) in the German context. On left activism and career choice, see Sherkat and Blocker 1997.

CHAPTER THREE

Nations, Classes, and the Politics of Professors

A Comparative Perspective

CLEM BROOKS

Resurgent scholarly interest in the politics of the professoriate is a welcome development. Ideas matter, and knowing the specific groups and occupations that control their production and dissemination is important. Because of their institutional locations, professors are perennially poised to exert influence.

Should the professoriate be understood as a resource for left-wing ideologies and activism? Are professors better viewed as reflecting the preferences of those holding similar positions in the class structure? When segments of the professoriate embrace radical or liberal views, is it due to conditions within their disciplinary fields or to tastes and preferences that prompted their career choices in the first place?

These questions have been at the center of renewed scholarly interest in professors' politics. We now know a good deal more about orientations, institutional settings, and demographic trends, particularly with respect to professors in the United States. American professors are, for one thing, heterogeneous. This is due not only to the considerable diversity of colleges and universities but also to differences in values and outlooks across individuals and disciplines (see chapter 1 of this volume; Fosse and Gross 2012). To be sure, there is much that is distinctive and tangible about "professorial" identity and styles of reasoning (Lamont 2009). And when it comes to political parties and national politics, while some disciplinary fields such as business have their fair share of Republican identifiers, the humanities, natural sciences, and social sciences are disproportionately Democratic in orientation. Overall, this lends the U.S. professoriate a distinctively liberal public profile, and such evidence has spawned wide-ranging commentary and debates surrounding charges of partisan "bias" among college faculty (Gross and Cheng 2011; Rothman, Lichter, and Nevitte 2005; Woessner and Kelly-Woessner 2009).

These debates demonstrate the high stakes in scholarship on professors' policy attitudes, and recent scholarship provides refined estimates and much-needed perspective. By the same token, it is notable that the recent state of the art has been based primarily on the United States. Yet there are numerous political, institutional, and cultural attributes that distinguish the American context from other nations. Indeed, a hallmark of comparative social science is that there is not one but multiple types of democracy, market economy, and nations, more generally (Hall and Soskice 2001; Lijphart 1999; Lipset 1981 [1960]). Might this rich variation be harnessed to the new literature on the politics of professors?

This scenario is my analytic focus in this chapter. A cross-national perspective has much to offer, extending and further situating the case of the U.S. professoriate. The comparative literatures I bring to bear also highlight some candidate mechanisms and instructive patterns of variation relating to the political institutions and class structure of nations. One focus of interest is the possible clustering of countries into ideal-typical regimes, an expectation that has been central to theory and research on welfare state development (Arts and Gelissen 2002; Esping-Andersen 1990; Huber and Stephens 2001). A second issue concerns the bearing of professors' class location on their outlooks and actions, a point of enduring contention in midcentury social theory (Gouldner 1979; Mannheim 1956; Shils 1968), as well as in the more recent literature on professorial liberalism in the United States.

To get comparative perspective, I use cross-national survey data from the International Social Survey Program (ISSP). The ISSP data are unique in providing a comparatively large sample of professors for analysis and enabling measurement of policy attitudes on key issues of relevance. The data cover a wide range of countries, including the North American, European, and Antipodean nations analyzed in this chapter. The ISSP data facilitate three points of constructive engagement between comparative scholarship and U.S.-centered research on the politics of the professoriate.

The first challenge is to situate U.S. professors cross-nationally. Is the overall liberalism of American professors more (or less) distinctive when gauged against their cross-national counterparts? Using the ISSP data, I offer detailed portraits as to where American professors fall with respect to five major policy issue domains. Looking at the degree to which professors' policy attitudes diverge from those of national publics, I also probe whether patterns of variation cluster into recognizable types of regimes.

What about the underlying issue of social class? This is the second challenge at hand, and here I probe interrelationships between the professoriate and the class structure of specific countries. Using the same policy issue domains, I examine whether professors' policy attitudes differ from those of professionals, the larger class location in which the professoriate is situated. This tells us how much the politics of professors is also a story about the politics of professionals, more broadly.

Finally, what accounts for the distinctiveness of professors'/professionals' policy attitudes? The possibility that U.S. professors' distinctive attitudes are the result of occupational self-selection has begun to resonate in recent scholarship. Earlier research pointed to compositional factors as buttressing the policy attitudes and overall liberalism of the professoriate. How much do these distinct types of factors contribute? Analysis of the ISSP data is again telling, and as before, results fruitfully engage the U.S.-centered state of the art.

Theory, Debate, and Cross-National Perspectives
The Phenomenon of Professorial Liberalism

Evidence for the partisan and ideological distinctiveness of the U.S. professoriate has been accumulating for some time. Early survey research on professors' politics during the postwar era found high levels of identification with the Democratic Party and with liberal policy ideas. In Lazarsfeld and Thielens's (1958) classic study, 46 percent of professors identified as Democrats and 16 percent as Republicans, with a near majority scoring high on a scale of positive attitudes toward communism. Research during the subsequent decade provided further evidence of professorial liberalism. In Lipset and Ladd's (1971; Ladd and Lipset 1976) faculty survey of 1969, nearly two-thirds of social science faculty expressed approval of "the rise of radical student activism," and even in the natural sciences, the corresponding level of support was 40 percent. Looking at issues of foreign policy and race, Lipset and Ladd found a large majority of faculty to be critical of the Vietnam War, and overall, half of all professors identified themselves as left or liberal.

A new strand of research in the 1970s went beyond the phenomenon of professorial liberalism, arguing for a more extensive pattern of radical beliefs and linkages to challenger social movements. This line of thinking took on its clearest and most contentious form in the theory of the New Class (Gouldner 1979; Konrad and Szelenyi 1979; Kristol 1972). Proponents argued that the underlying interests of intellectuals and professionals, particularly with reference to salaried and public sector locations, would dispose them to embrace radical ideas and pursue system-challenging forms of collective action.

Since this time, careful reconsideration and updated analysis of survey data have sought to illuminate these earlier claims. New Class expectations of professorial/professional radicalism and antibusiness orientations facilitating system-challenging activism received little support (Brint 1984). Reanalysis of the 1969, 1975, and 1984 Carnegie faculty surveys found the largest shift in professors' self-identification was from liberal to conservative (Hamilton and Hargens 1993), tracking a population-wide trend during this time. Attesting to a degree of diversity and complexity in professors' politics, disciplinary differences continued to be significant, with liberal attitudes and identification much more prevalent in the social sciences, humanities, and law than in business, engineering, and applied fields.

Together, these results lend important nuance to scholarship on the professoriate. They caution against theoretical interpretation or normative critique based on assumptions that U.S. professors are a monolithic and left-wing political bloc. By the same token, however, refinements of recent studies have reaffirmed much of the classic portrait of the American professoriate as relatively liberal in the aggregate and in many of its general orientations.

Gross and Simmons's 2006 survey found 44 percent of faculty identifying themselves as liberals, with 46 percent identifying as moderates and just 9 percent as conservatives.[1] Similarly, Zipp and Fenwick's (2006) analysis of 1989 and 1997 data from the National Surveys of Faculty found "moderately liberal" and "liberal" identifiers to outnumber "moderately conservative" and "conservative" identifiers, 56 percent to 24 percent. These estimates are compatible with an accompanying degree of ideological diversity across the professoriate. While there is thus little evidence that American professors are a homogeneous and radical political bloc, their overall degree of liberalism, particularly in contrast to the U.S. population, is an important phenomenon that calls for explanation.

Explanatory Themes

How have scholars sought to explain the phenomenon of professorial liberalism in the United States? In postwar scholarship, the organization and norms surrounding occupations were critical factors. Professions were seen as special because extensive educational requirements and apprenticeships exposed incumbents to abstract and flexible forms of reasoning, alongside a strong service orientation. Individuals in fields such as teaching, medicine, and the law were constantly brushing up against liberal values and ideas (McClosky and Brill 1983). This was far less common in other occupations and in professions like business management that were organized around different ideas and priorities.

Innovative surveys conducted in the 1950s and 1960s found evidence of a strong relationship between type of occupations/professions and degree of support for liberal values. During the height of McCarthyism, community leaders, often defined by their location in professions, were found to be far more supportive of civil liberties than were voters in general (Stouffer 1992 [1955]). Indeed, within this research tradition, the professions as a whole soon came to be seen as a key to building and maintaining democratic polities. The new middle class, in Lipset's (1981 [1960]) influential theory, provided stability to and a wellspring of support for liberal and democratic values.

For understanding causal mechanisms, a legacy of this classic scholarship was its focus on the learning of liberal norms through professional training. But alongside this point of emphasis was a secondary focus on the influence of liberalism as a causal force in its own right. A seminal theme in Lipset's (1996; Lipset and Ladd 1971) work was that subordinate groups at times sought status in higher education and a location in the professoriate, particularly in fields permitting social and political criticism. In complementary fashion, Lazarsfeld and Thielens's (1958) work highlighted subjective perceptions of minority status among U.S. professors, an orientation that they saw as facilitating support for ideas and policy platforms associated with egalitarian causes.

Revisiting this line of thinking, the occupational self-selection argument has been given a systematic restatement in recent work by Gross and colleagues. According to this thesis, individuals select careers and courses of study that they see as reflecting their ideological orientations and other tastes. In the twentieth century, U.S. universities came to increasingly value new knowledge over established dogmas, opening up space for the entrance of more independent thinkers. Later establishment of free speech and job protections furthered these processes, and academic fields within the social sciences and humanities came to be seen as powerfully animated by liberal and reform-oriented ideas. This disposed liberals to pursue careers within these fields, steadily tipping the professoriate in the direction of liberalism. Gross and Cheng (2011) also find interview-based evidence that liberal professors report their orientations as preceding their choice of careers. This sometimes operates *directly* through political motivations and at other times *indirectly* through motivations involving nonpolitical values such as job autonomy and creativity.

Complementing occupational learning and self-selection arguments is a third explanatory theme. Here, the focus is on demographic and group sources of policy attitudes (Kinder and Sanders 1996; Sherkat and Ellison 1999), where membership in and subjective identification with population subgroups can be expected to influence the attitudes of professors. If, for instance, a discipline gains, over time, a higher proportion of secular individuals, we may expect a trend toward less socially conservative attitudes. While self-selection processes would obviously be in operation, a treatment effect could also unfold if other individuals responded to the entrance of secular practitioners by adopting less socially conservative attitudes. Either way, demographic attributes and group memberships are critical mechanisms.

This is precisely the line of criticism and interpretation presented by Brint (1984, 1985) with reference to the New Class thesis. Focusing on liberal trends in attitudes among professionals, Brint argues that it is historical changes in professionals' generational, occupational, and educational composition that matter. Over time, professionals as a whole became more liberal as younger cohorts of individuals entered their ranks and as educational levels and number of creatively oriented professional jobs ratcheted up. Social and demographic changes of this sort are candidate mechanisms behind professorial liberalism (see also Smith 1990).

The Promise of Cross-National Scholarship

There is much to be gained from looking cross-nationally at the policy attitudes of professors. We can see whether the U.S. professoriate's degree of liberalism is high or low in comparison with college faculty in other nations. Also informative is whether gaps between professors, professionals, and national publics vary across countries. Finally, explanatory questions about occupational learning, self-selection, or demographic composition enable new insights when viewed through a cross-national lens.

Comparative Perspective and Cross-National Patterning

The politics of the professoriate and the phenomenon of professorial liberalism have received the most extensive attention in the United States. But when the policy attitudes of professors have been investigated in other national contexts, the results are provocative. Consider, for instance, a pair of studies focusing on the Canadian professoriate and Swedish social science professors. In the Canadian case (Nakhaie and Brym 1999), U.S.-themed findings concerning discipline-based diversity and an overall posture of relative liberalism can be readily discerned. Survey results for Sweden differ instructively (Berggren, Jordahl, and Stern 2010), insofar as the attitudes of social science faculty appear to be generally more conservative and to more closely resemble those of the Swedish public.

What might we expect when cross-national comparisons are systematically made across a wider sample of countries? We might expect a degree of patterning in professors' policy attitudes with respect to clusters of countries. Such expectations are informed by comparative theory and research, where the institutions and publics of nations develop in ways that are far from random and, instead, track similar historical experiences and conditions (Castles and Mitchell 1993; Garrett 1998; Katzenstein 1985).

A useful perspective on professors' politics is provided by scholarship on welfare regimes. According to theorizing on power resources and power constellations, polities in the developed world are usefully classified according to the patterning of inequality in the quantity and quality of welfare provisions (Esping-Andersen 1990; Hicks 1999; Huber and Stephens 2001). From this perspective, the social democracies of the Nordic region provide the most extensive public services and benefits, lowering individuals' reliance on markets and private institutions over the life course and leading to lower levels of class and gender inequalities. The Christian-democratic regime type found in continental Western Europe also has high levels of welfare benefits and public spending, but lower levels of service provision are viewed as facilitating greater gender and status inequalities. In the English-speaking liberal democracies, markets are typically less regulated, and generally lower levels of public spending and provisions leave intact more extensive patterns of inequality.

It is in the liberal democracies that welfare regime theorizing suggests larger gaps between the policy attitudes of professors (and professionals, more generally) and those of national publics. In social-democratic nations, and possibly also in Christian democracies, welfare state theorizing implies that lower inequalities tend to create more positive-sum patterns of interest and conflict (Korpi and Palme 1998; Svallfors 2006; see also Iversen and Soskice 2001). Put another way, policy attitude differences involving the professoriate should be smaller in social democracies than in liberal democracies because professors (and professionals) can be expected to share an interest with ordinary citizens in maintaining access to national-level public social provisions. To be sure, evidence to the contrary suggests the importance of alternative mechanisms, including early life course–related preferences and occupational selection processes. Policy gaps in professors' attitudes and those of national publics may have little to do with welfare regime factors. This is important to explore.

Comparative Perspective on the Question of Class

A long-standing issue within comparatively oriented social theory has concerned the relevance of professors' class locations to their outlooks and actions. Just how much do material and market-related interests ultimately explain such policy attitudes and preferences? Is the relationship between class location and orientation best understood as involving a close or a loose coupling?

Debates over intellectuals and issues of social class were central to mid-twentieth-century social theory. There, the focus was frequently on the larger category of intellectuals as a whole. As discussed by Kurzman and Owens (2002), this wide-ranging literature oscillated between a series of divergent perspectives on the influence of class location with respect to intellectuals' political orientations and behavior.

Implicitly rejecting a Marxist perspective on politics, for instance, scholars such as Mannheim (1956) and Shils (1968) viewed intellectuals (and thus professors) as largely free of the constraints imposed by class structure within specific nations. The key was instead to be found in nonmaterial considerations and motivations, and some commentators went even further to define "intellectuals" as those whose identities and attitudes were largely unanchored in class and social structure (Hofstadter 1963; see also Said 1994). What these otherwise diverse lines of theorizing shared was the view that class and market locations provided thin groundwork for understanding intellectuals' historical allegiances and any radical or authoritarian propensities in time and place.

But while, in most midcentury theorizing, class location was seen as doing little, post-1960s' scholarship took a different turn. In addition to the contentious theory of the New Class discussed earlier, the work of Bourdieu (1988 [1984], 1990; Bourdieu and Passeron 1979 [1964]) is important. Bourdieu used the concept of a field to capture institutional sources of influence among intellectuals. But contrasting with earlier claims about the limited bearing of social structure, Bourdieu argued vigorously for intellectuals and professors as an essential part, or "fraction," of the dominant class. In this way, intellectuals' political orientations would tend to situate them more closely with those of other dominant class actors, though class was nevertheless one of the several forms of capital.

This line of thinking has been influential in comparatively oriented social theory. As argued by Karabel (1996; see also Brym 1988), an instructive case is provided by intellectuals in Russia and Eastern Europe after 1991. There, the transformation of Soviet-style socialism provided a working historical experiment in whether the orientations of intellectuals placed them in closer proximity to the new institutions of market economies or toward egalitarian (or even authoritarian) alternatives.

For the current project, a key question is, in which national contexts do professors' policy attitudes resemble those of other incumbents sharing a similar class position? We can also engage the issue of whether the policy attitudes of the East European professoriate places professors in oppositional or dominant class–oriented alignments. Note that insofar as professors arguably occupy the most institutionalized and rule-bound positions of any intellectuals, empirical consideration of their policy attitudes represents an informatively demanding test for the relevance of class-related processes.

Cross-National Data and Methods
Research Design and ISSP Data

The International Social Survey Program surveys provide us with cross-national data on the policy attitudes of professors. Started in the 1980s and stretching up to the present, the ISSP has been a leader in seeking to implement survey items that are standardized as closely as possible with respect to question wording and response formats. This is critical to cross-national measurement of policy attitudes. Equally important is the availability of detailed occupational information with which to identify individuals employed as college/university professors.

I draw data from seven separate surveys (ISSP 1993, 1994, 1997, 1999, 2001, 2004, 2008) to address three questions. First is the issue of how U.S. professors' liberalism stacks up when we consider the policy attitudes of professors and national publics in other countries. Second is the question of social class, where I evaluate whether professors' attitudes situate them within the larger class category of professionals. Third is the challenge of explaining the policy attitudes of the professoriate, and here I gauge the relevance of explanations based on occupational learning, self-selection, demographic composition, and state-centered processes.

Professors, Class Locations, and Countries

I use ISSP occupation data for teachers in higher education / colleges / universities to identify professors who are full-time, current labor force participants. Countries having no respondents (or a trivial number) in the professoriate were dropped. Even so, professors typically constitute a small fraction of the samples, and that is simply a feature of most national surveys. These decisions effectively impose a methodologically conservative standard; this is preferable to the risk of type I errors.

In coding individuals' class locations, I apply a version of the scheme developed by Erikson and Goldthorpe (1992; Goldthorpe 2000), identifying class locations for professionals, managers, routine white-collar workers, skilled workers, and unskilled workers (with a sixth residual category for respondents not employed full-time in the paid labor force). As discussed earlier, professors are a subset of the class category of professionals, and the analysis returns evidence regarding professors' versus professionals' degree of similarity versus difference in attitudes.

The third major set of independent variables is for country location, where statistical models of policy attitudes control for country (and also survey year). Countries are also used to identify regime types, and I conduct tests for interactions involving social democracies (Denmark, Norway, and Sweden), Christian democracies (France, Germany, Portugal, Spain, and Switzerland), and liberal democracies (Australia, Britain, Canada, Ireland, New Zealand, and the United States). East European nations (Czech Republic, Poland, Russia, and Slovenia) are treated as a separate regime type, acknowledging the distinct heritage of formerly socialist countries.[2]

Other Independent Variables

Additional independent variables in the analyses are demographic and social group attributes that are candidates for explaining professorial liberalism. Education and generation are continuous variables, both coded in years. Four dichotomous variables take into account gender, marital status, homemaker status, and status as a retiree. A final variable is for church attendance level; this continuous covariate has five response categories that range from weekly (or more) attendance through nonattendance / don't know.

A Focus on Five Major Policy Domains

I consider dependent variables for five major policy domains. The first dependent variable, attitudes toward the welfare state, provides a benchmark for comparison with other policy domains. In particular, the four other domains tap into rights-related issues likely to elicit disproportionately liberal attitudes on the part of professors. By contrast, the welfare state domain may reveal relatively market-oriented and thus conservative attitudes, if the results of U.S. research (Brint 1985) on professionals' policy attitudes generalize.

To measure welfare attitudes, I scale together two ISSP items that ask respondents about their degree of support for government provision of jobs and reduction of income inequality.[3] Item responses are converted to z-scores, and reliability for the two-item scale is 0.65. Items were fielded in the 1990, 1991, 1996, 1998, and 2006 surveys. In the estimation sample, countries included are the United States, Australia, Germany, Britain, France, Ireland, New Zealand, Norway, Sweden, Switzerland, Spain, Denmark, Slovenia, Poland, Russia, and the Czech Republic.[4]

My second dependent variable is for civil liberties attitudes. This is a policy domain in which past research on both professors and professionals has found disproportionately liberal attitudes (Brint 1985; McClosky and Brill 1983). In the analyses that follow, I scale three ISSP items that ask respondents about their degree of support for First Amendment liberties or dissenting forms of collective action.[5] Item responses are converted to z-scores, and reliability for the scale is 0.75. These items were fielded in the 1990, 1996, and 2006 surveys, and in the estimation sample the countries are the United States, Australia, Germany, Britain, New Zealand, Norway, Spain, Denmark, Portugal, and Russia.

The third dependent variable is for attitudes toward gender. Gender represents a major policy domain and a key point of ideological conflict between liberals and conservatives in virtually all nations (Bolzendahl and Ólafsdóttir 2008). Gender attitudes are measured using a scale of two ISSP items asking respondents about their level of agreement with traditional family arrangements.[6] Item responses are converted to z-scores, and reliability for the two-item scale is 0.79. These items were fielded in the 1994 and 2002 surveys, and in the estimation sample the countries in the analysis are the United States, Australia, France, Ireland, New Zealand, Norway, Spain, Denmark, Poland, and Russia.

The fourth dependent variable is for the domain of sexuality. Here, ISSP data are more limited, and I rely on a single item asking respondents to evaluate sexual relations between two adults of the same sex.[7] This item was fielded in the 1991, 1994, and 1998 surveys. In the estimation sample, countries in the analysis are the United States, Australia, Canada, Ireland, New Zealand, Norway, Spain, Denmark, Russia, and the Czech Republic.

The final policy attitude domain is on religion. My measure is a scale of two ISSP items that ask respondents about their willingness to limit the influence of religious leaders on politicians and government.[8] Item responses are converted to z-scores, and reliability for the scale is 0.80. These items were fielded in the 1991, 1994, and 1998 surveys. In the estimation sample, countries are the United States, Australia, Canada, Ireland, New Zealand, Norway, Spain, Denmark, Russia, and the Czech Republic.

Results
U.S. Professors' Attitudes in Comparative Perspective

Just how unusual are American professors' attitudes? Let us start with the central issue of the welfare state. Figure 3.1 shows professors' attitudes toward the welfare state in the United States and fifteen other nations. Higher scores indicate greater support for the welfare state, so at 0.71, Russian professors have by far the strongest preferences for public social provision, followed by professors in Poland (0.37) and Norway (0.30).

Results for the U.S. professoriate are dramatic. With a score of –1.99, American professors are the second most *anti* welfare within the sixteen countries, followed only by Czech professors at –2.01.[9] This lends considerable cross-national support to U.S.-centered scholarship arguing for the relative economic

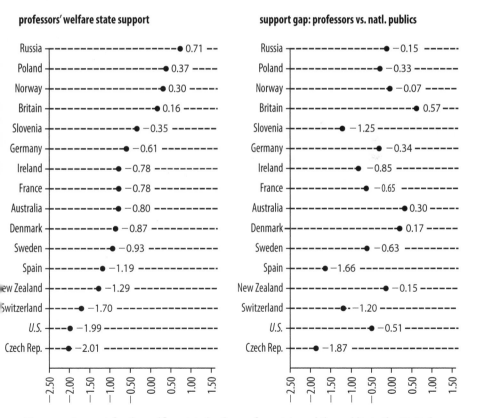

Figure 3.1. Support for the welfare state by the professoriate and the public in the United States and fifteen other countries

conservatism of American faculty. But could we be missing something by comparing just professors across nations? Is the U.S. professoriate relatively supportive of the welfare state in comparison with an American public that is even less so?

The second chart in figure 3.1 provides relevant evidence. This shows *gaps* in welfare attitude scores between the professoriate and the public in each nation. Higher scores again indicate greater relative welfare state support, and at −0.51, the size of the gap between professors and others in the United States is not particularly unusual. The negative sign of the estimate tells us that U.S. professors had lower support for social welfare compared with nonprofessors. But with a *t*-score of 1.42, the professors-public difference is not significant at the 0.05 level. This means that U.S. professors cannot be distinguished from the American public as a whole. U.S. professors stand out mainly for being so unsupportive of the welfare state in comparison with faculty of other nations.

What can we learn from the next issue, civil liberties? Figure 3.2 presents the results. As before, higher scores in the first chart indicate more left/liberal views, and higher scores in the second chart indicate that professors are to the left of national publics.

So, where do U.S. professors stand when it comes to civil liberties support? As the data in figure 3.2 show, the answer is much the same as for welfare state attitudes. The American professoriate's score of 1.28 places it third from the bottom in the ranking of civil liberties attitudes, ahead of only British and Russian faculty. Professors in seven other nations thus show higher measured levels of civil liberties support, with faculty in New Zealand and Denmark taking the first and second positions in the overall ranking.

What about gaps in civil liberties attitudes between professors and national publics? In contrast to the results for welfare state attitudes, professors in all countries are well to the left of their respective national publics, as shown by positively signed scores for all countries in the sample. Gaps in attitudes are smallest in Russia and largest in Australia and New Zealand. At 1.72, the gap between U.S. professors and the American public is clearly substantial,[10] but it also closely tracks the average measured difference (1.69) between all national professoriates and national publics. In the United States, then, professors' willingness to support civil liberties is much higher than that of the mass public, and this appears to be the case in several other countries as well.[11]

Looking at gender attitudes (figure 3.3), we can see that U.S. professors come in much higher in the country ranking of faculty attitudes. Indeed, only Danish and Spanish professors have more liberal gender attitudes. Initially, the gap in

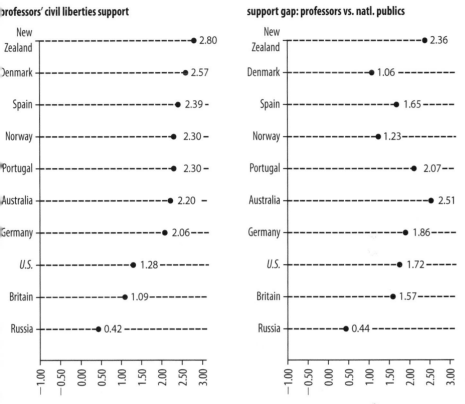

Figure 3.2. Support for civil liberties by the professoriate and the public in the United States and nine other countries

gender attitudes between the U.S. professoriate and the American public is among the largest in the sample. But additional analysis shows this difference is statistically illusory. Unlike the earlier case of civil liberties attitudes, the gender attitudes of U.S. professors (and other national professoriates) are indistinguishable from those of the national public.[12]

Turning to figure 3.4, we find that U.S. professors' attitudes toward sexuality appear conservative when viewed from a cross-national perspective. Given that sexuality attitudes are measured with a single item scored 1–4, the range of professors' attitude scores between the top (Denmark) and bottom countries (Russia) is substantial (1.83), and the U.S. professoriate's score is closer to the East European end of the sample.[13] Initially, gaps in attitudes place all faculty samples to the left of their national publics. But only in the Norwegian and Australian cases is there evidence that the gaps are significant.

professors' gender equality support   **support gap: professors vs. natl. publics**

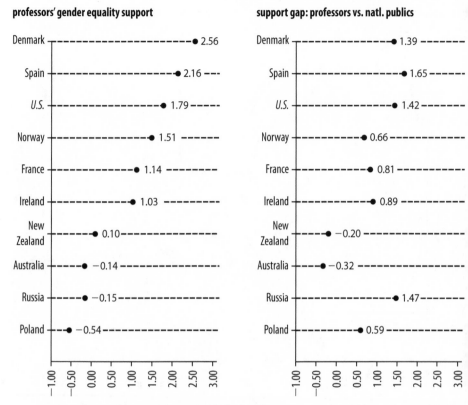

Figure 3.3. Support for gender equality by the professoriate and the public in the United States and nine other countries

The final domain concerns the issue of religious influence over government and politics. In figure 3.5, higher scores indicate greater support for *limiting* religious influence. With a score of 0.49, U.S. faculty are tied with their Irish counterparts for the third highest level of support for secular government. Danish and Spanish professors show much higher levels of support. Scores at the other end of the distribution suggest a high degree of polarization with respect to attitudes toward religion.[14]

In the second chart in figure 3.5, there are five cases in which national professoriates appear more supportive than national publics of limiting religious political authority. But statistical tests provide little evidence that these differences are significant. The same is true with respect to four of the five instances in which negative scores suggest that professors are *less* supportive than national publics of limiting religious political influence. Only in Norway does the measured gap in

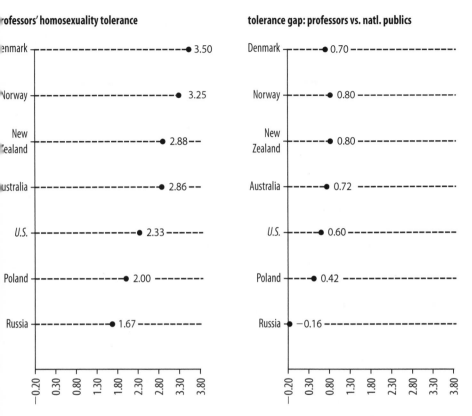

rofessors' homosexuality tolerance

tolerance gap: professors vs. natl. publics

Figure 3.4. Tolerance toward homosexuality by the professoriate and the public in the United States and six other countries

attitudes reflects a statistically significant difference in the attitudes of professors versus national publics.

Social Class and Cross-National Patterns

We now consider whether (and in which countries) professors' attitudes are shaped by their underlying locations as professionals. An intriguing possibility is that attitude gaps between professors and professionals vary among clusters of nations. I focus attention on social, Christian, and liberal democracies and East European nations.

Consider the coefficients and standard errors for two regression models of policy attitudes shown in table 3.1. The first model (left column estimates under each policy domain) takes into account the gap between professors and all others and any significant attitude gaps involving professors and national context

professors' support for church/state separation   **support gap: professors vs. natl. publics**

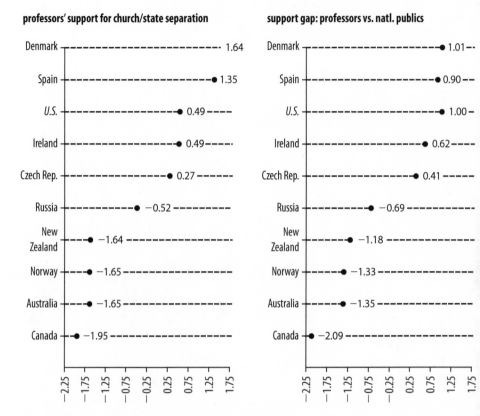

Figure 3.5. Support for limiting the influence of religion in government by the professoriate and the public in the United States and nine other countries

(main effects of country and survey year are controlled for and coefficients and standard errors are not reported, to avoid clutter).[15] The second model (right column estimates) adds the main effect of class and any significant attitude gaps involving professionals and national context.

Starting with the models of welfare state attitudes, we see that professors' attitudes differ significantly from others. There are also interactions involving the professoriate in liberal as well as social democracies. In both models, the negatively signed coefficient for the main effects of professors, when taking into account interactions involving regimes, pertains to the professoriate in Christian-democratic countries and East European countries. This means that relative to others, professors in countries such as France, Germany, Poland, and Russia are significantly more *negative* in their attitudes toward the welfare state. In contrast, the interaction effects tell us that professors in liberal and social-democratic

TABLE 3.1
Coefficients (standard errors) for Regression Models of Policy Attitudes among Professors and Professionals

Variable	Welfare state (N = 54,478)		Civil liberties (N = 22,663)		Gender (N = 14,915)		Sexuality (N = 18,714)		Religion (N = 15,450)	
Professors	-0.85* (0.17)	-0.45 (0.17)	1.74* (0.21)	1.18* (0.21)	0.72* (0.25)	-0.01 (0.25)	0.61* (0.15)	0.23 (0.14)	-0.48 (0.25)	-0.32 (0.25)
Professors × lib. dem.	0.78* (0.24)	0.73* (0.23)	—	—	—	—	—	—	—	—
Professors × Christ. dem.	—	—	—	—	—	—	—	—	—	—
Professors × soc. dem.	0.80* (0.30)	0.73* (0.30)	—	—	—	—	—	—	—	—
Professionals	—	-0.57* (0.02)	—	-0.19 (0.12)	—	0.82* (0.10)	—	0.34* (0.05)	—	-0.14* (0.04)
Professionals × lib. dem.	—	—	—	1.34* (0.14)	—	0.32* (0.11)	—	0.28* (0.06)	—	—
Professionals × Christ. dem.	—	—	—	1.26* (0.15)	—	0.45* (0.14)	—	—	—	—
Professionals × soc. dem.	—	—	—	0.88* (0.15)	—	0.36* (0.12)	—	0.27* (0.07)	—	—
Managers	—	-0.96* (0.03)	—	0.61* (0.06)	—	0.86* (0.06)	—	0.48* (0.04)	—	-0.07 (0.06)
Routine white-collar	—	-0.25* (0.02)	—	0.50* (0.06)	—	0.73* (0.04)	—	0.31* (0.03)	—	0.16* (0.05)
Skilled workers	—	-0.19* (0.02)	—	0.44* (0.05)	—	0.33* (0.06)	—	0.01 (0.03)	—	0.21* (0.06)
Unskilled workers	—	-0.05* (0.02)	—	0.35* (0.05)	—	0.21* (0.05)	—	0.01 (0.03)	—	0.09 (0.05)
Constant	-0.42* (0.07)	-0.21* (0.07)	-66.1* (4.8)	-60.9* (4.8)	-59.0* (10)	-36.2* (10)	-1.53* (0.34)	-1.10* (0.34)	-5.01* (0.55)	-5.16* (0.55)
R^2	0.18	0.20	0.07	0.09	0.17	0.22	0.07	0.10	0.04	0.04

Note. See text for description of the models. All models also control for survey year and country (coefficients not presented).
*$p < 0.05$ (t-test)

countries have relatively more positive attitudes toward welfare. Thus, not only do professors' welfare attitudes vary across countries, but this variation takes on a highly specific form of patterning.

Staying with results for the welfare attitudes domain, we see that coefficient estimates for the second model deliver two additional findings. On the effects of class, relative to non-full-time labor force participants, all five class categories are significantly more negative in their welfare attitudes. These differences are especially pronounced for professionals and managers. Returning to the −0.45 coefficient for the main effect of professors, this indicates that in East European and Christian-democratic nations, professionals employed as professors have welfare attitudes similar to those of managers. The welfare attitudes of professors in the liberal and social-democratic nations again differ, showing a considerably less negative posture.

The next set of results in table 3.1 is for civil liberties attitudes. In the first model (without controls for class), professors have considerably more liberal attitudes than nonprofessors ($\beta = 1.74$).[16] Two-thirds of this attitude gap remains when we take into account the main and interaction effects involving class. In all nations covered by these analyses, professors are much more supportive of civil liberties than others.

Table 3.1 shows something more. Taking into account the presence of interactions, the nonsignificant −0.19 coefficient for the main effect of professionals means that the attitudes of professionals do not differ from those of non–labor force participants in the East European countries. But in both liberal and Christian democracies, professionals have much more distinctively liberal attitudes; the attitude gap involving professionals in social-democratic nations is also substantial, if a bit smaller. We can thus see how professionals everywhere but Eastern Europe have comparatively favorable views of civil liberties. And in addition to this class-related gap is a professorial effect, operating over and beyond even the high level of support professors already give as professionals.

On gender attitudes, the results differ in two ways. First, while the professorial gap in attitudes is initially large, it vanishes entirely when class-related differences in gender attitudes are controlled. Looking at these class-related results, we see that professionals in all countries are significantly more liberal in their views of gender. These differences are magnified outside the East European nations, where attitude gaps between professionals and non–labor force participants are consistently larger.

Results for attitudes toward sexuality are generally similar to those for gender. Initially, there is a significant gap between professors and others, but it disappears when we control for class effects. As before, there is also a tendency for professionals to have relatively more liberal attitudes in all countries. This effect is accentuated in liberal and social-democratic nations, where the attitude gap involving professionals is larger.

In the final policy attitude domain, the results for religion reveal much smaller gaps involving professors and professionals. Indeed, the only significant difference is for professionals, and there is no evidence for interactions involving countries or aggregated regime types. Moreover, the −0.14 coefficient means that professionals are slightly *less* supportive of limiting organized religion's influence over government and elections. These results are notable as a point of contrast with thematic findings on the existence and cross-national patterning of attitude gaps involving both professors and professionals.

Explanatory Factors

What about sources of the professoriate's attitudes? I extend the regression analysis by considering a series of new factors in the model. These seven social and demographic covariates relate to compositional explanations of professorial attitudes. If coefficients measuring professorial (and professional) attitude gaps vanish, then it is primarily social groups and demography that are in operation.

What about scenarios in which, instead, the macro-effects of national institutions, or occupational learning, or occupational self-selection are at work? The relevance of national institutions would be implicated in patterns of interaction in which attitude gaps involving professors and professionals were consistently smaller in social (and possibly also Christian) democracies (due to the common interests and identities created by redistributive welfare states). Next, the occupational learning scenario implies that professors' attitudes will diverge significantly from those of other professionals (due to the institutional conditions that define professorial employment). Finally, the self-selection scenario relies on indirect evidence, where the preceding accounts offer little in the way of explanation.

In table 3.2, the first regression model is carried over from the earlier analyses, with the main effect of professorial employment, class, and any significant cross-national interactions taken into account. The new model adds sociodemographic covariates. Again, to avoid clutter, coefficients and standard errors for these variables are not presented.

Looking first at the results for professors' welfare state attitudes, we see a decline in the magnitude of coefficients across models. Professors' gaps in attitudes in the East European and Christian-democratic nations are approximately

TABLE 3.2
Final Models of Professors' and Professionals' Policy Attitudes

Variable	Welfare state (N=54,478)		Civil liberties (N=22,663)		Gender (N=14,915)		Sexuality (N=8,714)		Religion (N=15,456)	
Professors	-0.45* (0.23)	-0.29 (0.16)	1.18* (0.21)	1.00* (0.20)	-0.01 (0.25)	-0.01 (0.23)	0.23 (0.14)	0.17 (0.13)	-0.32 (0.25)	-0.26 (0.24)
Professors×lib. dem.	0.73* (0.23)	0.73* (0.23)	—	—	—	—	—	—	—	—
Professors×Christ. dem.	—	—	—	—	—	—	—	—	—	—
Professors×soc. dem.	0.73* (0.30)	0.87* (0.30)	—	—	—	—	—	—	—	—
Professionals	-0.57* (0.02)	-0.39* (0.02)	-0.19 (0.12)	-0.83* (0.13)	0.82* (0.10)	0.05 (0.09)	0.34* (0.05)	-0.06 (0.05)	-0.14* (0.04)	-0.15* (0.05)
Professionals×lib. dem.	—	—	1.34* (0.14)	1.32* (0.13)	0.32* (0.11)	0.27* (0.11)	0.28* (0.06)	0.34* (0.06)	—	—
Professionals×Christ. dem.	—	—	1.27* (0.15)	1.02* (0.14)	0.44* (0.14)	0.36* (0.13)	—	—	—	—
Professionals×soc. dem.	—	—	0.88* (0.15)	0.90* (0.15)	0.36* (0.12)	0.43* (0.11)	0.27* (0.07)	0.37* (0.06)	—	—
Managers	-0.96* (0.03)	-0.79* (0.03)	0.61* (0.06)	<-0.01 (0.07)	0.86* (0.06)	0.29* (0.06)	0.48* (0.04)	0.24* (0.04)	-0.07 (0.06)	-0.10 (0.07)
Routine white-collar	-0.25* (0.02)	-0.29* (0.03)	0.50* (0.06)	0.02 (0.07)	0.74* (0.04)	0.01 (0.05)	0.31* (0.03)	0.04 (0.03)	0.16* (0.05)	0.06 (0.05)
Skilled workers	-0.19* (0.02)	-0.11* (0.03)	0.44* (0.05)	-0.16* (0.06)	0.33* (0.06)	-0.08 (0.06)	0.01 (0.03)	-0.13 (0.04)	0.21* (0.06)	0.10 (0.07)
Unskilled workers	-0.05* (0.02)	-0.07* (0.03)	0.35* (0.05)	-0.14* (0.06)	0.21* (0.05)	-0.19* (0.05)	0.01 (0.03)	-0.11* (0.03)	0.09 (0.05)	<-0.01 (0.06)
Constant	-0.21* (0.07)	0.54* (2.57)	-60.9* (4.8)	-59.3* (4.9)	-36.2* (10)	-39.0* (9.3)	-1.10* (0.34)	-27.2* (1.34)	-5.16* (0.55)	-12.3* (2.3)
R^2	0.20	0.23	0.09	0.13	0.22	0.34	0.10	0.23	0.04	0.09

*$p < 0.05$ (t-test)

a third smaller in the second model, while the attitude gap in social democracies is, in contrast, larger in that model. The welfare attitude gap involving professionals shrinks in the second model, but still retains over two-thirds of its initial magnitude. Together, these results provide some evidence for the relevance of compositional differences to understanding professorial/professional gaps in welfare attitudes, yet the majority of these cleavages nonetheless remain.

In the civil liberties domain, professors' greater civil liberties support is even less unchanged across models. But for professionals, a change in the main effect coefficient from −0.19 to −0.83 indicates that attitude gaps involving professionals are much smaller in the second model.[17] This means that social and demographic differences help explain more of the distinctiveness in professionals' civil liberties attitudes in many national contexts. For their part, professors' unusually high relative support for civil liberties involves other factors, and the absence of cross-national patterning for professors' attitudes makes a state-centered explanation of limited relevance.

Turning to gender attitudes, recall that earlier results showed initially significant attitude gaps involving professors to be a product of class-related differences involving professionals. The extended results now show that attitude gaps involving professionals are mostly explained by compositional differences. Specifically, professionals' interactions with regimes remain significant, but a decline in the main effect coefficient from 0.82 to 0.05 indicates that most of the gender attitude gap involving professionals has disappeared.

Compositional differences are also relevant to sexuality attitudes. As in the case of gender attitudes, initially significant differences involving professors' attitudes toward sexuality evaporate when class location is taken into account (see again table 3.1). The additional results in table 3.2 show that the main effect of professionals now disappears when compositional factors are included in the model. To be sure, interactions between professionals and liberal/social democracies remain significant and are even slightly larger in table 3.2. But once the accompanying main effect estimate for professionals is taken (appropriately) into account in the calculations, we can see that these gaps shrink substantially when compositional factors are controlled for.

The final set of results is for the issue of religion. Throughout the multivariate analyses, there is little evidence that professors vary in their attitudes toward religious influence over government. For their part, professionals are slightly *less* supportive than non–labor force participants of limiting religious political influence. Table 3.2 shows that compositional differences leave this gap in attitudes largely unchanged. These results for religious attitudes caution against a portrait of professors (or professionals) as necessarily liberal/left or distinctive with respect to all policy issues.

Conclusion

Key to this chapter is the idea that we can learn from investigating the attitudes and orientations of professors in cross-national perspective. Building from a vigorous and increasingly sophisticated literature centered on the United States, I have analyzed the attitudes of professors and professionals with respect to five major issue domains. The International Social Survey Program data provide the foundations for cross-national insight. Results also speak to questions about the interrelationships between professors' and professionals' policy attitudes and some mechanisms that underlie patterns of these attitudes within and across countries.

Let us start by revisiting the findings that emerge from considering several different issue domains. It is striking that professors' attitudes are fairly heterogeneous across issues. This is also true for country rankings of national professoriates with respect to their degree of left/liberal attitudes. Whether and in what ways professors' attitudes are distinctive (or disproportionately liberal) hinges not only on the country context but also on the issue under consideration.

The case of welfare state attitudes is important. For twelve of the sixteen countries in this part of the analysis, professors' welfare attitudes are to the *right* of those of national publics. In this way, professors, much like professionals and managers, tend to be relatively inegalitarian in their attitudes within many countries. Class-related mechanisms have been brought into focus in scholarship on welfare state attitudes, where perceptions of market and material interests and risks are critical (Breen and Rottman 1995; Brooks and Svallfors 2010; Erikson and Goldthorpe 1992).

The welfare attitude results are notable in a second way. They represent the sole case in which professors' attitudes also vary systematically across regimes, suggesting the moderating influence of national institutions on policy preferences. In the four other issue domains, there is no evidence for a patterning of professors' attitudes with respect to specific countries or regime types. There are cross-national interactions involving *professionals*. But in two of these three cases, gaps between the policy attitudes of professionals and non–labor force participants are *larger* in social democracies than elsewhere. That result is inconsistent with the expectations of state-centered accounts of the formation of policy attitudes. Clearly, there is more work to be done here, in both cross-national theorizing and data analysis.

A second set of results concerns attitudes toward civil liberties. Attitudinal differences between professors and national publics are considerable, but explanations based on demographic composition and national/regime context shed little light. This means that the civil liberties results are suggestive of the self-selection scenario. This accords well with interview and survey-based evidence for the United States (Gross and Cheng 2011).

What of the remaining three issue domains? Neither occupational learning, nor self-selection, nor state-centered explanations are particularly helpful. It is demographic composition that is most illuminating. Initially, professors' attitudes on gender and sexuality differ significantly from those of national publics. But once class categories are considered in the model, professorial distinctiveness vanishes, and it is the larger category of professionals that shows disproportionately liberal attitudes. By itself, that result cuts against the occupational learning scenario, as this hypothesis implies that professors are exposed to different occupational norms than other professionals.

Social groups and demography enter the picture by effectively explaining away much of the sexuality and gender attitude gaps involving professionals. For both domains, significant interactions involving professionals and specific regime types remain. But even in the relevant national contexts, these interactions place the attitudes of professionals right next to those of managers and thus far less distinctive than in earlier models without compositional controls.

Results for rights-related issues are also informative with respect to country-level differences in professors' orientations. In particular, cross-national rankings of professors' attitudes differ across issues, and on rights-related issues, East European professors' attitudes consistently place them toward the less liberal end of the distribution.[18] These results resonate well with Karabel's (1996) comparative-historical analysis of social change processes that have tended to move East European intellectuals as a whole away from oppositional politics and toward dominant class alignments or traditional sources of authority. In the ISSP data, there is little evidence of left-wing or emancipatory orientations among the professoriate in this world region.

Underlying much of the continuing scholarly interest in the politics of professors is that their institutional locations give them a broad range of audiences and many potential arenas of influence. Thus it is perhaps not surprising that several generations of commentary have portrayed professors as a ready resource for left-wing ideas and activism, inside as well as outside the modern university. There are similarities between the contentious idea of a radical "New Class" of professors and contemporary critiques of a homogeneous status group seeking to exclude politically dissimilar scholars (Woessner and Kelly-Woessner 2009; see also Bruce-Briggs 1979; Kimball 1990).

New data collections and nuanced interpretation cast doubt on these scenarios for the United States. They document a degree of complexity and heterogeneity in professors' attitudes, also unveiling the importance of self-selection processes in generating high levels of liberal support and identification in some disciplines. While the current analyses should be viewed as a preliminary step in comparative research, three provisional findings are worth emphasizing in conclusion.

First is the tendency for many national professoriates to embrace centrist or relatively market-oriented attitudes toward the welfare state. This finding extends Brint's (1984, 1985) results for U.S. professionals. Professors' welfare state attitudes, in most nations, place them in close proximity to the attitudes of other professionals, particularly within most European countries (the Christian democracies and East European nations in this analysis). In many nations, there seems to be a poor fit between the social policy preferences of professors and the idea of an anticapitalist (or radically egalitarian) vanguard.

A second point concerns sources of gender and sexuality attitudes among professors. These issues have been central to partisan criticisms of "political correctness" among U.S. college faculty (D'Souza 1991). My analyses provide evidence for the importance of demographic and group-related factors in explaining liberal attitudes. For these issues, there is as yet little evidence for the occupational learning scenario in which it is workplace influence or even ideological conversion that accounts for liberal sentiments among the professoriate. In turn, this means that in many national contexts, any liberal tendencies in attitudes among professors and professionals can often be explained by the social identities of individuals who enter their ranks. Just how such liberal identities of this sort operate to prompt educational and career choices is an important, further question for scholars.[19] It may compel a reexamination of classic issues of early life-course and political learning (Alwin, Cohen, and Newcomb 1991; see also Jost, Federico, and Napier 2009).

The final point concerns the issue of civil liberties attitudes. Civil liberties seem notable for eliciting relatively big attitude gaps between professors and others across diverse national contexts. These results signal that individuals with a long-standing preference for both political and personal autonomy may tend to select into academic employment. If so, they may bring with them a strong initial orientation that colors much of what is politically distinctive about professors.

NOTES

This research was supported by grants from the National Science Foundation (SES-0830917) and the Russell Sage Foundation (RSF-83-08-04). I thank Neil Gross, Solon Simmons, Rune Stubager, and an anonymous referee for comments.

1. In chapter 1 of this volume, Gross and Simmons note that if response categories are reconceptualized to place all liberal identifiers together (and all conservative identifiers together), the percentage of liberals rises to 62, and the percentage of conservatives to 20.

2. While it bears emphasizing that the current study restricts itself to countries in Europe, North America, and the Antipodes, further work on the politics of professors may profit by broadening the cross-national scope, using ISSP (or other suitable) data.

3. Question wording for these items is as follows: "On the whole, do you think it should be or should not be the government's responsibility to: Provide a job for everyone who wants one?" and "On the whole, do you think it should be or should not be the government's responsibility to: Reduce income differences between the rich and poor?" Response options are in four categories: "definitely should not be," "probably should not be," "probably should be," and "definitely should be."

4. Note that not all countries were surveyed at each of the ISSP's five cross-sectional waves; controls for year and country are included in the regression models.

5. Question wording for these items is as follows: "There are many ways people or organizations can protest against a government action they strongly oppose. Please show which you think should be allowed and which should not be allowed by ticking a box on each line. Organizing public meetings to protest against the government? Organizing protest marches and demonstrations? Organizing a nationwide strike of all workers against the government?" Response options are in four categories: "definitely not allowed," "probably not allowed," "probably allowed," and "definitely allowed."

6. Question wording for these items is as follows: "Do you agree or disagree: All in all, family life suffers when the woman has a full-time job?" and "Do you agree or disagree: a husband's job is to earn money; a wife's job is to look after the home and family?" Response options are in five categories, ordered from "strongly agree" through "strongly disagree."

7. Question wording is as follows: "And what about sexual relations between two adults of the same sex, is it: 'always wrong,' 'almost always wrong,' 'wrong only sometimes,' 'not wrong at all'?"

8. Question wording for these items is as follows: "Agree or disagree with following statements: Religious leaders should not try to influence how people vote in elections [and] Religious leaders should not try to influence government decisions." Response options are in five Likert-type categories, ordered from "strongly agree" through "strongly disagree."

9. Overall country differences in national professoriates' welfare state attitudes are significant ($F = 3.73$, $p < 0.05$).

10. The t-score for gauging the significance of this score gap is 3.36 ($p < 0.05$).

11. In six of the remaining nine countries, civil liberties attitude gaps are significant. The three exceptions are Denmark, Portugal, and Russia.

12. Overall cross-national differences in professors' gender attitudes are, however, significant ($F = 2.27$, $p < 0.05$).

13. Overall cross-national differences in professors' sexuality attitudes are significant ($F = 3.05$, $p < 0.05$).

14. Overall cross-national differences in professors' religion attitudes are significant ($F = 3.82$, $p < 0.05$).

15. In the course of the analyses, I consider interactions involving professors and countries and interactions involving professors and country clusters aggregated into types of regimes.

16. Analyses of the civil liberties domain (and the three remaining policy attitude domains) find no evidence for interactions involving professors and either countries or regime-type clusters. Interaction effects, where significant, are thus for the larger category of professionals.

17. For instance, taking into account interactions, the predicted civil liberties attitude gap between professionals and non–labor force participants in liberal democracies is 0.49 in the second model (vs. 1.15 in the first model).

18. For their part, U.S. professors' attitudes situate them toward the less liberal/tolerant end of the distribution on two rights-related issues and with the more liberal of country faculties on gender attitudes.

19. In this context, consider again the findings about how location in the professions bears on attitude gaps involving professors for issues of gender, sexuality, and (to a lesser extent) civil liberties. What this finding suggests is that professors' exposure to occupation-specific cognitive (and other) stimuli matters less than the relevant experiences they share with other professionals.

CHAPTER FOUR

Political Bias in the Graduate School Admissions Process

A Field Experiment

ETHAN FOSSE, NEIL GROSS, AND JOSEPH MA

Because professors play an important role in imparting knowledge to the young, advising policymakers, and helping to steer national debates, much effort has been put into explaining why they tend to be on the political left, as the introduction and first three chapters of this volume show. Social-scientific theories of the phenomenon range widely, with some scholars highlighting the purported mismatch between the nature of the intellectual role and the cognitive demands of conservative ideology (Ladd and Lipset 1976); others, the distinctive class situation of the professoriate and the political and economic interests this establishes (Bourdieu 1988 [1984]; Karabel 1996); and still others, processes of self-selection into academe (Fosse and Gross 2012).

An additional line of thought focuses on political bias and discrimination. One hallmark of a profession, in sociological terms, is that its members, holding a monopoly over specialized knowledge, gain the right to collectively establish standards for entry into and practice in the field and to serve as the main evaluators of potential entrants, as well as of peers, according to those standards (Abbott 1988; Freidson 1986; Larson 1977). Some social scientists argue that in occupations organized in this way, there is inherent potential for social biases, objectively unrelated to performance, to influence evaluations and hence personnel decisions. More specifically, these scholars claim that if many members of a profession share a key social characteristic, then their natural tendency will be to evaluate more positively the competencies and work products of others with that characteristic. Even in the absence of an intention to bring about social closure, the operation of such a bias would, over time, yield a profession that reproduces itself in terms of social composition or becomes increasingly self-similar.

Social scientists such as Rothman, Lichter, and Nevitte (2005), Klein and Stern (2009), and Maranto (2009) see bias as contributing substantially to the enduring liberalism of American professors. In the 1960s, these researchers contend, there was an influx of leftists and liberals into the academy, such that in subsequent decades, left politics became a social characteristic of much of the professoriate. The result, they argue, is that a proliberal or anticonservative bias has tended to operate when professors evaluate applications to graduate school, the progress of graduate students, the potential of candidates on the academic job market, or the qualification of colleagues for tenure and promotion—especially in disciplines in which it is seen as legitimate to judge ideas in part by their political orientations. According to this line of thought, the main reason there are so few conservatives in academe today is that bias and discrimination hinder their entry.

The discrimination argument is important. If true, it would not only call into question the legitimacy of the American academic enterprise, which rests on meritocratic principles, but also throw doubt on other theories of professorial liberalism, some of which are integral to broader social-theoretical frameworks (such as that of Bourdieu). To date, however, few efforts have been made to test the discrimination argument empirically. Analyzing observational data from surveys of the professoriate, several researchers have reported that conservative professors do not fare as well as their liberal colleagues in the competition for prestigious academic appointments (Rothman, Lichter, and Nevitte 2005). Yet statistical differences are not necessarily evidence of bias or discrimination.

In this chapter we examine a key juncture in the academic evaluation process—admission to graduate school—in search of direct evidence that would support the thesis of political bias. Although there are many important evaluation points in academic careers, the one that results in students being accepted into doctoral programs is critical for explaining the politics of professors. Research shows that liberals are significantly overrepresented in the ranks of graduate students (see chapter 2), creating what Woessner and Kelly-Woessner (2009) call a "left pipeline" into the professoriate. Even if there were no biases in hiring and promotion, the overrepresentation of liberals among graduate students would result in a left-leaning academic profession. Given the limitations of observational data for testing theories of discrimination, we turned to an experimental design—to what is sometimes called a "field experiment." Field experiments "blend . . . experimental methods with field-based research, relaxing certain controls over environmental influences to better simulate real-world interactions" (Pager 2007b, 109).

We designed a study around the tendency of prospective graduate school applicants, especially in the social sciences and humanities, to write emails to directors of graduate study (DGSs) in the programs they are considering. The usual purpose of such emails is for students to introduce themselves and to ascertain whether they would be a good fit for the programs. During the fall of 2010, we sent two such emails of inquiry, three weeks apart, to DGSs in leading American graduate programs in sociology, political science, economics, history, and literature. The emails came from fictitious students, closely matched in their academic backgrounds and stated interests. We sent each DGS one control and one of two treatment emails: the control did not mention politics; the treatment email stated casually that two years earlier, the student had worked on either the Obama or the McCain campaign. To estimate the amount of political discrimination in the graduate school admissions process, we compare the average treatment effects for the Obama emails with those for the McCain emails, examining both frequency and timing of response, as well as the amount of information provided by the DGS, the emotional warmth of her or his email, and the level of enthusiasm shown for the prospective applicant. The last three outcomes were assessed by a politically mixed panel of three raters, blind to treatment condition. We find only the slightest hint—no significant evidence—of bias or discrimination.

The chapter begins by briefly reviewing previous research on political bias in academe. Then we turn to issues of study design and measurement before presenting the results. We conclude by discussing the limitations of our methodology and the implications of our findings.

Research on Political Bias in Higher Education

The claim that biases against conservative students, professors, and ideas are rampant in higher education is recurrent in the discourse of American conservatism. As mentioned above, several social scientists have pursued the thesis that such biases explain the continuing liberal tilt of the academy.

One of the first studies to advance this argument was Rothman, Lichter, and Nevitte's (2005) article "Politics and Professional Advancement among College Faculty." The authors examined survey data on the political views of professors teaching at four-year colleges and universities. They reported that 72 percent identified themselves as falling on the left side of the political divide and 15 percent on the right; that Democrats in academe outnumbered Republicans by a margin of 5:1; and that in terms of attitudes, faculty members displayed "an across the board commitment to positions that are typically identified with contemporary liberal ideals" (8). Beyond presenting these descriptive findings, a major goal of the article was to assess the hypothesis that political "homogeneity makes it more difficult for conservatives to enter and advance in the [academic] profession" (8). The authors regressed a measure of the prestige of their respondents' institutional positions on a variety of predictor variables: party affiliation, political self-identification, and political attitudes. They found that being a conservative or Republican is associated with teaching at a less prestigious institution, even after controlling for research productivity and other variables. In a follow-up study using the same data, Rothman, this time writing with Woessner and Kelly-Woessner (2010), reported that it was social, not economic, conservatives who were at a disadvantage; that the results of their models were little changed when the amount of time respondents devoted to research was removed from the index measuring productivity (as it should have been, given that this variable is collinear with institutional prestige); and that the effects of social conservatism on institutional location were small compared with the effects of productivity.

Klein and Stern (2009) offered a more elaborated version of the discrimination argument. Working with various coauthors, Klein has amassed evidence over the past few years of the liberalism of American professors, of the particular overrepresentation of liberals at high-prestige schools, and of the number of conservative PhD holders in the social sciences who do not wind up with academic appointments (e.g., Cardiff and Klein 2004; Klein and Stern 2004–5). In his chapter with Stern (2009), he sought to explain these patterns using Janis's (1982) concept of "groupthink." For Janis, groupthink, at its core, involves the emergence in a task-oriented group of strong pressures against dissent, born of "a desire to preserve the unity of the group" (Vaughan 1996, 525). Klein and Stern argue that such pressures operate in academic departments and keep professors from making job offers to candidates who are at odds politically with other faculty members.

A somewhat different take on the issue is provided by Maranto (2009) in a chapter on the politics of political scientists. Describing political science as a field that is "left but not quite PC," Maranto attributes the politics of political scientists mostly to self-selection. It is not, he claims, that intellectually oriented conservatives decide to avoid political science because they are naturally disdainful of the state, the field's main object of investigation. Rather, liberal political scientists display a "systematic bias" against conservative ideas that "emit distinct and perceptible signals" (211) to conservatives that they are not welcome. Among these signals, Maranto argues, are the composition of panels at meetings of the American Political Science Association, where conservative themes (such as "rights to school choice . . . or for the unborn") are rare; the informal evaluations offered to students about the importance of particular research topics; and the kinds of public stances the discipline has taken historically (216). When the occasional conservative does go into political science, Maranto claims, she or he will not be made to feel welcome, unless hired as a "house conservative" who is "used to prove the broad-mindedness of [a] department" (212).

These arguments are plausible on their face. We know from careful qualitative studies, such as Lamont's (2009) on peer review or Musselin's (2010) on academic hiring in Europe and the United States, that strong pressures toward homophily are often evident in academic settings where evaluations take place—although, as we discuss later, those same studies show that such pressures can be contravened by other group dynamics, norms, and practices about which theorists of political bias in higher education have had little to say. At the same time, research by political psychologists demonstrates that political commitments and identifications can influence and bias a range of judgments (e.g., Taber and Lodge 2006).

Yet little direct evidence has been amassed in support of the claim that liberal professors are biased against conservatives who would enter the academy and that they make decisions, individually or collectively, that have the effect of locking conservatives out. Rothman, Lichter, and Nevitte (2005) asserted that their findings were consistent with the hypothesis of discrimination, which is true; but if (as they acknowledge) "unmeasured factors," such as differing aspirations with regard to academic employment, had a strong enough effect on their outcome variable, their findings would be equally consistent with the hypothesis of no discrimination. Although Tobin examined survey data on professors that included several feeling-thermometer items and found that many academics hold negative views of one conservative group—evangelical Protestants (Tobin and Weinberg 2007)—and although it is easy to point to negative statements about conservatives and conservatism made by prominent liberal academics, it is not clear that such feelings and views systematically influence the evaluation of academic personnel and are at play in settings where resource allocation decisions are made. (Two more recent studies of the professoriate that report attitudinal evidence of bias against conservative scholars are Inbar and Lammers 2012 and Yancey 2011.) In the 2006 survey of the American professoriate described in chapter 1 of this volume, Gross and Simmons found that conservative professors are more likely than liberal ones to agree with the statement that academia favors professors with liberal views. But self-perceptions are not evidence of bias, and in any case, Rothman, Woessner, and Kelly-Woessner (2010) reported that the vast majority of conservative professors indicate they have *not* been discriminated against on political grounds. On the other side, Gross and Simmons also found that most American professors state that the political views of academic job candidates should have no bearing on decisions about hiring. Yet this could be similar to the insistence by most whites today that racial discrimination against African Americans is wrong: they may say that it is, and even believe it, but they might have implicit biases that nevertheless lead them to act in a discriminatory manner.

Methods

The problem of "unmeasured factors" is hardly unique to the Rothman, Lichter, and Nevitte study: it plagues every study of discrimination that relies on observational data. Unlike experiments, in which subjects are randomly assigned to treatment and control groups, in observational studies, treatment assignment (such as it is) is not manipulated by the researcher. Who happens to be poor or rich, or liberal or conservative, is a function of processes occurring in the world, and this is what leaves open the possibility of "hidden bias" in estimating causal effects from observational data (Rosenbaum 1991, 2002), since such processes, and the many social facts with which they are linked, could be systematically related to observed outcomes in ways for which it is difficult to control.

As recognition of this problem has spread, efforts at measuring discrimination have increasingly involved the use of experimental data. Although important experimental research on discrimination has been conducted in laboratory settings, field experiments have been more common in economics and sociology. The most frequently implemented type of field experiment in research on race and sex discrimination is the audit study (e.g., Bertrand and Mullainathan 2004; Neumark, Bank, and Van Nort 1996; Pager 2003; Pager, Western, and Bonikowski 2009), in which researchers lead resource allocators to make real-life decisions around fabricated cases.

Audit studies offer several advantages over other research designs. Unlike observational studies, audit studies let the researcher randomly assign subjects to treatment and control groups, allowing (in principle) for unbiased causal estimates. Unlike laboratory studies of discrimination, audit studies are conducted in natural settings, increasing external validity. For these reasons, audit studies are the current gold standard for research on discrimination, and we thought it only appropriate, given the importance of the topic, that something like an audit methodology be used to assess the claim that the liberalism of the American professoriate results from political bias.

There is, however, a significant limitation to audit studies: they only work in settings where nearly all the features of the experiment can be manipulated by the researcher. Applied to the study of political discrimination in higher education, this constraint made it impossible for us to conduct the first kind of audit study that came to mind: an audit of hiring practices in academe, in which we would send phony curricula vitae in response to academic job openings to determine whether liberal applicants are favored over conservative ones. As they work to put together "shortlists," members of academic hiring committees almost invariably seek information about applicants beyond that provided in their vitae, by reading their written work, for example, or looking closely at letters of recommendation, or sending informal emails to colleagues. Controlling for these stimuli would have been nearly impossible, and the chances of the experiment's being detected high. We also considered a study in which we would have phony students go through the graduate school application process to see who got in where, with what level of fellowship support; but, again, the decision-making context is such that too much information would be beyond our control. In addition, while the ethics of audit research are unclear, a general principle is that since respondents do not consent to participate, the amount of time and effort required of them should be kept to a minimum. (For a brief discussion of the ethics of audit research, see Pager 2007a, 76–78.) Reading and deciding on graduate school application files, much like deciding on shortlists of academic job candidates, are time-consuming, resource-intensive tasks.

To overcome this limitation, we decided to measure bias and discrimination by focusing on the informal emails that prospective applicants to graduate school often send to DGSs before they apply. Typically, DGSs in major programs in the social sciences and humanities read and respond to scores of such emails every fall, before applications are due in the winter, and usually they know nothing about the prospective applicant other than what is mentioned in the email. This means that all the stimuli for an experiment involving emails from prospective students would remain within our control, while the low-stakes nature of the response on the part of DGSs would lessen the ethical objectionability of the research design. There are substantive as well as practical and ethical reasons for our focus. As indicated earlier, there is good evidence that patterns of graduate school attendance are important in explaining the politics of the professoriate. Fosse and Gross (2012) found that the main factor accounting for professors' politics, compared with the politics of other Americans, is that a large proportion hold advanced degrees. Woessner and Kelly-Woessner (2009) discovered that liberal undergraduates are twice as likely as conservative ones to say they aspire to a doctorate. And again, Fosse, Freese, and Gross (see chapter 2) report that liberals are significantly overrepresented among those pursuing doctoral degrees and that liberalism in college helps to predict graduate school attendance.

Assessing how much of liberals' greater propensity to attend graduate school results from bias and discrimination is therefore critical in evaluating broader arguments about the role of bias in explaining professorial liberalism. And in this regard, informal notes from DGSs are important in three respects: they could indicate DGSs' biases toward liberal versus conservative applicants, which should matter greatly since DGSs make or influence decisions on admissions and funding; they could serve as indicators of the views of other department members, as the job of DGS generally rotates among the tenured faculty; and their content might figure among those "distinct and perceptible signals" that Maranto (2009) wrote about—signals that mark a department as off-limits to conservative applicants, thereby affecting self-selection.

Study Design

We examine political bias on the part of DGSs in the fields of sociology, political science, economics, history, and literature. We chose these fields because much of the controversy surrounding political bias in academe centers on the social sciences and humanities, which lean further left than other disciplines. For example, Gross and Simmons found that the ratios of Democrats to Republicans in political science, sociology, literature, and history are 8:1, 9:1, 25:1, and 21:1, respectively. Given this relative political homogeneity, if there is political bias to be found in the graduate school admissions process, it is likely to be found here. Economics is different from the other social sciences in that it is somewhat more conservative. We included it to assess whether our findings were robust to variation in political orientation.[1]

Our initial plan was to include a sixth field as well: psychology, which is strongly Democratic. We soon discovered, however, that it is not uncommon for psychology PhD programs to have several DGSs, one per specialty area (e.g., social psychology or behavioral neuroscience). Since specialty-area DGSs play organizational roles somewhat different from their counterparts' in other types of programs, potentially biasing our effect estimates, we decided not to sample psychologists. No other social science or humanities field, such as anthropology or philosophy, seemed to us a suitable replacement in terms of size or centrality to the contemporary university.

For each discipline, we drew up a list of the top seventy-five graduate programs as ranked in 2010 by *U.S. News and World Report*. Other rankings are available, but our goal was to focus on the programs that most applicants would be applying to, and our sense was that the *U.S. News* rankings remain the resource most commonly used by students. We chose to focus on seventy-five programs per field for three reasons: because of manpower constraints; because, though they may serve other valuable purposes, graduate programs ranked below seventy-fifth are not major providers of personnel to the academic profession; and because, as we discuss below, even after case exclusions, seventy-five programs in five fields results in a sample size large enough to detect even relatively small differences in outcome.

Early in the fall of 2010, we examined the websites for each program identified, recording contact information for the person listed as the DGS. In those few cases where DGS information was not available online, an undergraduate research assistant called the program, as an applicant might do, to ask who the DGS was. Typically this yielded the required information, but occasionally the research assistant was told that DGS information would not be given out and that prospective applicants should contact an administrative coordinator instead. These cases were dropped from the study.

Treatment and Control Conditions

The design of the study called for each DGS to receive two emails from a prospective student, one a control and the other either a liberal or conservative treatment. To this end we constructed two email templates for use in each discipline, in consultation with several former DGSs who showed us sample email inquiries they had received in previous years. The templates were designed with several goals in mind: ensuring that students' qualifications, social characteristics, and interest areas were similar between the two; making the treatment stimulus sufficiently obvious that DGSs would not fail to see it, but not so obvious that it would raise red flags; and ensuring that the language of the inquiries was, to some degree, tailored to each discipline but was otherwise the same across fields, allowing for comparability. The final templates involved two fictitious students, Kevin Cook and Jeff Allen, graduating seniors majoring in the focal field at the University of California, Irvine (UCI), and the University of California, Santa Barbara (UCSB), respectively (an example of each template is reproduced in the appendix). We chose these two schools so that we could hold region and institutional type constant: both UCI and UCSB are major public research universities located in Southern California, neither is a flagship school, and entering freshman classes have similar profiles of grades and test scores. In addition, in every discipline we planned to study, the UCI and UCSB programs are closely ranked, at least in the *U.S. News* rankings.[2] Southern California was selected because, unlike some regions of the country, it is known for both liberal and conservative politics, which we hoped would increase the plausibility of the emails. We excluded UCI and

UCSB graduate programs from our sample for fear that DGSs there would real-ize that Cook and Allen were not real students and because it is unusual for students to do graduate work at their undergraduate institutions.

In our templates, both students expressed interest in doctoral study and aca-demic careers and presented themselves as academically accomplished. But we decided not to mention honors work for either of them, out of concern that DGSs with pronounced political biases at lower-ranked schools might set such biases aside in order to attract University of California honors students. Cook and Al-len both asked the DGSs how well they would fit into their programs, along with more specific questions designed to elicit factual information and increase verisimilitude: Cook asked about opportunities for coauthorship with profes-sors, Allen about funding for original data collection (or, in English and history, archival work). The two emails were kept short (about two hundred words) to maintain DGS interest and to make sure the treatment prompt would stand out. After consulting academics in each discipline, we decided that for sociology, inquiries should express an interest in the sociology of culture; for politics, an interest in American politics; for economics, applied microeconomics; for his-tory, twentieth-century American political history; and for English, American modernism (e.g., Hemingway, Eliot, Faulkner). Although not every program in our sample had specialties in these areas, each specialty is well established in its discipline and, most important, is ambiguous as to political valence. Thus we hoped to avoid the problem that might arise, for example, if a conservative sociol-ogy student expressed an interest in the study of social inequality. Neither Cook nor Allen proposed a specific dissertation topic, as we could not have made these comparable in terms of academic promise and yet sufficiently different between the emails.

For the treatment conditions, we considered a variety of alternatives, including students' stating their leadership roles in Democratic and Republican student or-ganizations, overtly stating their identities as liberals or conservatives, or being older and either Peace Corps volunteers or military veterans. We rejected the last of these on the grounds that the stimulus was too indirect and open to multiple interpretations, and the first two because neither statement is plausibly the kind of thing a student would include in a short email to a DGS. On the heels of the 2008 presidential campaign, however, which involved a record number of young people, we thought it not implausible that a student might mention in passing his work for either candidate. The prompt we settled on, included about two-thirds of the way into the emails, was, "When I was a sophomore I also spent a few intense months working for the [Obama/McCain] campaign, which was quite a learning experience." It is true that McCain is seen by some as more a moderate than a true conservative, but our sense is that the vast majority of professors code him as being on the right, particularly given his association in the 2008 campaign with Sarah Palin. We worried that a stronger conservative prompt, such as being a George W. Bush supporter, might—if claims about the extent of hostility to conservatism in academe are true—lead some respondents to question the legitimacy of the email. (Of course, if such questioning had occurred in response to a very strong conservative prompt, that would itself evidence bias—but it would have undermined our attempt at systematic measurement.) We added the phrase "which was quite a learning experience" to signal that, though the student might be politically active, he was ultimately more oriented toward academics than politics. Emails in the control condition mentioned nothing about politics but rather volunteer work for unspecified local organizations.

Sending both a control and a treatment email, randomized as to treatment condition, to every respondent allows us to compare the average effect of an Obama treatment relative to control with the average effect of a McCain treatment relative to control. It does not, however, provide as firm a basis for estimating one of the counterfactuals—the response for any given DGS under the alternative treatment condition—as would sending each DGS a control and *both* treatment prompts. Yet our fear was that, despite the barrage of emails they typically receive during the fall semester, DGSs *would* notice two emails from students mentioning work on the 2008 campaign and get suspicious.

The templates completed, we randomized the treatment and control conditions. Whether the DGS would receive a McCain or Obama email, whether the treatment occurred in the first or second round of emails, and whether the treatment email came from Cook or Allen were all selected randomly. We then sent the emails, with the rounds timed at three weeks apart. After exclusions, our effective sample size became 68 in sociology, 62 in economics, 63 in political science and history, and 62 in English, for a total sample size of 318. For comparability, Cook and Allen both used Gmail addresses. Responses from DGSs were collected and analyzed as described below, and every response generated a short but courteous thank-you note from the respective student. We set three weeks as the cutoff for receiving valid replies to ensure that treatment and control emails would not be answered simultaneously and on the grounds that if a DGS takes three weeks to respond to a prospective student, the student is likely to get the impression that his application will not be much valued. In only three cases did DGSs respond after the cutoff. Those cases are treated as null responses in the analyses that follow, but including them in our models does not alter our results.

Outcome Variables

We measured the extent of political discrimination in the graduate admissions process by looking at both objective and subjective outcome measures. For objective measures, we examined whether or not the DGS responded to the student's query and how quickly. For subjective outcomes, we examined how much information about the program the DGS supplied in her or his response, the emotional warmth of the response, and how enthusiastic the response was about the student's application to the program. The first outcome, response, is a dichotomous variable. The second variable, timing, is measured in terms of elapsed hours between the sending of a student email and the response. As is conventional in audit studies, failure to respond within the allotted time is coded as a nonresponse rather than a missing case. All nonresponses on the timing variable were assigned a score of 504 (21 days × 24 hours) for the purpose of calculating treatment effects, although we experimented with a variety of alternative specifications (none yielded any substantive difference in results).

The subjective outcome variables—information, emotional warmth, and enthusiasm—were scored by three raters. The raters were recent graduates of undergraduate programs in the social sciences: one in sociology, one in economics, and one in political science. Two identified themselves as being on the left, the third as on the right. After initial training, the raters were given copies of all the emails received, with identifying information about the DGS and program removed. Raters were also kept blind as to whether a given case was in the control or the treatment condition. Rating was done independently, one round of emails at a time. All three raters scored every email. Amount of information and enthusiasm were scored on Likert scales ranging from 1 to 4, and emotional warmth from 1 to 5. Raters also scored the emails on several other measures, such as whether they contained any reference to the student's politics, but, as we describe below, there was not enough variation here for meaningful analysis of treatment effects. As with the timing variable, cases in which the DGS did not respond were not treated as missing but were assigned a score just beyond what an actual response could have received—a score of 0. Once again, we experimented with alternative specifications, such as assigning these cases a score of 1, but none affected our results in a meaningful way. Because assignment of a uniform score to nonresponsive cases would artificially inflate interrater reliability, we measured reliability before such assignment.

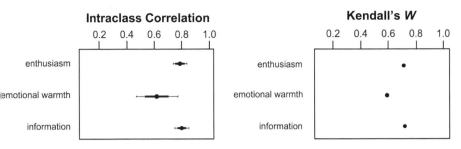

Figure 4.1. Interrater reliability measures for three subjective questions used in the study. For the intraclass correlation, thin lines indicate 95 percent confidence intervals; thick lines indicate 50 percent confidence intervals.

For the subjective measures, we averaged scores across the three raters. Inter-rater reliability for the scales is reasonably high, as can be seen in figure 4.1. Both measures of reliability are higher when closer to 1 and lower when closer to 0. The intraclass correlation, or proportion of the total variation within the scores of individual raters rather than across raters, is high for the information and enthusiasm scales and somewhat lower—though still within the range of acceptability—for the even more subjective emotional warmth scale. The error bars indicate 95 percent confidence intervals, with emotional warmth showing greater uncertainty in the reliability. The values of the intraclass correlations are mirrored by the relatively high values (again, lower for emotional warmth) on our other measure of interrater reliability, Kendall's W, a nonparametric rank statistic appropriate for ordinal data and multiple raters. Kendall's W ranges from 0 for no agreement between raters to 1 for complete agreement. We corrected for tied ranks for this statistic, assigning the average of the ranks that would have been given had no ties occurred.

Power Analysis

In designing our study, we attended to the issue of statistical power to ensure that we would be able to detect an underlying effect, if one existed. The power analysis we conducted is shown in figure 4.2, which maps the general relationship between effect size (also known as Cohen's d), sample size, and level of statistical power (which ranges from 0 to 1, from little power to a very high level of power). Larger sample sizes give one more power to detect small effects. We indicate the final sample size of our study with the horizontal line at $N = 318$. Given this sample size and assuming an underlying effect of approximately 0.2 (which translates to a 10-point difference, e.g., in percentage responding, assuming a standard deviation

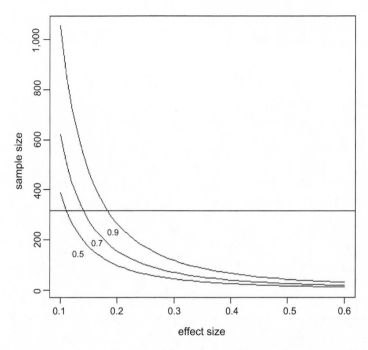

Figure 4.2. Power analysis: effect size (Cohen's *d*) plotted by sample size. Curved lines indicate levels of statistical power for combinations of sample and effect sizes. The reference line at N = 318 indicates the sample size of the study. With this sample, an effect size of 0.18 can be detected with a 0.9 level of statistical power; similarly, 0.15 can be detected with a 0.7 level of power, and 0.11 with a 0.5 level of power.

of 0.5), we can expect a high level of statistical power at 0.90. Similarly, given our sample size and an effect size of 0.15, we expect a statistical power of approximately 0.70, which is also considered relatively high. In the absence of previous studies examining political bias in graduate admissions, there was no way to estimate effect size in advance, but in general, an effect size of 0.2 in the social sciences is considered a "small effect," according to criteria set by Cohen (1988), and in the context of our research we surmised that if the effect were smaller than this, it would be of relatively little consequence. Increasing the sample size to detect an even smaller effect with an equivalent level of power would have required adding a cost-prohibitive number of cases and would not have made sense, given the limited number of major graduate programs in each of our selected fields.

Results

Overall, the response rate to the students' queries was high: 72 percent in the first round and 71 percent in the second. Taking the two rounds together, we find that

61 percent of DGSs responded to both queries, 22 percent to one but not the other, and 17 percent to neither. The cell sizes for individual disciplines are too small to draw reliable conclusions about observed differences, but patterns of response were similar across the fields, with the exceptions that a higher than average proportion of DGSs in economics replied to neither query (29%) and DGSs in English were somewhat more likely than their colleagues in other fields to respond to only one query (35%).

In nine cases in the first round of emails and twelve cases in the second, the student received a response not from the DGS but from someone else in the program, typically an administrative coordinator to whom the email had been forwarded. Since our focus is on bias on the part of DGSs, we cannot consider such cases in our analysis. Yet it would be inappropriate to treat them as equivalent to nonresponses. We therefore dropped from the sample those cases for which, in at least one round, there was a response from an administrator but not a DGS, while retaining those cases for which there was a response from a DGS *and* an administrator—but measuring our outcome variables based solely on the DGS's email. Of the seventeen cases so dropped, six were in economics and six in English, and, correspondingly, after the deletions, differences in overall patterns of response between English and economics and other fields narrowed.

Most of the responses our fictitious students received were quick and professional. Looking at both rounds together, 75 percent of the students' emails were answered within about twenty-four hours. According to our raters, about 80 percent of responses were either quite or extremely detailed in the amount of information provided about the program, even though they also tended to be concise, averaging 160 words.

As mentioned above, we asked our raters to score the emails on some variables that do not form part of our main analysis. The descriptive statistics here offer further evidence of professionalism, particularly when it comes to responses to students' politics. We recorded only six emails across both rounds in either of the two treatment conditions in which the DGS mentioned anything about the student's politics. In two of these cases (one an Obama treatment, the other McCain), the DGS interpreted the student's mention of involvement in a political campaign as evidence of the kind of research he was hoping to do (i.e., research on politics). In one response, a McCain treatment, the DGS mentioned the student's politics in the context of recruitment, saying that the state in which the school was located would be a particularly fascinating place to do campaign work in future elections. In another case, also a McCain treatment, the DGS praised the student for work on the campaign, saying it must have been great practical experience. In the last of these cases, also in the conservative condition, the DGS offered the advice that, while the department contained faculty and students of a variety of political stripes, the student should consider not mentioning his political work on his formal application (which the DGS encouraged him to submit), lest the application be judged as coming from someone more interested in politics than in research. Only the last case—and hence 1 of 450 valid responses—might be interpreted as advice to a conservative student to keep his views to himself. In no case did a DGS give any indication of disagreeing personally with the student's politics. What is more, according to our conservative rater—who might be expected to be particularly sensitive to such matters—in only 8 percent of emails could anything the DGS wrote be interpreted as signaling more indirectly a left political tilt to her or his program—for example, a mention of queer studies, women's/gender studies, or a departmental focus on race or class issues, or use of the terms *critical* or *social justice*. Of course, conservative applicants could get the message that they would not fit in a department politically simply by looking at lists of faculty members and their research interests. But focusing just on McCain treatments, we find that in more than 90 percent of cases, an applicant who presented himself as conservative received no such message from the DGS.

Is there other evidence of bias against prospective conservative applicants? We begin by examining the objective outcomes: response and timing. Figure 4.3 shows the results from paired *t*-tests between treatment and control conditions for the same individuals. The upper graph, pertaining to response, shows that while subjects given the Obama treatment were slightly more likely to respond, relative to control, than subjects given the McCain treatment, this difference is small and not statistically significant. The other two graphs in figure 4.3 show the results for timing. In the middle graph, in which nonresponse is adjusted for and scored at 504 hours, we see that subjects given the Obama treatment tend to respond slightly more quickly relative to control than those given the McCain treatment. Once again, however, the difference is not statistically significant. What is more, it appears to be entirely a function of the slightly lower response rate to the McCain emails. The bottom graph shows the results for subjects who responded to both emails. In this group, the McCain treatment was responded to a bit more quickly, but this difference is also not statistically significant.

For illustrative purposes, figure 4.4 shows the same results looking not at individual-level treatment effects but at means for the liberal treatment and control group and for the conservative treatment and control group, respectively.[3] The figure shows just how small the differences are between the groups. For example,

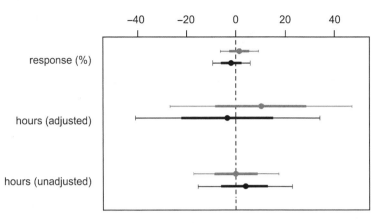

Figure 4.3. Paired *t*-tests for differences between participants in treatment and control conditions for objective measures. Black lines indicate conservative (McCain) treatment; gray lines, liberal (Obama) treatment; thin lines, 95 percent confidence intervals; thick lines, 50 percent confidence intervals.

we received responses to 70 percent of the McCain emails and 73 percent of the Obama emails. Likewise, in cases where we received a response to both the treatment and control emails, the McCain emails were answered about four hours more quickly, on average.

In figures 4.5 and 4.6 we examine the set of subjective outcomes used in our study. Figure 4.5 gives the results from paired *t*-tests between treatment and control conditions for the same individuals, while figure 4.6 shows group means. On the amount of information provided and the emotional warmth of the response emails, no differences are evident.[4] On overall level of enthusiasm, our raters scored emails in the Obama treatment condition slightly higher than those in the McCain treatment condition, but, again, the difference is small and not statistically significant: the mean scores on enthusiasm are 2.6 for the liberal condition and 2.5 for the conservative condition (on what is, with nonresponses scored at 0, a 5-point scale).

Could the lack of more meaningful differences for any of the outcome variables reflect the fact that economics—a less liberal field than the others—is included in our sample? Although doing so decreased our sample size and thus potentially decreased statistical power, we reran all our analyses excluding economics. As before, no statistically significant differences were found, and the results were substantively unchanged. Nor could we detect meaningful variation in our results across institutional strata (comparing the top twenty departments

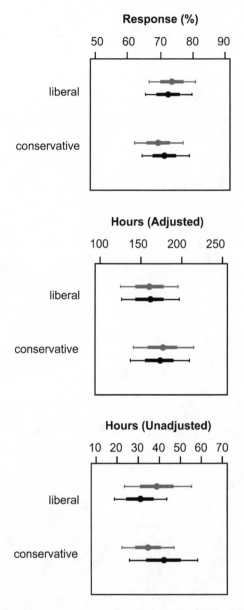

Figure 4.4. Means for objective measures. Gray lines indicate liberal (Obama) and conservative (McCain) conditions; black lines, control conditions; thin lines, 95 percent confidence intervals; thick lines, 50 percent confidence intervals.

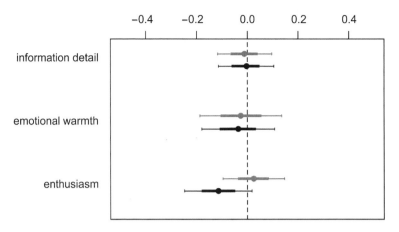

Figure 4.5. Paired *t*-tests for differences between participants in treatment and control conditions for subjective measures. Black lines indicate conservative (McCain) treatment; gray lines, liberal (Obama) treatment; thin lines, 95 percent confidence intervals; thick lines, 50 percent confidence intervals.

with others). In short, we find minor indications but, on the whole, no significant evidence of a proliberal or anticonservative bias on the part of directors of graduate study.

Conclusion

We used an audit/correspondence methodology to assess whether there is a political bias in the graduate school admissions process in five social science and humanities fields. Measuring responses received from directors of graduate study to inquiries from fictitious prospective applicants, we found that although liberal applicants have a slight advantage when it comes to whether or not a response is received, how soon it is received, and how enthusiastic that response will be, such an advantage is neither substantively nor statistically significant. In terms of the amount of information DGSs provide to students and the emotional warmth of their emails, there is no discernible bias (although emails to liberal students tend to be slightly longer). In response to a student's mentioning his conservative politics, the large majority of DGSs do not comment on this in any way or include subtle textual messages about their program's liberal tilt that might scare away conservative applicants.

Before discussing the implications of these findings, we note the methodological limitations of our study. First, our study focuses on bias in informal

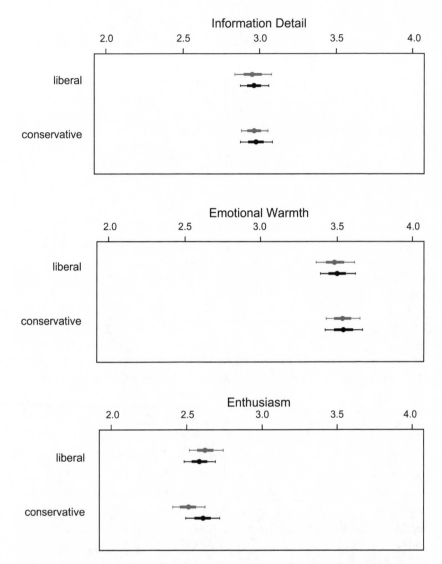

Figure 4.6. Means for subjective measures. Gray lines indicate liberal (Obama) and conservative (McCain) conditions; black lines, control conditions; thin lines, 95 percent confidence intervals; thick lines, 50 percent confidence intervals.

communications between DGSs and prospective students. It is possible that if self-identified conservatives were actually to apply to the programs we examined, forcing DGSs or other faculty members to make more consequential choices than whether to reply to an email, their experiences would differ from those of the fictitious students in our experiment. Second, the recent controversy over political bias in higher education, associated with the work of conservative activists like David Horowitz, may lead some DGSs to bend over backward to be supportive of a conservative student, out of a conscious or half-conscious fear that their email replies might become public. To the extent that this is true, our findings could underestimate the level of latent political bias. Third, while we made a case for the significance of patterns of graduate school attendance for explaining professorial liberalism, much of the literature on political bias and discrimination in academe is concerned not with graduate school but with hiring, tenure, and promotion. Our data do not speak directly to evaluation processes occurring at later points in an academic career. Fourth, as is true for all research, methodological choices may have affected our results. For example, had our treatment stimulus been different—had our conservative student not merely indicated his personal conservatism but also stated his intention to do conservatively themed research, say—we might well have found more bias.[5] Nor can we rule out the possibility of measurement error, particularly around the coding of the more subjective aspects of DGS response.

These observations suggest some caution in interpreting our findings. If political bias toward graduate students were very strong in the fields we studied, however, our methodology would probably have detected it. It is true that DGSs might behave differently in the context of actual admissions decisions, but research on stereotypes and social biases in general (Bargh 1999), as well as on political bias specifically (Lodge and Taber 2005), suggests that, when present, biases—as opposed to full-blown discriminatory ideologies—operate primarily in the domain of automatic cognition. Since responding quickly to prospective students' emails is, in the language of "dual process" models in psychology, more a matter of heuristic than systematic processing, one would expect political biases likely to affect a range of judgments to show up in our results.[6] Could DGSs be suppressing their biases out of fear that the content of their emails might become public? We cannot rule this out, but it seems unlikely. There was no clear evidence in the replies of any DGSs being suspicious of the emails. Although a few replies asked the students whom they had worked with at Irvine or Santa Barbara, which might be interpreted as a probe for veracity, overall we found no difference between the control and treatment conditions in the proportion of replies that asked the student for further information, and no difference in this regard between the Obama and McCain treatments. If anything, there is reason to believe that DGSs, when responding (or not responding) to students' emails, would think that nobody other than the student would be paying attention. Sociological research on the "opportunity structure for discrimination" (Peterson and Saporta 2004) demonstrates that discrimination is *most* likely to occur in such contexts—where people have no reason to believe they will be held accountable for their behavior. If this is right, replies to students' emails should be a particularly valuable data source for assessing biases.

On the question of the applicability of our findings to other evaluation settings in academe, such as those around hiring, tenure, and promotion, we cannot know for certain. Although a liberal academician may tolerate a conservative graduate student in the department, that same person may not tolerate a conservative colleague. But we note, again, that we would expect strongly held political biases relevant to the evaluation of academic personnel to be detectable with our methodology, and that DGSs represent a sample (if an imperfectly random one) of the tenured faculty who vote on hiring and tenure decisions. Furthermore, Gross and Simmons found that a majority of academics in the social sciences and humanities say they agree with the statement "The goal of campus diversity should include fostering diversity of political views among faculty members"—so it is not unreasonable to think that professors might be open to a more politically heterogeneous workplace. We do not doubt that there have been instances of discrimination against conservatives in hiring, tenure, and promotion. But we think our results establish a presumption—until further evidence can be found—against the idea that political bias and discrimination are rampant in the American academic profession, at least when it comes to personnel selection.

Nevertheless, given that much of the political tilt of the professoriate *is* a function of who goes to graduate school, our finding of no significant political bias toward prospective students on the part of DGSs in left-leaning social science and humanities disciplines (as well as in economics) means it is unlikely that discrimination is the key causal factor accounting for professorial liberalism. We believe that the theory with the most promise for explaining this phenomenon focuses on political self-selection into academe, and specific disciplines therein, from an already left-leaning pool of undergraduates (Fosse and Gross 2012; see also chapter 2 of this volume). As concerns this theory, a further implication of our findings is that DGSs do not play a major role in influencing self-selection by sending messages to conservative students that they are not wanted or to liberal students that they are. Our sense—consistent with the results presented here—is that for most people, such messages are communicated earlier in the undergraduate experience and have as much to do with the general reputation of the professoriate and of specific disciplines as with things said or done by individual scholars with whom students come into contact later.

Finally, our results identify an important puzzle. Although the politics of American professors are more complex than conservative critics charge, critics are right to point out that academe is a prominent institutional home of liberalism in American society. Given what we know about the dynamics of homophily and in-group preferences, we *should* expect to find significant political bias and discrimination on the part of professors. If our results are valid and generalizable beyond the graduate student context, we must ask why there is not more bias. Our best guess is that it is because of the well-institutionalized norms in place in higher education against evaluating personnel on criteria other than academic merit. Although academic merit in some fields is indeed defined in such a way as to be coextensive with left or liberal politics, this does not mean that professors, on the whole, fail to take seriously their responsibilities as carriers and upholders of distinctly academic values and ideals. If they did, the qualitative studies of academic evaluation mentioned earlier—Lamont's (2009) and Musselin's (2010)—would have revealed nothing but homophily and "horse-trading," with scholars consistently favoring other candidates precisely like themselves or supporting dissimilar candidates or projects only in the expectation of reciprocity by other members of evaluation committees. That is not what Lamont or Musselin found. Although there was ample evidence of social reproduction, these studies also revealed the operation of norms, linked to evaluators' sense of the legitimacy of the academic enterprise and their own self-worth as scholars, that could lead to more pluralistic evaluations. Understanding how such evaluative practices may work to counter the influence or even the formation of political biases that would directly affect personnel selection—one of many instances in social life in which cultural factors push back against seemingly structural imperatives—is an important task for further research.

NOTES

For their advice on the study and this chapter, we thank Chris Bail, Amy Binder, Frank Dobbin, Roberto Fernandez, Jeremy Freese, Andrew Gelman, Darrin Lehman, Devah Pager, and Paul Quirk. For research assistance we thank Chris Chiego, Rebecca Dickson, Andrew Le, and Laura MacDonald.

1. We consider below whether our findings change if economics is excluded from the sample.

2. The English Department at UCI is generally seen as particularly strong, but in the *U.S. News* rankings, it is ahead of UCSB's by only seven places.

3. With randomization, we can expect that the treatment and control groups are balanced, and thus a simple comparison of means will indicate a causal effect. Analyses show little standardized bias across treatment and control groups on observable covariates, confirming the adequacy of our randomization procedure.

4. To supplement our subjective measure of information, we also considered whether bias might be evident in the length of DGSs' replies, measured as number of words. Giving nonresponses a score of 0, we found that replies to the Obama treatment emails averaged 125 words, and replies to the McCain treatment emails, 110 words—a difference somewhat larger than the others observed but still not statistically significant.

5. Many prominent research paradigms in the social sciences and humanities are fundamentally at odds with certain strands of conservative ideology—in their assumptions, causal claims, and policy implications. It may well be that scholars whose conservative politics lead them to reject these paradigms are viewed negatively by their peers. But it is not clear to us whether this reflects political bias or discrimination per se or the same sort of intellectual judgment—colored by motivated reasoning, to be sure—that would lead supporters of any paradigm to be skeptical toward champions of an opposing paradigm. Indeed, as postmodernists, poststructuralists, and science studies scholars have long argued, the lines separating intellectual/scientific from political judgment can be blurry, especially in the social sciences and humanities. Our study measures only bias and discrimination that result directly from students' politics, leaving open the possibility that disadvantages for conservative students and scholars may obtain as a consequence of more run-of-the-mill scholarly judgment.

6. One possible objection to our methodology is that DGSs' responses to students' emails may involve *less* than heuristic processing: perhaps DGSs are just cutting and pasting boilerplate language, which would make their replies poor indicators of underlying attitudes. To test for this possibility, we used plagiarism-detection software to compare replies in which DGSs responded to both the treatment and control emails. While it was common for DGSs to use a few stock phrases, in only about 10 percent of cases was most of the text in the emails the same, and here DGSs typically included some individualized text before or after the boilerplate material.

PART THREE

THE STUDENT EXPERIENCE

CHAPTER FIVE

The Effect of College on Social and Political Attitudes and Civic Participation

KYLE DODSON

By many accounts, the postwar expansion of higher education represents one of the most dramatic and socially significant transformations of the past six decades (Schofer and Meyer 2005; Walters 1986). The percentage of young Americans enrolled in higher education increased from approximately 14 percent in 1940 to over 60 percent in 2008 (Arnett 2000). Scholars have linked this expansion to an array of outcomes, including economic growth (Walters 1990; Walters and Rubinson 1983), family change (Brewster and Padavic 2000; Thornton, Alwin, and Camburn 1983), and improving gender and race relations (DiPrete and Eirich 2006; Jacobs 1996).

Evidence that college plays a strong role in driving economic and social developments has also led scholars to examine many of the characteristics associated with higher education. Particularly in the 1950s and 1960s, when waves of protest were sweeping across college campuses, many observers—perhaps most notably, William F. Buckley Jr. (1951)—were worried that faculty in higher education were playing a central role in promulgating the rise and subsequent mobilization of anti-establishment sentiment. In response to these concerns, analysts set out to assess the political orientations of faculty. These early studies frequently arrived at a similar conclusion (Ladd and Lipset 1976). Yes, faculty in American colleges and universities were more liberal than the larger American public—but not overwhelmingly so. Moreover, the extent to which professors were liberal differed dramatically from one school to the next. Subsequent studies have reinforced these initial observations, indicating the presence of a liberal bent in academia, but one that varies considerably across institutional and disciplinary contexts (see chapter 1 of this volume; Fosse and Gross 2012). Nevertheless, contemporary observers (e.g., Horowitz 2006) have followed in Buckley's footsteps and used evidence of liberal tendencies within academia to suggest that faculty are indoctrinating students with a liberal education and waging a silent war on conservative thought in the process.

Against this backdrop, the issue of what effect college enrollment has on students' political orientations has received increased attention among analysts. Does going to college affect the political lives of students? How does it influence their political attitudes and their political engagement?

In seeking to understand how students are influenced by their time spent on a college campus, scholars have historically adopted a classic view of higher education. According to this approach, college attendance is seen as an incubator for both political liberalism and citizenship (McClosky and Zaller 1984)—one that fosters the values (such as egalitarianism and individualism) and practices (such as participating in elections and deliberating political issues) associated with the ideals of democracy (Bobo and Licari 1989). Lately, however, this view has come under greater scrutiny, with scholars challenging the argument that college exerts a real effect (Jennings and Stoker 2008; Kam and Palmer 2008). In contrast to the classic view, this emerging view argues that claims of a college "effect" rely on dubious methods that fail to control for potential sources of self-selection. Scholars in this more recent approach highlight the well-known findings that students who attend college are systematically different from those who do not (Featherman and Hauser 1978; Hout 1988; Jencks et al. 1972). According to this research, when compared with their noncollege counterparts, college attendees tend to have a higher class background, more political interest, and higher levels of cognitive proficiency (Verba, Schlozman, and Brady 1995). The revisionist view argues that these differences, in place before college enrollment, are the actual drivers of the perceived influence of college.

These divergent views have yet to be reconciled. On the one hand, studies continue to argue that college attendance is one of the largest predictors of political attitudes and behaviors (Dalton 2008; Miller and Shanks 1996; Rosenstone and Hansen 1993). On the other hand, mounting evidence provided by the revisionist work suggests that the effects of college may be overestimated (Brand 2010; Jennings and Stoker 2008; Kam and Palmer 2008). In this chapter, I explore this tension and argue that the two views can be reconciled by reference to a "contingent" view of college effects—one that acknowledges the multifaceted nature of a college education. I argue that the political effects of college depend on both the characteristics that students bring with them prior to enrollment and the extent to which they engage different aspects of the college environment. Indeed, while it may be overstated by some work, I contend that college attendance nevertheless does exert an influence—and occasionally in ways unanticipated by either view.

Competing Views on the Political Effects of College

The Classic View: College as a Transformative Institution

Early research on the effects of higher education on students' political orientations painted an impressive picture for the role of the university. A college education was associated with higher levels of political activism and more democratic orientations (A. Campbell et al. 1960; Converse 1964). With respect to political activity, college-educated individuals were found to be more likely to vote, discuss politics, and engage in protest behavior. In terms of political attitudes, they were more likely to support gender equality, individualism, and civil rights. These results led many researchers to conclude that colleges and universities were "transformative" institutions. Students come to college, they learn how to become citizens (along with other important skills), and then they graduate.

In explaining these findings, most scholars highlight three aspects of the college experience as relevant for political change: cognitive development, status acquisition, and social interaction. Students' cognitive development spurs democratic behavior because it helps students overcome the daunting barriers that could prevent participation (Verba, Schlozman, and Brady 1995). As one example, college students are required to navigate the bureaucratic aspects of higher education—registering for courses, applying for student aid, and so forth—which are not unlike what potential voters face when trying to register to vote. In other words, the cognitive skills that students develop at college are easily transformed to civic skills. College is thought, then, to reduce the difficulty of participation by endowing students with the skills necessary to navigate the complex political landscape.

Another important consequence of a college education is the status benefit it bestows on the recipient (Nie, Junn, and Stehlik-Barry 1996). For example, college graduates can anticipate securing more prestigious positions on entering the labor market than individuals who lack a college degree. College attendance also introduces students to new experiences and opinions, helping them develop middle-class lifestyles, one aspect of which focuses on the cultivation of a civic orientation (Bourdieu and Passeron 1990; Kingston et al. 2003; Lamont 1992; Pascarella and Terenzini 1991). Accordingly, students are exposed to important democratic values, such as participating in politics and tolerating different political viewpoints (Bobo and Licari 1989; McClosky and Zaller 1984).

Beyond the acquisition of cognitive skills and development of status orientations, colleges matter because they introduce students to new social networks

(Huckfeldt and Sprague 1987). While at college, students interact with a wide range of individuals, including other students, staff, and faculty. These interactions expose them to a diverse set of networks that promotes political tolerance (Huckfeldt and Sprague 1995; Knoke 1990).[1] The social interactions also bring students into contact with requests for participation (Rosenstone and Hansen 1993; Van Dyke 1998).

The Revisionist View: College as a Selection Mechanism

While most research on the relationship between college and political behavior has generally argued in favor of a college effects model—in which colleges and universities are thought to exert a real influence on the political development of students—some scholars have recently begun to challenge this view by arguing that college effects are more modest than originally thought (Brand 2010; Jennings and Stoker 2008; Kam and Palmer 2008). Rather than viewing college as a site for the cultivation of political attitudes and participation, these scholars argue that colleges select students who already possess the dispositions and characteristics that make participation more likely (Kam and Palmer 2008). They maintain that any observed difference between college and high school graduates in political activity is more a function of these preexisting conditions than any processes associated with a college education. In other words, colleges accept students who are already more politically active or liberal than their peers (see also Pallas 2002).

In formulating their argument, these scholars focus on the socialization experiences of students (Jennings and Niemi 1974). Their work thus has an affinity with the socialization arguments common to early sociological studies on the development of individuals' personalities (Adorno et al. 1950; E. Campbell 1969) and privileges students' *precollege* socialization experience, particularly as it relates to parental investments in different forms of human, social, and cultural capital (Cameron and Heckman 1999; Jencks et al. 1972; Morgan and Kim 2006; Steelman and Powell 1993). This view stands in contrast to the classic view that much of the political learning experienced by young adults occurs during college (Nie, Junn and Stehlik-Barry 1996). However, analyses drawing on the classic view tend to exclude measures of prior political involvement, class background, and academic preparation—measures that might explain the observed association between higher education and democratic behavior (e.g., A. Campbell et al. 1960; Miller and Shanks 1996).

Recent empirical work provides some support for the claim of a selection effect. These studies address some of the methodological limitations of prior work by using longitudinal data that include information on the characteristics that students bring with them to college—for example, their political interest, cognitive proficiency, or family resources. One such investigation focuses on the effect of a college education on political activity and finds, after controlling for precollege characteristics, that individuals with a college education are no more likely to participate in political activities than individuals without a college education (Kam and Palmer 2008). Another study examines the influence of college on political attitudes and suggests a similar process wherein students that go to college already possess the characteristics that make them likely to experience shifts in their political orientations (Jennings and Stoker 2008). Finally, one study, in highlighting the importance of selection effects, finds that college attendance does provide civic returns—but only to those individuals who are *least* likely to go (Brand 2010). That is, college would matter if the individuals who went to college had fewer family resources and less political interest.

The Contingent View: College as a Multifaceted Institution

These two views seem incompatible. One suggests that college endows students with important civic behaviors; the other argues that these behaviors were in place well before enrollment. How can they be reconciled? Here I argue in favor of a *contingent* view of college effects, in which the contested influence of college depends on the students in question and the college experience in question. Specifically, I argue that the influence of college on political attitudes and behaviors results from an interaction between the preexisting characteristics of students and how those students engage the college environment.

The revisionist view highlights many of the relevant student characteristics—for example, class background and academic preparation—but perhaps most important is the set of political preferences that students bring with them to college. As noted above, students who are politically active in high school (e.g., by discussing politics, participating in student elections, or joining community organizations) are much more likely to participate in civic activities in college and beyond (Frisco, Muller, and Dodson 2004; McFarland and Thomas 2006). The central insight of the *contingent view*, however, is not that students come to college with different orientations toward political involvement. Rather, the central insight is that different aspects of the college environment operate to either reinforce and strengthen those differences or to undermine and diminish them.

Studies of higher education help us understand why this is so, by highlighting the multifaceted nature of the college environment (Arum and Roksa 2011; Binder and Wood 2013). According to this research, colleges provide both an infrastructure for academic learning and sites for social development. These dual functions—intellectual and social development—are especially important for organizing the college experience. Yet these two sides of college do not operate in the same way. Research suggests that the academic side of college reduces differences among students, while the social side reproduces those differences (Armstrong and Hamilton 2013; Stuber 2011).

Looking first at the social side, we find that research on patterns of peer formation indicates a strong tendency among individuals to self-select into peer groups that reflect individuals' preexisting attitudes. This process of self-selection produces social networks that are similar in composition. This often has the effect of reinforcing individuals' prior beliefs and behaviors. In college, the homophilic preferences of students can be observed in a variety of social contexts, including the composition of their friendship networks and organizational affiliations.

The academic side of college operates differently. In part because students are required to take a variety of classes that span disciplinary objectives, the ability of students to self-select into a culturally homogeneous academic environment is reduced. Participation in the academic side of college frequently challenges students to engage in critical thinking from a diverse set of perspectives, which has the effect of forcing students to reevaluate their preexisting beliefs.

Together, these two aspects of higher education suggest that colleges operate as multifaceted institutions that simultaneously carry many different obligations, including both academic and social development. To the extent that it reinforces prior beliefs and behaviors, social activity during the college years probably exacerbates differences in the political orientations of students. By contrast, academic activity probably moderates differences in students' political orientations by introducing them to new opportunities and ideas. In many respects, it is this dynamic of colleges and universities—in serving as a context for multiple, sometimes competing processes—that political analysts occasionally overlook. Rather than asking *whether* college matters for political attitudes and behavior, perhaps the better question is *how* it matters for political attitudes and behavior.

Summary

Over the past five decades, research on student politics has been dominated by a singular view of how colleges affect democratic behavior. According to this view, colleges are transformative institutions that exert an exogenous force on the development of democratic behavior. While at college, students are exposed to a wide array of stimuli that foster the values, attitudes, and activities commonly associated with democratic citizenship. Recently, however, emerging work has started to challenge these causal claims. Drawing on past studies of political socialization and social stratification, the revisionist view maintains that much of the observed relationship between a college education and democratic behavior is due instead to the largely unobserved effects of students' backgrounds, including their social class and cognitive skills. In attempting to reconcile these two diverging views, I draw on new research in higher education to outline a more contingent view of how colleges matter for democratic behavior. I argue that students enter college with different orientations that influence how they engage the college environment. Specifically, this contingent view suggests that the two sides of college will have different effects on students' political attitudes and behaviors, with the academic side working to minimize differences among students' attitudes and behavior, and the social side working to exacerbate those differences.

An Empirical Illustration

How does the path-dependent view look in practice? In this section, I address the question by drawing on an underutilized data source—a series of panel studies that follow successive cohorts of students from the time they enter college as freshmen through their graduation as seniors.

The College Senior Survey

The panel study, the College Senior Survey (CSS), is administered by the Higher Education Research Institute at the University of California, Los Angeles (for more information on the CSS, see Franke et al. 2010). Since 1965, the institute has conducted an annual survey of incoming freshmen, referred to as The Freshman Survey (TFS). TFS covers a wide range of items, including students' *precollege* political attitudes and behaviors as well as their class background and academic preparation. Starting in 1993, the institute initiated the CSS to reinterview study participants when they became graduating seniors. When combined, the CSS and TFS form a panel study that allows researchers to examine the influence of college attendance on a variety of outcomes, including democratic behavior and attitudes, while controlling for several precollege characteristics.

One potential shortcoming of the CSS-TFS research design is that it lacks a proper control group. That is, everyone in the study receives the treatment of a college education. As a strategy to overcome this obstacle, I focus on variations in the extent to which students engage the college environment. While all of the survey respondents may have attended college, not all of the students were involved in college in the same way. Some focused more on academic pursuits, while others focused more on social activities. Variations in these "college biographies" provide a point of leverage for exploring how college may matter for the development of political identities.

Despite the absence of a proper control group, a primary advantage of the CSS is that the collection of information about both student and institutional characteristics readily supports an investigation into whether the effect of college depends on (1) precollege characteristics, such as political activity during adolescence; (2) college characteristics, such as the extent to which students participate in academic or social activities; or (3) an interaction between precollege and college characteristics.

In the analysis, I take advantage of the 1994, 1995, 1998, and 1999 CSS, along with the corresponding information derived from the students' responses to their TFS questionnaires. Compared with other longitudinal studies, the selected years of the CSS are unique in that the surveys asked respondents about their political behavior during their senior year in high school and their senior year in college, providing an excellent opportunity to investigate what aspects of college matter for democratic behavior.[2]

Methods

One of the primary critiques advanced by the revisionist perspective is that classic studies of college effects fail to control for background characteristics, which could generate selection bias. Panel data are particularly well suited to overcome this challenge because they contain information on a range of characteristics that students bring with them to college. Incorporating measures of these characteristics into models of political behavior allows an examination into the effect of college attendance net of students' backgrounds.

With panel data, analysts have two choices of estimation strategies, each with its own strengths and weaknesses. One approach is fixed effects (FE) estimation, and the other is random effects (RE) estimation. FE estimation takes advantage of multiple measures per individual to examine how changes *within* individuals in key independent variables influence changes in the outcome of interest. By focusing on within-person variation as a source of political development, these models automatically cancel out the influence of characteristics that are invariant within individuals—for example, their race, gender, or predispositions. This is both the strength and the limitation of FE estimation. Any characteristics that are time-invariant, regardless of whether they are observed or not, are automatically controlled for, reducing concerns over omitted variable bias. But at the same time, the influence of time-invariant characteristics, even if they are observed, cannot be directly estimated. In effect, FE estimation ignores variation between individuals, focusing strictly on variation within individuals. Ignoring the between-person variation means that FE estimation, while consistent, is nevertheless inefficient. Inefficient estimation can lead to spuriously large standard errors, which can raise the probability of a type II error (a false negative). Given the concern among conservatives that academics are influencing students, FE estimation may not provide a fair assessment of their claim since this method could be biased toward a false negative.

By contrast, RE estimation takes advantage of the variation that occurs both within and between individuals, making it a more efficient modeling strategy. But because it does not strictly focus on within-person variation, it is more vulnerable to omitted variable bias. As a result, it can generate inconsistent estimates when the model is not properly specified. As a compromise between the benefits and limitations of FE and RE models, Allison (2009) proposes a hybrid estimation strategy that incorporates the strengths of both FE and RE estimation while limiting their weaknesses. The hybrid model uses RE estimation but transforms the variables to focus on within-student variation, which yields a FE interpretation—that is, the focus remains on changes within individuals. This entails demeaning, or centering, the independent variables by subtracting their student-specific mean. Both the centered variables and the variables that measure the student-specific mean are then included in the RE model. The centered variables convey information on the influence of changes within students, as in FE estimation, while controlling for variation between students (due to the inclusion of a variable measuring the student-specific means). As Allison shows, this hybrid strategy yields estimates that are very similar to results obtained from FE estimation and also allows the estimation of time-invariant characteristics.

Measures

There are two dependent variables for this analysis: discussing politics, which is a measure of individuals' political engagement, and liberalism, which is a measure of individuals' political attitudes. Both outcomes are frequently examined in research on political behavior (Anderson, Curtis, and Grabb 2006; Huckfeldt and Sprague 1987; McAdam 1982; McFarland and Thomas 2006; Miller and Shanks 1996). Political discussion is measured as a binary variable, where a value of 1 indicates participation in at least occasional discussion and a value of 0 indicates no discussion. Political liberalism is measured ordinally, with five values corresponding to extremely conservative, conservative, moderate, liberal, and extremely liberal. Higher values indicate a more liberal ideology. Both outcomes were measured twice ($T = 2$), once when the students started college and again when they were finishing.

Two sets of covariates represent the key explanatory variables for this analysis. The first set reflects students' involvement with college—in particular, the academic infrastructure and the social scene. To assess how involved students are with these two facets of college, I use two measures of college involvement. The first is the extent of students' academic activity and measures the number of hours (divided by 10) in a typical week that a student reported spending on studying and interacting with faculty. The second reflects students' social activity and measures the number of hours (divided by 10) in a typical week that a student reported spending on socializing, partying, and playing sports. As noted above, the hybrid model proposed by Allison includes measures of both the student-specific mean and the centered activity level. Together, these measures of academic and social involvement help assess whether college exerts an influence on democratic behavior, net of the characteristics students bring with them to college.

The second set of covariates measures students' political background. For the political discussion models, I include a nominal variable that indicates the extent to which students talk about politics—not at all, occasionally, or frequently—measured prior to their freshman year in college. For the political liberalism models, I include a nominal variable that indicates the students political ideology—conservative, moderate, or liberal—also measured prior to their freshman year in college. In the analyses that follow, I incorporate a political background×academic engagement interaction and a political background×social engagement interaction. These interactions provide information on whether the political effects of a "college experience" operate differently according to individuals' pre-existing attitudes and activities. As such, this provides a direct test of the contingent effects perspective outlined above.

The regression models also include a variety of control variables to reduce threats to causal inference. Year of study (senior year or not) measures change in the outcome as students progress through college. Other control variables include the amount of time the student spends working (in hours), gender (female = 1), race (white is the reference category), and parents' income (measured in $1,000 units).

Results
Baseline Model: Civic Behavior by Academic and Social Involvement

Does a college education influence political attitudes and behavior? Or is college simply a proxy for the preexisting characteristics that individuals bring to college? Here I adjudicate between these two alternatives by estimating regression models that assess the influence of college involvement on political discussion and liberalism. Table 5.1 lists the results for a baseline model that includes covariates for academic and social activity as well as controls for other sources of political engagement.

Looking first at political discussion, we see that time spent on coursework (either by studying or by interacting with faculty) can yield positive returns for political engagement. Academic involvement has a positive and statistically significant effect on political discussion. These results are consistent with the classic view on college effects and highlight the potentially skills-building nature of a college education (Verba, Schlozman, and Brady 1995).

Perhaps more surprising is that involvement in the social scene fails to exert a positive effect on civic participation. The null finding is somewhat at odds with arguments that implicate the role of social networks in fostering political behavior. That is, the finding that social involvement has no influence on political participation stands in contrast to other research showing that social networks provide important cues and stimuli that make political activity more likely, either because individuals are subjected to personal requests for involvement or because they are exposed to the flow of politically relevant information (Huckfeldt and Sprague 1995; Rosenstone and Hansen 1993).

The control variables also yield some results that may seem surprising, at least initially. The coefficient for the students' year of study suggests that civic behavior *decreases* as students progress through college. While this may seem counterintuitive, further inspection suggests that the finding is consistent with work on social movements (e.g., McAdam 1986), which argues that biographical availability is a key driver behind movement participation. This research tradition argues that individuals who have the time necessary to participate in political activities are more likely to do so than those who have less time. Because high school students have more leisure time than college students, this view would anticipate a decline in political involvement from high school to college, consistent with the results reported in table 5.1.

TABLE 5.1
Regression Models of Political Discussion and Liberalism in College

	Baseline model		Interaction model	
	Political discussion	Liberalism	Political discussion	Liberalism
College involvement				
Academic activity (student centered)	0.100*** (0.019)	-0.002 (0.003)	0.810*** (0.031)	0.084*** (0.005)
Social activity (student centered)	0.014 (0.012)	0.005** (0.002)	-0.152*** (0.020)	-0.016*** (0.003)
Work activity (student centered)	0.049** (0.019)	0.016*** (0.003)	0.061** (0.019)	0.015*** (0.003)
Academic activity (student mean)	0.100*** (0.016)	0.009*** (0.002)	0.087*** (0.016)	0.009*** (0.002)
Social activity (student mean)	-0.011 (0.009)	0.006*** (0.001)	-0.012 (0.009)	0.006*** (0.001)
Work activity (student mean)	0.060*** (0.016)	0.005* (0.002)	0.063*** (0.016)	0.005* (0.002)
Controls				
Senior year	-0.433*** (0.025)	0.071*** (0.003)	-0.456*** (0.025)	0.071*** (0.003)
Female	-0.156*** (0.025)	0.053*** (0.003)	-0.158*** (0.025)	0.053*** (0.003)
American Indian	0.033 (0.313)	0.094* (0.041)	0.022 (0.316)	0.094* (0.041)

	(1)	(2)	(3)	(4)
Asian	−0.388*** (0.054)	0.038*** (0.008)	−0.398*** (0.054)	0.038*** (0.008)
Black	0.140* (0.057)	0.093*** (0.008)	0.138* (0.058)	0.093*** (0.008)
Hispanic	−0.095 (0.065)	0.063*** (0.009)	−0.102 (0.065)	0.063*** (0.009)
Other	0.221*** (0.063)	0.065*** (0.008)	0.059 (0.095)	0.069*** (0.013)
Multiracial	0.055 (0.094)	0.069*** (0.013)	0.225*** (0.064)	0.065*** (0.008)
Parents' income	0.001*** (0.001)	<−0.001** (<0.001)	<−0.001*** (<0.001)	<−0.001** (<0.001)
Prior political discussion				
Occasionally	3.355*** (0.025)		3.452*** (0.026)	
Frequently	4.675*** (0.051)		4.760*** (0.052)	
Prior political attitudes				
Moderate		0.817*** (0.004)		0.817*** (0.004)
Liberal		1.620*** (0.004)		1.620*** (0.004)
Interactions				
Occasional discussion × academic activity	−1.179*** (0.040)		−1.179*** (0.040)	
Frequent discussion × academic activity	−0.979*** (0.080)		−0.979*** (0.080)	

(*continued*)

TABLE 5.1 (*continued*)

	Baseline model		Interaction model	
	Political discussion	Liberalism	Political discussion	Liberalism
Occasional discussion × social activity			0.256*** (0.026)	
Frequent discussion × social activity			0.321*** (0.054)	
Moderate × academic activity				−0.086*** (0.006)
Liberal × academic activity				−0.184*** (0.007)
Moderate × social activity				0.022*** (0.004)
Liberal × social activity				0.046*** (0.005)
Constant	−1.167*** (0.052)	2.098*** (0.007)	−1.195*** (0.053)	2.099*** (0.007)
Observations	75,924	112,654	75,924	112,654

Source. Data on political discussion from the 1998 and 1999 CSS-TFS studies; data on political liberalism from the 1994, 1995, 1998, and 1999 CSS-TFS studies.
Note. Standard errors in parentheses.
*p < 0.05, **p < 0.01, ***p < 0.001 (two-tailed test)

What about political liberalism? Some conservatives argue that involvement with a left-leaning faculty can have a liberalizing effect on students' political attitudes. The second baseline model in table 5.1 assesses this argument. It indicates that changing levels of academic activity have no distinguishable influence on political attitudes. If anything, the negatively signed point estimate suggests that students' attitudes shift toward the conservative end of the spectrum. What aspect of the college experience does produce a liberal shift? In contrast to academic activity, the results indicate that increasing social activity can liberalize students, suggesting that conservatives' concerns about academic indoctrination may be misplaced.

Thus far, the baseline models suggest that attending college exerts a strong effect on civic participation, even after controlling for students' prior political dispositions. The finding thus appears to corroborate the claims of the classic perspective. While background characteristics certainly matter for democratic behavior, the results to this point suggest that college still represents a key source of political socialization. It provides students with important experiences that subsequently influence their political development. But research on higher education raises the possibility that a college effect is neither monolithic nor universal (Armstrong and Hamilton 2013). There are multiple facets to a college education, with each potentially having a different influence on college. Furthermore, the influence of a college experience may well depend on the characteristics that students bring to college.

Interactive Model: The Contingent Effects of Academic and Social Involvement

Turning now to the possibility that college effects vary according to students' backgrounds, the interactive model adds a lagged dependent variable × academic activity interaction and a lagged dependent variable × social activity interaction. These two interactions convey information on whether the influence of college involvement on political behavior and attitudes depends on students' political backgrounds.

The estimated coefficient for academic activity indicates that students with little prior involvement in politics receive a strong, positive return on increasing their academic involvement. However, the interactions for students who started college with high levels of political engagement show that their engagement *declines* as they become more involved in academics. These patterns are not a simple function of "floor" or "ceiling" effects, in which these exceptional students regress to the center of the distribution; indeed, as will be seen with some of the other estimates, these students exhibit different patterns in different contexts. Rather, these patterns suggest a "squeezing out" effect in which politically engaged students sacrifice some of their political activities in favor of more academic pursuits. Overall, these findings show that academic involvement during college matters more for students who were less politically active in high school, suggesting that the academic environment develops civic skills among those students who need it most. As such, this reduces overall differences in political engagement among students.

What about the social scene? Work on higher education suggests that peer networks and social activities on campus often work to strengthen differences between social groups as individuals self-select into homogeneous social networks (Astin 1993). Social activities, for example, are frequently implicated in research that highlights the role of higher education in reproducing social stratification (Featherman and Hauser 1978). They often serve the purpose of reinforcing the values and practices associated with an upper-middle-class lifestyle (Bourdieu and Passeron 1990). Might the social scene have a similar effect on political behavior, in which students' prior political dispositions are reinforced by their peer networks?

The estimates in table 5.1 seem to support such claims. Whereas the effect of academic involvement is positive for students with low levels of prior involvement in politics, the effect of social activity is negative for these students. This suggests that students who are disengaged from politics at the start of college become increasingly disengaged as they participate in more social activities. By contrast, the positively signed coefficients for the interaction terms indicate that for students with a high amount of prior civic involvement, more social activity leads to a slight increase in political activity. These patterns suggest that different aspects of college involvement can have different, even competing, effects on political behavior. On the one hand, involvement in the academic arena appears to mitigate the preexisting differences in political activity; on the other hand, participation in the social scene seems to exacerbate them.

The model for political attitudes yields similar results. The estimates indicate that academic activities generally moderate political differences. As the coefficients show, students who start college with conservative political attitudes drift to the left of the political spectrum as they participate in more academic activities. Conversely, students who start with liberal attitudes drift to the right as they become more active in academic pursuits. Moderates, however, largely remain the same.

As with political engagement, the influence of social activities largely reinforces political attitudes. Conservative students become slightly more conservative as a result of social activities, while liberal students become slightly more liberal. Moderates experience very little change. These results provide support for the contingent view of college influence and suggest that students' prior characteristics interact in complex ways with the college environment in developing students' political attitudes and behavior.

To further illustrate these findings, figure 5.1 shows the predicted probability of political discussion as academic involvement changes, by students' initial levels of discussion. As can be seen, academic involvement exerts differential effects according to prior history of engagement. Students with little history of political discussion receive a higher return on academic involvement than students who were initially more involved in political discussion. This suggests that the transformative effect of academics is greater among those students who need it most.

How does political discussion change as a result of social involvement? Figure 5.2 shows the predicted probability of political discussion for those who do and do not have a history of discussion. It indicates that the social scene exerts a differential effect on political discussion, depending on students' prior levels of discussion. Among students with a history of political discussion, involvement in social activities reinforces and strengthens their prior behaviors. That is, as they

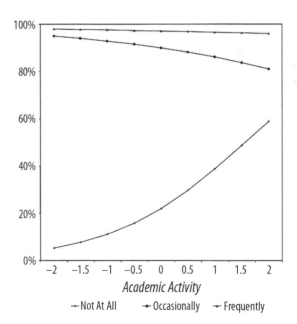

Figure 5.1. Predicted probability of political discussion, by academic activity and prior levels of discussion. Predictions derived from the interactive model (see table 5.1). All other covariates held at their mean.

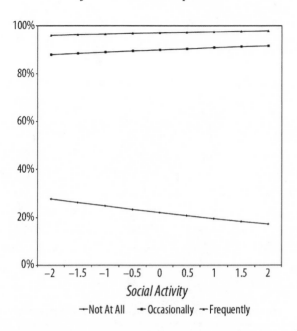

Figure 5.2. Predicted probability of political discussion, by social activity and prior levels of discussion. Predictions derived from the interactive model (see table 5.1). All other covariates held at their mean.

become more involved in social activities, they also become more active in discussions about politics. By contrast, students without a history of engagement become even less likely to discuss politics as they become more involved in social activities. As their social presence increases, their predicted level of discussion decreases.

Figure 5.3 illustrates the influence of academic activity on political attitudes. It shows that conservatives and liberals become more moderate as they more fully participate in academic activities. Political differences among the academically active (right side of the figure) are about half those of the academically inactive (left side). These results suggest that, far from liberalizing students, in general, faculty interaction provides a space for the cultivation of political moderation.

The final simulation, shown in figure 5.4, examines predicted levels of political liberalism as social activities change. As the estimates suggest, and as the figure makes clear, social activities reinforce and, to a limited degree, even strengthen students' political attitudes. As conservative students engage the social scene more fully, their attitudes maintain their conservative character. Similarly, as liberal students participate in social activities, their attitudes remain

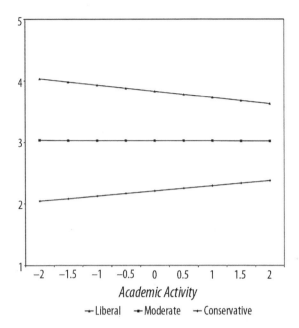

Figure 5.3. Predicted level of political liberalism, by academic activity and prior liberalism. Predictions derived from the interactive model (see table 5.1). The y-axis ranges from 1 (extremely conservative) to 5 (extremely liberal). All other covariates held at their mean.

solidly liberal. Moderates also retain their independent attitudes. Together, these divergent patterns provide a clear illustration of the importance of the social scene for reinforcing prior dispositions.

When viewed together, these results highlight the differential influence of academic and social involvement on students' political behaviors and attitudes. Moreover, they suggest that colleges are multifaceted institutions characterized by different internal dynamics. In the academic arena, students are guided by an infrastructure that focuses on critical thinking and exposure to an array of perspectives. Thus it is perhaps not surprising that exposure to this arena increases political activity among those who need it the most and reduces political inequalities in the process.

Yet the social component of college operates in a much different fashion. Whereas the academic side of college reduces political differences, the social scene works to reproduce them. As others have noted, social interaction exposes students to the preferences, tastes, and behaviors expected of upper-middle-class individuals. While many students arrive at college already equipped with

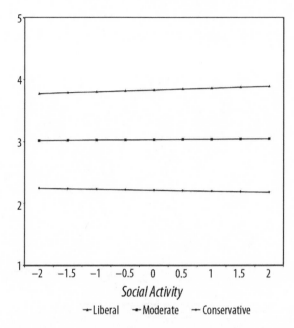

Figure 5.4. Predicted level of political liberalism, by social activity and prior liberalism. Predictions derived from the interactive model (see table 5.1). The y-axis ranges from 1 (extremely conservative) to 5 (extremely liberal). All other covariates held at their mean.

many of the requisite traits, social activities in college have the effect of reinforcing them. That is, college students self-select into largely homogeneous social networks that operate to strengthen the attitudes they bring from home. The results from this study provide further support for this view, indicating that the political norms and practices held by students when they enter college are largely reinforced by the social scene.

Discussion and Conclusion

Concern over the consequences of college for students' political attitudes and behaviors has a long history, both in the social science literature and in the mass media. Most scholars have articulated a position in which colleges and universities represent crucial incubators for the development of political attitudes and behaviors (Nie, Junn, and Stehlik-Barry 1996). Universities serve as a key site for the political socialization of young adults—one that, unlike other social institutions (such as the family), functions to reduce the social inequalities that students bring with them (Verba, Schlozman, and Brady 1995). As others have noted, colleges may well be the "great equalizer," insofar as they offset the exacerbating effects that other social institutions wield on social and political ine-quality (Hout 1988). One long-held belief among political scholars concerns the relevance of educational expansion for "leveling the playing field" and expand-ing political equality (Dalton 2008; Inglehart 1997; Powell 1986; Verba, Schloz-man, and Brady 1995).

Much of the sociological research on higher education, however, challenges the assertion that colleges and universities are meritocratic institutions that oper-ate independently of—or even actively reduce—background differences (Feather-man and Hauser 1978; Jencks et al. 1972; Meyer 1977). Instead, this research emphasizes the importance of students' backgrounds for all aspects of the col-lege experience, including admission, performance, persistence, and comple-tion (Bourdieu and Passeron 1990). Far from reducing social and political in-equalities, these scholars argue, colleges and universities can perpetuate them.

Perhaps more importantly, an emerging view provides a direct critique of the claim that colleges and universities exert a real effect on students' democratic activities (Brand 2010; Jennings and Stoker 2008; Kam and Palmer 2008). In-stead, the revisionists argue that students arrive at college already in possession of the relevant attributes needed to develop democratically appropriate attitudes and behaviors. In asserting this view, revisionists point to shortcomings in the methods used by researchers in the classic tradition. They argue that evidence in favor of a college effect relies largely on cross-sectional data. The problem with models that use cross-sectional data is that they are subject to estimation bias resulting from confounding variables that are unobserved. In the case of estimat-ing the causal effect of college attendance, potentially confounding variables in-clude measures of students' prior political dispositions.

An increasingly popular solution to the problem of omitted variable bias is to take advantage of panel data, in which units of analysis are observed at multiple time points (Halaby 2004). The benefit of panel data is that they allow for models that focus on variation within units of observation. Using this strategy as a point of departure for addressing the tension between the revisionist and classic views, the analysis in this chapter employed a series of random effects models to exam-ine how involvement with college influences democratic behavior. With a number of possible sources of self-selection ruled out, the results provided evidence of a robust effect of college involvement. Both the academic and social sides of college represent important sources of influence on how and to what extent students be-come politically engaged.

Drawing on recent research from higher education complicates the picture of college influence, however. This newer work highlights how students' backgrounds interact with different aspects of the college environment to create a unique college experience (Armstrong and Hamilton 2013; Arum and Roksa 2011). Models that incorporate these interactions indicate that the influence of college is highly contingent on students' political backgrounds. For the most part, the academic side of college promotes civic involvement among students with initially low levels of civic activity, while the social side generally reinforces students' preexisting political habits. That is, students who were civically engaged prior to college generally become more involved as a result of their involvement in the social scene, while students who were not civically engaged prior to college become more involved as a result of their involvement in academics.

In terms of how college influences political attitudes, the results indicate—in contrast to the concerns of many conservative commentators—that academic involvement generally moderates attitudes. While conservative students do become more liberal as a result of academic involvement, liberals become more conservative as a result of their academic involvement. Indeed, it appears that a critical engagement with a diverse set of ideas—a hallmark of the college experience—challenges students to reevaluate the strength of their political convictions. The social side of college operates much differently. As work on social networks would anticipate, social activities reinforce students' prior beliefs. As students become more active socially, the conservatives become more conservative and the liberals become more liberal. This finding suggests that students seek out and engage with familiar social environments—a choice that leads to the strengthening of their political beliefs.

What are the implications of these findings for relevant theories of political socialization and social stratification? With respect to socialization, the study of how individuals learn and adopt democratic norms and practices has a noteworthy intellectual history, particularly from the 1950s through the 1970s (Hyman 1959; Jennings and Niemi 1974, 1981). Scholars involved in this theoretical project initially focused on the importance of political learning during early childhood, providing evidence that the origins of adults' political behaviors and orientations could be traced back to the early, pre-adult experiences with their families, schools, and peer networks (Niemi and Hepburn 1995).

Since the 1970s, however, scholars have increasingly recognized the importance of later life events in continuing to influence attitudes and behaviors. For example, political scholars (e.g., Fiorina 1981; MacKuen, Erikson, and Stimson 1989) have demonstrated that individuals' political preferences, attitudes, and behaviors are marked by some degree of malleability during adulthood. They can also change in response to exogenous conditions such as new social networks, the onset of an economic crisis, or the experience of life-course transitions (e.g., divorce or parenthood).

The findings from the current study seem to shed further light on how socialization processes unfold over time. As others note, experiences during childhood and adolescence are clearly influential in forming an initial basis for students' values, dispositions, and habits, with families playing perhaps the most critical role. However, the results of this study suggest that later events can both reinforce and undermine the influence of these early events. The long-term effects of early socialization experiences are contingent on the paths that individuals take over their life course. In terms of the relationship between college and political behavior, this suggests that the causal status of both college characteristics and students' background characteristics is fluid and depends on how students engage the multifaceted environment that surrounds attending college. In other words, the influence of events that occur earlier in the life course—such as parental socialization—can be either exacerbated or mitigated by events that take place later in the life course, where college attendance represents an event of particular relevance. The results presented in this chapter suggest that students' experiences with the social side of college tend to reinforce their prior political behaviors, while experiences with the academic side tend to be more transformative.

NOTES

1. Note, however, that this exposure does not seem to extend to promoting participation (Mutz 2002).

2. For other years in the CSS, the data either do not have relevant information on important covariates (as in the 1996 and 1997 surveys) or are not yet publicly available (any survey after 1999).

CHAPTER SIX

"Civil" or *"Provocative"?*

Varieties of Conservative Student Style and Discourse in American Universities

AMY J. BINDER AND KATE WOOD

In 2004 and 2007, members of the College Republicans on a campus we call Western Flagship University staged an eye-popping event called the Affirmative Action Bake Sale.[1] The bake sale is a well-known piece of political theater that conservative students put on at many universities across the country, wherein members of right-leaning campus organizations sell baked goods at a higher price to white passersby than to, say, African Americans or Latinos/Latinas. The event is said to highlight, while also parodying, the deleterious effects on all students of affirmative action policies. Student sponsors argue that the event opens up discussion of an important topic that all too frequently remains unacknowledged on liberally biased campuses. But when they talk about what it is like to stage the event and to get others' reactions to it, it is clear that they also revel in the sheer fun and provocation that their activity stirs up. The Flagship students who put on events that we have labeled "provocative" are tickled to rile liberals at their universities as they make their political points. Moreover, they are supported in their theatricality by national organizations designed to foster such conservative activism on campus.

On a different college campus, two thousand miles away, which we call Eastern Elite University, such an event is considered verboten—not by campus liberals or college administrators and faculty, but by conservative students themselves. On this campus, most conservative undergraduates denounce the act of pushing liberals' buttons as sophomoric, as well as ineffective at recruiting potential fellow travelers or encouraging debate on an issue. Most conservative students at Eastern Elite argue that it is beneficial to conduct respectful arguments and to try to reach out to the other side, to learn from their political adversaries, and to create a well-tempered conservative presence on campus. They actively disdain the national conservative organizations that encourage theatrical events like the Bake Sale, accusing those organizations of having a populist reputation. Instead of engaging in provocative public actions, most students at Eastern Elite extol the virtues of what we have labeled "civilized discourse," to be used among themselves, as well as with faculty, administrators, and their liberal peers.

These dominant styles of conservatism on the Western Flagship and Eastern Elite campuses exist within a broader spectrum of activity that includes some other options. While the styles described above strongly dominate on their respective campuses, other approaches can be found as subordinate or submerged styles (DiMaggio and Powell 1991; Eliasoph and Lichterman 2003). At Eastern, for example, a conservative style of insurgency, or what we label "highbrow provocation," thrives mainly in the pages of the campus's conservative newspaper. Though often drawing the ire of campus conservatives practicing the dominant style, a subset of conservative students participates actively in penning the intense, philosophical, and at times vitriolic editorials within its pages.[2]

These differences in conservative styles across campuses are strong and stark and deserve sustained analysis. In some ways, the differences are surprising. As Robert Horwitz (2013) and others have pointed out, for decades the Republican Party has been pulled to the right by "antiestablishment conservatives" whose slash-and-burn tactics have become the style *du jour* of institutional politics. It is therefore possible to imagine that eighteen- to twenty-two-year-olds who have a proclivity for conservative ideology would participate in a shared system of national-level, right-of-center beliefs and use similar styles on their home campuses. After all, this population is wired in to multiple forms of widely disseminated technological media, from Facebook pages devoted to conservative causes to 24/7 streaming cable news channels and constantly updated right-leaning blogs. Were they interested in investigating "what is wrong with the liberal campus," they also would have encountered the ideas of "movement conservatives" (Tanenhaus 2009) located in right-leaning think tanks, foundations, and media outlets such as Fox News, which champion the cause of right-of-center undergraduates (Horowitz 2007; Kors and Silverglate 1998; Maranto, Redding, and Hess 2009). Students could even get their hands on the "Campus Conservative Battle Plan," distributed by the Young America's Foundation, which provides ready-made plans for actions like the provocative Bake Sale and, currently, for staging dramatic protests against the Obama administration.[3]

On the other hand, we also know that American conservatism, like any other political orientation, is a relational field. Conservatism has always been varied—in terms of the issues that fall under its umbrella, the organizations that are in place to advance its goals, and the styles to which its different advocates adhere. National political figures and pundits have long differed on issues and proffered different modes of political analysis. The same is true of conservative organizations targeting college students. While the national organizations sponsoring battle plans are the largest, most visible, and vocal purveyors of conservative ideology to undergraduates, a handful of other organizations such as the Intercollegiate Studies Institute educate, sponsor, and mobilize a more intellectual sort of student. These organizations espouse a type of conservatism more in line with the style of Edmund Burke (or in contemporary media, David Brooks), in which "corrections" to the established order are tolerated and the tempered disposition is valued. There is also a distinctive brand of conservatism that harks back to William F. Buckley Jr.'s "full-throated passion of the agitator" (Tanenhaus 2009, 43) in his book *God and Man at Yale* (1951), a brand that today can be found in such media outlets as the *Weekly Standard* and *National Review*.

In addition to the differences between types of conservatism that exist in the broader political culture, of course, there is also variation in the types of educational institutions that students attend, which lend themselves to distinctive styles. As Mitchell Stevens (2007) has pointed out, universities cultivate their own institutional characters. Selectivity in admissions, the quality and frequency of faculty-student interactions, differences in historical institutional sagas, variation in students' career aspirations, the very physical landscape of campus life—all of these affect the in-college experiences of students on any given campus and may be supposed to have an impact on the styles of political discourse and action. While these known campus features might lead to selection bias in some important ways—students choose colleges that fit with who they think they are now and who they would like to become, and, likewise, selective colleges choose students who they believe will enhance the institutional environment—we should also expect universities to influence students while they are enrolled in college. Further, though undergraduates certainly enter colleges and universities with differing personal histories, including varying experiences of social class, race and ethnicity, gender, religion, and sexuality, an extensive and long-established body of literature indicates that the campus as a meso-level institutional environment affects students' lives in significant ways (Armstrong and Hamilton 2013; Astin 1993; Clark 1970; Feldman and Newcomb 1994; Holland and Eisenhart 1990; Knox, Lindsay, and Kolb 1993; Pascarella and Terenzini 2005; Sanford and Axelrod 1979; Wallace 1966). To be sure, students' individual characteristics are salient; at the same time, however, the influence of the institutional milieu in which they find themselves immersed cannot be ignored (Einwohner and Spencer 2005; Yesnowitz 2010).

Understanding why an event like an Affirmative Action Bake Sale makes sense at Western but not at Eastern, then, as well as the more abstract issue of why conservative styles are different on these two campuses, is a complex matter. On the largest scale, it involves tracking the different national organizations with which conservative students across the country come into contact, with an eye to each organization's rhetorical styles and class cultures. At a middle level, closer to students' everyday experiences, conservative undergraduates also have extensive interactions with the different local structures and cultural practices on their school campuses. Finally, there is the micro-level of individual students' histories, experiences, beliefs, values, and interpretations, all of which are commingled with the campus- and national-level environments.

At present, social scientists know too little about the national or local organizational networks and cultural practices that leave an impression on conservative students. Nor do they understand conservatism generally (Lilla 2009) or conservative college students' thoughts about their education, let alone how conservative styles manifest distinctively on different university campuses. There is sparse analysis of how conservative students think and behave politically in college (Kelly-Woessner and Woessner 2006; Woessner and Kelly-Woessner 2009) or how these actions connect to their activities in college and beyond. We should know much more about who conservative students are and which parts of conservatism they identify with, how they become conservative and maintain their identities on campus, and whether and how they intend to be active politically in the future. Since college activism is often a first step to leadership in the larger political arena, knowing about students' activities in college is a crucial area of study.

We hope to fill this general gap in knowledge about right-leaning undergraduates and, in particular, their expressive political culture. In this chapter, and in greater depth in our book (Binder and Wood 2013), we argue that campuses create opportunities for particular forms of conservative student styles, largely at the expense of others. We demonstrate that political ideology and style are not characteristics that incoming freshmen simply transport to their college settings *fait accompli*; rather, these styles are in large part the organizational product of the many interactions that students have on the particular college campus they decide to attend. College students' commitments are elastic and undergo transformation once students arrive on campus, and they are largely based on the types of cultural repertoires, organizational resources, and social networks that students encounter at their universities. Higher education, from this perspective, plays a critical role in creating distinctive types of political selves.

In presenting this argument, we need to issue two caveats. First, to argue that political style is a form of organizational accomplishment is not to claim that students arrive in college with *no* ideological commitments based on family, community, and previous political and schooling experiences and media exposure, or that students are blank slates for institutions to imprint on; indeed, all this operates at the micro-level of the individual, as described above. Students' prior identities are important and must be accounted for, even while we observe that once students arrive on campus, cultural repertoires and resources funnel them into distinctive types of conservatism. Second and related, students are not automatons and molded seamlessly into these styles—there is plenty of agency to go around, as students strategically think about their identities on campus, their interactions with faculty and peers, and how their actions will ultimately sync with their future careers and social lives. There is evidence in our cases that students sometimes do actively defy predominant styles and create hybrids from multiple different styles.

Nonetheless, it is also clear that the informal and formal organizations and social networks that students belong to on campus present strong opportunities to lean heavily into the dominant style of their university and present considerable constraints against easily branching off into different group styles. Foregrounding these local settings of interaction and negotiation—and the cultural meanings that are shared in them—allows us to complicate the picture of how college affects students, revealing how neither individual identities nor institutional differences alone fully capture variation. Another way to say this is that we understand higher education to be a politically formative institution that hones preexisting ideological commitments into particular political styles. The importance of universities to students' politics goes far beyond affecting their "attitudes"—which is a rather thin account of political action. Rather, we see universities playing a fundamental role (at least for some students) in providing the cultural tools for constructing political *selves*: people who not only hold certain values or beliefs about the world but have learned how to express and practice those ideas in real time for real situations.

Higher Education's Role in the Development of Political Styles
College Effects: Large-N Studies of Political Attitudes

Sociologists long have been interested in the potential of higher education for influencing students' sociopolitical attitudes, values, and behaviors, both during the period of college attendance and after college ends. Most scholarship on this question—known as college effects or political socialization research—uses a social-psychological framework that makes the individual the unit of analysis and studies the effects of schooling on college students' and alumni's attitudes and behaviors (Pascarella and Terenzini 2005). National-level or institution-level data-sets are used to measure college's net effects on a large variety of political ideas and behaviors, from levels of political participation to whether education has the effect of "liberalizing" students on specific issues such as race, gender, and sexu-ality (Pascarella and Terenzini 2005). In their meta-analysis of three decades of research on these questions, Pascarella and Terenzini argue that scholarship dem-onstrates that higher education positively affects political participation levels and that college-educated members of society have greater knowledge of the political process.

As Kyle Dodson shows in chapter 5, however, some scholars recently have ques-tioned whether attending and graduating from college actually has significant effects on political awareness, net of precollege experiences, and have asserted instead that "differences in political sophistication . . . are already in place before anyone sets foot in a college classroom" (Highton 2009, 1564). Such research sug-gests that the most important factors in political awareness and knowledge are cognitive ability, parental characteristics, and pre-adult political engagement—meaning that the attitudes students express and the knowledge they demonstrate about politics while in college are quite similar to the attitudes and knowledge they come in with. Furthermore, since the 1980s, the literature has been considerably less consistent in demonstrating college's so-called liberalizing effect—that the more years of education people have, the more tolerant they are of social diversity and political dissent (Fosse and Gross 2012) or the less enthusiastic they are about probusiness or antiunion activities (Jennings and Stoker 2008). There also ap-pears to be decreasing empirical support for the proposition that between-college differences in the structure of institutions—such as size, mission, geographic re-gion, and public or private organizational control—are meaningful factors affect-ing students' political participation and attitudes. Together with decreasing faith in the liberalization thesis, these findings have caused some in the higher edu-cation field to doubt the discrete influence of college on students' political lives.

Where do findings such as these leave us in our argument that campuses are places where conservative discourses and styles are developed, shared, and sus-tained over time? Quantitative studies on political socialization might be inter-preted to present a challenge to our contention that the university setting signifi-cantly influences students' politics.

Not surprisingly, we disagree with this conclusion. One can think of style as a dimension of political experience that the quantitative literature on college effects simply has not captured and that such research was not built to describe. While political socialization research has measured students' attitudes and participation, it has ignored the more expressive, symbolic components of constructing a political self (such as modes of debating or framing arguments to mobilize adherents) and has paid no attention to the fact that the avenues for developing these styles may vary across universities. The largely quantitative social-psychological approach cannot describe interactional settings, which are the central places where meanings get made and styles are experimented with (Binder 2007; Fine 1984; Hallett and Ventresca 2006).

Pairing Institutional Accounts of Higher Education with Current Cultural Theory

Scholars working from a more institutional perspective within higher education research provide much-needed help. Kenneth Feldman and his colleagues have been at the forefront of specifying the main deficiencies of the social-psychological model, charging that the college effects approach gives primacy to the "characteristics of the individual organism"—in other words, the autonomous student (Kaufman and Feldman 2004, 463). This, they argue, effectively downplays the underlying constitutive forces of the campus's social environment and overlooks how unique college culture and structures shape students' thoughts and behaviors (Feldman and Newcomb 1994; Pascarella and Terenzini 1991). Due to these deficiencies, scholars in this area have worked to direct attention away from the student as the unit of analysis and toward the campus environment and its "subenvironments" as the objects of study. Looking at university students as existing in a series of interrelated organizational arrangements on campus—such as residential settings, major fields of study, peer cultures, and classroom settings—Feldman and his coauthors provide what they call a more sociological account of the influence of college on students' identities. They study campuses as "arena[s] of social interaction in which the individual comes into contact with a multitude of actors in a variety of settings, emphasizing that through these social interactions the identities of individuals are, in part, constituted" (Kaufman and Feldman 2004, 464). In sum, the theory of action in this institutional branch of higher education studies is that students, as they interact with one another in a variety of college-level organizational structures, learn how to be active, creative, and even appropriate members of different campus populations.

This is copacetic with current theoretical approaches in the areas of culture, organizations, and political sociology, which, when combined, further help us see how universities are places where systematically varying, shared political styles (not just individual identities) might be created and become available for use. Although disparate in their starting points and emphases, studies of group style (Eliasoph and Lichterman 2003; Mische 2008), cultural repertoires (Tilly 1995), and political culture (Lichterman and Cefai 2006) have important points of connection. All focus on "recurrent patterns of interaction that arise from a group's shared assumptions" (Eliasoph and Lichterman 2003, 737) and, in the case of Eliasoph and Lichterman, specifically, a group's shared assumptions about what constitutes good or adequate participation in the group setting. Such patterns of interaction are *culture*, as Eliasoph and Lichterman make clear: these patterns are not made individually anew from scratch but are publicly shared with others and durable over time. They structure action. Informed by broad institutional logics available in society at large (DiMaggio and Powell 1991), but always worked out through negotiation and renegotiation at the local level (Hallett and Ventresca 2006), these patterns are ways of doing things and of interacting with others that allow work to get done.

This theorization is well suited to interpreting the more specific subset of interactions relating to political cultures. According to Tilly (1995), group styles and organizational culture pertaining to politics consist of repertoires or, as Gross describes Tilly's work, "scripts for political performance that become institutionalized, sedimented in actors' expectations, and in the structure of institutions and intergroup relations" (Gross 2010, 3). Researchers have found that in different settings and at different times, groups might adopt styles of "avoiding politics" (Eliasoph 1998), engaging in contentious behavior (McAdam, Tarrow, and Tilly 2001), staging political theater (Gitlin 1980), or devoting themselves to highly institutionalized forms of political action like campaigning for candidates. There are different styles in different local settings; individuals in those local settings have shared understandings of the "rules" of the field (Fligstein and McAdam 2011), and, as Tilly points out, those styles have consequences for the styles that will be transposed into other settings and used in the future. The prevailing styles that we discovered at the Western and Eastern campuses—provocation and civilized discourse—are two different types of shared and ongoing political action that, although not the only forms of political expression on each campus, constitute the dominant styles at the respective universities.

Social and Cultural Capital in Two Relational Fields: Higher Education and Politics

Once we accept that universities may influence students' political development and that distinctive political styles exist in local settings such as on the university campus, a next question for our project is, what is it about the context of a particular university campus that leads to a unique conservative style in that location? What are the presuppositions and group interactions on a campus that combine to produce such distinctive modes of political culture, and what is their relationship to particular organizational and cultural facets of the university? Although we are not able to provide a complete analysis of this question here, we argue that a crucial factor contributing to a campus's conservative style is the university's reputation as a particular kind of place, which is derived from its location in the larger relational field of academic symbolic capital. People's shared understandings of specific colleges and universities shape students' assumptions about the kinds of people they are supposed to be, the ways they should express themselves, and the lives they are expected to lead in the future.

As Pierre Bourdieu and others have written, academia is a relational field in which different institutions of higher education occupy dominant and subordinate positions, depending on the specific resources they possess compared with other universities and colleges (Bourdieu and Johnson 1993; Naidoo 2004). These resources take many forms but include most prominently (though in no particular order) the historical legacy and traditions of the university; the research profiles and national reputations of faculty members; the size of the university's endowment; the visible connections that the institution sustains in the worlds of policymaking, business, and elite culture; and its admissions criteria for and future promise and actual social outcomes of its undergraduate and graduate student populations. Inhabitants of universities (students, faculty, administrators, staff) keep close tabs on their campus's position in this relational field, as do those outside its boundaries (Espeland and Sauder 2007).

While one of higher education's most visible charters is to cultivate students' human capital (Arum and Roksa 2011), another, less articulated but not inconsequential effect of universities is to reproduce class cultures through the distinctive development of students' social networks and cultural dispositions. Most of the literature on the reproduction of class culture has focused on elite universities (Bowen and Bok 1998; Karabel 2005; Massey et al. 2003; Stevens 2007) and how they cultivate privilege and distinction. Universities ratify and reproduce social and cultural capital among those already habituated to social advantage (Cookson and Persell 1985; Khan 2011; Lareau 2003) while also introducing their less privileged students to cosmopolitan discourses, practices, and tastes (Granfield and Koenig 1992). Students come to have a feel for the kinds of persons they ought to be academically and socially by virtue of being a member of this elite educational institution, as well as the types of careers and futures they are expected to have.[4] Few studies of non-elite postsecondary settings address elite formation, although recent work by Elizabeth Armstrong and Laura Hamilton (2013) shows the varied cultural dispositions and social networks that are in place in one university on the lower end of the relational field (very much like our Western Flagship), which produces particular types of social and academic lives.

As significant as these studies of capital acquisition and reproduction in university settings have been, they mostly have not been brought to bear on the forms of *political* capital that are being created in universities. Indeed, several recent qualitative studies of college students argue that students more or less turn their backs on political commitments (Clydesdale 2007; Nathan 2005). The question we bring to the table is, how do two universities—which are differently located in the higher education status hierarchy, cultivate in students different forms of social and cultural capital, and are home to unique organizational arrangements where student interactions take place—serve as the settings where students can burnish their distinctive styles of conservatism?

Data and Methods

In this project we study the political ideas and styles of self-identified right-of-center college students, with a focus on two universities: Eastern Elite University, a single campus, and the Western Public University system, which is home to a flagship campus, a land-grant university, and smaller satellite campuses. Our main focus in the Western system is on the Flagship campus, though we draw on data from three other campuses in the system, which are more conservative than the Flagship campus. The names of campuses, campus organizations, and individual students and alumni used here are pseudonyms. To preserve the institutions' anonymity, specific characteristics of our two universities are pulled from school profiles carefully created by amalgamating attributes of the actual universities we studied with the attributes of two of their peer institutions.[5]

During 2008–9 Binder conducted seventy in-depth interviews with members of the two universities' communities. More than two-thirds of these interviews were with students and recent alumni; other interviewees included faculty, administrators, and donors.[6] Of the conservative student/alumni interviewees on the Western campuses, fifteen respondents were current students and seven were alumni (four within four years of graduating, three within ten years of graduating), for a total of twenty-two. Of the conservative student/alumni interviewees on the Eastern Elite campus, ten respondents were current students and fourteen were alumni (twelve within four years of graduating, two within seven years of graduating), for a total of twenty-four. Interviews lasted from one to two hours.

Initial student and alumni interviewees were selected on each campus after we read on the Internet about campus conservative activities and then located students who were active members in such clubs as College Republicans, anti-abortion groups, and campus newspapers. Early respondents were asked for the names of other conservative students and alumni they knew, and interviews were conducted with all students/alumni on these lists who were willing to participate. This chain-referral sample methodology mostly ruled out students who were not visibly active in conservative politics on campus, since it was more difficult to find out about them. However, a few such respondents were located on each of the campuses. In general, the people we interviewed were known on campus for the conservative politics they wrote about, ran political campaigns on, or otherwise expressed in their campus political activities. They were generally active members in their organizations, if not always activists or leaders of those groups. We do not argue that they were representative of all conservatives on campus, but as active members of conservative organizations on campus, they showcased the prevailing style of conservatism at their university. After the interviews were completed, Wood systematically coded all interviews so that both authors could identify trends and generate concrete empirical claims about the findings.

Interviewees varied along many axes. The majority of students and alumni interviewed at both Western and Eastern were white men, but nonwhite students and women were represented within the sample. Students and alums from both schools came from a range of class backgrounds. Subjects' social class—nearly always a difficult variable to deal with in this type of study—was determined using qualitative data. Rather than inquiring as to individuals' net worth or specific cultural competencies, we asked interviewees about the occupations of any co-residing parents or guardians during their precollege years. We also inquired about the highest level of education completed and the institution(s) that parents or guardians had attended. With data as complete as possible (some participants avoided questions about their family backgrounds), we found that while Eastern respondents tended to come from families with higher socioeconomic status, students at both Eastern and Western showed extensive variance. Both groups included parents who had received graduate degrees as well as parents whose highest level of education was a high school diploma or its equivalent. Correspondingly, parents' jobs ranged from unskilled labor to the professions. Interviewees also varied considerably in their religious beliefs, with Catholicism the most common faith among religious students from Eastern and various forms of Protestant Christianity among those from Western. More students/alumni at Western said they were not religious at all, perhaps correlated with the larger number of libertarians at Western than at Eastern. Interviewees at both schools represented all regions of the United States. Though students at Western campuses were more likely to come from within the state, Western also attracts a large population of out-of-state students. Likewise, extensive regional variation was represented among the Eastern students, with more than half coming from outside of the Northeast.

The logic of the comparison of Eastern and Western rests on several axes of institutional similarity and difference. Both Eastern Elite and Western Flagship are prominent examples of campuses that conservative critics point to as paradigmatically liberal strongholds. Both are also Research I, religiously unaffiliated universities. Differences lie along the dimensions of geographic region, the public-private divide, and admissions selectivity, among other distinguishing features. In its selectivity and prestige, Eastern Elite does represent somewhat of an outlier or an extreme case compared with the Western campuses, as well as with our understanding of other campuses as gleaned from pilot interviews. But using this extreme case provides considerable analytic leverage, revealing institutional attributes that would be difficult to tease out among more similar institutions (for example, between campuses in the Western system, where differences, though present, were more subtle). Although it is not possible to generalize from these two case studies, the findings are suggestive for understanding the lives of conservative students as they have gone through college in the first decade of the twenty-first century.

Results

To address our empirical questions about the experiences of conservative college students and to engage the literatures overviewed above, we now go through the conservative styles present on the two campuses, noting their marked differences. We trace these differences to a variety of organizational structures and cultures that conservative students encounter and participate in on their respective campuses. Beginning with a look at the students themselves as they enter college, we move outward from the individual to look at conservative campus organizations, then finish with a discussion of some of the overarching cultural and organizational features marking each campus, which go a long way toward explaining cross-campus variation in political styles. Given the space constraints here, we cannot closely examine students' direct experiences with national-level conservative organizations once they are in college (as we do in our book [Binder and Wood 2013]), but throughout we do refer to the macro-level discourses produced by these organizations.

Individuals Entering Institutions:
Varied Political Identifications and Styles

In describing our sample, we mentioned several demographic characteristics of our student respondents, including their racial, social class, and religious backgrounds. Here we look more carefully at the precollege *political* backgrounds of students on the Western campuses and at Eastern Elite to demonstrate that prior to matriculation, these students had more in common than might be supposed. Students at both schools varied in terms of their political identification, as well as—among those students who identified as conservative before attending their universities—their political style.

While most students interviewed at both schools entered the university identifying as some form of conservative, several did not. Western and Eastern each boasted one student who identified as moderate and one who identified as libertarian. More strikingly, each school had five interviewees who identified as liberal prior to their college experience. Similarly, students entering college as conservatives varied in how they described their early political affiliations. Most commonly, interviewees at both Eastern and Western adopted the opinions of their conservative and/or Republican families. But there were several who had one or more liberal parents and/or close family members, as well as interviewees whose parents, while conservative, were much less politically active than they, themselves, became at Eastern or Western.

For students at both schools who identified as conservative before arriving at college, a single issue often initially galvanized their conservatism. In many cases, issues that concerned interviewees were related to their own biographies or family histories. Two students described being drawn to conservatism by examining the impact of Republican economic policies on their parents' businesses:

> And my dad always says that . . . he became Republican when he started to make money. And I get that, and really see how those policies, especially tax policies, they're more friendly to small business. My dad owns his own business, so . . . I

see how that party benefits my family. And you kind of vote your pocketbook sort of thing. (Stephanie Cohen, Western Flagship)

[My father] is heavily involved in the auto industry. He . . . talked to me a lot about industry in America and about what it takes to have a successful business. I have taken those lessons to heart and developed sort of a fiscal or economic conservatism from that side of things, by seeing how he has been able to succeed, and specifically how his company is able to succeed . . . That is where the economic conservatism stems from. (Darius Norton, Eastern)

Other students described being motivated by issues that were less directly related to their personal experiences but about which they felt no less strongly. Abortion and the events of September 11 were the most frequently mentioned, with the former slightly more common among Eastern students and the latter among those from Western. Students who did not have a "lightning rod" issue described developing their political views through reading influential books or simply having "always been interested" in politics.

Among respondents who described themselves as conservative before matriculation, we saw considerable variation in precollege political *styles*. Across the two universities, styles varied from students describing themselves as uninvolved in politics to those fully engaged in conservative activism as high school students. We saw a spectrum of political behaviors that ranged from relative apathy (identifying as conservative but remaining otherwise politically uninvolved) at one end to active engagement at the other. Among the politically active precollege conservatives, we found that some students from each campus described early political behavior that could be described as fitting the "provocative" style we identify as typical of Western students as well as the "civilized discourse" style we see commonly at Eastern.

Some students described themselves as leaning to the right before heading to college but not having acted on their beliefs. Those who said they had been politically inactive in high school often attributed this to the zeitgeist in their home communities, which was uniformly conservative. This caused them to be unreflectively conservative and not act on their inchoate beliefs, such as when a Western student said, "I feel like when I went to college I was conservative because I came from a small town and everybody was conservative" (Christina Young, Western Flagship). Similarly, one Eastern student reported, "In a place like —— where I grew up, conservatism wasn't something that was really part of my identity because everyone around me was basically conservative" (Molly Nash Downing, Eastern). Others explained that an apathetic climate in their schools had caused them to be sluggish about really thinking about or investing in their own ideological positions or political manners. As one interviewee explained, "[politics] really didn't ever come up. My school was very apolitical . . . I was never even challenged on those beliefs before I came to Eastern" (Elizabeth Tennyson, Eastern).

Even before heading off to college, some of the more politically active respondents—at Eastern as well as Western—pointed to early stylistic proclivities closely related to the provocative style of conservatism. On one occasion for an Eastern student, the development of a Fox-style mode of political expression happened quite literally, when he worked on a class project that earned him an A:

> The real thing that got me involved in news and politics and journalism, that sort of thing, was in eighth grade we had to do a book report, nonfiction. At that moment, Bill O'Reilly was kind of taking off on Fox News and we had just gotten Fox News on our cable TV. He came out with a book version of his show, *The O'Reilly Factor* . . . and I read it and I thought, "I really like this a lot" . . . My friend and I did a mock *O'Reilly Factor* show [for our project] . . . We did a split screen and I played the liberal and he played the conservative. (Calvin Coffey, Eastern)

Other students described these inclinations as largely picked up from their families' habits of consuming right-wing media, as one Western student noted:

> Growing up my parents were always conservative and they would listen to Rush Limbaugh and watch the news a lot, my mom basically. And she would have the radio on AM all day or have it on Fox News. Like whenever we're together there was always at least one TV on Fox News . . . And so I'd be in the car with them and mostly Rush Limbaugh and I'd hear him talking and everything. And I was, "Okay, good." (Victor Irwin, Western Satellite)

In a few cases, family influence was even more direct, with family members actively recruiting our respondents into political activism. As one Eastern interviewee described, his mother had him and his siblings out on the front lines of conservatism from a young age: "As soon as we could walk we were holding campaign signs for pro-life candidates and that sort of thing" (Kingsley Griffith, Eastern). Thus at least some interviewees from both Eastern and Western were well-schooled in confrontational styles before setting foot on campus.

We also heard descriptions of precollege political styles from interviewees at both Eastern and Western that fit with the civilized discourse style of conservatism. Again, in some cases families were influential, as a Western interviewee explained:

My dad and I definitely have that political bond in common. I talked with him a lot about it . . . some of his heroes are people like Ronald Reagan, people like Milton Friedman. And those people are [the] books I grew up reading, philosophies I grew up understanding. (Lindsey Nicholson, Western Satellite)

For many interviewees, their earliest type of political expression came in the form of debating their own family members. In other cases, this style was institutionally sanctified through local organizations for high school–aged conservatives or high school debate clubs. One Eastern interviewee described attending Young Republicans meetings in high school as when he "started to critically evaluate my own views. I think that is when I sort of began to make my views my own" (Derek Yeager, Eastern). Other early proponents of the civilized discourse style described this as being the result of autodidactic reading, researching the Austrian economists (a Western student) or absorbing *Atlas Shrugged* (an Eastern student) on their own and then debating their newfound knowledge with family and friends. In all, civilized debate and discussion marked the early political lives of at least some of our interviewees at both Western and Eastern, although slightly more Eastern students—particularly those from homes with greater levels of high cultural capital—exhibited this style.

In sum, we find that our student and alumni interviewees from both Eastern and Western varied in largely similar ways prior to attending college. Respondents at both schools described a variety of precollege political identifications, not always coming to college already on the right. Among those from both universities who *did* identify as conservative before matriculation, we saw considerable variation in political style. A good number of our interviewees from both campuses were familiar with the style of provocation: their families listened to and appreciated Fox News and Rush Limbaugh and/or were active in protest politics. Others from both campuses had experience with the civilized discourse style, reading seriously about political ideology, debating with family and friends or in high school clubs, and finding their own distinctive conservative voices. What this means is that the high school students who ended up in conservative clubs at Western and Eastern were not remarkably politically different from one another when they entered college. It is more accurate to say that incoming freshmen on each campus were internally varied in similar ways. As our data demonstrate, our two campuses welcomed students with varied political identifications and stylistic tendencies, but then, through culturally shared experiences—where they became acquainted with coherent group styles, or repertoires, for political action—conservative students on each campus became more stylistically homogeneous.

Conservative Clubs: Fitting in on Campus

Once arriving on campus, students at both Western and Eastern find a similar array of like-minded organizations available for them to join; both schools offer a College Republicans chapter, a conservative newspaper, a pro-life group, and other right-of-center, issue-oriented, student-run clubs (College Republicans are the focus in this chapter). At both schools, the College Republicans clubs are representative of the dominant discourse of conservatism on campus, and conservative newspapers and, to some extent, other clubs provide a venue for a subordinate or submerged style. However, the roles that College Republicans play in the lives of the two campuses differ greatly.

To join and thrive in these clubs—which, if nothing else, is often seen as a social imperative for students who feel ideologically and socially isolated (Binder and Wood 2011)—conservative undergraduates need to learn what is and is not acceptable within these groups on the two campuses. They generally stray from those dominant styles at some personal peril, much as theory on group style would predict (Eliasoph 1998; Eliasoph and Lichterman 2003; Mische 2008). Forays into actions that are deemed beyond the usual boundaries of acceptable style—which do happen—are often met by other students with a good deal of additional debate and even censure. Whatever their prior experiences of national-level institutional logics and styles of conservatism, students must come to understand themselves as members of *this* campus community, meaning that they must select carefully from the varied repertoires and adapt to the local campus level. In our discussion here, we briefly describe the two dominant styles across the campuses, then offer an analysis of the particular university characteristics that contribute to them.

WESTERN FLAGSHIP COLLEGE REPUBLICANS:
PROUD TO BE PROVOCATIVE

The College Republicans group at Western Flagship, whose Affirmative Action Bake Sale was briefly described at the beginning of this chapter, is the most vibrant and active of all those on the campuses in the Western system. Interviewees on other Western campuses spoke admiringly of this group and described its success as being the result not only of the skillfulness of the individuals running the club but also of the club's vocal liberal opponents on campus and within the community where Western Flagship is located. Said one interviewee of the

2004 Bake Sale, "there was like a lot of talk on campus about it, [people saying] I'm shocked that Flagship is allowing it. But I can't believe people were shocked. I mean Flagship allows so much ridiculous behavior on the *other* side, you know" (Stephanie Cohen, Western Flagship). The provocative events staged by the Flagship Republicans can always expect an equal—or in some cases, outsized—reaction from left-wing student groups, attracting local media attention to their events and, they argue, spreading their message much farther than they could on their own.

Western College Republicans generally strive to be a visible, vocal presence on campus both during and outside their events. Since the early 2000s, when a new leader took over a bedraggled group of "ten people sitting around, literally talking about how they hated Hillary Clinton" (Chuck Kelley, Western Flagship), the organization has been equated with provocation. The group sells T-shirts designed to irk their Democratic counterparts ("Join Us Now Or Work For Us Later") and regularly dispatches campus-wide emails that this same leader described as calculated to drive campus liberals wild. College Republican members are highly critical of all things political at Western Flagship, from what they see as the campus's over-the-top environmentalism to its student-run Funds Board, which the Eastern group describes as typically bloated big government.

Even those Western conservatives who do not think provocative action is a good idea understand it to be necessary on the Western Flagship campus, which they describe as absurdly liberal. As one conservative student explained, "the College Republicans are really important . . . because they provide, in my opinion, really the only contrast to the professors. They're the other side" (Hunter Devine, Western Flagship). Thus, he elaborated, even if he disliked the combative tactics of events like the Affirmative Action Bake Sale—or Catch an Illegal Alien Day (where students marked as illegal immigrants are mock-imprisoned by citizen students) or the Global Warming Beach Party (where environmental concerns are ridiculed with suntan oil and beer)—he participated in the Western College Republicans and adapted to their style in order to counteract the effects of a liberal professoriate.

As we further describe below, Western Flagship's College Republicans share with those at Eastern a view of themselves as providing a necessary counterpoint to the marginalization of conservative viewpoints on campus. However, the manner in which they go about redressing this imbalance by creating a conservative presence demonstrates a stark difference. College Republicans at Western make clear that "the only way to get that message out is to do something controversial." This student continued:

Sometimes you have to do something controversial to get your word out. If we had just released a press release saying, "By the way, we don't support Affirmative Action," no one would have cared . . . The day that we announced [the 2007 Bake Sale], I had about five newspapers call me for interviews . . . We got a lot of press coverage out of it, and that's exactly what we wanted. (Kody Aronson, Western Flagship)

Thus the majority of College Republicans at Western see provocation as by far the most effective, if not the only possible strategy for bringing attention to the conservative perspective. This stands in sharp contrast to the style of their fellow College Republicans at Eastern.

EASTERN ELITE COLLEGE REPUBLICANS: A CIVILIZED PRESENCE

Though likewise located on a campus and within an area known for its liberal leanings, Eastern Elite's College Republicans have little in common with their peers at Western Flagship in terms of political style. Their relationship with the campus and its community is far from combative (at least to the extent that *any* level of conservatism could be seen as noncombative on their campus); instead, the College Republicans at Eastern emphasize the importance of civilized discourse in spreading their message. Even though they occasionally bring in potentially divisive or controversial speakers, members of the College Republicans give credit to their liberal peers for their respectful audience at these events. Describing one such invited speaker, a prominent member of the George W. Bush administration, one student said, "When he came, obviously . . . [students] challenged him on the Iraq War and [were] asking tough questions. But it was fine. That's the whole point of being on campus, seeing that debate and having it. It was civil" (Calvin Coffey, Eastern).

Indeed, the Eastern Republicans seem to see it as part of their mandate not only to create a space for conservative ideas on campus but also to allow the merit of those ideas to be debated openly, as a possible invitation to less conservative listeners to see the wisdom of their political stances. This is reflected in the type of events they put on: In addition to inviting speakers, the Eastern College Republicans fundraise for conservative causes, write op-ed pieces in the mainstream campus newspaper, host debates with the Eastern Democrats club, and hold social events (including a popular annual bowling night with the Democrats). While other campus conservative groups at Eastern learn through their occasional mistakes what not to do—such as papering the campus with flyers depicting developing fetuses, which generated hostility and controversy for the

Pro-Life group—the Eastern College Republicans did not appear to take such incautious steps. Reflecting on the type of events the Eastern Republicans see as most successful, a recent group leader said, "I think good events are events that are intellectually stimulating, that influence the people that are there that may not be Republicans [and] that will cause them to question their beliefs or their political views" (Derek Yeager, Eastern).

This interest in winning over other students, and even faculty, through persuasion rather than provocation is seen even in events that might appear more similar to those conducted by Western students. Describing an anti–illegal immigration rally that the Eastern College Republicans organized, one student recalled that "we had a few signs 'We Support *Legal* Immigration.' Again, we couched our campaign using terms that are not like, oh, 'Kick the Hispanics Out' or something like that" (Kyle Lee, Eastern; emphasis added). Eastern College Republicans carefully selected the frames they used in this event to highlight a less provocative style than students on other campuses might use. Although students at Western always point out that they also provide valuable information at their events (for example, handing out pamphlets at their Global Warming Beach Party that explained their opposition to the Kyoto Treaty) and claim these are effective vehicles for recruiting members, their provocative spectacles appear to be oriented more toward inciting nonconservative students than converting them.

Eastern College Republicans' interest in gaining the support of their peers by not offending them is related to another concern that was not seen among the College Republicans at Western: the opportunity to foster future leaders for the national Republican Party. Discussing the function of the College Republicans, another recent group leader mentioned "being part of the broader discussion . . . as to where the Republican Party goes from here. Bringing in speakers to talk to young Republicans in our club about what they believe about the Republican Party and how they think it should be structured and what they believe is important going forward" (Darius Norton, Eastern). Though students at Western are attuned to gaining the attention of local media and politics, they do not share this sense of themselves as significant to the national arena. As we discuss below, this difference is distinctly related to students' understandings of their campuses and their future career paths.

Campus Cultures and Dominant Styles

The dominant conservative political styles of provocation and civilized discourse seen, respectively, on the Western Flagship and Eastern Elite campuses are more than simply a function of the individuals within the student-run organizations. They are the result of shared local culture through interaction, much of which gets worked out in informal conversations and negotiations about what is the appropriate group style on each campus. This can be gleaned from the fact that, despite the transitory nature of student leadership—with new freshmen coming in every year, and seniors graduating—these organizational styles endure over the course of multiple cohorts of students. As a former editor of the conservative newspaper at Eastern put it, each new cohort's group leaders need to "learn" what works for their group (Henry Quick, Eastern). Similarly, group members who try to change the direction of their group—for example, a recent leader of the Western Flagship College Republicans who attempted a more civilized style—find they face an uphill battle, inviting critiques from past organization officers.

Much of the dominant style on each campus can be attributed to the universities where these groups are found. Though comparable to other similar universities, Western and Eastern are two quite different types of campuses. Examining each school's reputation, as well as students' experiences with a variety of organizational arrangements—from their interactions with professors and peers in classrooms to their social life in the dorms—and their aspirations for the future reveals a logic to the dominant conservative styles in place on those campuses.

FUN WITH A PURPOSE—AND PROVOCATION—AT WESTERN

Students at Western Flagship go to a large state university with a reputation for being a party school, one where fun and recreation predominate in the local definition of what it means to be a college student. As indicated by sources such as *U.S. News and World Report*, Western Flagship is known for football, fraternities, and most of all, a good time. As a state school with mid-level admissions criteria and a party reputation, Western objectively does not sit atop the relational field of academia where elite intellectual or cultural capital is developed and reproduced. Conservative students indirectly refer to this as a problem when they share their perceptions of faculty's unprofessionalism on their campus. As we document elsewhere (Binder and Wood 2011, 2013), conservative students at Western talk at great length (compared with their Eastern counterparts) about their sense of being a marginalized population, which contributes enormously to their taste for provocative political action. Western conservatives are significantly more suspicious of their professors' motives in the classroom than are conservative students at Eastern: They castigate faculty as unreasonably politicized liberals who seem to be either clueless that their students might have different political commitments from their own or disdainful of said commitments, sometimes singling out particular students as "the conservative girl" in the lecture hall. Western interviewees described specific negative experiences that they or their acquaintances had had with faculty, such as feeling they had to write papers in such a way as to not betray their views and receive a punitive grade or to keep their thoughts to themselves in the lecture hall or in smaller discussion sections ("I didn't feel like it was a safe environment"; Christina Young, Western Flagship). Our interviewees mostly did not know individual professors well, and there was low esteem for the faculty in general. Large class sizes—a hallmark of large state universities—contribute to this level of disregard.

Also contributing to Western conservative students' sense of political marginalization is a high level of suspicion about university structures. Conservative students at Western believe that the funding practices of their university are strongly biased against them, such that they have to fight much harder than liberal clubs for monetary resources to bring their preferred speakers to campus and to organize other activities. Members of student groups like College Republicans at Western likewise have far darker assessments of their liberal classmates' potential to be fair and nonjudgmental interlocutors in discussions of political ideas. Perhaps because so few students at Western live on campus, where they can get to know one another in more intimate settings (the university guarantees first-year housing only), there is greater self-segregation. Whether students opt to live in off-campus apartments or join the Greek system, the net result appears to be political homophily, and students do not have to socially encounter, let alone interact with, people who are unlike themselves politically. This creates a weak set of community norms for friendly and respectful political debate.

Further, conservatives at Western are confident that regardless of their future paths, they will be able to write off their exploits as the folly of youth on an as-needed basis. There is a sense among Western students that college represents a liminal stage in which "anything goes" and a wider range of behavior is acceptable. In addition to allowing these students to strategically create a conservative presence on campus that would be unacceptable at other schools, this sensibility allows conservatives to mix the pleasures of being a college student with their politics, as one student described:

> Yeah, I mean the best part about standing up in front of a group, people that are protesting you or . . . calling you names, whatever, is that besides believing you're on the right side of the issue, it does give you a charge, gives you a certain

energy. And you know, it's fun . . . you're standing up for what you believe in and you're not backing down just because someone else tells you that you're wrong . . . if you wake up and come to school in the morning and someone calls you a bigot, you know you're going to have a good day. (Karl Hayes, Western Satellite)

This sensibility extended to their understanding of the wider political arena. As one student explained, "the function of a lot of College Republicans chapters is that we are the ones who are crazy enough and don't have as much to lose to make points that the national party really can't afford to make" (Bryan Carhart, Western Satellite). Thus conservatives at a school like Western can choose to take advantage of their status as college students in order to "get away with" hosting controversial speakers or otherwise raising the hackles of campus liberals.

Various aspects of Western's undergraduate structures and campus-wide culture help to make the "gotcha" provocative style of conservatism appealing to these students. The institutional attributes of large classes, relatively little personalized faculty interaction, off-campus housing, and student-run funding of student activities and clubs, combined with conservative students' sense that the surrounding college town exists inside a liberal bubble and their belief that being at Western is supposed to be a "fun" experience, together create an environment in which a civilized political style would hardly make sense. This constellation of factors also helps us understand Western conservatives' more extensive connections to national conservative organizations like the Young America's Foundation, which are thrilled to lend monetary and ideological support to provocative conservatism. *Someone*, our interviewees said, needs to provide an opposing point of view, and they must do whatever it takes to be heard within what the students perceive as their overwhelmingly liberal milieu: best to connect with an organization that sponsors conservative action "battle plans" and a speakers' stable that features Dinesh D'Souza, Ann Coulter, and Bay Buchanan, and one that will happily hand over funds when the liberal university is unwilling or unable to write the checks.

In sum, students' emphasis on blending fun, pragmatism, and political partisanship creates the Western campus's dominant style of provocative conservatism. The provocative group style fits in with Western conservatives' understandings of themselves, both generally as *college* students, more specifically as *Western* college students, and most centrally as *conservative* Western college students.

PLANNING FOR THE FUTURE AT EASTERN

Eastern Elite University holds a different place in the field of higher education than does Western, which is strongly reflected in our interview data. Eastern is known above all for academics, having a reputation as an elite school even among elite schools, with a lengthy roster of famous alumni in numerous fields. Conservative students entering Eastern are keenly aware of its place within the institutional pantheon, as are their parents and peers. As one student explained, "There is an incredible mystique to [it] . . . It was like this wonderful place where everyone was really smart and talked all the time, learning these great ideas" (Keaton Townsend, Eastern).

Eastern conservatives cited numerous reasons for wanting to attend the school, with the most common being faculty and academics, their future careers, and interestingly, their fellow Eastern students. These undergraduates share an understanding that their peers are talented and exceptional people who are destined to follow the tradition of Eastern alums and become leaders in their fields. Students anticipated building extensive social capital, as one student described:

> There's something to be said for studying with these people and entering into that crowd. It's not for everybody. But I think, I mean before I went to Eastern I think I did fairly clearly think that that was what I should do, and that *was* sort of what I wanted to do. So it was more a matter of Eastern's the best and I *wanted* to go to the best. (Nate Quinn, Eastern; emphasis in original)

This future-oriented perspective, combined with a strong sense of Eastern's importance as an institution, colors the interactions of Eastern conservatives at every level, including their political style. They are interested in having lengthy conversations with their exceptional peers and learning from them.

The many well-resourced subenvironments on the Eastern campus provide plentiful opportunities for such conversations to happen. Eastern conservatives report feeling much more at home on their campus than do conservatives at Western. The housing system at Eastern, where students live with their classmates on campus for much of their college careers, seems to modulate conservative students' willingness to engage in high-profile, provocative action, as do the dining halls where students congregate night after night to discuss politics with their worthy peers. Conservative students' assessment of faculty's world-class prominence in their fields all but obviates the need to ferret out bias in the classroom, and they have little interest in potentially embarrassing themselves by protesting in the quad. Eastern's vast monetary resources further contribute to conservative students' comparatively civilized tone. Our interviewees were adamant that they suffered no funding shortfalls for their student activities when compared with their liberal counterparts. As a consequence of these campus characteristics and still others (an extensive freshman orientation; many campus traditions that bring all students together at different points in the year), Eastern conservatives feel that they are part of the university's deep and manufactured special community.

This sense of being part of a small, special community plays a large role in the university's reputation, which many of the interviewees acknowledged as opening doors for them socially and for future careers. An understanding that community members uphold this esteemed institutional legacy informally bars most Eastern students from adopting a provocative style. Even those students at Eastern who came to college with a background in watching the Fox News channel and picketing Planned Parenthood learn the civilized style; the few students who choose more provocative tactics show restraint in fighting their battles in student newspaper columns rather than on the quad—although the latter *do* show a high degree of agency in being even that provocative.

The institutional characteristics present at Eastern contribute not only to a respectful community of students, faculty, and alumni but also to pressures for Eastern undergraduates to further bolster the institution's reputation through their own success in elite careers. Compared with Western, few interviewees expressed interest in baldly political careers. Instead, politically inclined conservative students hoped for positions where they might be able to draw on their passion for politics (for example, as high-powered policymakers) but where political affiliation was not definitional to the position.[7] Overall, the strongest consensus among Eastern conservatives' speculations on their futures was about their likelihood of success in their chosen career. Whether set on one path or selecting from a variety of options, virtually none expressed doubt in their abilities to enter into or prosper in their given field. Much of this can probably be attributed to their status as Eastern Elite students. The university's reputation in some sense preceded them; as Eastern students, these undergraduates did not feel that college is a time where "anything goes" and that inappropriate behavior can be written off as youthful folly. Instead, Eastern conservatives in some sense needed to fulfill their half of the bargain; just as their Eastern diploma and social networks would assist them in their future careers, so too did they need to comport themselves in a manner worthy of the Eastern imprimatur.

These factors combine to explain the supremacy of civilized discourse as the dominant style of conservatism at Eastern, in spite of its being at odds with the prevailing styles in current Republican politics and well-funded national conservative organizations. As a College Republicans leader explained, this style is best suited to the type of student found at this university:

> At Eastern . . . the way that you get to students is much different, because people are willing to go to a discussion seminar with an eminent academic, or people are willing to come to a speaking session . . . with a big-name speaker. You don't have to sort of be out on [the quad] protesting in order to get people's attention. I think that gives us the ability to make a more nuanced and supported argument than some other people on other campuses. (Darius Norton, Eastern)

Although Eastern students understand that a markedly different conservative style often is deployed on other campuses to gain attention, conservatives at Eastern adopt a unique repertoire because their highbrow fellow students will best receive their message in this way.

Eastern conservatives also expressed concern that provocative action is not suited to conservatism in general. In explaining why he opts for a style of civilized provocation rather than activism, one student said:

> I mean there's something inherently radical about that [kind of activism] and not quite with the conservative aesthetic . . . I mean we bring in speakers and they're provocative as far as being a conservative at Eastern is provocative. But it's nothing for its own sake. It's in order to have a good discussion about some issue that would otherwise be ignored at school. (Drew Metcalfe, Eastern)

This concern, which underscores the type of high-culture discourse drawn on by Eastern conservatives, is not seen among students at Western. As described above, there the focus is on provoking rather than persuading their liberal peers.

As one might expect, conservative students at Eastern have a different idea of fun than their peers at Western. Though one student acknowledged that provocative actions are "fun I guess" (Nate Quinn, Eastern), the majority of Eastern conservatives hardly relished the thought of aggravating their peers:

> We have a bowling night against the Democrats. I think that kind of fun is more productive than fun that involves you screaming at the top of your lungs at someone. I enjoy a good debate . . . But I like debating when I can get my message across in a way that I can feel like people are respecting [me]. It is no fun for me to have

people walk by and leer or gaze at me or yell at me that I am bigoted or whatever it is, because I'm not . . . I would rather argue with them in a more reasonable level to say here is why I'm not and here is why we can agree to disagree, but I will not respect you calling me something that I am not. (Darius Norton, Eastern)

This fits in not only with the dominant style of conservatism on campus but, again, also with Eastern students' understanding of themselves as part of the Eastern community and of themselves and their peers as significant within the wider scope of U.S. culture. The identity of being a college student—and having college as a liminal space in which to enjoy a broader scope of acceptable behavior—appears to be trumped for them by their identity as *Eastern* college students. For the most part, Eastern conservatives are unwilling to compromise their cultural and social capital or their futures as elite professionals in order to engage in what they consider to be more lowbrow forms of provocation.

Conclusion

Conservative students at Eastern Elite University and at the Western Flagship campus of the Western Public University system exist in a larger institutional environment that is home to an overarching political logic—the Republican Party's current loyalty to movement conservatism (Blumenthal 2009; Tanenhaus 2009)—as well as a variety of ideological and stylistic positions beneath the level of that one dominant logic. Students on both campuses are aware of this complex repertoire of available discourses in the world at large but are, themselves, enabled and constrained by the distinctive group style shared locally on their campuses. While we do find certain students on each campus who engage in a "submerged style" at their university, our point here is to look at the dominant styles in place on the two campuses. On each campus, some elements of the national discourses get labeled as appropriate by the local conservative group style, so much so that particular conservative types dominate cohort after cohort, while other styles of conservative identity do not gain much traction. There is variation across these campuses in what is considered to be generally legitimate conservative identity and action, informed by students' understandings of themselves as college students; their involvement in campus clubs, classes, faculty's office hours, and other subenvironment settings; their ties through these organizations and/or individually to national organizations; and their sense of what they are likely to be doing in their future careers. Each of these components is connected to varying levels of social and cultural capital—

both the students' own burgeoning sense of themselves as endowed with particular types of capital and each university's location in the relational field of academia.

While elements such as students' backgrounds—particularly social class—and their self-selection into specific universities have important effects, we contend that the institutional environments and subenvironments found on these campuses provide greater explanatory power than those precollege factors alone. In particular, social class background and previous political styles cannot account for the consistency of the differences between these campuses. Students and alumni/alumnae in our sample at both schools varied substantially in terms of their class backgrounds, came from many different regions of the country, and described differing styles of political engagement prior to matriculation. We thus argue against the position—advanced by scholars who locate students' college politics firmly in their precollege attributes (Highton 2009)—that we are simply seeing students' early proclivities reinforced on whatever campus they attend. Instead, we can make a strong argument for campuses as a significant force in encouraging the production of different kinds of cultural capital, and indeed *political* capital, and for these resulting in distinct types of outcomes for students. Just as conservative students at Eastern—regardless of class of origin—learn dispositions that enable them to thrive in elite national political environments, Western conservatives who find themselves in similar positions through internships or conferences often become disillusioned. However, these Western students are able to prosper in the contentious political environment of the state where their university is located, both before and after graduation.

Our findings are important from the vantage point of both sociological theory and the study of American political life. First, we pay attention to empirical terrain that far too few social scientists have explored: the formation of political ideas and style among conservatives at the college level. To the extent that social scientists have studied collegiate politics, they have been far more interested in the origins of ideas on the left than those on the right. We also locate the experiences of politically active college students in several campus organizational structures, each of which provides additional layers of meaning to their unfolding political ideologies. We find that students are active agents in their cultivation of political styles—they talk about and debate their political ideas, they experiment with other styles, they hone their identities. But they are also restricted in their individual proclivities by the organizational resources and cultural repertoires differentially available to them, in interaction with one another, and within a relational field of cultural and social capital. We argue that styles of campus conservatism are much less the result of natural inclinations that students simply bring with them to campus, or a mirror of students' social class origins, than dispositions developed on campus—they are the products of interaction in organizations, built up through multiple networks of shared culture. Marshaling rich data from these campuses, we extend theory on political socialization, group styles, cultural capital, the reproduction of elite status in higher education, and the origins of political styles and discourse.

This is important in itself, but our study also helps make sense of the battles currently taking place in the United States, in the midst of political contentiousness surrounding immigration, the environment, the national debt, and numerous other debates in the larger body politic. The tensions we see among students over populist provocation and elite civilized discourse are being played out not only on college campuses but in the highest levels of government decision making, as well.

NOTES

This chapter is adapted from our book *Becoming Right: How Campuses Shape Young Conservatives* (Princeton University Press, 2013). We thank the Spencer Foundation Civic Learning and Action Initiative and the Academic Senate of the University of California, San Diego, for financial support for this project.

1. The names of campuses, campus organizations, and individual students and alumni are pseudonyms. Some identifying details have been altered to protect their anonymity.

2. We discuss these subordinate styles in our book (Binder and Wood 2013).

3. Other organizations sponsoring this conservative style include the Leadership Institute, David Horowitz's Students for Academic Freedom, and the Heritage Foundation.

4. We should note here that students select into specific universities with aspirations and senses of self already partly formed—they do, after all, choose to apply to and attend one university over another. Meyer (1977) even writes about "anticipatory socialization" that occurs for students entering elite colleges. Nonetheless, campuses clearly have an impact on students' future plans.

5. For example, to come up with specific descriptions of residential arrangements and student-to-faculty ratio and so on, we combined information from three public universities most like Western Flagship to describe Western Flagship, and three private universities most like Eastern Elite to describe Eastern Elite. This does not mean that we are arguing that either Eastern Elite or Western Flagship is representative of these schools.

6. Binder also conducted interviews with many individuals outside the two universities, particularly with leaders of conservative organizations that lend support to conservative students.

7. Eastern interviewees who adopted the submerged style of highbrow provocation were more likely to aspire to elite careers where their identity as *conservatives* was explicitly relevant (e.g., becoming journalists at national-level conservative publications).

PART FOUR

FORMATIVE PERIODS

CHAPTER SEVEN

Naturalizing Liberalism in the 1950s

ANDREW JEWETT

In the 1950s, Paul Lazarsfeld's pioneering analysis of the American professoriate's political commitments coincided with the consolidation of a substantial shift in those commitments. After the late 1930s, the political culture of the American academy changed as the Depression-era dynamics of economic recovery and antifascism gave way to a global struggle against communism. Most strikingly, social scientists increasingly celebrated American institutions and values rather than challenging them (Abbott and Sparrow 2007; Adcock 2007; Haney 2008; Isaac 2007; Jewett 2012; Wall 2008).[1]

Although this shift is typically described as a move toward the political center, we miss key features if we stick to the conventional left-right spectrum defined by views of state-market relations. Changes in political theory and rhetorical style shaped the establishmentarian tenor of the postwar social sciences as much as new economic policies. In this chapter, I explore a key feature of postwar academic culture, a widespread interpretive tendency that extended into the natural sciences and infuriated conservative and radical critics: liberal professors knit their own political views into the very fabric of reality and dismissed their political opponents as hopelessly out of touch with the world—perhaps even clinically insane (Cohen-Cole 2005, 2009). This realist stance, along with Keynesian economics and, in some circles, an emphasis on individual rights, set the tone of postwar academic liberalism (Fowler 1978; Pells 1985).

Postwar liberals portrayed natural and social scientists as the spokespersons for reality in the political process. They littered their writings with phrases like "history reveals," "experience tells us," "responsible observers agree," "the truth of the matter is," and "deeply ingrained in the structure of." Silently turning oughts into ises, these veiled normatives filled the academic discourses of the 1950s with a welter of "to be" verbs and passive, agentless phrasings. According to this necessitarian outlook, professionals with the proper training and technical skills could easily discern the meanings of social phenomena. Yet the realist stance was politically flexible. It united under the banner of liberalism scholars ranging from the critical Marxist émigré Theodor Adorno to the ardent New Dealer Arthur M. Schlesinger Jr. and the proto-conservative Daniel Boorstin. Postwar liberalism assigned to key components of Cold War political thought the implicitly normative quality that Boorstin termed "givenness."

Practitioners of science and technology studies have theorized and chronicled such processes of rhetorical naturalization, wherein actors unconsciously reinterpret human choices and values as structural features of an empirically given world (e.g., Hackett et al. 2008; Young 1981). Naturalization impulses figure centrally in the history of the scientific disciplines, which typically claim to identify the boundaries between those features of experienced reality that are open to human intervention and those that are not. To the extent that these scientific disciplines serve as sources of cultural, intellectual, and legal authority, major political consequences follow.

Here, I explore a series of overlapping modes of naturalization that operated among the American professoriate in the early Cold War years. Academic liberals projected the core values of postwar liberalism onto five aspects of natural or social reality: individual biology, psychological maturity, American political culture, Western civilization, and a distinctive set of modern institutional structures. In each case, a potent adjective—human, mature (or healthy), American, Western, or modern—performed the normative work that the term "liberal" would have done in a more open and self-reflective political discourse. My analysis of each naturalization strategy focuses on a few key texts that, while not necessarily the most influential among disciplinary professionals, both embodied the central claims of that dynamic and spoke to a broad, educated audience. A final section further elucidates the postwar cluster of naturalization strategies by indicating how liberal professors hoped to change the minds of students and how they portrayed Senator Joseph McCarthy and other anticommunists on the right. My intention throughout is not to posit timeless characteristics of the professoriate as such but simply to describe certain contingent features of mainstream academic thought in the "long 1950s" and to explore their political ramifications.

Most importantly, the naturalization moves that were so common in postwar academia allowed liberal professors to describe themselves—and see themselves—as objective and nonpartisan, even as they threw their intellectual weight behind the policies of Truman, Eisenhower, and especially Kennedy.[2] Postwar academic liberals largely eschewed normative arguments for their political views—arguments explaining why Americans *should* embrace New

Deal liberalism—and hewed instead to the naturalizing assertion that the political structures created by Roosevelt comported uniquely well with human nature and contemporary industrial conditions. "Within the limits set by industrial democracy," the Columbia University historian Jacques Barzun (1952a) characteristically cautioned, "any proposed change must fit such facts as are immovable and must suit such needs as are widespread and genuine" (76). Leading postwar scholars agreed with Barzun that, in the wake of industrialization, humanity's very survival depended on embracing welfare state liberalism (Gilman 2003).

Other words also performed important political work in the Cold War era, for both defenders and critics of postwar liberalism. For example, commentators stuffed all manner of normative content into the terms "civilized," "democratic," and "free" during the 1950s. But the adjectives "human," "mature," "American," "Western," and "modern," along with the accompanying naturalization strategies, defined the conceptual space of postwar professorial liberalism. Not coincidentally, these terms also marked important axes along which left and right critics would challenge postwar liberalism with ever-greater effectiveness after 1960. As the 1960s and 1970s would reveal, radicals and especially conservatives retained sufficient power to block the further spread of the postwar complex of liberal ideas and institutions. Indeed, the naturalization strategies employed by liberal professors in the early Cold War years helped to create the intellectual and cultural conditions for the left-wing backlash of the 1960s and the broader, slower-moving reaction from the right that reshaped American politics by the 1980s.

Human Nature

Most of the postwar naturalization strategies operated at an extremely abstract level, presenting liberal policies as deductions from lofty principles such as individual dignity and the value of diversity. Such values can justify any number of policy approaches, whether conservative, liberal, or radical. Yet the relatively generic values that postwar scholars projected onto reality meshed easily with a form of liberal humanism that described the New Deal state as the needed instrument for harmonizing individual freedom with material prosperity.

This dynamic can be seen in the work of many biologists, who expressed the postwar naturalization impulse in its most literal form. They updated for an age of social diversity the long-standing practice of deriving a vision of the ideal society from human physiology. Yale's Edmund W. Sinnott wrote in 1945 that "tough-minded" moderns instinctively doubted all established institutions and claims to authority and could not be moved by "abstract appeals," "declarations of the rights of man," or "panegyrics upon liberty." Thus, he reasoned, "any plan for human society must have a sponsorship transcending the changing and fallible wisdom of mankind. It must conform to nature and her laws, must be in harmony with the very structure of the universe itself. In short, it must be grounded on scientific fact rather than passion, emotion or intuition." Fortunately, Sinnott continued, the core democratic tenets of "freedom, progress and the worth of individuals" flowed from "the fundamental character of protoplasmic structure and activity" (62–63). Other prominent biologists joined Sinnott in finding evidence for their political commitments in the natural world (Allee 1951; Dobzhansky 1956; Emerson 1954; Muller 1958).

Sinnott's particular derivation of political prescriptions from human biology, which he developed in several books during the 1950s, rested on a distinction between a materialistic, deterministic interpretation of human behavior and one that deemed the individual morally free and self-determining. Mid-twentieth-century liberals frequently identified biological determinism as the intellectual root of both laissez-faire capitalism and Soviet communism, arguing that it led governments to stress material comfort at the expense of individuals' higher needs—including the need for meaningful democratic participation.[3] Sinnott sought to break the link in the public mind between science and determinism by arguing that all living entities—from human beings down to sea sponges, pine trees, and even slime molds—guided their own behavior by projecting purposes and choosing ends (Sinnott 1950, 1951, 1953, 1955, 1956, 1957).[4]

Sinnott's emphasis on the purposive character of life justified an argument that dated back to the late nineteenth century and took firm hold in the American social sciences between the wars: that the human species had moved onto a separate track of cultural evolution wherein culture replaced biology as the primary determinant of behavior and human decisions became the motor of social change. Human beings set the direction of the cultural process by articulating and pursuing goals in accordance with consciously held values (Sinnott 1953, 85–86; see also Cravens 1978; Degler 1991). Sinnott thought the needed values comported with Christian teachings. "Love is the climax of all goal-seeking, protoplasm's final consummation," he wrote. "To love your neighbor as yourself is the only basis for human relationships" (Sinnott 1955, 155). For Sinnott, biology validated a society in which individuals, busily projecting their purposes without excessive interference by an authoritarian state, welcomed their differences and aimed at the highest development for all.

In *On Being Human* (1950), the Rutgers anthropologist Ashley Montagu drew a distinction between cooperation and competition out of biology in a different manner. According to Montagu, who was widely known for his antiracist writings, scientists could prove that "there are certain values for life which are not matters of opinion but which are biologically determined" (54). Chief among these was the lesson of universal brotherhood (109). "Man does not want to be independent, free, in the sense of functioning independently of the interests of his fellows," Montagu declared. "This kind of negative independence leads to lonesomeness, isolation, and fear. What man wants is that positive freedom which follows the pattern of life as an infant within the family—dependent security, the feeling that one is a part of a group, accepted, wanted, loved and loving" (80).[5] The experience of childhood dependency persists in deep organismic memory and provides both a model and an impetus for social relations (30). The "tissues of every organism," Montagu asserted, "remember their dependency and interdependency" (30) from early childhood and seek to maintain or recapture that state. Every fiber of being points toward loving cooperation, whereas aggressive competition is a learned trait alien to the species' biological heritage (92).

This dichotomy of cooperation and competition and the associated naturalizing claim that "humanity has moral goodness built into it as insistently and biologically as hunger" (Robertson 1956, 174) dated back to the Progressive Era and continued to find adherents in the postwar universities. After the 1930s, however, much of the academic mainstream moved toward a rights-based liberalism that clearly distinguished American democracy from Soviet communism as well as laissez-faire capitalism. They held that a general, universal, and prepolitical right to individual self-determination authorized a suite of specific "human rights" standing prior to all concrete political systems (Ciepley 2006; Jewett 2012).[6]

The Columbia paleontologist George Gaylord Simpson offered a biologically grounded version of rights-based liberalism in his 1949 blockbuster *The Meaning of Evolution*. Like so many liberals of his era, Simpson favored a polity in which science set the broad outer boundary of normative discussions of policy questions. Ironically, however, he arrived at that political conclusion by criticizing biological determinism in its usual form. Simpson posited an incontrovertible principle of "self-responsibility": a "nondelegable" obligation to determine individually one's own actions and even values (318–319). This principle stemmed in turn from the very fact that "the workings of the universe cannot provide any automatic, universal, eternal, or absolute ethical criteria of right and wrong" (345). According to Simpson, the moral indeterminacy of the world generated a corresponding duty "to recognize the integrity and dignity of the individual and to promote the realization or fulfillment of individual capacities" (315) for all members of the species. Simpson presented both human rights and a program of global economic development as outgrowths of the solemn obligation of moral responsibility borne by the occupants of a universe that met their chosen purposes with an implacable ethical neutrality.[7]

At the same time, Simpson used a strong assertion of scientific objectivity to convert his principles of self-determination, tolerance, and human flourishing into an "ethic of knowledge" (313) that demanded deference to professional experts. He argued that granting authority to anything other than empirical evidence entailed attempting the impossible: delegating self-responsibility to another person or group. By contrast, in hewing to the empirical findings of the scientist one did not alienate one's responsibility and bend to the will of others; one simply obeyed—voluntarily, of course—the dictates of reality itself. Simpson's expansive ethic of responsibility thus boiled down to a simple imperative to promote and heed the work of scientific experts and to eschew the alternative decision mechanisms of "pure intuition," "authoritarian dogma," "revelation," and "emotional reaction" (315).

Turning to the more concrete side of politics, Simpson steered the usual course between totalitarianism and laissez-faire. Under each, he contended, the individual abdicated—to a ruling party or to the market—the "responsibility to choose what he considers right directions for social and for biological evolution" (330). Between the poles, Simpson saw the biologically correct path: a "socialized democracy" featuring "controlled capitalism without improper exploitation" (322).[8] Science, he argued, could harmonize collective action with individual freedom by producing a body of knowledge about the general direction of cultural evolution on which all interpreters could agree without coercion. In his view, this unforced consensus would leave plenty of room for individual and group diversity. The citizens of Simpson's ideal democracy would choose freely from the range of theological and philosophical frameworks—"reading[s] of meaning into the history of life" (339)—that had proven compatible with research findings, just as they did with policy orientations. In his view, empirical evidence rarely validated a single set of policies, let alone a full-blown religious outlook. Yet science, by revealing the contours of reality—including the inescapable fact of individual interpretive responsibility—set the terms for both political debate about what should be done and philosophical-theological debate about the meaning of it all. Like Sinnott and Montagu, but via a different path, Simpson found an apparently inarguable justification for postwar liberalism in scientific teachings about the human organism.

Psychological Maturity

Many psychologists and anthropologists adopted a closely related naturalization strategy in the early Cold War years by making assertions about the character of the normal human being and the implications for politics. These figures embedded the normative content of postwar liberalism in the concept of psychological maturity and an array of associated adjectives: "mature," of course, but also "adult," "responsible," and, most potent of all, "healthy." Liberal theorists of maturity suggested that an inexorable developmental process would, if left unblocked, produce adults attuned to the values and institutions of the New Deal order.

"The characteristic knowledge of our century is psychological," declared the City College of New York philosopher Harry Allen Overstreet in his widely read book *The Mature Mind* (1949). Overstreet identified "psychological maturity" as not only "the master concept of our time" but also the ultimate *telos* of all past philosophies and religions (14). He defined the "maturity concept" as the empirically grounded observation that "the business of man is to mature: to mature psychologically as well as physically, to mature along the line of what is unique in him and what he healthily shares with all his fellows, and to continue the maturing process throughout his life" (41) by creating ever-expanding bodies of knowledge and networks of social relations based on that knowledge (43). Overstreet attributed all of the world's ills to the immense and largely subterranean havoc wreaked on society by "child-minds" operating in adult bodies and enjoying adult privileges and powers (15). "*Not all adults are adult*," he stressed repeatedly (19).[9]

What form of society did the maturity concept entail? At one point, Overstreet implied that a truly human society would peg voting and other rights to psychological age rather than chronological age (20). Usually, however, he spoke of a meritocratic society wherein careers mapped onto innate talents. According to Overstreet, psychologists had proven that "a man is at his best when he is doing his best at what he can do best" (34). He further asserted that the democratic ideals of freedom and equality obliged Americans to provide this experience of maximal functioning to all by opening every career to talented individuals from any background (113). Overstreet spoke of an "unalienable right" to "grow in an environment conducive to growth" (75). Largely eschewing talk of the state's role in the economy, he differentiated American democracy from communism and laissez-faire conservatism by arguing that it alone could steer individuals into the jobs for which they were psychologically equipped.

The Berkeley psychologist Erik Erikson connected psychological maturity to social policy in a different manner, through the phenomenon of prejudice, in his influential book *Childhood and Society* (1950). Political debates were never far from Erikson's mind as he walked analysts and other readers through clinical case studies and anthropological observations that buttressed his modified Freudian approach. According to Erikson (1950), implementing genuine democracy and developing a healthy self were simply the collective and individual phases of a single, broad "evolution in conscience structure" (282). Political aberrations such as machine politics represented "a danger to the American identity, and thus to the mental health of the nation" (281; cf. Fromm 1955).

Indeed, Erikson (1950) held that political machines and other civic abnormalities had fueled both fascism and conservatism by preventing individuals across the West from developing personalities appropriate to the age of industry. Having bounced from Germany to Austria to Denmark before emigrating to the United States, Erikson insisted that only a coherent culture with clearly defined adult standards could instill a healthy sense of self in its young members through normal socialization processes rather than laborious therapeutic interventions (368). Those deprived of such forms of socialization became easy marks for aristocrats and reactionary church leaders, who were rapidly losing their social dominance but still wielded the main weapon of all successful ruling classes— namely, the "ruthless exploitation of infantile fears" (238). Against these threats, Erikson urged Westerners to imbue their children with "judiciousness," a mindset that was "tolerant of differences, cautious and methodical in evaluation, just in judgment, circumspect in action, and—in spite of all this apparent relativism— capable of faith and indignation" (371). Tracing the labor-management struggle and conflicts of political ideology to deep-seated patterns of prejudice ("prejudged values and dogmatic divisions" [371]), Erikson called for the formation of psychologically healthy citizens who were neither tempted to use their power to exploit those below them nor susceptible to exploitation by those holding power over them and could thus safely hold the positions of both strength and weakness that were required by modern democracies.

At Berkeley and elsewhere, many of Erikson's contemporaries—especially Jewish émigrés from Central Europe—joined him in defining Nazism and conservatism as parallel psychological diseases generated by the crisis of industrialization. The massive 1950 volume *The Authoritarian Personality*, written by the émigré social theorist Theodor Adorno and three other Berkeley scholars, codified this interpretation. Like Erikson's work, *The Authoritarian Personality* read political conflicts through the dichotomous psychological categories of judiciousness and prejudice, tracing both fascism and free-market conservatism to pathological mental rigidity. Famously ignoring communism, Adorno's group sought to identify the psychological conditions under which citizens would actively join the cause, or at least passively fail to resist, if American business leaders—like their German counterparts before them, the authors averred—adopted the fascist strategy of abridging democratic freedoms in the name of the people (7). Like other theorists of maturity, the authors described defective personalities as a dire threat to the nation and childrearing as the ultimate locus of social reform. Adorno wrote that democracy's fortunes rested entirely on whether children were "genuinely loved and treated as individual humans" (975). Grounded in reams of survey and interview data rather than Erikson's clinical cases and anthropological field notes, *The Authoritarian Personality* profoundly shaped the 1950s discourse on the relationship between psychological maturity and politics (Cohen-Cole 2009; Roiser 2001). Like Overstreet and Erikson, Adorno and his collaborators naturalized postwar liberalism by describing it as the normal response of psychologically healthy individuals to industrial conditions.[10]

American Consensus

It is harder to see naturalization processes when these involve the projection of political values onto social phenomena rather than biological or psychological characteristics. Yet the underlying dynamic is the same, and the effects can be enormously powerful. Whereas the above naturalization strategies rooted political commitments in the essential characteristics of the human person, viewed as either a biological organism or a psychological being, other 1950s liberals projected their values onto an idealized cultural or institutional matrix within which, they insisted, Americans already lived.[11] Commentators identified three different, though overlapping, aspects of social reality as the vectors for their ideals: a political culture found only in the United States, a broader cultural complex shared across "Western civilization," or a set of institutions that Americans used to distribute resources and careers. Each of these strategies portrayed modern liberalism as the expression of a fundamental condition of American life, a condition so firmly established as to be practically innate for those raised on the nation's soil.

The first version of this naturalization approach posited a deep-seated "liberal consensus" shared by all Americans since their earliest days on the continent (Brinkley 2001; Gilman 2003; Jewett 2012; Wall 2008). A celebratory attitude toward American culture was largely new in the postwar universities. Between the wars, most liberals in the social sciences and philosophy and many in the natural sciences had urged a sharp break with existing cultural configurations. In many cases, this critical stance carried into the late 1940s. Shortly after World War II, the demographer Philip M. Hauser (1946) characteristically complained that "our folkways, our mores and our institutions have not originated in the laboratories of the social scientist" (379). The agricultural economist Carl C. Taylor (1946) added that true democracy would emerge only when "scientific and expert knowledge" entered "the blood stream of the masses" and "the ideals of the intellectuals" shaped "the aspirations and desired standards of the common people" (386–87). By contrast, the liberal consensus orientation described the New Deal order as continuous with principles that had been foundational to American national life since the colonial era. In this portrait, there was no need for new values; Americans could solve their problems by simply rediscovering and implementing their deepest ideals.

Although the immediate theoretical roots of consensus liberalism lay in the "national character" concept pioneered by anthropologists and social psychologists in the 1940s—the view that a single personality type defined each national culture—political scientists and historians crafted its most influential expressions in the 1950s.[12] Yet Erikson (1950) also adopted the main tenets of consensus liberalism in *Childhood and Society*, illustrating the permeability of postwar naturalization strategies. In colonial America, he wrote, the combination of "Protestantism, individualism, and the frontier" (355) had fostered an egalitarian climate that produced "undogmatic people, people ready to drive a bargain and then to compromise" (276). Erikson contrasted these practical, genial Americans to Europe's "uncompromising ideologists," with their abstract, quasireligious, and thus bitterly contested politics (277). Postwar political scientists and historians routinely employed this contrast between temperamentally realistic Americans and dangerously utopian Europeans as an analytic tool. Like Erikson, they combined the concept of national character with the increasingly dominant assumption that the colonial experience had set the terms for contemporary American culture.

In the hands of its more celebratory advocates, such as the University of Chicago historian Daniel J. Boorstin and the Yale historian David M. Potter, the idea of an American cultural consensus threw the weight of the nation's very being on the side of a centrist politics that could shade over into conservatism. Surprisingly, given the Cold War setting, Boorstin's *The Genius of American Politics* (1953, 1; see also Gilman 2003, 65–66) denied that American ideals—more properly, Americans' lack of ideals—could be exported, because they had been produced by the intersection of a uniquely exploitable continent with "a peculiar and un-repeatable combination of historical circumstances." Boorstin described the entirety of American history as an experiential validation of the measured, anti-utopian sensibility of the conservative theorist Edmund Burke. "Our geography and history," Boorstin wrote, had instilled in Americans "the axiom that institutions are not and should not be the grand creations of men toward large ends and outspoken values; rather they are organisms which grow out of the soil in which they are rooted and out of the tradition from which they have sprung." By contrast, he continued, Europe had succumbed to the "romantic illusion" that "man can better his condition by trying to remake his institutions in some colossal image" (6–7).[13] Potter's *People of Plenty* (1954) likewise portrayed a people constitutionally—in both senses of the word—resistant to the abstract, ideological principles that threatened a politics of compromise and negotiation.

A much more ambivalent version of consensus liberalism emerged in the writings of the Harvard political scientist Louis Hartz and the Columbia historian Richard Hofstadter. A resigned, ironic tone that could verge on bitterness permeated their work. Hartz and Hofstadter identified the liberal consensus as a rigid constraint on American politics—a "national subjectivism" that rendered Americans incapable of grasping reality as it was (Hartz 1955, 306). Still, each held that the path to a more satisfying polity ran through the dominant form of liberalism, not around it. As Hartz (1955) put it, America's "natural liberal mind" (6), despite its monumental irrationality and oppressiveness, possessed a "power for transcending itself" (309) that was utterly absent in Soviet totalitarianism. Hartz (1955) and Hofstadter (1948), who were attracted to the common sense realism of the Burkean center and deeply worried by the persistence of utopian tendencies among their former interlocutors on the left, defended the New Deal order as the best system for the current stage of humanity's moral growth. Theirs was a naturalization approach with regrets, holding that a melioristic, individualistic form of liberalism was so deeply sunk in the soil of American culture that, for the time being, it functioned as a permanent structure and could not be challenged at its roots.

Consensus history also proved compatible with other varieties of postwar liberalism. The Harvard historian Arthur M. Schlesinger Jr., who in political terms stood between the proto-conservatives Boorstin and Potter and the disaffected socialists Hartz and Hofstadter, demonstrated the power of the consensus approach to shape even historical narratives that apparently contradicted it. Schlesinger's *The Vital Center* (1949) identified class conflict as the central dynamic in the nation's political history. A fierce partisan of the New Deal, Schlesinger followed his father, a leading Progressive historian, in describing the American past as one long clash between "the people" and narrow-minded business interests. Yet, he explained, social stability nonetheless prevailed because neither side viewed the struggle as a zero-sum affair; each sought to negotiate with, rather than eradicate, its opponents. According to Schlesinger (1949), the colonial experience and subsequent developments had fostered a practical, empirical mindset that steered the combatants toward compromises rather than winner-take-all political warfare. This practical orientation funneled class conflict into the arena of political negotiation, militating against a violent politics of abstract principles and fixed social blueprints.

As political historians and historically minded political scientists built up the school of consensus history, literary scholars and cultural and intellectual historians articulated the closely related concept of an "American mind" (Gleason 1984; 1992, 188–206; Marx 2005). Particularly revealing is the 1950 classic *The American Mind*, in which the Columbia historian Henry Steele Commager faced head-on the challenge of squaring the consensus paradigm with the dramatic political shifts of the previous half-century. He framed his narrative as an explanation of how "The Nineteenth-Century American" became "The Twentieth-Century American." Yet Commager argued that the similarities across the centuries outweighed the differences, even as he presented considerable evidence to the contrary. Employing a psychological analogy common at the time, he asserted that a nation's character, like that of an individual, took form in its youth— during the colonial period, in the American case. Commager acknowledged that subsequent generations had gone through major cultural contortions to accommodate their inherited views to modern science, industry, and city life. Indeed, his book described those changes at great length. But in the end, he insisted that the American mind of the twentieth century was essentially continuous with its nineteenth-century predecessor, despite the new "environment" in which it operated. The "American character" remained "substantially the same," wrote Commager; "the differences are quantitative and material rather than qualitative and moral" (409; cf. Commager 1951; Gabriel 1956).

This claim of historical continuity, which portrayed the New Deal as the embodiment of characteristically American values, was not the only politically consequential element of the liberal consensus / American mind approach. Equally powerful was its assertion of an "underlying cognitive unity that permeates all sectors of American life." Within this "basic unity," according to theorists, could be found many alternative "value orientations" that were "distinctly different" but shared a family resemblance (Gottlieb and Hodgkins 1963, 267). This postulation of an underlying cultural unity led Commager (1950) to identify "art, education, criticism, psychology, anthropology, business, science, technology, and a dozen other" areas of national life as merely "manifestations" of a coherent, underlying "American culture" (vii). According to such portraits, the nation hung together—literally thought and felt together—as a single psychic entity. That harmonious image, even divorced from claims about the determining influence of the colonial frontier experience, rendered both radicalism and conservatism fundamentally un-American. The emphasis on continuity across the centuries merely made the American consensus seem even deeper and less consciously chosen—a product of quintessentially human behavior in a highly congenial environment rather than a matter of contingent political choices. In short, it made postwar liberalism seem necessary and inevitable.

Western Civilization

Whereas consensus liberalism projected political commitments onto a primordial stratum of American experience, "Western civ" liberalism looked back to the classical world. Its advocates discerned a strong line of cultural continuity from ancient Greece, Rome, and Palestine through medieval and early modern Europe to the United States and Western Europe of their time (Allardyce 1982; Segal 2000).[14] In a typical expression, the philosopher Irwin Edman (1947), a stalwart of Columbia's fabled "Contemporary Civilization" course, cautioned his readers that the origins of democracy could not be found in the modern histories of England, France, and the United States. Its "human and moral meaning" (26) had instead taken shape in the ancient world. Edman's interest in the classical roots of liberal democracy resonated widely in the 1940s and 1950s. Although most theorists of Western civilization identified distinctive phases in its growth, all discerned "a culture that is historically one since the Greeks" (Barzun 1952a, 75).

The author of those words, Jacques Barzun, used the Western civilization framework to carve out space for the arts and literature at the heart of modern liberalism. However, he did so in a manner very different from the better-known "Great Books" project of the University of Chicago's Mortimer Adler. Barzun lambasted Adler's desire to reduce Western civilization to a single, spare set of philosophical tenets. According to Barzun (1952b), Adler's overly rationalistic canon offered a "joyless, dehydrated" portrait of "western man" (84). Barzun instead rooted Western civilization in a tense but fruitful dialectic of two ultimately incompatible elements: Adler's rationalism and the creative, imaginative energies that drove artistic production.[15] Although Barzun spent much of the 1950s writing detailed pieces on the history of musical forms rather than crafting a broad, synthetic narrative, his numerous publications in popular magazines (e.g., Barzun 1954a) and his very persona as an émigré Frenchman who adored baseball kept the vision of a unified, aesthetically tinged Western heritage on display for wide audiences. So, too, did his paean to American culture, *God's Country and Mine* (Barzun 1954b; see also Rubin 2006).

Other intellectual and cultural historians compiled massive textbooks for the "Plato to NATO" offerings that proliferated in American colleges and universities after 1940. Each tome listed innumerable details and conflicts while touting the basic unity and continuity of the overall picture. For example, Yale's Franklin Le Van Baumer (1952) stated in a well-known sourcebook that the events of the 1940s and 1950s had led Americans to finally recognize that their nation was "part of a much larger cultural whole" (9). Despite recounting major shifts in which the medieval "Age of Religion" had given way to the "Age of Science" and then the twentieth-century "Age of Anxiety" (9), Baumer held that the West had featured "the same culture" through the centuries (3). The Western civ textbooks posited a single "western mind" that extended across time and space, transcending national differences and historical changes as extensive as the Protestant Reformation, the emergence of democracy and capitalism, and the rise of modern science and industry (3; see also Allardyce 1982; Segal 2000).

Even natural scientists plumped for Western civilization after World War II. For example, the Harvard biologists Leigh Hoadley and George Wald joined humanistic colleagues such as the philosopher Raphael Demos, the literary critic I. A. Richards, and the historian Arthur M. Schlesinger Sr. in authoring one of the Western civ framework's most forceful and influential early statements: the "Redbook," a 1945 Harvard report formally titled *General Education in a Free Society* (Harvard University Committee 1945). The Harvard committee identified a crying need for "a unifying purpose and idea" in American higher education (43). Although the authors equated the "Western civilization" rubric with Adler-style "education in the great books" and ostensibly rejected it in favor of "the character of American society" as the needed central thread, they identified the American ideals of human freedom and dignity as inheritances from a "Western tradition" dating back to antiquity. "We are part of an organic process, which is the American and, more broadly, the Western evolution," wrote the committee. "Our standards of judgment, ways of life, and form of government all bear the marks of this evolution." The Redbook gave a powerful boost to Western civ liberalism by urging students and educators to "recognize the huge continuing influence alike on past and present of the stream of Jewish and Greek thought in Christianity" (45–46).

Postwar theorists routinely gave political specificity to such broad pronouncements by referring to Western civilization's area of influence as "the liberal world." In a particularly forthright statement, the City College of New York historian J. Salwyn Schapiro (1958) argued that the classical Greek heritage had finally revealed its true political meaning during the eighteenth-century Enlightenment, when liberalism had become "the accepted pattern of life" across the West (26). Western thought, Schapiro added, had then proceeded naturally through the evolutionary stages of classical liberalism and democratic liberalism (32–38) before achieving its highest expression as contemporary social liberalism: "the recognition by the government of its responsibility for the welfare of the 'small man'" (83). Schapiro described the American people as "now definitely committed to the Welfare State," the recalcitrant Republican Party having finally gotten on board with social liberalism (86).[16]

Social Structure

The final mode of postwar naturalization was much more institutionally specific than its counterparts. Its proponents argued that liberal—American or Western—values were manifested in a set of social structures that characterized all modern societies but had found their highest expression in the post–New Deal United States. Whereas the liberals who spoke of an American consensus or invoked Western civilization rarely explained how values such as freedom and dignity were institutionalized in the modern United States and focused instead on broad assertions about their wellsprings, the social-structural liberals identified a set of basic institutions as the carriers of those political values and largely bracketed the historical question of their origins.

Social-structural liberalism took shape in the newly named "behavioral sciences" of the 1950s, as political scientists and sociologists incorporated insights from psychology and anthropology into composite portraits of the American political and social system. Social-structural liberals asserted that this system of institutions had long since solved the puzzle that Schlesinger (1949) described as the task of the present day, namely "ordering society so that it will subdue the tendencies of industrial organization, produce a wide amount of basic satisfaction and preserve a substantial degree of individual freedom" (171). Many behavioral scientists argued that Americans had resolved this knotty political problem by bringing together four basic elements: first, the industrial mode of production; second, a career structure allowing all individuals to find positions suitable to their abilities (including political offices, where appropriate); third, a political apparatus sufficiently decentralized and fluid to allow each occupational group to pursue its interests peacefully rather than violently; and fourth, a deep commitment among the population to preserve these institutional arrangements. Interpreters of the American institutional structure typically described it as the purest expression of a social-political form—industrial modernity—that had already emerged across the democratic and communist nations and would soon spread to the developing "Third World" (Gilman 2003; Latham 2000).

In keeping with their assertion that American institutions already worked well, social-structural liberals proved surprisingly eager to label the United States a class society and even to urge readers to stay in their inherited places. "Social class permeates all parts of our existence," averred the anthropologist W. Lloyd Warner and two of his University of Chicago colleagues (Warner, Meeker, and Eells 1949).[17] Their textbook introduced readers to the "American status system," which made the mythic "American Dream" of equal opportunity available to many—though not all, they cautioned (v). Picking up on Henry A. Wallace's "Century of the Common Man" slogan, Warner and his coauthors argued that "un-Common superior and inferior men" were needed in order for "Common Men to exist as a class" (5). They introduced students to the operation of the American status system, explaining how readers could "adapt themselves to social reality and fit their dreams and aspirations to what is possible" (5; cf. Kahl 1953, 1957; Queen, Chambers, and Winston 1956).[18] Like many other behavioral scientists of the era, Warner and his coauthors presented accommodation to existing American structures as the only possible path to social progress.

Social-structural accounts revealed one of the few overt fault lines between the postwar modes of naturalization. To the Chicago sociologist Edward Shils (1954), the obvious stratification of American society undercut the purely psychological approach of *The Authoritarian Personality*. Political life, he protested, reflected much more than basic personality traits. Psychological analyses missed the "differentiated behavior in a system of roles" that channeled individual tendencies into routinized forms of practice (45). Indeed, Shils insisted that a liberal democracy would fall apart if operated solely by "democratic liberal personalities" of the kind celebrated by Adorno and his collaborators. Shils explained that the tasks and roles necessary for social order demanded a whole range of personality types, including even the authoritarian type, which he regarded as positively helpful in certain roles and relatively harmless in others (48–49). Shils found the psychological concerns of *The Authoritarian Personality* irrelevant to the task of ensuring democracy's stability under modern conditions. Like any other functioning society, he asserted, a democracy required leaders, followers, and experts suited to a vast range of specialized tasks.

Erikson's *Childhood and Society* (1954), however, showed that social-structural liberalism could comport with a psychological approach despite Shils's sense of a fundamental opposition between the two. Erikson argued that psychologically healthy interactions would lead to social relations of "mutual regulation" (219), not of substantive equality. In his view, the labor struggle and other powerful emancipatory movements that had arisen during the industrialization process aimed at "the recognition of the divided function of partners who are equal not because they are essentially alike, but because in their very difference they are both essential to a common function" (373). All cultures featured "special leader classes," Erikson declared. "In order to approach or experience integrity, the individual must know how to be a follower of image bearers in religion and in politics, in the economic order and in technology, in aristocratic living and in the arts and sciences" (232–33). Although Erikson sought a substantial redistribution of material resources, he did not foresee the flattening of all economic and social distinctions. Indeed, he held that equipping individuals with a judicious temperament would fit them for the detailed division of labor that characterized a healthy society.

The Barnard College sociologist Bernard Barber reiterated that a democracy required social distinctions as a condition of survival in the modern era. Although Harvard's Talcott Parsons and Columbia's Robert K. Merton were the key theorists of the "structural-functionalist" orientation that underlay social-structural liberalism, Barber, a student of Merton, played a crucial role in popularizing that approach. His 1957 textbook offered an accessible portrait of a stratified but psychologically satisfying and normatively unified society. Barber stated that every modern society faced the same problems of stability and addressed them through the same means: "a system of more or less differentiated roles." Of course, he continued, the occupants of these divergent roles did not and could not enjoy the same prestige, status, or monetary rewards. Rather, the roles represented nodes in a hierarchical structure that was functionally interrelated and sustained by normative judgments regarding the relative worth of the various pursuits. "Carpenters need kings," Barber summarized, "and kings, carpenters" (1–2).

Despite its emphasis on differentiation and specialization, social-structural liberalism meshed well with the idea of an American consensus or a coherent Western civilization. Barber explained that each society's judgments of worth—its divergent valuations of the various social roles—represented a shared framework of values that bound the society together by adding the powerful glue of like-mindedness to the thinner form of solidarity derived from functional interdependence. Without "common values" to regulate social interactions and determine social stations, Barber declared, society would degenerate into a Hobbesian "war of every man against every man" in which individuals treated one another solely as means to their selfish ends. Every successful society was a Durkheimian "moral community," its shared commitments ensuring that individuals felt justly placed within the overall structure of roles. Barber argued that, although the value orientations of various social groups inevitably diverged, these differences operated within an overarching normative consensus. That consensus produced cultural and social institutions that shaped personality formation so as to harmonize individual needs with the conditions of societal stability by fitting individuals into the functional roles for which they were best suited (2).

Making Students Liberal and Critics Crazy

All five of the naturalization modes located certain values and institutions of postwar liberalism prior to politics and assumed that a political system needed to incorporate them in order to be normatively valid and functionally successful. In short, they deemed liberalism—like the human rights that many postwar liberals also invoked—objectively true rather than simply a good idea. From this perspective, liberalism and conservatism appeared to be entirely different kinds of entities: apples and oranges, not mirror-image opposites. The distinction between the two was the distinction between reality and ideology, truth and lies, rather than left and right.

This approach portrayed liberals as nonideological, despite their vigorous commitment to one of the contending forces in the political arena. In their eyes, liberalism operated on a different level from party politics and the details of governance. No mere set of policy prescriptions or ideological preferences, liberalism was instead a spiritual outlook or character type—an orientation toward experience, toward one's fellow citizens, and toward truth itself. To be sure, many scholars argued that in an industrial age, the liberal attitude identified an extensive suite of welfare provisions as the only means of providing a dignified existence for all. Still, they presented the welfare state as a mere deduction from a thoroughly nonpartisan and essentially human ethical tradition. To the endless irritation of conservatives and radicals alike, liberal professors of the 1950s routinely charged that their political opponents mistook or denied the nature of the human person and that American social and political institutions, as they de-fined them, faithfully reflected human nature.

The vision of postwar liberalism as a spiritual outlook rather than a political platform came through most clearly in the meanings ascribed to the venerable concept of liberal education after World War II. Professors of the era called openly and without self-consciousness for "education in liberalism" (Harvard University Committee 1945, 57). They prided themselves on their ability to move students' beliefs and values in a particular direction and saw this ability as central to the operation of modern society. Yet these academic liberals believed that they were instilling broad-mindedness and combating ideological rigidity, not making politicians, party operatives, or ideologues. To most postwar advocates, liberal education meant turning students into nonconservatives and nonradicals—and nonfundamentalists and non-Catholics as well.

The impulse to educate for liberalism informed the controversy surrounding the so-called Jacob Report of 1957. *Changing Values in College*, penned by the peace activist Philip E. Jacob, caused great consternation among commentators on higher education because it claimed that collegiate study had no perceptible liberalizing effect. According to Jacob, American students were not assimilat-ing the needed "civilizing values," despite the best efforts of the professoriate (xi). They remained *"gloriously contented"* with the surrounding society, mouth-ing platitudes about intellectual freedom and diversity but in fact conforming blindly to the prevailing beliefs (101). Rather than learning to think freely, Jacob contended, the students swapped their idiosyncrasies for the genial relativism of the professional class. Outside a few distinctive institutions such as Antioch, Bennington, and Sarah Lawrence (100), he lamented, "American college students today tend to think alike, feel alike and believe alike" (12).

The Jacob Report prompted vigorous rebuttals. It directly contradicted a well-known study by the left-leaning psychologist Theodore M. Newcomb (1943)—carried out at Bennington—which found that undergraduate course-work profoundly altered the average student's mindset. Some critics com-plained that Jacob ignored attitudinal changes revealed by his own evidence (Edelstein 1962; Penister 1958). Others undertook new studies in search of a direct and potent faculty influence on student character or called attention to earlier studies that had found such an influence (Bloom and Webster 1960; Eddy 1959; Edelstein 1962; Goldsen 1960; Pace and McFee 1960; Stanley 1961). By 1962, a writer summarizing the post-Jacob burst of research declared with palpable relief that "a predominantly liberal faculty culture has had its liberal-izing impact upon college youth" (Edelstein 1962, 573; cf. Stanley 1961, 95).

Jacob's critique cut to the heart of faculty liberals' understanding of their social role.[19]

On both sides of the Jacob Report controversy, one sees the theologically potent assumption that value commitments were inescapable in collegiate teaching, obliging faculty to cultivate liberal commitments in students and challenge alternative viewpoints. The conception of liberalism on display in the debate overlapped substantially with the psychological discourse of maturity (e.g., Sanford 1956, 1962), and commentators on the Jacob Report, like many theorists of maturity, strongly correlated political positions with theological views. Edmund Sinnott (1953), who was less guarded in his religious claims than most, argued forthrightly that neither Catholic doctrine nor the biblical literalism of the fundamentalists comported with the "Great Tradition" of the West, despite the Catholic Church's instrumental contributions to that tradition's survival over the centuries. In the final analysis, wrote Sinnott, the Great Tradition boiled down to "the faith of religious liberalism" (224–27).

Not every formulation of postwar liberalism referred so openly, or even at all, to liberal theology. But many liberals joined Sinnott in viewing the American or Western heritage as a compound of two elements: a set of putatively noncognitive, spiritual commitments echoing the ethical lessons of the Sermon on the Mount and a second-level, epistemological claim about the unavailability of absolute cognitive truths in both science and religion (Commager 1954, 155; Harvard University Committee 1945, 50; Schapiro 1958, 9; Sinnott 1953, 209). According to Sinnott (1953), any individual who refused to "renounce dogmatism in his beliefs" (223) stood outside the Western tradition and posed nearly as great a threat to freedom and progress as did the advocates of Soviet Marxism (229).[20] This view of cognitive truths as fallible human creations gave a clear theological coloration to faculty liberals' portrait of the Western tradition.

When postwar liberals used concrete political commitments to sort between the enemies and friends of democracy, these commitments likewise tended to have religious resonances. The Inventory of Beliefs and Critical Reasoning, which was widely used in surveys of undergraduate attitudes, identified agreement with the following statements as evidence that subjects lacked "mental and emotional maturity":

1. Literature should not question the basic moral concepts of society.
2. We are finding today that liberals are really soft-hearted, gullible, and potentially dangerous.
3. Anything we do for a good cause is justified.

4. We should impose a strong censorship on the morality of books and movies.
5. Science is infringing on religion when it attempts to delve into the origin of life.
6. Americans may tend to be materialistic but at least they aren't cynical and decadent like most Europeans.
7. No one can really feel safe when scientists continue to explore whatever they wish without any social or moral restraint.
8. Political parties are run by insiders who are not concerned with public welfare (Moss 1960, 155).

It is little wonder that many religious leaders joined political critics in viewing postwar liberals' vaunted rejection of ideology as a self-serving sham.

Although few faculty liberals drew out the religious implications of their positions, many forcefully attacked political conservatives by calling them psychologically imbalanced and dangerous to the nation. Historians usually view the postwar spate of naturalization strategies and the accompanying assaults on dogmatism, authoritarianism, and ideology primarily as attempts to discredit dissent on the left.[21] Yet in the age of McCarthy, the American right seemed much more dangerous to many liberals (Rogin 1967). In response, leading scholars placed conservatism outside the democratic pale and described their own politics as a natural outgrowth of centuries-old values and institutions.

The concept of psychological maturity proved especially attractive for this purpose, although it often operated in tandem with other naturalization moves. Studies such as *The Authoritarian Personality* concentrated disproportionately on the pathology of conservatism. To be sure, Adorno's group insisted that a political "phoniness" derived from "father-fixation" could and did appear across the political spectrum (Adorno et al. 1950, 679–680, 971).[22] Yet the study focused so strongly on the right that Edward Shils (1954, 38) accused the authors of failing to recognize parallel disorders on the communist left. In Adorno's chapters, especially, the features of the democratic personality overlapped almost completely with the policy preferences of the social democrat (cf. Shils 1954, 29). *The Authoritarian Personality* (Adorno et al. 1950) clearly targeted conservatives when it listed as central characteristics of the antidemocratic personality an "ultimate respect for the existent," an "idea of unchangeability," an "assumption of a 'fighting instinct,'" and a failure to express "pity for the poor" (696–98). Democratic individuals, by contrast, harbored a "rational insight into the necessity of some governmental interference" with free enterprise (713). Other parts of the volume explained that the true democrat worked to "eliminate an unequal distribution of power" (44) and to foster "affectionate, basically equalitarian, and permissive interpersonal relationships" (971). *The Authoritarian Personality* described post-war liberalism as the only psychologically healthy response to the inequalities fostered by industrial capitalism and saw nothing but psychological instability in the political alternatives.

Such psychological presuppositions informed the many studies of conservatism that followed McCarthy's exit in 1954. In the late 1950s, liberal scholars devoted considerable energy to dissecting the unprecedented eruption of right-wing agitation into respectable political circles. Why had major social groups neglected their economic interests and gone in for seemingly outrageous conspiracy theories? To many interpreters, psychology explained the lapse of political rationality. Attacked as "eggheads" in the conservative press, liberal professors replied that their critics were utterly deranged (Cohen-Cole 2009).

This tendency to psychologize and pathologize conservatism found its most influential expression in *The New American Right*, a 1955 volume edited by the Columbia sociologist Daniel Bell. Its authors steered, as Bell put it in the dedication, "to the right of the left, and to the left of the right, seeking always the road of freedom and intellectual decency." The book is best remembered for its authors' use of the concept of "status anxiety"—a nervous and even paranoid state caused by a rapid change in a group's status position—that Richard Hofstadter had recently popularized. However, Hofstadter and other contributors to *The New American Right* also drew heavily on *The Authoritarian Personality* (Cohen-Cole 2009, 233), stressing "the neglected social-psychological elements in pseudo-conservatism" (Hofstadter 1955, 39–40). Hofstadter borrowed the "pseudo-conservative" label and the accompanying psychological analysis directly from Adorno and his collaborators, tracing the right's populist resentment to personality defects as well as shifts in social status. The McCarthyites, Hofstadter wrote, exhibited neither "the temperate and compromising spirit of true conservatism" nor the "dominant practical conservatism" of the Eisenhower crowd (35). Rather, they possessed authoritarian personalities. These pseudo-conservatives lacked "the capacity to criticize justly and in moderation the failings of parents" and were thus "profoundly intolerant of the ambiguities of thought and feeling" that characterized everyday interactions. In short, McCarthyism was "a disorder in relation to authority" (47). Neatly capturing the core claims of postwar liberalism, *The New American Right* portrayed a political struggle between right-wing crazies and a sober, mature, nonpartisan, liberal mainstream.

The Aftermath

"No one has to worry that the colleges are producing radicals," one commentator wrote during the Jacob Report furor (Abrams 1958, 313). Only a few years later, the rejuvenated student left would give the lie to that statement. Meanwhile, conservatives, consigned to the dustbin by liberal critics, would climb out and begin their long ascent to political power. Did the naturalization arguments of liberal professors contribute to these twin reactions against the New Deal order? Can we speak of a dynamic of liberal overreach in the intellectual realm as well as the policy sphere?

Assessing the long-term impact of scholarly arguments is difficult at best. Yet it seems like more than a mere coincidence that the post-1960s left and right have shared a deep suspicion of claims to academic disinterestedness (Brick 1998; Solovey 2001). This preoccupation with the question of value-neutrality suggests that the intellectual-political formations of the 1950s may have cast a long shadow. Surely the brief flare of revolutionary sentiment in the 1960s and the slow burn of right-wing populism that took its place in the 1970s gained some of their shape from the fact that postwar liberals enlisted reality itself on the side of their political values. In at least one case, a direct connection is apparent: the reduction of political commitments to psychology that characterized *The New American Right* still rankles American conservatives (Buchanan 1993).

More specific, short-term connections to the upheavals of the 1960s and 1970s also come to mind. For example, the naturalization strategies of the liberal professors may have helped to widen their perceived distance from radicalized students. As Howard Brick (2006) has shown, many student activists shared with their liberal elders a "postcapitalist" sensibility centered on the expectation that a more socialized society was gradually emerging from the chrysalis of capitalism. Yet the liberals' naturalization efforts were easily misread as forthright defenses of the status quo, particularly when they projected liberalism onto existing cultural commitments or social institutions. For example, radical critics of the "system" could hardly have seen much potential in Talcott Parsons's (1955) call to lodge political power in a "leading stratum" (139) that was drawn heavily from business and other practical pursuits and closely connected to academic and religious leaders. Indeed, Parsons and his mainstream contemporaries may have done as much as C. Wright Mills and other 1950s gadflies to define how young radicals saw that system, shaping their image of its power, its pervasiveness, and its essentially liberal character. Whatever the cause, many

1960s activists mobilized the rhetoric of human nature—especially psychological nature—and their own, radicalized readings of American ideals against the liberals' consensus claims and paeans to America and the West (Brick 1998; Herman 1995).

Postwar scholarly liberals also bequeathed to the younger generation a portrait of American conservatives as a backward-looking and rapidly vanishing fringe group whose views bore no relation to reality, let alone the formation of national policy. Listening to their elders, student radicals could not have been particularly frightened of any conservative opposition they might face after defeating the faculty liberals, whose ideological work appeared to sustain the whole political system. An imaginary political landscape featuring only Kennedy Democrats and Eisenhower Republicans might have led students to think a great deal about academic neutrality but worry far less about combating conservatism. Similarly, liberal arguments might have led young radicals to highlight the political impact of cultural and psychological phenomena and downplay the continued relevance of economic power. In obscuring key elements of the political situation from radical activists, the postwar liberals' strategy for staving off right-wing attacks on the New Deal may have backfired just as badly as it did in fanning the flames of conservatism.

All of this is sheer speculation, of course, although hints can be found here and there in the historical literature. Still, when scholars explore the connections between the apparently quiescent 1950s and the tumultuous 1960s, they should look beyond civil rights activism, the Beats, the mass culture critique, and even C. Wright Mills. In the heart of the academy, at the very highest levels of scholarly production—and scholarly abstraction—important lines of conceptual continuity and reaction radiated outward from the academic liberalism of the 1950s and deserve further study as potential influences on the subsequent course of American politics. We can hardly understand the situation of the professoriate today without grasping the contours and consequences of those earlier developments.

NOTES

1. The natural sciences and humanities present a more complex picture, and hard numbers are scarce all around. But the social sciences as a whole clearly became more centrist.

2. Between the wars, by contrast, important groups of American scholars had challenged the naturalization claims offered by colleagues and portrayed science as a culturally embedded practice (Jewett 2012).

3. In this view, laissez-faire arbitrarily placed economic exchange, a key realm of collective action, beyond the reach of conscious, ethically grounded choices.

4. Through the twentieth century, and especially in the 1920s and 1930s, an impulse to find a biological explanation of conscious, purposive action contended against harder-edged, hereditarian theories of human behavior (e.g., Jewett 2012).

5. Historians have argued that the American social sciences liberated themselves from biology when they abandoned biological determinism and adopted the culturalist perspective of Boasian anthropology in the 1920s (Cravens 1978; Degler 1991). In fact, a biologically informed view of the person as the locus of powerful, if vaguely defined, needs and drives still underpinned much postwar liberal thought. By naturalizing the mind and sometimes even the soul or spirit, interwar biologists gave the imprimatur of natural science to a range of social sciences resting on a view of human beings as goal-oriented, purpose-driven creatures whose social and cultural activities could be studied empirically (Jewett 2012).

6. Whereas most postwar liberals steered a course between American conservatives and the Soviets, Montagu (1950) ignored communism and targeted the right. He attacked "moneytheism" (114)—"the religion of economics" (115), which measured human action by the "externals" of material possessions (108). In portraying the cooperative polity he sought not as an expression of normative liberal principles but rather as "a society based on human relations" (118) rather than spurious economic laws, Montagu showed how much work the adjective "human" did for postwar liberals.

7. By contrast, Sinnott (1945) reasoned from the "stubborn inborn differences" of human genetics to the need for political freedoms: "the basis of our diversity is sunk deep in the constitution of living stuff itself, safe from totalitarian attempts to regiment us into an army of standardized robots" (66–67).

8. Sinnott (1945, 72; 1953, 93), on the other hand, barely even mentioned his axiomatic belief that freedom required progress in the social sciences and institutions that placed boundaries on market behavior.

9. Simpson employed the language of maturity on occasion (e.g., Simpson 1949, 346), and Sinnott (1953, 5) cited *The Mature Mind* directly. The discourses of biological humanity and psychological maturity cross-fertilized easily, as the shared political framework obviated any need to resolve implicit tensions over the disciplinary locus of final moral authority (e.g., Sinnott 1955, 83–92).

10. Like many postwar liberals, Adorno and his colleagues (1950, 8) distinguished between a rational politics of "material interests" and an irrational politics of undisciplined emotions and empty symbolism. Bridging Marxist class analysis and interest-group pluralism, this understanding of rational political interests helped to constitute the distinctive milieu of postwar liberalism.

11. Advocates of these modes of naturalization simply took for granted the transhistorical, if highly flexible, picture of human nature outlined by the biologists and psychologists and focused instead on concrete mediating structures that, in their view, gave human nature full expression and embodied an authentically human politics.

12. A particularly important precursor is Mead (1942). Potter (1954) outlined the national character approach for historians.

13. Boorstin (1953) thus scorned the "modern abolitionists" (188) who saw no cause other than anticommunism and no solution other than the Americanization of Russia.

14. Consensus liberalism and Western civ liberalism could be reconciled. Theorists of consensus often spoke, with Ralph Henry Gabriel, of "the American variant of Western civilization." They posited continuity between the United States and Europe at the broad level of the Western axiom of "human freedom and dignity" but discontinuity in specific "social beliefs" stemming from colonial conditions (Gabriel 1956, v–vi). "The story of America is the story of the impact of an old culture upon a wilderness environment," explained Allan Nevins and Commager (1956, v) in a popular textbook. This approach presented America as exceptional in the purity of its Westernness due to environmental factors (Commager 1950, 4–5; cf. Curti et al. 1953, 2; Schlesinger 1949, 8).

15. In a parallel move, Sinnott (1953) defined Western civilization as the product of a dialectical interaction between science and religion.

16. The economist and administrator Alvin Johnson (1949) likewise called the welfare state "the state of the common man" (111), produced by "the genius of the whole underlying population" (109) under the influence of Western civilization's unique "concern for the masses" (99).

17. "Your personality is a part of the class from which you have come," another group of authors told their readers (Naftalin et al. 1953, 11). Yet "you probably know less about yourself, if you are a man, than you know about the inside of a Model A motor, or, if you are a woman, about the baking of a cake" (4).

18. "The ordinary man can no more be Secretary of State as of tomorrow morning than he can be a professor of higher mathematics," another text explained (Ross and Van den Haag 1957, 751).

19. This literature on student attitudes, values, and beliefs was partly intertwined with the body of work on professorial politics explored in this volume's introduction. Indeed, Paul Lazarsfeld wrote the introduction to a critical study of the Jacob Report's methodology (Barton 1959). In turn, both literatures were part of a wider discourse on the role of the intellectual in society that took much of its shape from McCarthyism and the postwar expansion of American higher education.

20. Sinnott was rare among postwar liberals in viewing the human person dualistically as composed of a body and a soul. He defined the soul as a protoplasmic capacity to grasp spiritual truths directly, bypassing the laborious, fallible processes of sensory perception and logical reasoning (Sinnott 1953, 221).

21. This goal certainly operated as well. Schlesinger (1949), for example, listed Gandhian nonviolence alongside "the restoration of feudalism" (7) as quixotic ideals that produced only individual self-satisfaction.

22. Schlesinger (1949) employed the more colorful terminology of "neanderthal conservatives" and "responsible conservatives" (42).

CHAPTER EIGHT

Challenging Neutrality

Sixties Activism and Debates over Political Advocacy in the American University

JULIE A. REUBEN

In 2003, David Horowitz launched the organization Students for Academic Freedom to rid the university of what he saw as political preaching (Horowitz 2007). Horowitz has used this group as a platform to lobby state legislatures to investigate charges of political indoctrination at public universities and to pressure colleges and universities to adopt the "Academic Bill of Rights," a document that many within higher education believe, contrary to its name, threatens academic freedom by inviting outside interference in college classrooms.[1] Horowitz is one of several conservative critics who over the past few decades have attracted public attention by arguing that American higher education is being destroyed by radical professors. According to these critics, leftist professors distort scholarship to promote their political causes, use the classroom to indoctrinate students in their political ideology, and block the appointment and promotion of faculty members who hold opposing political positions. These critics trace the abuses back to the 1960s, arguing that former student activists are today's powerful professors. No longer protesting against the university, these professors are instead pushing their political causes from within the academy. Critics believe that these professors, by hiring like-minded colleagues, now control large portions of the academy and the professional societies that set standards for their disciplines. Administrators, in this view, either support the professors' agenda or have been unwilling to rein them in. Hence, conservatives have called on the public to apply pressure in whatever ways it can to help reverse this situation.

The response within higher education to these conservative critics has been mixed. Some of the critics are themselves academics and have like-minded colleagues in organizations such as the National Association of Scholars. But many within higher education find the threats of outside intervention dangerous and believe that conservatives' portrait of America's universities is highly distorted.

Academics have tried to combat conservatives' critique in various ways: some have pointed out its inaccuracies and exaggerations, others have offered alternative analyses of power dynamics in the academy, and still others have questioned its fundamental assumptions about the nature and purpose of scholarship and education. But the underlying historical narrative has not been carefully examined. Did campus activism of the 1960s fundamentally change the political role of the university? Are conservatives correct that the 1960s marked a turning point after which the university became a tool for leftist politics?

This essay explores these questions by examining debates in the 1960s and 1970s over institutional neutrality, the idea that universities should not assume political roles or advocate political positions. Activists did attack the ideal of neutrality, arguing that it was both untrue, because universities were in fact political actors, and wrong, because universities should commit themselves to positive social change. Although activists gained advocates within universities, the ideal of neutrality was not abandoned. On the contrary, it was reaffirmed but redefined. For most of the twentieth century, the ideal of institutional neutrality was closely linked to norms of individual professorial neutrality: for a university to be trusted to be nonpartisan, its faculty would also have to be free of partisan attachments. As the Red Scare made abundantly clear, though, this equation could have negative consequences for faculty. Some professors recognized the challenge to institutional neutrality as an opportunity to sever this link. Instead of joining the call to end institutional neutrality, they defended it but reinterpreted it to allow for individual partisan activity. They argued that institutional neutrality created a "free market" that protected faculty members' right to political advocacy of all kinds.

This redefinition proved to be a popular middle ground in the debates over institutional neutrality. Thus, conservative critics' historical analysis contains some truth and some exaggeration. Sixties activism did change norms governing professors' political advocacy, and this made certain political positions more visible on and off campuses. But critics wrongly portray the 1960s as the beginnings of a newly politicized university. The ideal of institutional neutrality was preserved, and the nature of universities' interactions with society did not change significantly.

In the late nineteenth century, the creators of the modern university insisted that the new university—as distinguished from the traditional college they were trying to reform—should be free from outside control and be autonomous. They were particularly concerned about religious control because colleges at the time were typically associated with a particular religious denomination that could determine who was hired and fired and what was taught. University reformers found this arrangement intolerable because it did not guarantee the intellectual freedom that they believed was essential to the discovery of new knowledge and the teaching of new, perhaps controversial, ideas. They therefore declared that their institutions should be nonsectarian, outside the control of a particular religious group. They extended this idea to politics, arguing that universities should not be associated with any organization that was committed to particular positions. Thus, they also declared that true universities were nonpartisan, independent of any group that was committed in advance to a set of principles.

Originally, the notion of nonsectarian and nonpartisan simply meant that members of a particular religious or political organization did not control the university's governing board and did not apply religious or political tests to its faculty or students. The institution would not require its faculty or students to accept certain contested beliefs as truth. But as university leaders elaborated on the conditions necessary to produce and disseminate new knowledge and gained experience putting their ideals into practice, the principle of nonsectarian/nonpartisan morphed into the ideal of neutrality. University leaders emphasized freedom and openness as the fundamental condition for the discovery of new truths. Scientific inquiry, they believed, was distinguished by openness combined with strict empirical verification. They maintained that openness must be a characteristic not only of the institution but also of the faculty who made up the institution. True scholars must be willing to question any idea, must subject it to rigorous tests before adopting it, and even then, must be open to the possibility that the idea might be proven untrue. By temperament, then, scholars should be skeptics not advocates. Like the university that employed them, professors should be nonpartisan. Both the individual and the institution should remain neutral (Reuben 1996b).

University reformers wanted knowledge produced at their institutions to contribute to social progress. They defined this broadly to encompass research that might produce a better train engine or might elevate people's appreciation of beauty. But in whatever fashion, they firmly asserted that the institutions they led would improve the world. They thus encouraged their faculty to be engaged with the world outside the university. Initially, university reformers conceived their promises to produce new knowledge and to serve the practical needs of society as completely consonant. They believed that intellectual progress would automatically result in material, social, and moral progress because scientific inquiry would produce sound consensus on the full range of human concerns. But by the turn of the century, this expectation began to seem simplistic as it became more apparent that scientific consensus was not quickly achieved and did not easily translate into social progress (Reuben 1996b).

This exposed a tension inherent in university leaders' expectation that faculty members serve society and remain neutral: when professors researched controversial political topics, they frequently became engaged in partisan debates. In the 1890s, several universities dismissed social scientists who took radical stands on current political issues. Outraged colleagues accused university leaders of violating their own commitment to intellectual freedom. University leaders denied that they fired the faculty for their political beliefs, citing instead the professors' failure of judgment. In discussing academic freedom, they stressed that professors must always express themselves in a scholarly, temperate, and reasoned manner. They did not acknowledge that this might make it nearly impossible for faculty to express opinions that sharply challenged the status quo. Social scientists, for their part, responded to these dismissals by trying to curb substantive disagreements within their ranks. The solution promoted by a generation of rising leaders in the social sciences was to transform their fields into objective sciences by excising value judgments from research. True science, they argued, was strictly limited to questions of what *is* not what *ought to be*. This fit nicely with university leaders' emphasis on a scholarly manner of expression because both tended to silence positions that seemed extreme (Furner 1975; Reuben 1996a).

The emphasis on objectivity and temperate modes of expression favored one interpretation of institutional neutrality over another. The term *neutral* can be understood in different ways. A neutral party in a war, for example, is one that remains uninvolved in the conflict. In an argument, neutral ground is the area on which the various parties can agree. In this sense, neutrality means the avoidance of conflict or existence of agreement. But neutral can also connote disinterestedness or lack of favoritism. According to this view, neutrality entails tolerance, which might result in a multiplicity of conflicting positions rather than agreement. In the first meaning, neutrality evokes the notion of consensus; in the second, it entails the possibility of pluralism. Following the conflicts of the 1890s, the ideal of institutional neutrality definitely took on the connotation of consensus. University leaders wanted their institutions to be involved in society but to avoid areas of conflict. They wanted their faculty to be sound, solid, safe scholars who did not attract controversy or seek to inflame it. They did not choose a pluralistic understanding of neutrality in which they might seek out and hire partisans of different stripes and make the university into a space in which multiple views, even those seen as extreme, were protected, explored, promoted, and disputed. This notion of neutrality would come later.

Faculty leaders in the early twentieth century largely accepted the consensus view of neutrality and the link between institutional neutrality and individual neutrality (Reuben 1996a; Slaughter 1980). In 1915, a group of professors founded the American Association of University Professors (AAUP) to protect academic freedom and advance the professional interests of faculty. The association's defining document was the 1915 Statement on Academic Freedom. The document (AAUP 1915) began by affirming the view that nonpartisanship and institutional neutrality were the lynchpin of intellectual freedom for faculty. Faculty could not enjoy academic freedom at institutions controlled by outside bodies committed to particular positions. Indeed, the report argued that faculty members' research should be independent of all lay opinion; evidence and expert judgment should be all that influenced scientific inquiry. Professorial autonomy, though, demanded corresponding responsibilities. Although the AAUP argued that faculty must be able to report the findings of their research no matter "to what extent they come into conflict with accepted opinion," it adopted norms for faculty conduct that made controversy suspect (37). According to the report, university faculty should refrain from anything that might seem to involve their institutions in "party antagonisms" (33). The report maintained that professors, when teaching controversial topics, should present multiple points of view, refrain from advocacy, and adjust their presentation to account for students' "immaturity." Faculty should have the right to engage in public affairs as private citizens, but even then, they should "refrain from intemperate or sensational modes of expression" (29). Thus, the AAUP promoted professional norms that respected universities' consensus-oriented interpretation of neutrality.

University leaders in the early twentieth century aggressively sought opportunities to demonstrate that the knowledge they produced and disseminated served society. They held onto an idea that there was a public interest above partisan interests, a national good or a transcendent human benefit, with which they could safely align. In the Progressive Era, urban universities developed local alliances with institutions such as public schools and settlement houses. Their faculty researched social conditions such as housing and workers' safety and weighed in on plans to reorganize local government. State universities happily took federal funding for agricultural research stations and sought to establish extensive ties to state government. University leaders leapt at the opportunity to serve the nation during World War I, literally turning their campuses into military camps. Despite mostly abhorring the policies of Franklin D. Roosevelt's New Deal, many academic leaders proudly hailed the use of faculty as advisors to the federal government during the Depression. Their ideal of service to the nation dampened their own partisan doubts (Diner 1980; Gruber 1975; Loss 2012; Marcus 1985; Tugwell 1968).

University leaders became willing partners in government planning in preparation for World War II. Not surprisingly, university faculty and facilities became an integral part of the war effort. The most famous of the World War II military research projects, the Manhattan Project, relied heavily on research done at university facilities, such as the Metallurgical Laboratory at the University of Chicago, and on the leadership of university scientists, such as University of California professor J. Robert Oppenheimer. Although physicists and chemists were the stars of the war research effort, university professors served the war in many capacities. The Office of Strategic Services (the precursor to the CIA) needed experts on the countries occupied by Germany, Italy, and Japan. It relied heavily on anthropologists who knew the culture, geographers who could prepare maps and explain the physical terrain, and language experts, among others. In addition to supplying experts for government, universities were heavily engaged in training military personnel. ROTC programs, set up during World War I, now expanded, and new, short-term educational programs were created for military personnel (Allen 2011; Bird and Sherwin 2005; Cardozier 1993; Herman 1995; Kevles 1987; Rudy 1991).

The government, the media, and university leaders widely perceived universities' wartime service as mutually beneficial. Most analysts believe that the expertise provided by universities made a significant contribution to the Allies' victory. University leaders enjoyed the material and status benefits of their work with the federal government. And, unlike after World War I, when ties to the federal government largely dissolved, these connections held and were strengthened after World War II. Although the wartime science-coordinating bodies were shuttered in 1947, the three branches of the military, the newly created Atomic Energy Commission, and the National Institutes of Health developed their own systems for contracting research with university scientists. The quick transition from World War II to the Cold War ensured that the military's demand for research remained high.

Some academic leaders, including Harvard's James Bryant Conant, questioned the propriety of universities continuing to support research that was defined by outside agencies and often classified, but most university administrators welcomed the opportunity (Conant 1970; Keller and Keller 2007). Research universities aggressively sought government contracts and used the income from these projects to expand and upgrade their academic programs, particularly in fields likely to yield more opportunities for sponsored research. Competition among universities for funds and the prestige that went along with growing research programs made it difficult for any institution to limit the types of research activity on its campus. Scientists actively participated in this competition, and the availability of large grants sustained the growth of "big science" and reoriented the research agendas of some disciplines (Doel 2003; Leslie 1993; Lowen 1997). In 1950, Congress created the National Science Foundation to support basic, researcher-initiated projects, but even this basic research was justified in terms of possible long-term, unknown technological advances (Kleinman 1995). The federal government increasingly appointed academic scientists to high-level government positions, and the students they trained took new positions in the growing government bureaucracy. All this activity signaled a now lasting integration of academic science with national interests.

While the physical and medical sciences continued to be the primary partners in this relationship, social scientists' ties to government and foundations also increased in these years. Social scientists served in high-level government positions in even higher numbers than their natural scientist counterparts, reflecting government's growing respect for academic analysis of economic and social problems and the increasing prominence of policy-oriented research within the social science disciplines (Townsely 2000). The federal government and foundations encouraged the development of new interdisciplinary fields of study, most notably area studies such as Soviet studies and Latin American studies. Although funding for area studies ultimately supported a wide range of research in the social sciences and the humanities, it helped forge a strong connection between Cold War concerns and the trajectory of new scholarship in the postwar decades (Engerman 2009; McCaughey 1984; Simpson 1998). As a result of these connections, increasing numbers of social scientists did classified contract research for the military and other government agencies (Solovey 2013; Solovey and Cravens 2012). As with the natural sciences, secret research raised ethical questions for universities, which were formally committed to openness and free inquiry, but these concerns did not gain much traction in this period. Instead, social scientists and the universities that employed them delighted in the new research opportunities and saw them as the fulfillment of their long-held dream of establishing expertise in service to the nation.

One of the negative consequences of university ties to government was increased scrutiny, particularly as the Cold War fueled fears of security threats. Universities and their faculty became targets of the House Un-American Activities Committee investigations. The ideals of neutrality and openness were used to make professors vulnerable to political witch hunts. Most university leaders, with the acquiescence of the AAUP, adopted the reasoning that membership in the Communist Party required absolute loyalty to a political ideology and thus party members had given up their freedom of thought in favor of partisan loyalty. This allegiance, university leaders argued, disqualified people from a faculty position that demanded freedom from partisanship and an openness to new ideas. University leaders viewed faculty who refused to cooperate with investigatory committees as violating the institution's commitment to openness and also unfit for a university position. Hundreds of faculty members lost their jobs and scientists lost their security clearances during the Red Scare (Schrecker 1986).

As McCarthyism played itself out, more academics became wary of the logic that justified the dismissals. Did the ideal of neutrality protect faculty or establish professional norms that made them vulnerable? Did universities strong alliance with government compromise their neutrality and limit faculty members' academic freedom? Some academics began to question the ideal of neutrality that linked objective scholarship with service to society, arguing that the focus on service was a threat to pure scholarship or that the claim of objectivity was a cover for support for the status quo. But these questions did not disturb the main discourse about universities until the second half of the 1960s.

Instead, Clark Kerr's book *The Uses of the University* (1995 [1963]), based on the Godkin lectures he delivered at Harvard in 1962, captured the main mood of higher education. This book, an insightful and compelling account of the development of the service-oriented research university, remains a classic analysis of higher education today. Kerr claimed the mantle of objectivity, asking his readers in the preface not to confuse "analysis . . . with approval or description with defense" (xii). But nonetheless, he conveyed intense enthusiasm and pride in the postwar university. In his eyes, it truly had become a powerful instrument of progress. The knowledge it produced and disseminated fed economic growth, helped the nation in international competition, and supported "political and social as well as cultural development" (xv). Although Kerr maintained that the university was transformed in the process, becoming—in a term he would later regret—a "multiversity," higher education was finally fulfilling the dreams of the founders of the modern university.

Kerr expressed this zeal despite cataloguing numerous problems and educational dilemmas created by the transformation of higher education. He even acknowledged critics of the service role: "There are those who fear the further involvement of the university in the life of society. They fear that the university will lose its objectivity and its freedom" (87). But he dismissed these concerns in a paragraph. All of the shortcomings of the multiversity either were technical, so adjustments would right them, or were well worth the benefits. This attitude suffused the higher education establishment. Leaders in higher education thought about university relations with government—how to maintain good overhead rates for contracts, how to reduce regulatory demands, how to ensure a position of relative power within the partnership—but they did not really entertain fundamental philosophical questions about the relation between service and neutrality, on both an individual and institutional level. For them, the old identification of neutrality with consensus still sufficed in the new era of national service.[2]

Five years later, Kerr's optimism would seem naive. By 1968, debates about the university's neutrality raged within the academy. Kerr's position depended on a degree of political consensus that made service to government seem above politics. There were, of course, critics of government policies during the two decades after World War II, but those ideas did not gain much traction in either public discourse or the academy. Consistent with the ideal of institutional neutrality forged in the early twentieth century, those to the far left or far right could be easily dismissed as partisan, while those occupying a broad middle ground could be viewed as nonpartisan and neutral. Disagreements existed within this middle ground, but they could be understood as technical problems, soon to be resolved by more data or improved methodology. But this view became untenable as political protest movements won adherents and legitimacy during the 1960s. Support for the status quo no longer seemed to be "above" politics. Activists argued that universities' ties to the national government and support for well-established social arrangements were political positions, and odious ones at that. They pushed universities to make their politics more explicit and more oppositional.

The movements that destroyed the political consensus of the 1960s took shape a decade earlier. By the late 1950s, the civil rights movement began to shake national politics and force social changes, including on college campuses. In the South, movement activists began the long process of desegregating white colleges and universities. At black colleges, students, sometimes with the support of faculty members, organized sit-ins and other protests against segregation and black disempowerment. Often facing harsh reprisals from their campus administration, these students also explicitly and implicitly challenged campus rules limiting their political rights and the academic freedom of faculty. Although ostensibly designed to keep colleges free from politics, these rules were invoked in this period to crush activists' challenge to white supremacy. Thus, challenging those rules was an implicit challenge to the ideal of neutrality (Wallenstein 2008; Williamson 2008).

In other areas of the country, small groups of activist students also tried to challenge the segregation that existed on their campuses and in their communities. Small protests against segregated fraternities and sororities, the benching of black athletes when competing against segregated southern colleges, discriminatory hiring practices at local businesses, and other instances of racial discrimination peppered campuses in the late 1950s and early 1960s. Although students generally enjoyed much greater political freedom at these institutions than at their counterparts in the South, in some cases activists did face reprisals and restrictions. The most famous example was the rule against political advocacy on the University of California, Berkeley, campus that provoked the Free Speech Movement (FSM; Rorabaugh 1989). Activists in that movement directly challenged the idea that restrictions on political advocacy protected institutional neutrality. For example, student Bettina Aptheker argued that the chancellor's effort "to clamp down on political activism on the campus . . . is doing the opposite to achieve neutrality . . . [it] is yielding to government and business pressure to stifle free debate" (ja [1965]). Students concluded that neutrality was a sham, hiding the university's true political alliances with corporations and the state.

While convincing to many students, this argument divided faculty. Some faculty members opposed the FSM in the name of neutrality. Carl Landauer (1964), professor of economics, wrote to the executive committee of the FSM: "The political neutrality of the university is a very precious thing . . . safeguarding of the neutrality . . . seems to me vastly more important that the question of whether money can be collected on the campus for political purposes, tables set up at the Bancroft entrance without permit, speakers be invited by student organizations without the latter having to pay a policeman's wages, and so on." Landauer viewed restrictions on students' political activity as an inconvenience, not worth threatening university neutrality for. Other faculty members, however, came to side with the FSM, in part because they saw it as related to their own fight against the California state loyalty oath and their ongoing struggle to prevent the dismissal of a colleague charged with communism. Stifling political advocacy in the name of neutrality was the logic that allowed communists, who had supposedly abandoned their own neutrality and become committed partisans, to be summarily dismissed. Faculty members, therefore, had their own reasons for beginning to question the ideal of neutrality as it had been traditionally defined.

The growing antiwar movement was instrumental in challenging the ideal of neutrality. In 1965, Students for a Democratic Society (SDS) helped organize a national march protesting U.S. involvement in Vietnam. The success of the march energized SDS members and greatly enhanced the group's reputation. Seeking to build on this momentum, SDS fell upon a strategy of linking opposition to the war to the university's ties to the military. As SDS veteran Todd Gitlin (1971 [1967]) wrote:

> It seems that SDS people are caught in a serious tension: on the one hand, they want to do something about the war and the garrison state; on the other, they have a commitment toward transforming the institution at hand, the university. It might make sense, then, for SDS to consider a strategy that joins the two concerns. The natural synthesis would be a national movement to expel the military from campus. (127)

SDS adopted this approach as a national policy in June 1967 and referred to it as "resistance" to "university complicity." But even before it became official SDS policy, individual campus groups, inspired in part by teach-ins organized by antiwar faculty and students, were targeting university ties to the military. In the spring of 1966, student activists began protesting universities' cooperation with the Selective Service's new requirement that they submit students' grades and class rankings to determine draft deferment eligibility. Protests against other military ties followed. University of Pennsylvania students protested the presence of "chemical and bacteriological war research" on campus. In 1966, Harvard students surrounded the car of Robert McNamara when he spoke on campus and refused to let him pass until he answered their questions about the war. The same year, students at UC Berkeley protested the presence of a Navy recruiter in the student union by setting up an antiwar table next to his. The students' table was promptly removed, escalating the protest to a free speech issue. ROTC programs, Dow Chemical (the maker of napalm) recruiters, and stock in GE (a major defense contractor) also became common symbols of universities' ties to the military and thus targets for protests (Davidson 1971 [1967]).

The charge of "university complicity" spread from the war to other issues. Black activists claimed that the absence of black faculty, the small number of black students at traditionally white colleges, the neglect of blacks in scholarship and college curricula, and universities' physical expansion into poor urban neighborhoods were all proof of institutional racism. Feminists viewed the stereotypical treatment of women in research, the steering of women into traditionally feminine fields, condescending rules that restricted the social activities of female students but not their male counterparts, and the lack of women as faculty and administrators as signs of sexism. Protests against these various forms of "university complicity" ranged from petitions to pickets, sit-ins, building takeovers, strikes, and occasionally, the destruction of property such as the burning of ROTC buildings. Most protests were peaceful, but some intentionally disturbed university activities. Activists justified this disruption, arguing that it was necessary to interrupt normal university functioning to draw attention to how it used its power to bolster injustice. Universities commonly reacted to disruptive demonstrations by arresting students. The presence of police often mobilized other students, who viewed arrests as a violation of students' political rights, and sometimes led to violence. This upheaval made it impossible to ignore the question of university neutrality.

Activists pushed the university to stop hiding behind the myth of neutrality and become a different kind of political actor, to use its power, resources, and prestige to fight against the war and for justice. For example, pressure on universities to take a stand against the war intensified in the fall of 1969 when antiwar faculty joined students demanding that administrators honor the October 15 Moratorium, a protest calling on people to cease normal activity for a day, by closing their institutions. At Harvard, the undergraduate student council asked the university to honor the moratorium by canceling classes. In response, Everett I. Mendelsohn, then an associate professor of the history of science, sponsored a faculty resolution that softened the students' demand by making the cancelation of classes voluntary. The compromise proposal would have the university declare its support for faculty members who canceled their classes in protest of the war but would not force unwilling professors to participate. Feeling that the Mendelsohn resolution did not go far enough, the liberal caucus of the faculty introduced a motion to have the Harvard faculty officially call for the withdrawal of troops from Vietnam. Members of the liberal caucus at Harvard, like groups of faculty at universities across the country, believed that "neutrality" in the case of the war really entailed support and that universities needed to cut their ties to the military and officially pressure the government to end the war ("Members of Liberal Caucus" 1969).

But many Harvard professors rejected this logic and saw the resolution as a clear violation of institutional neutrality. One hundred and fifty Harvard faculty signed a petition that called "official and collective involvement of the Faculty—sitting as a Faculty—in political debate" dangerous. In their view, it threatened the independence of the university, which would become increasingly embroiled in political conflicts, and the freedom of individual faculty members, who would be forced to accede to the political views of the majority. Eventually, they argued, such action would lead to the imposition of political tests in the selection of faculty and would undermine all legitimate educational activity. In other words, deviations from institutional neutrality would produce a partisan university. The petition attracted the support of professors who were members of the conservative caucus of the faculty as well as many who affiliated with neither the liberal nor conservative camps. This latter group included faculty who opposed the war but believed that their political views should not influence their professional responsibilities (Fallows 1969).

The petition tried to shift the discussion away from the substance of the resolution—formal opposition to the Vietnam War—to the question of political neutrality. Supporters of the resolution countered that a university is inevitably political. "The university does function politically, willingly or unwillingly, by virtue of the fact that it exists in the world and has effects on it," one tutor asserted. "The question is thus not 'am I or should I be political?' but . . . 'what sort of politics must I engage in?'" (Glassberg 1969). These arguments, however, remained unconvincing to many faculty. Professor Martin Kilson, for example, derided this argument as "the erroneous SDS view of the university as a political system, or the equivalent of such" ("Kilson on Resolution" 1969). Faculty members who defended the ideal of institutional neutrality tried various means to prevent the antiwar resolution from coming to an official vote. "Preponderantly harm will come from putting the Faculty in a position where it will be forced to comment on a problem not directly related to the conduct of University business," asserted Robert Dorfman, an economics professor who led the effort to block the vote. But supporters of the resolution insisted that since the war affected the university and the university affected the war, it was university business. "The resolution is profoundly related to the business of the University—the Vietnam war has had a poisonous effect on U.S. life in general and University life in particular," explained John T. Edsall, professor of biological chemistry (Blum and Janis 1969). Not only did the university contribute to the war effort, but the war infiltrated the educational activities of the university.

When a last-ditch effort to preserve neutrality—a motion to allow faculty to vote as individuals rather than speaking for the university—failed by a one-person margin (215 to 214), the antiwar resolution came to a vote and passed 255 to 82, with 150 abstentions. The faculty committed the university to officially oppose the war (Reinhold 1969). This clear rejection of the principle of neutrality sent shock waves through the academic community. Since antiwar activists at more than six hundred colleges and universities pressured their institutions to honor the October moratorium in some way, academics across the nation had to consider the appropriateness of taking institutional and/or individual positions on the war and, by extension, had to debate the question of institutional neutrality ("More than 600 Campuses" 1969). A decade earlier, institutional neutrality was a truism that most academics honored without much thought. But vigorous protest movements had shattered the political consensus that had made it possible for universities' service to society to appear to be above politics, and campus activists forced universities to defend their claims to being neutral institutions.

Suddenly, institutional neutrality was the topic of intense debate. What did neutrality entail? Was it possible? Was it desirable? What was the relationship between institutional neutrality and individual neutrality? Could universities remain neutral and be engaged in society? Out of this tumultuous debate emerged groups with four distinct positions: radicals who thought that the university used its political power to prop up a corrupt society and that the university should therefore be destroyed and radically reconstructed; liberals who thought the university was inherently political and wanted to reorient its influence to achieve greater social good; conservatives who thought the university had, to its detriment, become political and believed it needed to shed its service role to restore neutrality; and moderates who defended neutrality but redefined it in pluralistic rather than consensual terms.[3] Although the question of institutional neutrality was never completely settled, the moderates came to dominate academic discourse by the end of the 1970s.

Student activists associated with SDS and its various splinter groups articulated the radical critique of neutrality most forcefully. At the beginning of the 1960s, students in SDS tended to view the university positively, as a potential resource in their fight for a more just world. By the end of the decade, the critique of neutrality pushed some of them in the opposite direction: they came to view the university, with its extensive ties to corporations and government, as an essential tool of an oppressive society, and as such, they vowed to fight the institution. This view justified the disruption of campus activities and, in more extreme cases, the destruction of campus property such as the bombing of Sterling Hall, the location of the Army Mathematics Research Center, at the University of Wisconsin and the burning of ROTC buildings on several campuses. This never became a common position among professors, even those who considered themselves to be radicals, because it was fundamentally at odds with their choice of vocation. Nonetheless, small numbers of radical faculty members gravitated toward it. For example, New University Conference (1969), an organization of faculty and graduate students, prepared a pamphlet on the "Student Rebellion" and identified both with radical students' vision of a transformed society and with their despair about the university as an agent of change: "We have hoped that the university could be a center of work toward these ends. That hope, however, seems increasingly illusory. We have all come to realize that through the veil of 'official neutrality' and protestations of innocence, the universities—including the 'great centers of learning'—are partners with the most pernicious forces in our society." Far from being neutral, New University Conference saw universities, in large part through their service roles, as strongly linked to oppressive social institutions. The group imagined a thoroughly reconstructed university but realized that such deep changes would be unlikely until society itself was transformed.

Liberals agreed with radicals that the universities were not in fact neutral, but they were more optimistic that universities could be reformed to serve what they saw as positive social ends. Liberals argued that universities were inevitably intertwined with society and, therefore, would always be engaged in politics to some degree. For example, Yale Law professor John G. Simon and doctoral students Charles Powers and John P. Gunnemann, in their book *The Ethical Investor* (1972), pointed out that universities had to interact with the outside world whenever they engaged in basic administrative tasks such as managing real estate and money. These activities, they noted, involved choices that were value-laden: "The university cannot avoid participation in the prevailing economic system. And in so doing, it usually reflects the values of the system" (72). But, they argued, this did not need to be so; universities could and should challenge the values of the system to protect people and improve society. They believed that universities, instead of hiding behind the mantle of neutrality, should conduct their affairs for good ends not destructive ones. Recognizing that it might be difficult to get agreement in universities on a common positive social program, they suggested that, instead, universities use a minimalist standard of avoiding "social injury" when making decisions about their interactions with the world.[4]

Liberals pointed to other practices that they believed undercut institutional neutrality: funding from corporations, foundations, and government skewed the knowledge produced and taught; standards of objectivity in scholarship favored moderate views and produced narrow, technical, uncritical research; and the economic class, race, and gender of trustees and administrators shaped institutional policies and practices. They argued that the question was not neutrality versus political involvement but rather political involvement for what ends. For example, in his 1969 book *The University in Turmoil*, Columbia sociology professor Immanuel Wallerstein wrote that "the university is willy-nilly involved in the political arena. If there is turmoil today, it is because so large a segment of the university community is discontented with the manner in which the university is presently involved" (141–42). He argued that struggle over the political direction of university policies would be good for the university because it would turn the university into a social critic rather than a supporter of the status quo. He wanted to mobilize his colleagues to reorient the university's relation to urban poverty. He thought that by ending their own destructive practices in urban neighborhoods, changing their admissions and hiring practices, providing direct services, and lobbying for federal support for these efforts, universities could help transform their urban communities. Liberals did not view themselves as politicizing the university but, rather, thought they were redirecting political activities that the university inevitably engaged in to serve new ends.

Liberal professors also argued that making universities take explicit political positions would empower faculty. They maintained that university administrators and boards of trustees currently determined universities' unstated political positions. If the faculty was to have a significant role in academic governance, it, as a body, needed to weigh in on these issues. In addition, they argued that educational and political questions were tightly interlinked. Consequently, professors could not fulfill their educational responsibilities without considering political issues. Donald Koster, an English professor at Adelphi University, explained that "when political and moral issues are so inextricably tangled with issues of educational policy . . . faculties are not only justified but indeed obligated to take positions" (Koster and Solberg 1970, 11). Since liberals believed that neutrality was impossible, they thought it would be better for students' education and for society if political issues were debated and decided directly rather than left to funders and administrators to decide covertly.

Conservatives also saw the contemporary university as political, but they viewed this as a perversion rather than a necessary state. Some conservatives blamed radical and liberal activists for the politicization of the university, but many saw deeper roots. For example, in his 1971 book *The Degradation of the*

Academic Dogma, sociologist Robert Nisbet agreed with activists that neutrality had become a myth and that the university was deeply entwined with politics: "Members of the student left in the 1960s spoke truly when they declared they were not the first to insinuate politics into the universities. That work, they properly argued, had already been done by agencies of government working directly with universities and with individual members of the faculty" (146). Nisbet agreed with activists that the university's external ties compromised its neutrality. Government funding, particularly, harmed universities because it politicized them. According to Nisbet, universities' involvement with government had ripple effects: institutional interests became intertwined with politics; faculty member's identification with national politics and their efforts to relate politics to university issues increased; political factions on campuses developed and the conflicts among them intensified; and relations between campus constituents became more litigious.

Nisbet laid out a history similar to the one told by his former colleague, Clark Kerr: after World War II, the university transformed itself by rapidly expanding its service to society. But instead of being a story of triumph, Nisbet's was a tale of despair. The availability of grants from government and foundations, Nisbet argued, turned professors into entrepreneurs, ceaselessly searching for "new sources of capital, new revenue, and taking the word in its larger sense, of profits" (73). This quest for "profit" eclipsed the university's commitment to its true purpose, "the dispassionate and objective study of nature, society, and man" (xiii). In addition, these new academic capitalists created "institutes, centers, [and] bureaus" (72), new institutional forms that fragmented the university and produced fissures that made it vulnerable to protesters' challenges.

Nisbet made it clear that he did not oppose government service because it supported the military and a misconceived war: "This is like decrying the pustule in a smallpox epidemic and giving no thought to the larger contexts" (82). All forms of social engagement, he argued, even those devoted to morally attractive causes such as "ethnic uplift" and "environmental purification," would have deleterious effects on the university; this would pull professors and institutional resources away from pure research and teaching (136). The only solution, he thought, was to restore university's rightful relation to society, one in which the university served society *indirectly* through the future actions of the students it educated. This limited form of service could not be directed and controlled; it had to happen freely from the inclinations of alumni. The university would shield itself from society and focus solely on objective scholarship and intellectual training. In this way the university could be neutral.

Many within academia wanted to defend the principle of neutrality, but not at the cost of eliminating the university's service function. They therefore rejected conservatives' conclusion that institutional engagement with society necessarily compromised the university's neutrality. They argued that activists distorted how universities functioned by falsely asserting that wealthy trustees controlled universities and that donors determined institutional agendas. For example, in 1970, McGeorge Bundy, then president of the Ford Foundation, looked back at his experience as dean of the School of Arts and Sciences at Harvard University in the 1950s and flatly contradicted the activists' critique. Harvard, he stated, "was not the tool of its trustees . . . They did not run the place in the interests of the ruling class" (531). Nor was Harvard "the tool of the military-industrial complex, the C.I.A., or a foreign policy establishment" (537). Donors facilitated what faculty wanted to do; they did not direct them or limit them. According to Bundy's recollection, independent-minded faculty members used outside money to pursue their own agendas, not vice versa. To the extent that any group controlled the university, Bundy contended, it was the faculty.

Although critical of conservatives, these academic defenders of neutrality also distrusted the liberal position because they believed it would pull the university into constant political struggles. Internally, constituents would struggle over whether university resources should go to urban renewal or public health or racial conciliation or economic development or weapons research or many other potential causes, and this would split the academy and leave it embroiled in constant conflict. To the extent that the university was able to take stands, it would then alienate those members who disagreed and therefore create an orthodoxy from which people could not dissent. "Were an individual college or university to assume the posture of a lobby or a pressure group with respect to some special issue," wrote Edward Shoben Jr. (1970), then vice president of Evergreen College, "it would be declaring itself the opponent of those who dissent from its stance and therefore the opponent of an environment in which a critical forum can genuinely thrive" (695). In addition, this would invite outside interference as different political groups vied to change and control the political position of universities. Bundy (1970) warned, "No institution which depends on society for its resources will be allowed—as an *institution*—to choose sides in the general contests of the democratic process" (555). Such actions would lead outside groups to seek to take control of universities and use them for their own political ends.

When defending institutional neutrality, some academics echoed the traditional consensual notion that linked institutional neutrality with individual neutrality. For example, in 1968, the American Political Science Association issued a report on professional ethics strongly proscribing political stands by departments or schools. It also maintained that a professor "must be very careful not to impose his partisan views—conventional or otherwise—upon his students or colleagues" (11). While the association acknowledged a faculty member's right to be politically active, it warned that "even when he is openly in the political arena the professor may not entirely forget his professional standards of skillful and scrupulous inquiry and rational utterance" (13). Paul D. Carrington (1969), a law professor at the University of Michigan, shared this traditional view: "Engagement in the politics of social change is destructive to an institution of what is called 'higher learning' because it is inconsistent with the idea." For him, this meant limiting individual faculty activism as well as prohibiting institutional stands. "I am not saying that there is no place in the classical university for scholars who have made up their minds and are ready for action," Carrington conceded. "There may even be a need for some individuals of that kind, but their actions ought to be individual and carefully framed to involve the institution as little as possible" (16). But, he continued, "an institution that long shelters a dominant group of social activists of whatever stripe does so at the expense of the spirit of inquiry" (17). The university, to maintain its own neutrality, must have a faculty that maintains a scholarly distance from the larger society.

Some academics, however, viewed the debate over institutional neutrality as an opportunity to replace the consensual view of neutrality with a pluralistic one, by decoupling the traditional association between institutional and individual neutrality. For example, the psychologist Kenneth Keniston (1968), then an associate professor at Stanford, opposed universities' taking political positions because he thought it would limit the range of political opinion and expression among faculty members and students: "Acting as a lobby or pressure group for some particular judgment or proposal, a university in effect closes its doors to those whose critical sense leads them to disagree, and thus destroys itself as an environment in which the critical spirit can truly flourish" (161). Keniston believed that an important function of university professors was social criticism and that they could not fulfill this role if the university took positions as an institution: "The task of a university as an organization, then, is to be neutral, objective, and dispassionate in order to preserve an atmosphere in which students and faculty members can discuss, evaluate, criticize, judge, commit themselves, and, when they choose, act" (161). Neutrality, according to this view, was intended to provide a safe haven for the advocacy of multiple perspectives.

Keniston's pluralistic understanding of institutional neutrality had implications for academic freedom. Academic freedom, he asserted, could not be limited to protecting only "objective" scholarship; it had to cover all modes of expression and action, no matter how intemperate: "Any attempt to distinguish between 'objective' and 'partisan' criticism ignores the role of judgment and values in the critical process: for all judgments and values can be deemed 'partisan' by those who reject them" (161). Keniston's defense of institutional neutrality expanded the meaning of academic freedom. Commenting on these views, Frederic Ness (1968), president of Fresno State College, argued that Keniston assumed "the provision of more liberty than may have been intended by the doctrine of academic freedom, and perhaps more than society, to which we must ultimately be accountable, will be willing to give" (166). While Keniston and other like-minded colleagues defended institutional neutrality and thus affirmed traditional proscriptions against the university's taking official political positions, they did so in a way that gave academics, as individuals, much more political freedom than they had traditionally been granted.

This pluralistic position was commonly expressed when the AAUP, in 1969, considered taking an official position on institutional neutrality and asked members to weigh in on the issue. For example, Thomas Ford Hoult (1970), a sociologist at Arizona State University, wrote a letter on behalf of five other members of the executive committee of the university's chapter of the AAUP supporting the pluralistic understanding of institutional neutrality: "The academic setting that officially favors one side of an ideological question almost inevitably degenerates into a propaganda institute" (128). But Hoult and his colleagues did not favor neutrality in the sense of faculty members' objectivity in teaching and research. They urged faculty "as individuals" to take a stand "on relevant social issues" and to bring this critical attitude into their classes: "Since we want to encourage skepticism about dogma, it should be clear that we do not advocate neutrality. We feel colleges and universities serve society best when they teach their participants to engage in social criticism and to register dissent when necessary" (129). This position transformed traditional notions of academic freedom to protect not only "proper" scholarly discourse but also partisan political advocacy in and outside the university. Unlike traditional consensual notions of institutional neutrality that labeled "extreme" positions as "partisan" and therefore unprofessional and unacceptable within the academy, this conception saw the presence of "extreme" positions as proof that the institution tolerated all ideas and therefore was truly neutral.

Whereas in the Progressive Era and the Cold War, the ideal of institutional neutrality had been used to exclude radical beliefs from the university as unacceptable forms of partisanship, in the late 1960s and early 1970s, some academics redefined institutional neutrality in ways that could protect radicalism. Columbia University philosopher Robert Paul Wolff somewhat cynically made this connection in *The Ideal of the University* (1992 [1969]). Wolff believed that institutional neutrality was a myth: "A large university in contemporary America simply cannot adopt a value-neutral stance, either externally or internally, no matter how hard it tries" (70). But he believed that it was a myth that could be used to the advantage of the political left. If the university abandoned the ideal of neutrality and openly took political positions, faculty and students—who, Wolff believed, were "conservative in their leanings"—would move institutional policies even farther to the right, and "conservative forces in society at large" would seek to use the university more directly for their own purposes. But under the myth of neutrality, universities could function as "sanctuaries for social critics who would find it very hard to gain a living elsewhere in society" (74–75). While he believed it to be impossible in practice, then, Wolff argued that institutional neutrality, defined pluralistically, was an advantageous ideal because it could support an expansive definition of academic freedom that protected political radicals.

While the pluralistic conception of neutrality offered protection to radicals, it represented a moderate, compromise position in the context of late 1960s and early 1970s debates over neutrality. Unlike the radical and liberal positions, it reasserted prohibitions against institutional stands. Contrary to the conservative position, it maintained the university's service activities. As a compromise, it gained traction over the course of the 1970s. While no consensus emerged around questions of neutrality, objectivity, advocacy, and service, the pluralistic conception of neutrality achieved widespread acceptance within American academic discourse by the end of the decade. Derek Bok, then president of Harvard, took this position in his highly regarded book *Beyond the Ivory Tower: Social Responsibilities of the Modern University* (1982). He maintained that the university should remain engaged in society as long as its service activities had an educational justification. He asserted the necessity of institutional neutrality to prevent the university from being dragged into political battles. And he strongly defended academic freedom, which he understood as protecting political advocacy within and outside the university.

Conservative critics of contemporary higher education correctly note that the 1960s marked a turning point in American higher education. Campus activists forced academics to reexamine the ideal of institutional neutrality and related ideas about scholarly objectivity, academic freedom, and institutional service.

As a result, the ideal of institutional neutrality was redefined in pluralistic rather than consensual terms. This newer understanding of neutrality tolerated a wider range of political views and political behaviour on the part of professors. Universities began to accept faculty who actively combined their scholarship and teaching with political advocacy. Although professors remained sharply divided on whether scholarship should reflect their political views and only a small percentage of faculty came to view the classroom as a place to advance their political views, this still represents a significant shift from the first half of the twentieth century, when unorthodox political positions or impassioned modes of expression were labeled partisan and viewed as unprofessional (Gross 2011).

Although conservative critics correctly note a broadening of professional norms regarding faculties' political advocacy, they exaggerate the extent to which the 1960s changed universities' relation to society. Universities continue to be involved in a wide range of service activities, many of which have political implications that are not examined or defended. Thus, activists' critique that the ideal of institutional neutrality hides the political consequences of universities' ties to government and business has had little impact on university policies. In addition, conservative critics ignore how much they have adopted the pluralistic conception of institutional neutrality and used it for their own ends. Conservatives such as David Horowitz blast universities for having programs in gender studies that assume gender inequality is bad, but they use the notion of the university as a free market of ideas to press for the hiring of more conservative faculty and to justify the creation of academic programs based on conservative beliefs. Ironically, the pluralistic conception of neutrality that opened the academy to forms of scholarship that conservatives abhor also provides the platform from which they critique higher education.

NOTES

I thank the Spencer Foundation for funding some of the research used in the chapter and Jal Mehta, Meira Levinson, members of the Boston Area History of Education Group, and members of my writing group for comments on an earlier version of this essay.

1. See www.studentsforacademicfreedom.org/documents/1925/abor.html.

2. For an example of the obliviousness of another leader in higher education to the coming critique of neutrality, see Perkins 1966.

3. These positions did not align perfectly with conventional politics. For example, almost all of the people who took the radical position on institutional neutrality were politically radical, but not all political radicals held the radical position on neutrality. Conversely, political conservatives generally gravitated to the conservative position on neutrality, but

a good number of political liberals and moderates joined them. Academic politics overlapped with but did not perfectly mimic national politics.

4. Simon and coauthors (1972) wanted their program to be acceptable to administrators who still believed in the ideal of institutional neutrality. To avoid being accused of politicizing the university, they limited their critique of institutional neutrality to the administrative functions and called for the avoidance of social harm rather than active pursuit of social good. They showed that the critique of institutional neutrality could be narrowly focused or globally defined.

PART FIVE

INSTITUTIONAL CHANGE AND ITS LIMITS

CHAPTER NINE

Activism and the Academy

Lessons from the Rise of Ethnic Studies

FABIO ROJAS

The twentieth century witnessed numerous profound transformations of the academy, ranging from the rise of the American research university (Vesey 1970) to the global expansion of higher education (Frank and Gabler 2006) and its increasing integration with the for-profit sector (Powell, Owen-Smith, and Colyvas 2007). One important development was the proliferation of disciplines and areas of study (Brint et al. 2009). In addition to the ever increasing complexity of science, the growth of new academic programs was driven by political and social trends such as the civil rights movement, which instigated ethnic studies. The appearance of ethnic studies and other identity-based fields of study raises some important questions. How, exactly, did ethnic studies activists succeed in forging a new discipline? What are the long-term consequences of establishing a field that defined itself in both intellectual and political terms? What lessons should scholars draw from studying the institutional development of ethnic studies?

This chapter addresses questions about ethnic studies from an organizational perspective. Higher education is a system of organizations and practices that regulate work within these organizations. A new type of academic unit, the ethnic studies program, can be established only if proponents successfully navigate this bureaucratic system. Thus, the creation of ethnic studies is a political and bureaucratic process. It is political in the sense that students and scholars are using political tools such as campus protest to obtain a new academic unit. It is bureaucratic in that an ethnic studies unit can survive only if it can satisfy the goals of the university and successfully obtain resources such as staff, students, and funds. Consequently, scholars interested in the institutional development of ethnic studies have often adopted a process model of program adoption (Clark 1968; Rojas 2007b; Yamane 2001). This chapter is organized around the different stages in the implementation of ethnic studies programs and the issues raised by this process.

Ethnic Studies: Definitions and Debates

"Ethnic studies" denotes the field of study that examines the history, culture, and social organization of ethnic groups. This area of study usually focuses on American racial groups, even though many adherents have called for a "diaspora" perspective situating American ethnic groups in a global perspective (Gilroy 1993). Ethnic studies is sometimes cast as an interdisciplinary area that draws from more established fields, such as history, to describe the life and culture of African Americans, Native Americans, and other minorities. The field is organized into subdisciplines focusing on a single cultural group, such as African American studies or Asian American studies. Sometimes there are academic specialties focusing on more specific groups, such as Puerto Rican studies or Filipino studies.

The first ethnic studies units were proposed in 1966 when students at San Francisco State College asked the administration to create a department of black studies (Rojas 2007b, 2010; Rooks 2006). This new unit would act as an organizational umbrella for traditional courses and student-run courses that explored African American topics. This proposal was not accepted or implemented until students staged a strike on behalf of ethnic studies in the fall of 1968. The College of Ethnic Studies, which included black studies, was started in the fall of 1969, an event that triggered student strikes for ethnic studies on other campuses. Almost two hundred black studies programs were started in the next decade, as were dozens of programs in cognate fields such as Native American studies, Asian American studies, women's studies, queer studies, and gender studies (Rojas 2007b, 170–71).

Ethnic studies programs were motivated by two conflicting political ideas. Many activists thought that ethnic studies could encourage racial integration, a core goal of the civil rights movement (Rojas 2007b, 140–43). Both white and nonwhite students could attend ethnic studies programs and be exposed to different cultures. Activists also relied on ethnic nationalism to justify their proposed reforms. By "ethnic nationalism," I refer to the theory that ethnic groups should retain their autonomy by exerting control over cultural, educational, economic, and/or political institutions (Dawson 2001). Within the context of the late 1960s, many civil rights activists became disappointed with civil rights and thought that the white mainstream would not cede resources or status to African Americans or other minorities. The response of ethnic nationalists was to claim that ethnic groups such as African Americans should promote their own agendas through dedicated institutions, such as black studies programs. Thus, there was a tension between those who saw ethnic studies as a tool for erasing racial boundaries and those who wanted these programs to be a place where students and scholars could cultivate their knowledge and appreciation of the history of particular ethnic groups.

The academic units representing ethnic studies vary a great deal in their internal organization and identity. Some present themselves as multipurpose "ethnic studies" units where students can concentrate on specific cultural groups, such as Native Americans. An example is the American Ethnic Studies department at the University of Washington (2011). Other programs specialize in a single group. For example, most African American studies programs focus on people of African descent, whether they are in the United States, Brazil, or elsewhere. There are also important bureaucratic differences in the operation of ethnic studies programs (Ford 1973). One model is the department, which contains its own teaching faculty. In contrast, the interdisciplinary program is staffed mainly by professors with joint appointments in other programs and departments. These organizational differences often correspond to philosophical differences. It is not uncommon for ethnic studies professors to claim that the organizational format of their program indicates a sort of intellectual status. The program staffed by faculty with joint appointments indicates a field that does not have intellectual maturity or autonomy. Ethnic studies is also often cast as a boundary-transgressing field that draws from but is not constrained by traditional disciplinary fields.

Aside from organizational structure, ethnic studies is characterized by debates over the mission of the field. One common debate concerns the importance of nationalism and the relationship to other disciplines (Chiang 2009; Rojas 2007b; Van Deburg 1992). It is often argued that ethnic studies represents a specific point of view that is not captured within existing disciplinary frameworks. The history taught in an African American studies program emerges from an intimate encounter with racial oppression, an experience not found in traditional historical accounts. This example shows the close relationship between values and organization. The ethnic studies program is needed because of the lacunae in traditional research. Of course, there are those who dispute this position. Logically, critics have argued, African American studies, or any other type of ethnic studies, can be grouped within the larger framework of the humanities and social sciences.

By the 1980s, the debates over ethnically conscious academic work evolved into arguments over multiculturalism (Asante and Ravitch 1991; Bryson 2005; Kalu 1991). Definitions vary, but multiculturalists share the belief that educational institutions should represent the views of multiple ethnic groups. The underlying logic of multiculturalism is accommodation and institutionalized tolerance of ethnic differences.

Sociological Theories of Organizational Change

Organizational scholars offer two crucial insights for those who wish to understand how ethnic studies emerged in the university: organizations are embedded in larger social systems, and organizational change is a constant process of change and adjustment. This suggests that the story of a new organizational form such as ethnic studies programs is about both political mobilization and bureaucratic expansion. The trajectory of a new academic field is defined by the strategies and resources available for helping programs and departments survive and prosper inside larger educational institutions.

First, organizational sociology tends to view universities in terms of larger populations defined by common practices, beliefs, and relationships. For example, neo-institutional scholars argue that organizations such as colleges are embedded in larger political systems that impose constraints (DiMaggio and Powell 1983; Meyer and Rowan 1977). These social structures, in turn, are predicated on the values that legitimize the organization. A single university belongs to a larger "field" that includes other universities, accreditation agencies, the state, and the public. Collectively, these actors articulate the values that legitimize universities, such as academic freedom or scientific rigor, and encourage universities to adopt practices instantiating these ideas. Thus, the ability to promote ethnic studies depends on how scholars and student activists defend the field to the publics that govern academia. Resonance with academic culture helps promote ethnic studies, while explicit rejection of academic culture would suppress the field.

The second insight is that organizational change is a complex, ongoing process that has no clearly defined terminal point, especially in academic settings (Clark 1968). A new organizational unit such as an academic program must show that it is compatible with the ever-changing goals and culture of the organization. The earliest stages of change involve arguments about missions and values, in addition to the assessment of multiple, possibly viable alternatives. Then, staff and funds must be obtained, and this is followed by implementation. Over time, organizational units and policies are subject to criticism and financial pressures as well as planned changes. Proposing change, staffing, budgets, and periodic evaluations all offer opportunities for allies and critics to either appropriate or undermine ethnic studies programs.

Conditions Creating the Potential for Change

The analysis of movement-initiated organizational change starts with a description of the broader social trends that created political opportunities. The most basic fact about ethnic studies is that it was an outgrowth of the civil rights movement (Rojas 2007b; Rooks 2006). The civil rights movement facilitated the push for ethnic studies in multiple ways. On a national level, the movement created an environment particularly conducive to race-based structural reform within universities. Americans, in general, were changing their attitudes toward race. Educators, in particular, were willing, for the first time, to consider reforms aimed at bringing minority issues into the curriculum.

The civil rights movement also facilitated ethnic studies through desegregation. For the first time, predominantly white colleges had significant numbers of black students (Willie and Cunnigen 1981). Even though intellectuals had discussed something like ethnic studies for decades, there were not enough students to stage a movement. By the 1960s, many colleges had hundreds of black students rather than dozens. This shift meant that it was possible to create a politically motivated community of black student activists (Rojas 2007b, 22–44).

College desegregation also enabled the transmission of tactics from the civil rights movement to the college campuses. As reported in many histories of the civil rights movement, students would often participate in projects such as voter registration drives in the South (e.g., McAdam 1988; Rojas 2007b, 34–42). The consequence was that students returned to their schools with a radicalized perspective and with experience in protest tactics. The original Freedom Ride was in 1961 and other civil rights projects continued into the late 1960s. It is not surprising that campus mobilizations escalated shortly thereafter. Accounts of the ethnic studies / black studies movement at San Francisco State College found that student leaders had spent their summers in the South working for the Student Nonviolent Coordinating Committee, a central civil rights organization. More research needs to be done on the connections between civil rights actions and college student leadership, but it is surely the case that students in the late 1960s were exceptionally well versed in political action.

Another crucial factor in the rise of ethnic studies is that universities were already very liberal places by the 1960s. Numerous studies of professorial attitudes have shown that professors are more likely to vote for Democrats and more likely to consider themselves politically liberal, and this was so even before the 1960s (see the introduction and chapter 1 of this volume). Given this political stance, combined with the turbulent political environment, it is no surprise that many professors were responsive to demands for ethnic studies. Approving ethnic studies was one way to show that campuses were open to all and were serious about desegregation.

Universities themselves acted as incubators for protest. As numerous observers have noted, higher education dramatically expanded in the 1960s (Bayer and Astin 1969; Buchanan and Brackett 1970; Lipset 1976; van Dyke 1998). Campuses increased enrollments and constructed large housing units. The sudden and unprecedented concentration of students lowered the costs of political activism. It became relatively easy to summon thousands of students for a demonstration. Universities were now providing facilities for students' clubs, which could easily be used as gathering places for political groups (Rojas 2007b; for a discussion of university geography and campus protest in China, see Zhao 2001). The university in the 1960s was a place with lots of people, ample resources, and weak administrative control over students. In retrospect, a "perfect storm," a confluence of ideal conditions, made ethnic studies a highly likely if not inevitable outcome of the civil rights movement.

Where Protest Happened and How It Happened

Contentious behavior was crucial in the push for ethnic studies. Early studies of this period, focusing on interviews with department chairs, found that many programs—probably a majority—were created after rallies, student strikes, and sit-ins (Blake and Cobb 1976). Later studies find a large correlation between black student protest and the creation of black studies programs (Rojas 2006). A single protest by black students nearly triples the odds that a black studies program was formed. These findings draw attention to an extremely important issue: the ubiquity of student uprisings and their impact on universities. In this section I summarize what is known about student protest in general and how it facilitated ethnic studies.

One of the strongest findings is that student protest most frequently occurs in research-intensive institutions (Rojas 2006; van Dyke 1998). Anecdotally, there is much evidence to support this. The most well-known examples of campus unrest tend to be at research universities, such as the University of California, Berkeley, Columbia University, and Cornell University. Scott and El-Assal (1969) found that being a research university was a strong predictor of having campus unrest in the 1960s. A 1970 study by the Urban Institute found similar results (Buchanan and Bracket 1970). In a survey of college presidents and student body presidents, the probability of reporting protest of any kind was much higher in research institutions than in other types of colleges. Among respondents at community colleges, for example, the reported rate of protest was almost zero percent. Alexander Astin's (1975) research on college protest found similar patterns: protest was more likely at research-intensive schools than others, and protest was more likely to lead to curricular change. Similar findings are reported in contemporary research. For example, studies of new student protest tactics show that they are more likely to appear at research universities (Soule 1997).

Research on protests supporting ethnic studies finds similar patterns. Even though ethnic studies was invented by students at San Francisco State College, the universities most likely to have an ethnic studies program were the research universities. The available evidence suggests that non-elite schools may be the site of innovation but ethnic studies demands were most commonly fulfilled at research universities. For example, by 1998, about 50 percent of research universities had degree-granting African American studies programs (Rojas 2007b, 171). In contrast, 20 percent of selective liberal arts colleges had these programs. The program creation rate was much lower at other kinds of colleges, such as master's colleges and less selective liberal arts colleges. Similar patterns can be found for other kinds of ethnic studies. A casual glance at the *Index of College Majors*, a College Board publication listing institutions offering specific majors, shows that Asian American studies programs are likely to be found at research universities on the West or East Coast, Puerto Rican studies programs at research universities in the northeast, and so forth. This does not imply that there are no ethnic studies programs in nonresearch environments. These programs do exist at non-research-intensive schools, but at a lower rate. If the school teaches ethnic studies, it is likely to do so in specific courses and not in specially designated programs.

Why is the research university such a hospitable place for student activism and ethnic studies? It might be hypothesized that research universities have more resources. Wealth, as measured by financial endowments, is correlated with having ethnic studies units. In statistical models, however, the effect of being a research university persists even when accounting for wealth (Rojas 2006), suggesting that wealth is not the only factor. Multiple regression analyses using wealth as a control variable still yield a significant and substantially large effect for research institutions. Similar analyses show that black student enrollments, university size (as measured by total enrollments), and other factors do not completely account for the correlation between student protest and ethnic studies. There seems to be something distinctive about the research university environment that promotes ethnic studies.

Case studies suggest that research universities are good places for ethnic studies because they have a distinctive student population and a culture that is open to new academic disciplines (Rojas 2007b, chaps. 4 and 5). Students can take the time to protest because they have financial support, and they already have the inclination toward politics. Research universities attract students who have stronger academic credentials, come from wealthier families, and are less likely to be commuter students. Given that many student activists in the 1960s later rose to political prominence, this might also be an early expression of a political career. Furthermore, universities are places with faculty members who are searching for new topics and ideas (Bryson 2005). As long as there is a small but dedicated intellectual constituency at the research university, a new field has a chance at survival.

Another question here is how protest disrupted the status quo in the research universities, making new academic fields possible. Sociologists and political scientists have long recognized that the way in which protest happens is important; the type of protest matters a great deal (Rojas 2006). Protest is more likely to be followed by curricular change than no protest, and a nonviolent protest by black students, such as a rally, is more likely to lead to an African American studies program than violent action, such as property damage. The importance of nondisruptive protest suggests that protest has mattered when it fruitfully addressed the moral framework of the university. When student protestors did violent or disruptive things, they could easily become stigmatized and subsequently marginalized from the academic community. In case studies of disruptive protests by black students, it has often been found that violence destabilizes college administrators. For example, in the Third World Strike at San Francisco State College, numerous administrators quit because they could not control campus protest, which sometimes led to violence (Rojas 2007b, chap. 3; 2010). Administrators were often under pressure from trustees to do something drastic or to resign in the face of highly disruptive actions. These political pressures prohibited university leaders from negotiating with activists or offering compromises. In contrast, nondisruptive protest gave students a chance to air grievances, develop relationships with faculty and administrators, and start the complex process of setting up an academic program.

The Menu of Options

The push for ethnic studies generated a wide range of options, from ethnic-themed courses to separate institutions. Perhaps the most common proposal was that colleges and universities should start offering courses on ethnic topics, which entailed a modest change in the orientation of existing academic work as it was then expressed. In some disciplines, the demand for courses and research did not require much effort. Sociology and anthropology, for example, have always addressed ethnicity in some way. It is not surprising that some early black studies scholars, for example, had earned their doctoral degrees in sociology, such as Joyce Ladner (1998) and Abdul Alkalimat (2009). In other disciplines, focusing on ethnicity was seen as contrary to the spirit of the discipline. In literary studies, ethnic studies scholars insisted that works by African American authors such as James Baldwin and Langston Hughes deserved the same status as works by other canonical authors. Demands to expand the scope of American literary scholarship were met with substantial resistance, as critics insisted that literary merit could not be tied to political claims for curricular reform. These arguments evolved into disputes over multiculturalism in the 1980s and 1990s, when arguments about the enduring value of classic texts altered the terrain of American literary writings (for a summary, see Bryson 2005).

Insisting on more teaching and research on American ethnic groups was the most successful proposal to come from the ethnic studies movement. Despite bitter debate over multiculturalism in the 1990s, it is now routine for a wide range of departments to teach courses that might be called ethnic studies (Brint et al. 2009; Cole 2006). These topics are no longer considered controversial, but rather, they are viewed as standard elements of research and teaching in the humanities and social sciences.

One interesting outcome of the demand for ethnically focused teaching and research is the existence of multiculturalism requirements on some college campuses. In the 1990s, some student groups asked that college administrations require all students to take courses on an American ethnic group. David Yamane's *Student Movements for Multiculturalism* (2001) documents the student mobilization around multiculturalism requirements at the University of California, Berkeley, and the University of Wisconsin–Madison. Yamane's account focuses on how students promoted multiculturalism courses by appealing to the mission and liberal culture of universities. These courses are now standard elements of the undergraduate curriculum at some research universities.

Multicultural course requirements are an example of incremental institutionalized change that has now become a routine and "taken for granted" part of the curriculum. It is no longer the case that "culture studies" or "multicultural" course requirements generate much controversy, except from long-standing conservative critics who tend to criticize most race-based educational practices. There is even the distinct possibility that these courses will become extremely common, especially as Asian and Latino immigrants increase their numbers and their children enroll in the higher education system. Ethnic studies and multicultural courses, required or not, may be a relatively simple way for administrators and professors to show that a college education remains relevant to these populations.

The ethnic studies movement also generated proposals for permanent, structural changes in universities, some of which were, and remain, much more controversial. Activists routinely demanded ethnic studies programs, departments, and research centers (for an extended discussion, see Rojas 2007b, 93–129). As noted earlier, many types of academic units were proposed, entailing different levels of commitment by the university and motivated by different strategic and intellectual concerns (Bankole 2006; Daniel 1980; Ford 1973). The proposal requiring the least commitment was probably the interdisciplinary program. This type of academic unit brings together courses on a specific topic, such as African American studies, and jointly appointed professors and adjuncts teach them. The attractive feature of this program model is that the university administration does not have to hire many new faculty members. Instead, scholars who are already interested in ethnic studies agree to be listed in the new unit's faculty roster. By drawing instructors from existing disciplines, one can avoid a contentious debate over whether ethnic studies is a legitimate field that deserves to be recognized as distinct from others.

The second kind of academic unit is the department, which has its own faculty members, can award tenure, and can be a graduate training center (Aldridge and Young 2000; Ford 1973; Kamoche 1980). In debates over the bureaucratic organization of ethnic studies, departments are often seen as the alternative to the interdisciplinary program. Departments almost always have tenured professors and represent disciplines that have attained a high degree of autonomy. Doctoral programs in the arts and sciences are usually located in departments, another sign of their status. The intellectual argument for the department is that it signals that ethnic studies is a distinct area of study and not merely a marginal topic in other fields. Departments require a higher level of commitment from a university. Tenured faculty need yearly salaries and graduate programs require financial support. These units are not easy to contract, or eliminate, once they are established.

A third kind of academic unit is the research center (e.g., Rojas 2007b, 151–55; White 2004). In this model, teaching and staffing issues remain in the hands of the traditional arts and sciences departments, but interested academics can participate in a separate unit built around common research interests. These academics units are removed from the traditional needs of teaching and research and can be flexible. The research center can, as administrators deem necessary, offer seminars, conduct surveys, pay for research, publish journals and books, and/or hold public lectures.

A fourth kind of academic unit is more innovative—the "cultural center." In this model, the university creates a student support center on campus that is aimed at students interested in a particular ethnic group. For example, an African American–themed dormitory was created at the University of Pennsylvania (Glasker 2002, 115–28). Cultural centers did not have to be residential; they could be aimed at educational activities that do not fit well with the mission of a typical degree program, such as student counseling or the performing arts.

In practice, the distinctions between these different kinds of academic units were blurred. Some programs became departments, and departments were often linked to cultural houses and research centers. On some campuses, the ethnic studies departments kept their distance from the cultural centers, while on others, they kept in close contact.

The most radical ethnic studies proponents promoted separate institutions. For example, at the beginning of the ethnic studies movement, some activists promoted the "black university" as an alternative to the predominantly white university and the traditional historically black college (McWhorter 1968; Rojas 2007b, 24). The argument was that white institutions were too dominated by racist values, while the historically black colleges were too strongly tied to conservative religious groups (Watkins 2001). The alternative was to create an autonomous institution that was designed to promote black values and pursue a black mission, such as helping poor inner city residents or developing Africa.

Not surprisingly, these proposals met with very limited success. For example, there was a proposal in 1969 at Antioch College for the creation of a black studies college (Thelwell 1969). This proposal enjoyed some support, but it also alienated many faculty members and ultimately failed. At the University of Illinois, Chicago, the education faculty proposed an ethnic studies college to be controlled by "members of the community," which meant people in poor Chicago neighborhoods. This proposal was rejected in favor of a more traditional academic unit completely contained within the university (Rojas 2007b, 112–16).

There were some independent ethnic studies institutions that managed to be created and survive for some period of time. Nairobi College was a short-lived college in East Palo Alto, California (Hoover 1992; Van Deburg 1992). Founded in 1969 to develop black leadership and push a "third world" perspective, Nairobi

College admitted a few dozen students who wished to learn college-level materials from a radical black perspective. The college also began a day school for younger children, which focused on teaching black English and black history. In North Carolina, activists associated with Duke University started Malcolm X Liberation University. It had goals similar to those of Nairobi College—to train black leaders and serve the black community. Like Nairobi College, Malcolm X Liberation University explicitly employed a nationalist perspective on education (Belvin 2004). A third example is the Institute for the Black World, an off-shoot of the Atlanta University Center. Founded in 1969 by scholars associated with the university center, the institute would become a think tank where teachers and scholars could develop a new intellectual agenda. It was perhaps the first and most prominent ethnic studies think tank (Rojas 2007b; White 2004).

All three of these institutions closed. By 1972, Malcolm X Liberation University had collapsed when funding disappeared. After the media critiqued the school for being racist, few people were willing to donate. Nairobi College closed in 1979, after years of declining enrollments and factionalism. The Institute for the Black World closed in 1984 in the face of similar problems. What these three examples show is that ethnic studies did not fare very well in settings independent of the traditional university system. Their strong ideology made it hard to attract donors and maintain a steady income stream, especially in the recession of the 1970s. In contrast, ethnic studies institutionalized within the university system survived, though not without problems, until the present.

Deradicalization

An important theme emerging from social scientific analyses of ethnic studies is deradicalization. That is, for ethnic studies to be implemented and gain acceptance, it had to be stripped of its most political trappings. Specifically, proponents had to distance themselves from ethnic nationalism and promise that all courses would be open to both black and white students. Furthermore, ethnic studies courses and departments had to frame their mission in terms of bringing new knowledge to the university, not advocating a political ideology or promoting any particular group.

Reformulating ethnic studies as a race-neutral enterprise was not a simple process, given that the field's early history was strongly intertwined with the surge of ethnic nationalism in the 1960s and early 1970s. For example, the first black studies courses were probably African American history courses at Merritt College in Oakland, California. These courses were demanded by a student group that included Huey Newton, the future leader of the Black Panthers (Seale 1970). The explicit goal of the course was to teach black history to black students and promote a nationalist perspective. Later in 1968, at San Francisco State College, black studies courses were taught in ways that promoted a nationalist perspective. Eyewitness accounts of the first black studies courses indicated that instructors often promoted nationalism (Rojas 2007b, 61).

While some departments and institutions maintained a nationalist stance, many did not. As early as 1969, it was becoming clear to ethnic studies advocates that nationalism was not going to be a framework that would ensure integration into the university. On numerous campuses, ethnic studies proposals were rejected for being too political (Rojas 2007b, 100–108). In other cases, autonomous ethnic studies institutions, such as Nairobi College, disbanded because the constituency for them was too small (Van Deburg 1992). There simply were not enough people willing to donate money for a consciously nationalist and radical organization. The nonprofit sector exerted significant pressure, as well. Philanthropic groups such as the Ford Foundation preferred to support ethnic studies programs that promised to teach integrated classrooms. Studies of Ford Foundation documents show that grant applicants were rejected if they were perceived as too "political"—a code word for nationalist (Rojas 2007b; Rooks 2006).

In addition to rejecting nationalism as a legitimate justification for their field, ethnic studies scholars altered the content of their courses and texts. This isn't to say that nationalism and other ideological perspectives are absent in modern ethnic studies. It is still possible to find prominent radical voices from every strand of ethnic studies. Molefi Asante developed "Afrocentric theory" in the 1980s as a response to the perceived shortcomings of Eurocentric scholarship (Asante 2006; Small 1999). Leonard Jeffries (2011), an advocate of "Nile Valley scholarship," argues that essential elements of classical Greek culture were first innovated in pre-Hellenic Egyptian societies. Ward Churchill (2007), the controversial former ethnic studies professor, has defended violent resistance by indigenous peoples. The typical ethnic studies program, however, is staffed by scholars with traditional academic credentials who approach ethnic studies in ways that would seem normal to their colleagues in related disciplines, as is apparent from quantitative data on African American studies professors. Survey evidence shows that over 60 percent of African American studies professors, for example, were jointly appointed in other departments (Rojas 2007b, 190). Analyses of the publication records of faculty in African American studies doctoral programs show that many scholars at elite universities tend to publish in disciplinary journals rather than black studies journals such as the *Black Scholar* (Rojas 2008).

The shift to interdisciplinary and value-neutral scholarship might be linked to the drive for status in the academy. Chiang (2009) makes this claim with an analysis of the Asian American studies field. Employing Bourdieuian sociology, Chiang notes that academia is a social system built around reputation, and success requires that professors obtain the right type of symbolic capital. Specifically, professors need ideas that will allow them to show superior technical and academic skills, not their allegiance to social movements. Therefore, Asian American studies, as a discipline, is ill served by an exclusive reliance on nationalist ideology, such as evaluating books in terms of relevance to the community, because nationalist frameworks provide few opportunities for intellectuals to demonstrate technical mastery of their discipline's core methods. Asian American studies "for the community" was simply not a viable way to acquire status in the academy.

Chiang's analysis of the history of Asian American studies illustrates the argument well. Like most other kinds of ethnic studies, Asian American studies was strongly associated with the student movements of the 1960s. The first proposals for Asian American studies came out of the Third World Strike at San Francisco State College, which also spawned African American studies, Native American studies, and Chicano studies. Scholars were committed to a nationalist perspective in the field's formative phase. The anthologies that defined the Asian American studies canon stated that their purpose was service to the Asian American community.

As time passed, the tenor of scholarship in Asian American studies changed. Scholars began to focus on books that permitted a more technical and thus more prestigious approach to the field. One of Chiang's examples is *Dictee*, a book written by California performance artist Theresa Hyak Cha. The book is written in a mixture of English, Korean, and French; it mixes prose and poetry and combines text and visual arts. For these reasons, the book is often described as difficult and postmodern because it does not contain a traditional narrative or linear plot (Wong 1993). Though it does reference colonial politics, it cannot be described as a conventional narrative of immigrant assimilation or political resistance. Publication of this text allowed Asian American studies scholars to claim that their field had matured. Scholars were now producing readings of texts that were just as demanding as any associated with other kinds of literature. The expertise required to read and interpret *Dictee* exemplified the intellectual capital needed to help Asian American studies grow into a more respected field.

The Long 1970s

An emerging theme in historical scholarship on the civil rights movement is the 1970s as a time of political retrenchment. In a relatively successful period from the mid-1950s to approximately 1968, civil rights groups scored a series of important victories, such as the Brown decision of 1955 and the 1964 Civil Rights Act. Starting in 1968, there were visible signs that the movement was entering a new era. From the radical flank, nationalist organizations such as the Black Panthers captured national attention. At the same time, conservative groups were forming, partially in reaction to the civil rights movement. The 1970s are seen as a time when liberal politics gave way to more radical tendencies, while conservative groups made progress and formed winning electoral coalitions. Historians call this period, from 1968 to Reagan's election in 1980, the "long 1970s" and view it as a transitional period between a more liberal and a more conservative political climate (e.g., Cowie 2005; Strub 2008; Zanini 2010).

Ethnic studies had to survive in this new environment, and it is worth asking how the field's deradicalization was tied to the shifting political climate. Historians have noted that the Third World Strike of 1968, the event originating modern ethnic studies, occurred during an election year when political candidates were campaigning on a "law and order" platform. At that time, this was advantageous in the short term. Ethnic studies proponents at San Francisco State College could portray themselves as an embattled, righteous group fighting for minorities. However, the acrimony of the late 1960s consumed liberal allies and encouraged opponents. The political environment became a liability because it resulted in a generation of administrators who were actively opposed to ethnic studies, some of whom worked to repress the field (Rojas 2010). As protest receded in the late 1970s, these administrators retained a cautious, often contentious, stance toward ethnic studies.

While the backlash and retrenchment of the 1970s is certainly important, it is by no means the only factor behind the abeyance and deradicalization of ethnic studies. For example, the 1970s were a time of economic crisis. Inflation decimated budgets, and even the most enthusiastic university leaders found it hard to provide additional funds for ethnic studies. There is also the issue of "protest cycles." As coined by movement scholar Sidney Tarrow (1994), a protest cycle denotes the pattern of emergence, peaking, and decline experienced by a political movement. By the 1970s, the civil rights movement had gained its biggest victories and attention shifted elsewhere; it had reached the end of its cycle. In interviews with black studies professors, I have been told of the differences between the students of the early 1970s, who were politically engaged, and later cohorts that were more vocationally oriented. Finally, ethnic studies is but one field in a crowded university system with dozens of social science, humanities, and professional fields. Deradicalization may have been a way to reach out to more students in the competition for enrollments.

The Uses of Ethnic Studies

Ethnic studies developed different relationships with the various audiences that constitute the American university system. At the highest levels, administrators did not support ethnic studies. Case studies of particular programs and historical accounts show that administrators ranged from ambivalent to hostile (Cunningham 1991; Frye 1979; Rojas 2007b, 2010; Small 1999). Before the Third World Strike that began the modern ethnic studies movement, administrators initially supported proposals for black studies and ethnic studies, but the academic programs were delayed in committees. The administrative delays strained relationships between students and deans, which contributed to the conflict. Settlement of the Third World Strike established ethnic studies, but there were still substantial conflicts between ethnic studies faculty and the administration. Tension and distrust characterized the relationship between ethnic studies programs and college administrators on many campuses.

The Ford Foundation, which funded many ethnic studies programs, published a report on black studies that remains one of the few extended discussions of administrators and their relationship to ethnic studies programs in the 1970s and 1980s (Harris, Hine, and McKay 1990). The report notes the hostility felt by many administrators because ethnic studies was brought to campus by protest. The report also notes that administrators tolerated ethnic studies for pragmatic reasons. Disbanding these programs would lead to a public outcry, and they retained their symbolic value despite perceived shortcomings as an academic discipline. Administrators also thought that ethnic studies might help with campus diversity problems. A black studies unit, for example, was bound to bring African American scholars to the campus and showed that administrators cared about affirmative action and black undergraduates.

Even though administrators have had a historically tense relationship with ethnic studies programs, there are moments when administrators have been more receptive. For example, in the early 1990s, administrators at Harvard University decided to rejuvenate their program, which had very low enrollments and a small staff (Rojas 2007b, 116–27). The departing dean of Arts and Sciences thought that Harvard's Department of African and African American Studies deserved another chance at improving its reputation. This effort culminated in the hiring of Henry Louis Gates Jr., a well-established literary scholar, as department chair. A literary intellectual with an impeccable reputation, Gates quickly hired a cohort of high-profile scholars, who became known at the "Harvard Dream Team" of African American studies. Shortly thereafter, college administrators at other campuses initiated efforts to rejuvenate their black studies programs.

The 1990s boom in ethnic studies was not limited to African American studies. A glance at a listing of Asian American studies programs shows that they doubled their numbers in the 1990s, from about twenty programs to nearly fifty. Other types of ethnic studies programs also were created in recent years. Why did ethnic studies experience a renaissance of sorts in the 1990s? Perhaps the answer is generational. For decades, ethnic studies had been closely associated with student politics. It is possible for an academic field as a whole to acquire a stigma. By the 1990s, many hostile professors and administrators who were present in the 1960s began retiring, and memories of protests faded. Thus, sympathetic administrators could now argue that it was time for a new push, and there was probably much less opposition. Once this happened in a prestigious institution like Harvard, ethnic studies could make gains at other institutions.

Research on ethnic studies units and instructors depicts a small but embattled field that has found a very specific niche. Data on unit staff size show that ethnic studies programs tend to be small. The average degree-granting African American studies program has only seven professors (Rojas 2007b, 3). Other ethnic studies units are smaller and, in some cases, are bundled with other programs such as American studies. These programs rarely grant graduate degrees and have heavy undergraduate teaching obligations. Ethnic studies programs occupy narrow niches, unlike other generalist fields such as history that attract large numbers of students. These units offer a few popular introductory courses or multiculturalism requirements that attract many curious students, but few of them enroll as majors.

Research also addresses how ethnic studies professors understand their own profession. For example, survey data indicate that African American studies professors think their field is independent of other fields and has unique methods, suggesting that ethnic studies has created a distinct professional culture (Rojas 2011). These attitudes vary greatly by race, with little else correlating with such attitudes. The data do not explain why these differences exist, but one might conjecture that black professors feel a stronger personal attachment to the field or have had different professional experiences than white professors. The racial differences, according to recent data, seem to be disappearing (Rojas and Byrd

2012). The youngest white Africana studies professors have begun to resemble their black counterparts.

Another finding about African American studies professors, which may also be true for other kinds of ethnic studies, is that the typical professor has a joint appointment in another field (Rojas 2007b, 190). As noted earlier, there are advantages to this strategy. A controversial area of study may need to justify its existence by allying itself with more established areas. The cost of the strategy is that the cohort of professors in charge of the field may not have the luxury of devoting all of their time to ethnic studies. Collectively, these findings show that ethnic studies professors work in small academic units, have appointments in multiple areas, and have a heightened professional identity.

Surprisingly, there is almost no research addressing the students who enroll in ethnic studies courses. Most research on ethnic studies students is historical and focuses on the central role played by students in motivating ethnic studies (Nelson 2000; Rooks 2006). One of the few contemporary studies of ethnic studies pupils is a survey of African American studies students at three large universities (Rojas and Shaffer 2009). The key finding is that students are attracted by the content of the course and the desire to acquire academic skills, while few report an interest in multiculturalism or more abstract justifications for African American studies. The starkest finding is that students almost never hear about the course from other students, professors, or advisors. Africana studies courses are disconnected from the social relationships that typically channel students into particular courses.

A Counter Center

Despite pressures for conformity with the rest of academia, ethnic studies scholars still retain a radical, if qualified, stance. Ethnic studies is an example of a "counter center," an organizational space within a mainstream institution that embodies alternative discourse. Perhaps the most notable example is Temple University's Department of African American Studies (Rojas 2007b, 216–17; Small 1999). Established in the 1970s after student protest, Temple's program developed into a center for Afrocentric theory, which claims a distinctly African approach to knowledge. The program was the first to offer doctoral degrees, in 1983, and has hosted journals and conferences. Temple University remains a beacon for scholars interested in African American studies that does not rely exclusively on other disciplines.

An important question is whether this position—an institutionalized oppositional stance—is sustainable in the years to come. More research must be done on this matter, but there are some indications that the field will experience more pressures to deradicalize. For example, recent research on the publications of Africana studies professors in doctoral programs shows that there is a serious bifurcation of the field (Rojas 2008). Professors in Ivy League Africana programs tend to publish in disciplinary journals and almost never publish in the journals that define black studies, such as the *Journal of Black Studies* or the *Black Scholar*. Non–Ivy League faculty professors are much more likely to publish in the core black studies journals. This suggests that the more elite programs are staffed by scholars with strong attachments to the traditional disciplines. Thus, one might expect that graduates of these doctoral programs will be trained by scholars who do not share the view that black studies is about maintaining a radical voice in the academy.

Another issue is whether the people trained in the more distinctive doctoral programs, such as that at Temple University, are continuing this tradition in other programs. If a doctoral student wrote a dissertation from an Afrocentric perspective in the Temple department, would she or he continue teaching and researching from an Afrocentric perspective? If so, what impact do such scholars have? Will they be able to maintain African American studies programs as radical spaces? Without more research, this question is nearly impossible to answer. But there are some indicators that things are changing. Survey data from black studies professors show that more recent PhD graduates are less likely to think that their field is unique in comparison to other fields. They are less likely to assign radical texts such as Asante's *The Afrocentric Idea* (Rojas 2007b). Though more research is needed to assess these hypotheses, the preliminary evidence suggests that newer cohorts of ethnic studies scholars are more professionalized, which may change the field in the years to come.

The Permanent Interdiscipline

Ethnic studies achieved its status with an interdisciplinary stance. The academy accepted ethnic studies if it promised that its main ideas would be tied to traditional disciplines. What were the consequences of this interdisciplinary strategy? What happens to an insurgent academic field if it is required to maintain a constant investment in other disciplines? What are the risks in being a permanent interdisciplinary field?

One immediate consequence is that ethnic studies must draw its faculty from other, related fields in the social sciences and humanities (Rojas 2007b, 190). Since ethnic studies programs are usually undergraduate units whose courses are defined in terms of disciplines (e.g., the sociology of black America), there are almost no "native" PhD holders. Most of the ethnic studies professoriate is drawn from fields like history or sociology. About 6 percent of professors in African American studies earned their doctoral degree from an African American studies program (Rojas 2007b, 186). Since there are only a handful of doctoral programs in other types of ethnic studies, there must be a similarly small number of PhD holders in fields like Native American studies or Asian American studies.

A second consequence of an interdisciplinary stance is a modest suppression of disciplinary solidarity. Analysis of survey data shows that African American studies professors, if they have a PhD in a social science discipline, are less likely to believe that African American studies is a field with its own distinctive methods or ideas (Rojas 2007b, 198). This correlation may be due to the fact that social science disciplines usually address ethnicity in some way. In contrast, many humanities fields are organized around canons that until recently included few works by ethnic minorities.

A third consequence of the interdisciplinary strategy is that ethnic studies has competing allegiances within the university. Again, a majority of ethnic studies professors have a PhD from outside the field, and a majority of faculty have joint appointments with programs outside ethnic studies. This means that professors in ethnic studies units must often teach in other units, have administrative responsibilities in other units, and are often evaluated for tenure and promotion by professors in other units. The overall impact is that faculty members often have divided loyalties. This can appear in several ways. The "other" department may require publication in different journals than those found in ethnic studies, which leads to promotion problems. In interviews with African American studies professors conducted for my own research, it was not uncommon for interviewees to claim that they have only a casual connection to their program and are "really" in some other field.

What is the future of this interdisciplinary strategy? Avoiding the label of political radicalism was certainly useful for ethnic studies activists. But, as I have described in this chapter, ethnic studies now faces a different environment. There has been a renaissance of sorts, and many administrators, in research institutions at least, have encouraged an expansion of ethnic studies. Even though the interdisciplinary strategy was useful during the creation of ethnic studies, there is little evidence suggesting that it remains useful. As noted above, a reliance on interdisciplinary scholars means that ethnic studies instructors have multiple loyalties in the university and a relatively weak attachment to the field. These tensions exacerbate promotion problems and other issues for professors (Cunningham 1991; Rojas 2007a).

The alternative is not clear. One option would be to recruit faculty from within the ethnic studies field. As of early 2013, there were eight doctoral programs in African American studies and only a few in other areas such as Asian American studies. Collectively, these programs produce perhaps twenty PhDs per year. Considering that there are approximately nine hundred tenure or tenure-track faculty positions in African American studies alone, it would take over forty-five years to produce a professoriate composed entirely of faculty with ethnic studies doctorates. This estimate is very generous. It assumes that all graduates go into university teaching immediately and choose to teach in ethnic studies units, instead of related areas such as American studies.

This analysis suggests that ethnic studies might be served by other strategies. One approach might be to more closely integrate ethnic studies graduate training with existing doctoral programs. Rather than have autonomous doctoral programs, universities might have programs that require concurrent enrollment with other programs. This is the approach taken at Yale University. It is not possible to obtain a doctoral degree only in African American studies. Graduate students must gain simultaneous admission to the African American studies units and a second graduate program from a preselected list.

A hybrid approach to doctoral education in ethnic studies has several advantages that stem from being halfway between an autonomous department and a program recruiting from existing disciplines. First, it guarantees that graduate students have an intense exposure to both an older discipline and ethnic studies. Graduates of this program will not be recruits with a secondary interest in ethnic studies. Presumably, they will have a strong attachment to the field. Second, these programs require much less investment on the part of the university than a full-fledged doctoral program. If the university does not have an existing African American studies program, it can still have a dual doctoral program. Third, this type of program sends the signal that the university wishes African American studies to have the same status as other departments. The dual program requires constant collaboration with other programs, and graduates have the stamp of approval of two disciplines. It remains to be seen whether this type of doctoral training will gain popularity.

Ethnic Studies Spill Out

Overall, the evidence suggests that the ethnic studies movement was a modest success as an autonomous institution. Ethnic studies programs tend to be small, and they have moved in a less political and more interdisciplinary direction. At the same time, it would be misleading to say that ethnic studies did not have broader effects on the academy. To the contrary, ethnic studies had one very profound effect, which was to significantly expand the scope of debate in the humanities and social sciences by insisting that the history and culture of nonwhite ethnic groups is worth studying (Bryson 2005; Rooks 2006). Among the affected disciplines, the humanities appear to have had a very strong engagement with ethnic studies. It is common to find specialists in American ethnic literature in a wide range of departments. History programs have developed specialties in areas such as African American or Native American history. Even philosophy, a very technical discipline, has scholars who study issues related to race, such as nationalist political philosophy (Shelby 2007) and the nature of ethnic identity (Appiah 1993). The greatest triumph in the humanities for the ethnic studies movement may have been the adoption of multicultural course requirements, which are often history or humanities courses.

Ethnic studies has also spilled out into selected types of nonresearch universities. For example, one study found that Native American tribal colleges are more likely to have ethnic-themed courses than predominantly white colleges or even historically black institutions (Cole 2006). These schools have ethnocentric courses not only in humanities disciplines such as history but also in natural science areas. The argument offered is that Native American tribal colleges were created in the 1960s and 1970s, at a time of heightened attention to race. For that reason, they have a distinctive culture that is particularly open to the politics represented by ethnic studies. This is not the case for white institutions or for historically black institutions, which were created in the late 1800s and early 1900s and retain ties to conservative religious groups.

The influence of ethnic studies on sympathetic disciplines and colleges is important, but it should not be overestimated. While many scholars may be sympathetic to the calls for more racially conscious education, ethnic studies has not become the dominant mode of academic thought in America. There is little evidence suggesting that a majority of scholars in the humanities disciplines have adopted ethnic studies. A routine examination of history department graduate programs, for example, shows that many offer specialization in American ethnic history but it is one offering among many. Similarly, while American ethnic literature is a popular topic, there is no evidence that it has displaced other, more traditional specialties in major journals. The *Proceedings of the Modern Language Association* carries numerous articles on ethnic literature while simultaneously publishing research on more canonical authors.

Ethnic Studies as Educational Policy

This chapter has addressed questions about the development of the ethnic studies field. Here the focus is on a different question: did ethnic studies achieve its stated policy goals? Answering this question requires a discussion of what, exactly, the activists of the 1960s intended when they demanded ethnic studies programs.

The politics behind ethnic studies were complex. As noted in the introductory portions of this chapter, leading activists and scholars were often nationalists, which meant they wanted these programs to serve the "community," but they also viewed themselves as motivated by the civil rights movement, which was centered around racial harmony and integration. Ethnic studies brought these two, often conflicting tensions into the academy. From this perspective, ethnic studies has a mixed record. Deradicalization means that ethnic studies professors abandoned calls for single-race classes and their scholarship deemphasizes distinctly racial perspectives. Few programs promise service to urban ethnic populations, meaning that the community mission has receded.

While ethnic nationalism has not succeeded in becoming established and is thus an unsuccessful policy, there is the question of ethnic studies courses and their impact on students. One policy question is whether ethnic studies actually brings students of different ethnicities together. Some scholars have noted the increasing number of white students and faculty in ethnic studies programs. This finding has led to some hand-wringing in the field, with observers wondering whether ethnic studies programs might be viewed as a failure or whether the programs need a different mission for a new multicultural age (Rooks 2006). This response suggests that diversifying the student population in ethnic studies conflicts with the lingering image of ethnic studies as a service to minority students. At the very least, integrated ethnic studies classes have raised new and important questions about the purpose of the field.

The policy that speaks the most to the civil rights movement is the multicultural course requirement discussed earlier. These courses may be the only exposure to ethnic studies that many students are likely to have. The question is whether enrolling in one or two undergraduate courses has a lasting impact. There is a substantial body of research claiming that students emerge from these courses with an enhanced sensitivity to racial issues and more interracial tolerance (e.g., Chang 2002; Hogan and Mallott 2005). The research on this topic does not follow students over the long term, nor are students who enrolled in multicultural courses compared with similar students who did not have to enroll in these courses, nor does the research take into account selection effects (i.e., more tolerant students enroll more often). For these reasons, there is no definitive answer to the question of whether multiculturalism courses are a policy with a strong and sustained impact.

Conclusion

This book is dedicated to research on the politics of the academy. The story of ethnic studies speaks to the question: what happens when liberals mobilize and try to change the system? The contrast between ethnic studies as structural change and as intellectual change shows the complexity of politics in the academy. If liberals, or any other political group, intend to change higher education, they face a system that is highly stable and only occasionally susceptible to dramatic alteration. Should academic liberals ever decide to mount a challenge as they did in the 1960s, they will have to decide whether subtle, but palpable, intellectual change is worth the effort.

CHAPTER TEN

Rationalizing Realpolitik

U.S. International Relations as a Liberal Field

PATRICK THADDEUS JACKSON

According to the traditional tale that international relations (IR) scholars tell their students in introductory courses,[1] U.S. international relations ought to be among the most politically conservative of the social sciences. After all, the usual IR "lore"—"its ritualized understandings of the titanic struggles fought and challenges still to be overcome" (Ashley 1986, 259)—revolves around three supposed "great debates" that shaped the contours of the field over the course of the twentieth century (Wæver 1996), the first of which is said to have pitted a small and courageous band of geopolitical "realists" against liberal "idealists." Many of those remembered as "realists"—according to the traditional tale, those whose immersion in the realpolitik tradition of diplomatic history allowed them to understand the unique dangers of international life posed by the absence of a global sovereign—were either émigré intellectuals from Europe or those decisively influenced by the brand of great-power political history made famous by German and British scholars. These "realists" are said to have triumphed over a broad swath of liberal American "idealists," whose naive and utopian hopes for a peaceful world had to be put aside in favor of a concerted effort by the United States to assume the responsibilities of a world power. The anarchic character of international life meant not only that there could be no international counterpart to domestic political theory and its concerns with rights and justice (Wight 1960) but also that geopolitical realities needed to trump progressive aspirations of all kinds (Walker 1993).[2]

Hence, U.S. IR might be expected to be the refuge of political conservatives, holding the line against efforts to transform the world in a more ethically progressive direction by pointing out the limits of even the most well-intended schemes: the last redoubt, perhaps, of the tradition of developmental historicism and a grimly stoic resignation to the world's imperfections. But this is untrue, whether we look at the declared political leanings of IR scholars or at the most common kinds of research undertaken in U.S. IR. The 2009 report of the Teaching, Research, and International Policy survey project indicates that only 10 percent of U.S. IR scholars self-identify as being anywhere to the right of the center of the political spectrum, and a majority—56 percent of those surveyed—self-identify as either "slightly left/liberal" or "left/liberal" in their political ideology (Jordan et al. 2009, 26).[3] And although the same report suggests that the percentage of self-reported realists in U.S. IR is 21 percent, this is less than the percentage of respondents claiming no allegiance to a particular research tradition at all—26 percent—and only a single percentage point higher than self-identified IR liberals.[4] Nor do most contemporary U.S. IR scholars celebrate the large military budgets and preemptive wars advocated by contemporary right-leaning U.S. politicians, and a perusal of the latest issues of *International Studies Quarterly* or *International Organization* would not yield any articles that would be identifiable as politically conservative—or, indeed, that would display much of an overt partisan orientation at all.

By the same token, contemporary U.S. IR scholarship, by and large, does not look like the kind of realpolitik historical-critical elaboration of "theory" as the distilled wisdom of experience that the émigré IR scholars advocated. Gone are the days when IR scholars could follow Hans Morgenthau, one of the seminal figures in the early IR field in the United States, in rooting their analysis in the contention that "the political act is inevitably evil" and that therefore "to choose among several expedient actions the least evil one is moral judgment" characteristic of "the tragic contradictions of human existence" (Morgenthau 1946, 203). Allusions like this, or references to Reinhold Niebuhr's (1932) distinction between the "moral man" capable of behaving ethically and the "immoral society" fated to sustain itself by unethical means, function in contemporary IR more as shibboleths than as core intellectual commitments with methodological and theoretical implications. As with U.S. political science more generally (Adcock and Bevir 2010), U.S. IR has, by and large, quite enthusiastically participated in the "modernist empiricist" and "behaviorist" turns in social-scientific scholarship, focusing on systematic empirical claims to the detriment of sweeping characterizations of social and political life.[5] So, although the traditional tale of U.S. IR's origins is correct in one respect—the injection of émigré scholars and scholarship at midcentury was, in fact, an important chapter in the field's formation—the idea that these scholars, largely formed by the substantive concerns and theoretical orientation of traditional realpolitik, simply and unequivocally triumphed over naive and native American liberal idealism and thus definitively set the course for a conservative IR field is somewhat mistaken.

To the contrary, scholars influenced by the realpolitik tradition arrived in the United States only to confront an indigenous tradition of thinking about world politics that was far from idealist or utopian. Yes, it placed a great deal of emphasis on cooperative global institutions and international law—traditionally "liberal" themes—but it rooted that emphasis in a broadly pluralist critique of the notion of the state, a critique revolving around the contention that "the constitutive elements of the theoretical discourse of the state were no longer consistent with the reality it [the discourse] sought to explain" (Schmidt 1998, 187). This indigenous U.S. tradition *did* regard the international realm as distinct from the domestic realm because of the lack of an overarching and authoritative global sovereign, but it did *not* regard this as an insurmountable obstacle to rational cooperation intended to solve pressing global problems. The shapers of this indigenous U.S. tradition seized the mantle of "science" for their claims, suggesting that their pluralist approach to politics was, as Charles Merriam (1921) put it, "modern equipment supplying the rapid, comprehensive and systematic assembly and analysis of pertinent facts" (175); these scholars claimed the sanction of the facts, not the blessing of morality, for their contentions. Hence, while their specific claim about international cooperation may have appeared utopian and idealistic to those in the realpolitik tradition, the basis on which the claim was articulated purported to be at least as "realistic" and grounded in experience as the contrary claim that international anarchy called for a more militaristic and altogether grimmer response.

This amendment to the traditional tale immediately throws into doubt the main conclusion of the traditional story of early U.S. IR: that the field, once the domain of fanciful idealist utopianism, became decidedly more concerned with global political realities as it shed its liberal progressive character to become more of a conservative discourse about the limits of social and political action. Instead, scholars influenced by the realpolitik tradition made some headway in the United States only by seizing precisely the same commonplace—"reality," best apprehended through systematic "scientific" study—that was fundamental to the scholars and scholarship they sought to supplant or supplement. It is thus perhaps better to read this episode in the early formation of U.S. IR as a scholarly field as an episode of *translation*, in which some of the central substantive concerns of the realpolitik tradition (such as the relative balance of military capability between sovereign states) were framed as "IR realist" empirical generalizations that could more or less directly compete with the indigenous pluralist tradition. Along the way, however, something was *lost* in translation: where realpolitik was rooted methodologically in a kind of historical and philosophical pessimism, IR realism consisted of a set of testable propositions about the character of international life—propositions that could, if empirically grounded, serve as the foundation for a science of world politics of the sort that would have been completely alien to genuine philosophical conservatives.

In this chapter, I argue that this kind of translation of realpolitik into terms more acceptable to Americans—both U.S. scholars and the broader U.S. public, especially that portion of the public directly concerned with policymaking—is a more appropriate way of thinking about the formation of U.S. IR than the traditional tale whereby IR looks like the last likely redoubt of conservatives. The variant of realpolitik that appears in U.S. IR in the 1940s and 1950s is, broadly speaking, an *empiricist* kind of realpolitik, in which scientific knowledge, not the unfettered clash of power-laden decisions, provides the last word on how political strategies unfold. The emphasis on scientific practice as providing a master key to understanding world politics, in turn, is closely related to a broader sensibility in the U.S. academy about the proper relationship of science and politics: a philosophically liberal and progressive sensibility in which the role of science is to put an end to political controversy by providing objectively correct knowledge that can shape decisions. Viewed in this light, U.S. IR looks less like a conservative stronghold and more like a field shaped by a series of negotiations between a philosophically conservative realpolitik tradition and an indigenous American liberal tradition.

But this translation of realpolitik into a liberal idiom was not limited to questions of methodology or epistemic authority. Liberalism, broadly understood, certainly foregrounds a commitment to reason as the ultimate source of action; indeed, much of the liberal Enlightenment project was about replacing modes of authority grounded in religion and tradition with modes grounded in the exercise of reason in scientific empirical study, and this commitment resonates loudly through the writings of Hobbes, Locke, Kant, and other seminal figures. But philosophical liberalism, broadly understood, is also about the centrality of *individual* reason and the notion that individuals acting on their rational interests are the foundation of social order. The translation of realpolitik into U.S. IR also involved an embrace of this kind of individualism, such that what had originally been an account of world politics based either in the corruption of human nature or in various systemic social forces became, largely, a perspective focusing on the incentives facing individuals and states alike. Irreducible tragedy was replaced by remediable bargaining challenges, to the point where contemporary U.S. IR scholarship largely consists of alternate specifications of the utility functions and preference schedules of global actors, and it is possible to seriously ask whether anyone is still a realist (Legro and Moravcsik 1999).

In characterizing IR this way, I am not suggesting that all IR scholars deliberately set out to construct a field on these twin liberal premises of scientific rationality and individualism. Rather, the translation of realpolitik into a liberal idiom was affected by the efforts undertaken by scholars influenced by the realpolitik tradition to legitimate their claims in the eyes of traditional American scholars and policymakers. Realpolitik first became a science, and then became a theory about individual preferences, as émigré scholars sought to make their claims comprehensible in a novel context. Like the rest of U.S. political science, U.S. IR is constitutively liberal in its individualism and its rationalism, and it remains that way because of the ongoing demands of legitimation—but this does not mean there are any specifically partisan-political commitments built into the structure of U.S. IR. Indeed, U.S. IR as a field remains extremely sensitive to charges of "politicization," clinging to its scientific credentials both as a way of avoiding any necessity to make political interventions and as a way of bolstering its credibility with policymakers. The constitutive liberalism of the U.S. IR field thus works to depoliticize the field and to mute potentially transformative claims, a tacit status quo bias that might be mistaken for conservatism by casual observers lacking awareness of the complex history of legitimation behind this constitutive commitment.

Legitimation and U.S. International Relations

The kind of legitimation I am referring to is a causal mechanism that involves the provision of publicly acceptable reasons for a given course of action. *Action* here means socially meaningful behavior, and as such, action is always and already embedded within a specific social and cultural context, a context out of which action arises and into which action flows. This pragmatic emphasis on the meaningful social context of action is to be distinguished from various kinds of structuralisms precisely by the fact that the context in question is *created* through action rather than standing outside or before action and controlling it.

> Action constantly encounters unexpected obstacles: goals show themselves to be unattainable; simultaneously pursued goals prove to be mutually exclusive; attainable goals have doubts cast upon them by other actors. In these various crises of habitual action, the action situations have to be *redefined* in a new and different way. This involves defining that which is as yet undefined, rather than simply making a different selection from a reservoir of situation components that are either

already defined or have no need of definition . . . Every situation contains a horizon of possibilities which in a crisis of action has to be rediscovered. (Joas 1997, 133)

Crises of habitual action are continual in that no two situations are exactly alike and hence no action can be a pure repetition of an earlier one; adaptation and localization are ongoing. Andrew Pickering (1995) refers to this ongoing process of the mutual adjustment of anticipation and outcome as the "mangle of practice" and notes that it is fairly ubiquitous in knowledge-producing endeavors broadly understood (21–23). The central point here is that "there are no general, substantive principles that we can hang on to in understanding cultural extension" (202), and action is never completely predetermined by an existing set of fixed parameters. Instead, what emerges in any concrete situation is the result of a contingent combination of social and cultural resources to deal with the omnipresent crises of everyday life.

Legitimation is one response to a crisis of action, and like all such responses it involves the creative deployment of elements of the "living tradition" (Shotter 1993, 170–71) in which the actor is embedded so as to shape an acceptable response. Legitimation allows the actor to "go on," to make the next move, even when uncertainty and ambiguity characterize any such next steps; it does so by foregrounding issues of *identity* and linking some claim about that identity to a specific course of action. "Because we are at war, you should support the government" is a fairly standard example of a political legitimation claim; "because we are scientists, you should listen to our policy recommendation" is equally standard and more directly relevant to the social and political context within which advocates of realpolitik articulated a distinct approach to the study of world politics.[6] Contexts matter because they provide the raw materials out of which novel claims can be constructed and because, while open-ended, contexts are almost never completely elastic (Krebs and Jackson 2007, 45). The specific historical configuration of a given context provides certain conditions of possibility and not others, and empirical investigation is required to explain why and how certain kinds of legitimation claims are advanced and how and why they exercise their effects.

Another way of saying this is to simply observe that not all possible cultural resources are available at all times and places. Justifying a course of action with reference to an imminent extraterrestrial invasion is unlikely to have much political resonance if used in the course of a contemporary debate about national security policy, but justifying a course of action with reference to the imminent threat posed by communists or terrorists might have quite a bit of political resonance at particular historical junctures. The cultural resources out of which plausible reasons can be generated have specific histories that result in their being variously available to concrete actors and their audiences; as Clifford Geertz (2000, 25) once famously quipped, "You can't castle in dominoes." It follows that the specific articulation of a given theme, such as the more or less objective dangers of an anarchic international environment and the consequent need for responsible state leaders to focus on power instead of morality, will look different depending on the specific vocabulary and grammar of the locally available cultural resources. The task of translation thus involves rendering a theme in terms that, quite literally, *make sense* in a particular local context.

With these considerations in mind, we can understand the strange U.S. career of the realpolitik sensibility about world politics, a career wherein a deeply conservative appraisal of the limits of reason becomes a set of empirical propositions about the behavioral motivations of states operating in an anarchic environment, thus helping to support an IR field that is just as liberal as any other subfield of U.S. political science. There are two phases to this career: a first phase in which a broad realpolitik sensibility becomes the IR realist scientific theory of world politics, and a second phase in which IR realism shifts from being a theory about structural features of world politics to being a specification of the interests of state actors. In both phases, realpolitik is translated into a decidedly liberal idiom, but an important difference between the two phases is that in the first phase it is the self-proclaimed "realists" themselves who are responsible for translation, while in the second phase it is a misreading of IR realism that is responsible. The result, however, is the same in both phases: what starts off as a decidedly nonliberal approach to world politics ends up looking considerably more liberal as a result of its translation into the basic vocabulary of U.S. political science and the broader society in which it is embedded.

The Indigenous Tradition

As I have hinted at already, it matters quite a bit for this story that international relations—the study of world politics as a discrete object of analysis—is, in the United States, largely organized as a subfield of political science. As such, U.S. IR is not isolated from broader trends within U.S. political science and shares many of the preoccupations of that discipline, as well as participating in its constitutive and distinctly liberal orientation toward politics. This liberal orientation was and is less about any specifically partisan stance on contentious issues and more about the idea that a scientific approach can put political controversies to rest. This commitment was especially prominent in the late nineteenth and early twentieth centuries, when the discipline—along with other social-scientific disciplines like economics—was first being organized in the United States as a progressive way to comment on social problems without getting wrapped up in political controversies.

Social science, in many of its dimensions, began as a reform movement. Lacking political authority, it sought purchase in the authority of knowledge, which in turn led to specialization, differentiation, and gravitation toward the university to ensure its claim to science (Gunnell 1993, 23). "Social scientists could offer counsel not in the guise of wise, interested elites but as mere mouthpieces for a disembodied science. They could disarm suspicions that their advice was self-interested by intoning the phrase *scientific method*" (Porter 1994, 148). The commitment to "science" served as a way to separate social scientists from their object of study but, somewhat ironically, did so in order to promote political change through the application of scientific principles to social life.

This is a distinctly liberal position, wherein the proper application of scientific reason can claim political authority by separating itself from politics per se.[7] Reason, not power-laden struggle, was to be the arbiter of political decisions, and the arbitrariness of actual social and political life could be brought to order in a scientific manner (Ross 1994, 181). This commitment is ubiquitous in calls to update the study of politics in the early part of the twentieth century, including calls for a "positive" approach to international law that could ground progressive reforms (Schmidt 1998, 104–7), and in virtually every presidential address of the American Political Science Association (APSA; organized in 1903). As Woodrow Wilson (1911)—president of the APSA before he went on to become president of the United States—put it in his presidential address of 1910, the task of political science was to articulate the common rational interest that underlay particular controversies, "not a mere task of compromise and makeshift accommodation, but a task of genuine and lasting adjustment, synthesis, coordination, harmony, and union of parts" (6). According to this conception, science and reason could contribute to political reform by putting mere politics to rest, in favor of progressive and technocratic certainties.

But the separation of science and politics can unfold in at least two, rather distinctive ways. The liberal and progressive way of separating and relating the two domains of practice is to hold science apart from politics for the ultimate purpose of gaining political authority and thus the ability to advance particular programs of progressive reform under the banner of a nonpartisan scientific rationality. The proper stance of the liberal scientist is to provide unbiased expertise to guide political decisions. There is another version of this separation, however, which continental émigré intellectuals would have been more familiar with: associated with Max Weber and summarized most clearly in his famous "vocation" lectures of 1917 and 1919 (Weber 1992 [1917/1919]), this position divided science from politics, not to subordinate politics to science, but to foreground the irreducibly *political* character of important controversies and the extent to which they elude purely rational solutions. In this account, social scientists have the freedom—perhaps even the obligation—to engage in systematic value-clarification, pointing out the likely consequences of adopting a particular set of goals and a particular set of means to achieve those goals. Such value-clarification, however, is likely to disappoint partisan ideologues on all sides, as it will refrain from offering context-independent solutions to thorny social and political problems, but it might contribute to the formulation of more nuanced and realistic policies.

That early U.S. political science took the liberal option rather than the Weberian one is perhaps most clearly glimpsed in the annual presidential addresses of the APSA from its beginnings. Presidential addresses are interesting symbolic moments, in which the character of the discipline is most explicitly on display; APSA presidents typically take the opportunity to address their professional peers as an occasion to reflect on the character of the discipline as a whole and to identify the distinctive qualities of the discipline and its approach to politics. Appeals to "science" figure prominently in these moments, with seventeen of the thirty-nine presidential addresses delivered between the founding of the association and the end of World War II taking up the theme of how a scientific study of politics can contribute to political reform and progress. The second president, Albert Shaw (1907), used his 1906 address to characterize the association in decidedly liberal terms: "This organization of ours is not partisan, or sectional, or propagandist in its nature. It is, nevertheless, made up of men who are both willing and eager to see the results of their scientific study of political life and conditions converted to the practical ends of statesmanship" (180). Along similar lines, Jesse Macy's (1917) admonition in his 1916 address that a new "spirit" was needed in politics so that it could follow in the footsteps of medicine and be "revolutionized, changed from the occult and the empirical to the scientific" (4) stands as an illustration of the liberal hope for improving political life through scientific study: only in this way could partisan controversies be put to rest, as political figures worked to enact the solutions discerned by political scientists. And at the end of World War II, John Gaus (1946) used his address to describe "the urgency and importance of our job" as political scientists: "It is to record, to explain, to invent, as carefully, as honestly, and as responsibly as we can, the significance of physical, social, and intellectual change upon govern- ment as an instrument by means of which people first may live at all, and live better" (226). All of which shows quite clearly how political science in the United States was, from its beginnings, animated by a commitment to provid- ing a scientific corrective to political practice. Remaining apart from the day-to- day press of politics itself and remaining firmly located in the university setting was a means to that end—a means to exerting some measure of influence over the course of political controversies, by standing outside them and pronouncing their "scientific" resolution.

How Realpolitik Became a Science

The primary exponents of a realpolitik perspective in the United States—émigré scholars who came to the United States in the 1930s and 1940s—partook of a kind of cultural pessimism characteristic of antiliberal declinists like Oswald Spengler and felt that a surplus of decontextualized rationality was partially to blame for the problems of contemporary political and social life (Schmidt 1998, 210). In direct contrast to local U.S. scholars' embrace of scientific reason as a way to civilize and modernize political life, these thinkers, by and large, maintained that politics ought to remain the domain of contextual wisdom and judgment. Hans Morgenthau, the German émigré whose work was seminal to the found- ing of the field of international relations, gave voice to this skepticism in his 1946 book *Scientific Man versus Power Politics*:

> [Science] has discovered the causes of many isolated things. But it has not even searched for a meaningful connection of all those isolated things, nor for their na- ture, let alone their purpose and value for man . . . even the problems of living have not been solved, except in the meaning of a mere technical possibility. Art, reli- gion, and metaphysics have endeavored to give an answer to the problems of life although, from the rationalistic point of view, it was an unverifiable and illusory one. Still, they at least saw problems where the Age of Science sees none. (125)

Rejecting the notion that scientific reason can provide objectively superior solu- tions to political problems, Morgenthau suggested that politics in general, and international politics in particular, was an irreducible domain of "the struggle for absolute power" (108) and that scholars and politicians alike ignored this at their peril.

Given this strong indictment of science and reason, one would suspect that Morgenthau would be dismissive of the very idea of a science of world politics.

And indeed, Morgenthau concludes his book with a contrast between the rationalist engineer and the statesman, concerned not with general principles but with "the contingencies of the social world" (220). But he also argues that even this wise statesman needs to grasp "the eternal laws by which man moves in the social world," which suggests a role for some kind of generalizing account of world politics. Science and reason might be to blame for the problems of politics, but Morgenthau does not articulate a complete abandonment of systematic investigation. Instead, he proposes a different kind of science, a *conservative* science:

> Whereas the conservative of the modern age turns to the historic past and expects from the science of history the answer to the riddle of the present, the liberal sees in history only a process through which reason realizes itself in time and space. The scientific approach is common to both. For the liberal, science is a prophesy confirmed by reason; for the conservative, it is the revelation of the past confirmed by experience. (32)

Morgenthau places himself on the conservative side of this ledger, suggesting that the proper role of a science of world politics is to convey the timeless lessons of the past to modern political leaders—even though chief among these lessons is a skepticism about the powers of science itself to solve political problems! Instead of pressing his critique of science as far as it could go, Morgenthau pulls up short, legitimating his critical endeavor in the name of science itself.[8]

This ambiguity persists throughout Morgenthau's work. The first section of his seminal textbook *Politics among Nations* (first published in 1948)—which served as the introduction to the study of world politics for generations of American students—contains a fairly strident articulation of six putatively timeless principles of political realism, even though the third principle stresses the historical variability of notions like "power" and "interest" while the sixth principle emphasizes the irreducibility of political controversies to universal principles. Similarly, Morgenthau's (1955, 452) evaluation of the evolution of the discipline of political science both critiqued scientistic formalism and called for the formalization of a set of general theoretical propositions about politics, because "political science, as any science, presupposes the existence and accessibility of objective, general truth" (Gunnell 1993, 242).

Morgenthau was hardly the only self-identified political realist who engaged in this "gambit" (Guilhot 2008) of simultaneously claiming the cultural prestige of science *and* critiquing the existing U.S. articulation of the science-politics relationship. A 1955 Rockefeller Foundation–sponsored conference on theory and

IR gathered many luminaries articulating just this position: world politics was a realm characterized by the irreducible clash of great powers and could not be reduced to a rational synthesis, but to make progress, the field of IR needed "a base or fixed point upon which analysis can be founded" (Thompson 1955, 738). IR realism, it would seem, had adopted, by and large, the notion of science as part of its critique of science, seeking to yoke the existing prestige of the notion of scientific rationality to its campaign against the position that science could provide answers to political quandaries.

It is certainly not necessary that this position inevitably lead to a more or less liberal definition of IR scholarship. Indeed, the hope of the realpolitik-inclined scholars who initially articulated it seems to have been that they could import something like a Weberian definition of science into the U.S. scholarly and political discussion. But the difficulty of such a gambit is that once one has expressed a commitment to science, one is vulnerable to subsequent specifications of what it means to be scientific. And this is precisely what happened, as political scientists committed to the liberal vision of science as a corrective to politics advanced a narrower definition of "science" that emphasized quantitative measurement and falsifiable general hypotheses for the purpose of generating objective knowledge useful for differentiating among policy options. Because IR realists had already claimed the mantle of science in their effort to legitimate the study of the machinations of power among sovereign states, they had little recourse when confronted by a version of science that contradicted their own, more Weberian use of the label.

The subsequent transformation of IR realism into a more liberal kind of science—a science that could provide generally valid claims about the political world on which to fashion more or less reasonable policy responses to various situations—stemmed from two sources, one inside the academy and one outside the academy proper. The source inside the academy was a movement among political scientists to adopt a more abstract and formal approach to the production of social knowledge and to engage in the systematic elaboration and evaluation of general propositions rather than spending their time explicating classic texts or describing political institutions. The movement called itself "behaviorism," perhaps because of a lingering fear that the very term *social science* implied socialism (Kruzel and Rosenau 1989, 18),[9] but the basic idea was in many ways a continuation of the initial constitutive liberal impulse of U.S. political science (Gunnell 1993, 141–42). In the terms preferred by these behaviorist scholars, notions about the irreducibility of political conflict became not the philosophical grounds of a perspective but hypotheses to be tested against empirical evidence: *did* states struggle against one another for power, or did they find ways to cooperate and advance their mutual interests?

So potent was the attraction of scientific behaviorism in the United States that subsequent controversies became largely tempests in teacups about the best way to generate and evaluate hypothetical propositions about world politics. The mid-1960s clash between "traditionalists" and "scientists" remembered in IR lore as the "second great debate" (Kratochwil 2006) was largely a disagreement about the relative contribution to the understanding of world politics of formal propositions and abstract models, on the one hand, and detailed historical reconstructions, on the other—but all sides of the debate agreed that the point of studying world politics was to produce empirically grounded and justified claims. All participants in the debate wanted to be "scientific" in the broad sense and to produce coherent and orderly knowledge, but they disagreed on which techniques were actually "scientific" in the relevant sense. Thus, the actual result of this so-called second great debate in IR—which the "traditionalists" lost—was to link the notion of science with quantification, formal models, and general propositions, replacing Morgenthau's more Weberian notion of science with something more narrowly construed, while retaining the cultural prestige of the notion. Self-identified IR "scientists" made numerous references during this debate (e.g., Levy 1969; Singer 1969) to the successes of physics and economics, holding out hope that IR could enjoy similar successes by becoming equally "scientific." In that way, they continued the basic commitment of U.S. political science to a methodology that was distinct from the historicist techniques of the realpolitik tradition; IR realists, having already accepted the idea of science as controlling, had little defense.

The unavailability of a IR realist defense against this call for a more formal, high-tech kind of science was reinforced by the way the ecosystem of grant agencies and other sources of funding for IR scholarship had developed over the postwar decades. It is perhaps unsurprising that U.S. governmental agencies supporting work in IR, and in political science more generally, were interested in obtaining knowledge that they could use to promote particular policy goals; as such, the work supported by such agencies was closely tied to the foreign policy of the United States, especially with respect to the opposition between liberal democracy and communism (Oren 2002, 12–15). While the substantive orientation of that policy was something to which realpolitik-inclined scholars were generally sympathetic—indeed, a typical component of their criticism of liberal science was that it was incapable of providing a sufficiently transcendental justification for democracy against fascism and communism (Gunnell 1993,

140–41)—the methodological mode of expression for the knowledge sought by policymakers was worlds away from the historical-critical idiom of classic realpolitik. Alexander George, who spent most of his career trying to bridge the worlds of IR academia and government-contracted "think tanks" such as the RAND corporation (Abella 2008, 32–34), described the challenge to IR academics:

> Scholars should recognize that for their research to be more relevant and useful in policymaking they should not define concepts and variables at too high a level of abstraction. The more abstract a concept, the more remote it is from its referent in the real world, and the greater and more difficult the intellectual demand on the practitioner to make that linkage and to benefit from it. (George 1993, 139–40)

In George's view, it is incumbent on scholars who want to affect the policy process that they downplay, or even provisionally abandon, any ambition to produce conceptually rich accounts of phenomena in world politics, instead focusing on the provision of specific analyses of a more concrete variety. From the perspective of practitioners, scholarly research is often too remote from actual events to inform real-time deliberations and too concerned with conceptual syntheses rather than with case-specific particularities. The adjective that practitioners use to denigrate scholarship they don't find particularly useful? "Theoretical." Thus defined, from the perspective of its critics, *theory* seems to mean abstraction, generalization, and remoteness from concrete situations, and it is precisely these attributes that George argues have to be attenuated or abandoned to produce scholarship that is of genuine relevance for policymakers.

All of which means that however important transcendental justifications of democracy or critiques of technocratic modes of social organization were to realpolitik-influenced scholars, their political supporters simply did not want to hear much about that. What they *did* want to hear about was concrete recommendations for courses of action: they wanted, in terms I have used elsewhere (Jackson 2010), "experts" rather than "scholars," researchers who could tell them what they should do rather than researchers who simply clarified thorny policy choices while steadfastly refusing to remove the necessity for decision. Obviously, the notion that IR research was "scientific" lent credence to these kinds of expert claims, and it was on this basis that funding was secured for large data-collection and data-analysis projects like the Correlates of War project at the University of Michigan—a project that aspired to solve the riddle of war, once and for all, by collecting massive amounts of quantitative information on conflicts of all types around the world and then mining those data to see whether, for example, alliances prevented a state from becoming involved in major wars, or which kinds of conflicts were most likely to escalate into major wars. Along similar lines, Karl Deutsch—trained in mathematics, optics, and law before emigrating to the United States and obtaining a PhD in political science from Harvard in 1951 (Gunnell 1993, 184)—developed a remarkable "cybernetic" theory of social and political organization as involving feedback loops and information exchange, then put this model to work in seminal studies of international integration and political authority (Deutsch 1957, 1963) by collecting massive amounts of quantitative information to infer the necessary and sufficient conditions of functional political communities at various scales. In these and other cases, the mantle of "science" underpinned the expert status that U.S. IR scholars brought to their discussions with policymakers and funding agencies. Although some funding agencies were willing to support work in political science that was not as heavily invested in and sometimes explicitly critical of its putatively scientific status, even that support was ordinarily contingent on the idea that theoretical and philosophical work would have long-term scientific payoffs of the sort sought by the policy establishment (Hauptmann 2006, 645–46).

The efforts of realpolitik-inclined scholars thus backfired, inasmuch as their efforts to legitimate their work in terms that other political scientists and the agencies supporting them would understand and accept opened the door for a subsequent critique of that work for not being scientific enough, as well as its transformation into a very different and more liberal way of conducting scholarly research on world politics. Although some of the substantive positions of realpolitik, such as skepticism about the role of international institutions, survived the translation process, the philosophical and historicist sensibility did not.

The Triumph of Individualism

The extent to which U.S. international relations had become self-evidently scientific after the 1960s is perhaps best illustrated by the fact that the writing of, arguably, the most important piece of U.S. IR theory—Kenneth N. Waltz's *Theory of International Politics*, first published in 1979—was funded in part by the National Science Foundation. *Whether* IR should be a science was no longer an open question, although *how* it should become more scientific was still very much a matter of debate and discussion. Waltz's book thus served as an occasion for rearticulating the realpolitik sensibility in more contemporary terms—and the story of its reception is instructive for an appreciation of the impact of liberal presumptions, not just on methodological issues, but on substantive issues as well.

There are important continuities between Waltz's depiction of world politics and the depiction offered in the realpolitik tradition, as both emphasize the political limits of deliberate social action as well as the unavailability of a global rational solution to conflict. More importantly, both anchor their analyses in global systemic factors rather than in a failure of individual will or a lack of sufficiently rational calculations of self-interest. But Waltz's theory was badly misunderstood by critics *and* supporters alike, since they persistently recast it in reductionist, liberal individualist terms. Through a close reading of the exchanges between Waltz and his interlocutors, we can see the resilience of a particularly American kind of commonsense liberalism—what Louis Hartz (1991) refers to as "irrational Lockianism"—which understands the social world only in terms of its constituent individuals. It is this liberal individualism that, in effect, rewrites Waltz's theory to make it more compatible with a set of broader social assumptions dominant in U.S. social and political life. And it is the self-proclaimed "scientific" status of U.S. IR that rendered more philosophical or conceptual objections to this rewriting ineffectual.

Instead of beginning with observations and correlations and seeking to induce a theory from those patterns, Waltz sought to conceptualize world politics as a discrete domain so as to make it available for distinct empirical study. Perhaps unsurprisingly, his distinction between the realms of the international and the domestic involved the familiar notion that the domestic realm was characterized by hierarchy while the international realm was a domain of anarchy, "formed by the coaction of self-regarding units" (Waltz 1979, 91). For Waltz, the absence of hierarchy in international politics placed certain distinct pressures on states, pressures summarized in the notion that an anarchic system is a "self-help" system in which each individual state has to provide for its own security:

> A self-help system is one in which those who do not help themselves, or who do so less effectively than others, will fail to prosper, will lay themselves open to dangers, will suffer. Fear of such unwanted consequences stimulates states to behave in ways that tend towards the creation of balances of power. (118)

But a theory of political structure "can tell us what pressures are exerted and what possibilities are posed by systems of different structure, but it cannot tell us just how, and how effectively, the units of a system will respond to those pressures and possibilities" (71). Hence it cannot completely explain what an individual state does, and the theory's main prediction—the recurrent emergence of international balances of power—depends not on a specification of the motivations or the deliberate goals of particular states but on the overall structure of the system: "Notice that the theory requires no assumptions of rationality or of constancy of will on the part of all the actors. The theory says simply that if some do relatively well, others will emulate them or fall by the wayside" (91). Here we see a respecification of the classic realpolitik notion that rational plans and desires will not translate directly into beneficent outcomes; international politics, for Waltz, is just as frustrating to noble reformist wishes as it was for Morgenthau. In this way, Waltz's account of world politics is a clear example of a translation of a realpolitik sensibility into the detached and abstract terms of U.S. social science. Continental lyricism is replaced, in Waltz, with analytic precision, and even though the substantive expectations of the theory are quite similar to those of older realpolitik, the skepticism about science has vanished, leaving only a skepticism about political progress—a skepticism for which Waltz, speaking scientifically, offers rationally defensible grounds. Waltz's account is thus rather unproblematically liberal in its embrace of scientific reason as the best instrument for clarifying the character of international politics (Shimko 1992), even as its conclusions about the infeasibility of rationalist reforms distance it from more conventionally liberal progressive understandings of politics.[10]

But in another way, Waltz's account is distinctly nonliberal. Contrary to the main thrust of liberal social theory, Waltz lodges his explanation of social and political outcomes not at the level of individuals but at the level of social structure. In Brian Barry's (1970) terms, Waltz's account is "sociological" rather than "economic," inasmuch as it does not begin with a series of constitutively autonomous individuals whose actions produce the appearance of social order but with a set of patterned social transactions that are analytically autonomous from any particular individual. Because Waltz's theory is a *systems* theory (Goddard and Nexon 2005), this should not be surprising; Waltz is working in a social-scientific tradition that extends at least as far back as Talcott Parsons's seminal formulations of the coherence of social life in decidedly nonindividualist ways.

But because of its variance from the classic liberal presumption that society is an amalgam of more or less rational individuals—a kind of Lockian state of nature where social order emerges from individual agreements—this sociological tradition was always subjected to enormous amounts of criticism in U.S. scholarly circles, criticism intended to link social arrangements more firmly to the motives and decisions of individuals. The most (in)famous example of such a critique in U.S. political science is undoubtedly Mancur Olson's *The Logic of Collective Action* (1965), which sought to more or less completely revolutionize any focus on public institutions and social groups by calling for any account of such institutions and groups to be firmly grounded in the rational decision-making processes of individual people. Olson's targets were those theories of social and political behavior that reasoned from a similarity of individual-level attributes to a politically viable solidarity between individuals sharing those attributes, but his critique—which also came with the prestige of economics attached to it, since Olson's model was none other than the model of the rational consumer that had held sway in microeconomics for decades—had a much more far-ranging effect on political science than simply the reform of accounts of social groups. Olson's liberal individualist critique served to reaffirm the notion that discussions of social outcomes and phenomena *needed* to be in some sense reduced to discussions of the individuals participating in them; in the jargon of the profession, the analysis of social phenomena required "microfoundations."

In his book, Waltz (1979) had considered and rejected just this line of argument, devoting an entire chapter (chap. 2) to criticism of "reductionist" arguments in IR that sought to explain world politics through a focus on the properties and decisions of individual state actors, and another chapter (chap. 3) to putatively "systemic" arguments in IR that, on closer examination, turned out to be more about individual actors and their behaviors than about the structure of the international system as a whole. Waltz's relentless focus on the condition of the system as a whole instead of on the individual decisions made by actors in the system is an element that he preserved more or less intact from the realpolitik tradition. Where a concentration on individual decisions could easily lead to a liberal criticism that if actors had made more rational decisions, then adverse consequences could have been avoided, a concentration on system-wide structural factors emphasizes limits rather than choices. Instead of looking at microfoundations, scholars are admonished to pay closer attention to the persistent and perennial ways that plans go awry and noble goals are foiled.

So one would think that this would set up a significant clash between Waltz's scientific and systemic restatement of IR realism and a variety of liberal alternatives. But although, for along while, Waltz's account became the favorite target of criticism for non–realist IR scholars of all kinds, what the vast majority of IR scholars spent their time arguing against was not Waltz's actual argument but a profound *misreading* of his argument as involving a specification of state preferences under conditions of anarchy. That this was not Waltz's argument— indeed, that he spends considerable amounts of time in the book railing against this kind of individualist reductionism—was lost in the shuffle.

Instead, the U.S. IR field spent the next two decades fencing with a decidedly liberal and individualist reconstruction of Waltz's claims, in which state actors were constrained by the structure of the international system to pay attention to questions of relative power. The main vehicle for the promulgation of this (mis) reading of Waltz was the volume *Neorealism and Its Critics*, published in 1986 and edited by one of the most prolific liberal theorists in all of American IR: Robert O. Keohane. Already the coauthor of a major study conceptualizing world politics in terms of complex interdependence between states (Keohane and Nye 1977), Keohane produced a volume that brought Waltz together with a series of critics and shaped the contours of the mainstream IR debate for the next several decades. The volume accomplished this in part through the simple expediency of reprinting four chapters from Waltz's book up front, before a set of critical engagements and a reply by Waltz to his critics; this made the book ideally positioned for assignment in IR courses. But significantly, Keohane's book omitted the two chapters of Waltz's book (chaps. 2 and 3) in which Waltz most exhaustively criticizes reductionism through detailed engagements with other IR theorists; it also omitted the chapters in which Waltz sought to apply his theoretical conceptualization to actually existing world politics by gathering and analyzing system-level positional data about interstate relations. As such, the version of Waltz presented in the edited volume is somewhat truncated, and his important critique of reductionism is minimized.[11]

Cementing this liberal individualist reconstruction of Waltz's argument is Keohane's own summaries of and engagement with Waltz in the edited volume. In his introduction, Keohane (1986) characterizes Waltz as covertly relying on an assumption that states are rational actors, since only that assumption would "enable the theorist to predict that leaders will respond to the incentives and constraints imposed by their environment" (167). Keohane elaborates:

> Waltz recognizes that any theory of state behavior must ascribe (by assumption) some motivations to states, just as microeconomic theory ascribes motivations to firms. It is not reductionist to do so as long as these motivations are not taken as varying from state to state as a result of their internal characteristics . . . For his balance of power theory to work, Waltz needs to assume that states seek self-preservation, since if at least some major states did not do so, there would be no reason to expect that roughly equivalent coalitions (i.e., "balances of power") would regularly form. (173)

But this is a deeply misleading characterization of Waltz's argument, one that makes Waltz into a liberal individualist rather than a theorist concerned with system structure above all else. What Waltz actually says is that states that survive have responded appropriately to their environment, with *appropriately* in this context meaning only that the states have acted in a way that enhances their own survival; whether they have done so accidentally, or at random, or deliberately after careful forethought is completely irrelevant to the logic of Waltz's theory.

The point is that the causal logic of Waltz's account takes place outside individual state actors, whereas in Keohane's summary, the causal logic has moved inside those state actors and become a motivation. As such, *Keohane's version of Waltz* forecloses the possibility of a clash between a liberal individualist and a nonliberal individualist account of world politics. Instead, Waltz's argument is transformed into an alternate way of defining what is important to individual states—specifying their utility functions, so to speak—and its systemic character simply vanishes from view.

Perhaps unsurprisingly, it was Keohane's version of Waltz's argument rather than Waltz's actual argument that became so influential in U.S. IR circles— even if one of its primary lines of influence lay in provoking people to articulate alternatives. Both Waltz's supporters and his detractors relied on the liberal individualist version of his argument and sought to supplement Waltz's deliberately spare theoretical formulation with a variety of other factors to help in making more specific predictions about the behavior of individual states (e.g., Elman 1996; Walt 1987). This liberal individualist reconstruction, which was perhaps easier for U.S. scholars to apprehend, became the received wisdom about Waltz's theory, despite his constant restatements of his theory and his equally constant effort to distance himself from those IR scholars who tried to make his theory do things it was not designed to do (for a particularly good example of this, see Waltz 1997). Like the notion that science provides answers to political controversies, the notion that good social explanation requires microfoundations was so much a part of the scholarly context of U.S. IR that alternatives were simply assimilated into it—in this case, through systematic misreading.

The irony should be noted here: by being recast in liberal individualist terms, Waltz's theory appears considerably less "political" and more "scientific" than it might if it were correctly understood as a *challenge* to the default assumptions of a constitutively liberal society. Indeed, there is a not insignificant way in which the "political" character of an account is wrapped up with its relationship to tacit assumptions; simply restating those assumptions looks natural and obvious, not "political" (Abbott 2001, 85). A theory or account that challenged the commonsense notions of American liberalism would have to ground itself, not in the activities and behaviors of putatively autonomous individuals, but in some broader aspect of the overall character of social life—precisely what the older realpolitik tradition, as well as Waltz's systems theory, tried to do. But the successful reception of those approaches involved translating their most challenging parts into terms more readily comprehensible to other U.S. political scientists and their audiences. Accepting the constitutively liberal assumptions of science and individualism enabled IR as a field to claim the kind of detached objectivity on which its epistemic authority rested.

As a further irony, consider that it was the IR scholars most directly influenced by the realpolitik tradition who first came out as critics of U.S. intervention in Vietnam during the 1960s, and their intellectual progeny who first came out against the U.S. invasion of Iraq in the early 2000s. Morgenthau, most famously in a 1965 *New York Times Magazine* article, suggested that the United States was deluding itself by failing to correctly evaluate the power struggle going on in Indochina, and Waltz regularly dismissed U.S. military adventurism in the developing world as distracting from the main challenge of maintaining a stable bipolar balance of power between the United States and the Soviet Union. Neither Waltz nor Morgenthau grounded his critique of the Vietnam War in an ethical denunciation of imperialism or the other arguments common to the more leftist critics of U.S. foreign policy at the time (indeed, their criticism might be summed up as: Vietnam *doesn't matter* so the United States shouldn't be expending resources there), but both took positions that were sharply critical of the anticommunist crusading mentality characteristic of U.S. domestic "Cold War consensus." Their skepticism about the power of liberal science to resolve problems in a progressive manner, a manifestation of a broader dissent from the liberal modernization narrative (Ninkovich 1994), thus placed them in the unenviable position of trying to fight liberalism from the inside—a position shared by the group of IR realists who took out a newspaper ad in early 2003 warning that "war with Iraq is *not* in America's national interest." In all of these instances, we see U.S. IR scholars reaching conclusions broadly similar to those reached by left-wing domestic critics, but doing so on grounds that those critics would probably reject and receiving flak from professional colleagues for doing so.[12]

That none of these critiques resulted in policy change is testimony to the limits of the liberal strategy for establishing the epistemic authority of social science: dissent from broadly shared substantive assumptions falls on deaf ears, dismissed as "political." The philosophical liberalism that animates U.S. political science and its IR subfield therefore does not generate a bias in favor of partisan-political liberalism but generates more of a "do-nothing" attitude behind which all manner of political opinions and positions might flourish as long as they don't culminate in partisan activism. That U.S. IR scholars are self-identified partisan-political liberals has less impact on IR scholarship than do the shared assumptions of scientific neutrality and the need for individual microfoundations, both of which work to channel potential political expressions into avenues less threatening to the general consensus in U.S. society about political life.

Conclusion: The Shape of U.S. International Relations

Pierre Bourdieu (2004) suggests that we think of academic disciplines as fields in which impersonal forces push and pull people to and fro. But this strikes me as a dangerous metaphor, inasmuch as it runs the risk of reifying the present configuration of a discipline and imbuing it with more solidity and stability than it perhaps warrants. Instead, I would much prefer that we think about academic disciplines as ongoing products of social action and, in particular, as occasions for reworking existing cultural resources to make sense of novel situations. Individual scholars have some autonomy here, but it is not as though Morgenthau could have avoided the critique from behaviorists by simply refusing to use the word *science* to legitimate his endeavor, or Waltz could have avoided being recast as a liberal individualist who thought that rational individuals would conform to the dictates of their environment by simply stating his position more plainly. Let me be clear: either individual *could* have taken those positions, but I do not believe that their work would have been anywhere near as influential as it was. Science and individual-level microfoundations are such integral parts of U.S. political science that alternatives are not likely to be recognized as alternatives but are instead likely to be assimilated into a dominant liberal standard. The availability of a traditional vocabulary emphasizing these claims provides the mechanism missing in too-quick attempts to summarize an academic field: one uses the available resources, and if the available resources are all about science and individuality, it is not surprising that the final articulation of a position is also all about science and individuality.

By focusing on specific moments when U.S. IR scholars had to legitimate their scholarly enterprise, I have sought to explain how the need to justify one's concerns and point of view to specific audiences shapes one's scholarship. IR scholars seeking to put themselves in a position to speak to the powerful and to perhaps influence their policies adopted the language of "science" in order to differentiate their work from merely partisan opinion. They also adopted a way of explaining events in world politics that resonated with the basically individualist assumptions of the discipline and, as such, were not worthy of much comment or notice. It is not as if these scholars had much of a choice, however; this is the vocabulary they were handed, and out of that vocabulary they crafted a field that maintained some of the tragic sensibility of classic realpolitik, even while becoming more palatable to American audiences. Saying something completely alien simply means that one gets ignored, however, so what came out from these scholars was a justification that, at first grudgingly, then more enthusiastically, embraced one or both of these notions. In that way, U.S. IR remains a liberal enterprise.

NOTES

Note for IR-knowledgeable readers: This book is targeted at an audience wider than international relations, which I hope explains some of my extra explication of IR terminology in the text. Thanks to Robert Adcock for his close reading and careful engagement with an earlier draft.

1. I follow common practice in the field and use the term *International Relations*, or *IR*, to refer to the ensemble of scholars and scholarly activities engaged in seeking to make sense of world politics. The precise boundaries of what "counts" as IR are a matter of some considerable debate; the point of the label is merely to differentiate the scholarly enterprise from the realm of practical world politics.

2. For IR scholars, *international anarchy* is a term of art meaning the absence of a global sovereign or world state.

3. The 2011 survey disaggregates this question into "economic" and "social" components; only 8 percent of U.S. IR scholars identified as any degree of conservative on social issues, and while 16 percent identified as some kind of conservative on economic issues, 18 percent identified as very liberal and 31 percent as liberal.

4. Jordan et al. 2009, 31. In the 2011 survey, 16 percent identified as realists and 20 percent as liberals, and 26 percent claimed no particular research tradition.

5. As in the other subfields of U.S. political science, such concerns have increasingly been relegated to "political theory" (Gunnell 1993), showing up in mainstream IR journals (if at all) under the heading of "international ethics." Space does not permit me to go into the resulting, sometimes contentious relationship between "ethical" and "empirical" IR scholarship; for a recent overview, see Price 2008.

6. Note that I am eliding an analytically significant difference between these two examples: the former ("because we are at war . . .") invokes a group identity to which both speaker and addressee are held to belong (they are both "nested" within a single identity), while the latter ("because we are scientists . . .") invokes a relationship between different but related identities held by speaker and addressee. Erving Goffman (1959) would have a lot to say about the scene-setting aspects of the latter; for an extended empirical example of the former, see Jackson 2006. For my purposes here, the distinction is less important than the overall point that legitimation deploys cultural resources to shape the contours of acceptable action by configuring identity.

7. As such, it should be stressed again that the "liberalism" with which I am most concerned throughout this chapter is philosophical rather than partisan-political liberalism and, in particular, the dimension of the former that privileges notions of scientific progress and their contributions to social and moral progress.

8. Michael Williams (2013) refers to this as the "IR Enlightenment," linking it to the "political studies Enlightenment" discerned by Ira Katznelson (2004) in anglophone

postwar political science, especially in the United States. But Williams emphasizes less the philosophical and rhetorical tensions inherent to the project and more the contrast between the project and the thinner rationalist/behaviorist U.S. IR that succeeded it. I would rather call attention to the continuities stretching from the indigenous U.S. scholarly tradition into the present-day incarnation of IR realism.

9. Many historians of the discipline, however, think this largely a myth (Robert Adcock, personal communication).

10. Like other IR realists who trace the distinctive character of international political life to its anarchic character, however, Waltz (1979, 111–14) is also clear that anarchy and self-help preserve the autonomy and freedom of individual states. As Deborah Boucoyannis (2007) has argued, this argument itself has great precedent within the tradition of classic liberal political philosophy, such that the notion of a balance of power is not an inextricably antiliberal one. While this raises some questions about the extent to which liberalism and realpolitik are implacably opposed on this particular issue, the fact remains that the dominant thread of IR realism when it comes to the balance of power is more of a weary resignation to its inevitability than a positive defense of its virtues.

11. Arguably, the other thing that Keohane's presentation of selected chapters from Waltz minimizes is the extent to which Waltz's conception of science is considerably more ideal-typical than Keohane's own preferred falsificationism (see the discussion in Jackson 2011, 111–14, 149–51). But that's a separate issue.

12. Indeed, there is evidence to suggest that Morgenthau lost the election for president of the APSA in large part because of his outspoken opposition to the Vietnam War (Frei 2001).

CHAPTER ELEVEN

The Merits of Marginality

Think Tanks, Conservative Intellectuals, and the Liberal Academy

THOMAS MEDVETZ

Since the 1960s, the loosely bounded organizations known as public policy "think tanks" have multiplied in many countries around the world (Garnett and Stone 1998; McGann 2012; McGann and Weaver 2000; Stone and Denham 2004; Weaver and Stares 2001). Although think tanks defy easy classification, the United Nations Development Program (2003, 6) defines them provisionally as "organizations engaged on a regular basis in research and advocacy on any matter related to public policy." In the United States, where the growth of think tanks has been the most pronounced, a clear ideological unevenness marks the think tank landscape. As scholars and nonprofit researchers have shown, think tanks with conservative missions and reputations outnumber their liberal and progressive counterparts by wide margins and consistently enjoy advantages in the competition for funding, publicity, and political attention (Callahan 1999a, 1999b; Covington 1997; Dolny 2000; Krehely, House, and Kernan 2004; Rich 2004; Rich and Weaver 1998).

This chapter considers the relationship between the growth of conservative think tanks in the United States and the predominantly liberal attitudes of professors. Are the ideological imbalances in these two spheres linked in an intelligible way? More specifically, did conservative activists establish think tanks in response to the perceived dominance of liberals in the academy, particularly after the political upheavals of the 1960s? Can think tanks of the right therefore be counted as part of a "counter-establishment" project in the sense described by journalist and political aide Sidney Blumenthal (1986)? I will argue that, notwithstanding the appeals of the counter-establishment narrative, conservative think tanks are better understood as connectors in a political-intellectual network that incorporates mainstream or "establishment" institutions. Extending from within the academic sphere, through the emergent subspace of "policy research," and into the field of official politics, this network confers on its members certain advantages not available to academic scholars, whose professional closure is more likely to isolate them from public and policy debates.

What is novel or noteworthy about this argument? Put simply, it runs counter to the two most commonly cited explanations for the growth of conservative think tanks in the United States. The first explanation, often found in journalistic and scholarly writings, is that conservatives built think tanks in response to a powerful "liberal establishment" centered in the major culture-producing institutions of American society, including the media, the universities, and the spheres of art, entertainment, and philanthropy. This view received its first extensive treatment in Blumenthal's (1986) study of the conservative movement. Blumenthal cited many specific think tanks as key operators in this movement, so it is not surprising that his "counter-establishment thesis" soon became the standard narrative for describing their origins and purposes. For example, in their history of the American conservative movement, Micklethwait and Wooldridge (2005) describe right-leaning intellectuals of the 1950s as already poised to create a set of extra-academic institutions to rival the authority of liberal professors: "If the Right was going to have a hard time getting its voice heard in universities, then it would invent conservative institutions of its own" (49–50). Over the years, the same authors argue, think tanks came to fit this bill, eventually becoming the "general command center for the intellectual Right" (160). A similar view informs historian Kim Phillips-Fein's (2009) study of the postwar business activist movement. Among other observations about think tanks, Phillips-Fein notes that the "ultimate vision" of American Enterprise Institute architect William Baroody Sr. was to build "a network of conservative think tanks that could *rival the university system*" (66; my emphasis). Sociologists Aaron McCright and Riley Dunlap (2003, 353) similarly identify conservative think tanks as indispensable "countermovement organizations." In these and other writings, the suggestion is that conservative think tanks derive their identities largely from their detachment from and opposition to the liberal academy (see also Diamond 1995; Himmelstein 1990; Jenkins and Eckert 1989; Pierson and Hacker 2011; Stefanic and Delgado 1996).

The counter-establishment thesis offers a useful starting point for understanding the birth of conservative think tanks, not least because it is consistent with the self-accounts of many conservative activists, who attributed their earlier defeats to the presence of a well-organized liberal establishment. On the conservative view, liberal professors collectively played an important role in this establishment not only by imposing their political attitudes on students, but also by training an emerging "new class" of technocrats, bureaucrats, and professionals who shared a stake in expanding the federal government (Bruce-Briggs 1979; King and Szelenyi 2004). Technocratic organizations such as the Brookings Institution, which would later come to be known as think tanks, also figured prominently in this network.

Despite these useful observations, I would argue that the counter-establishment thesis ultimately proves incomplete as an explanation for the post-1960s growth of conservative think tanks. The main problem lies in its overemphasis on the themes of *separation* and *rivalry* between conservatives and the university system. In the first place, an exclusive focus on these themes leaves us hard-pressed to explain why many of the leading postwar conservative intellectuals, including those involved in the creation of think tanks, actively worked to fortify and extend their ties to the academic world. This was true of William F. Buckley Jr., for example, who helped establish campus outreach groups such as the Intercollegiate Studies Institute, even as he "railed against liberal academe" (Fosse and Gross 2012, 127). Accordingly, the counter-establishment thesis leads to an oversimplified image of conservative think tanks as "anti-academic" organizations. This is a significant problem, I would argue, because the most successful think tanks have thrived not simply by distancing themselves from the world of academic scholarship but by carrying out a complex game of separation and attachment vis-à-vis the university. Think tank–affiliated "policy experts" continuously signal both their differences from and similarities to professors by imitating the forms of academic production and proclaiming their scholarly competence (Medvetz 2012).

But if it will not do to portray conservative think tanks as unambiguously "anti-academic" organizations, then neither can we describe them in the opposite terms—that is, as part of a conservative attempt to "infiltrate" the university and increase their influence within it. Doubtless, conservatives have made some notable efforts to strengthen their presence in the academic world since the 1960s. The founding of new colleges and universities dedicated, as the Young America's Foundation puts it, to "discovering, maintaining, and strengthening the conservative values of their students"—including Liberty University (incorporated in 1971), Regent University (1978), and the Thomas More College of Liberal Arts (1978)—is vital to this project.[1] Another sign of campus conservatism's recent vitality is the growth of right-leaning student government, activist, and leadership groups, internship programs, and campus newspapers (Binder and Wood 2012). Nevertheless, if the past few decades have seen significant efforts by "conservative groups . . . to 'take back' universities from the 'grip of the left,'" as Nagy-Zekmi and Hollis (2010, xxv) argue, then think tanks have not been consistent contributors to this effort. Put simply, conservative think tanks have dedicated few resources to the goal of influencing scholarly debate, whether by publishing in academic journals or by working to increase the number of conservative faculty members. It would make little sense, then, to speak of them as involved in a project of academic "infiltration."

Given these points, how should we grasp the relationship between the university system and the conservative think tank–building project? To answer this question, I begin by setting aside the images of the "counter-establishment" and of academic "infiltration." Instead, I depict conservative think tanks as members of a diffuse organizational network that traverses, links, and overlaps the more institutionalized spheres of politics, philanthropy, academics, business, and the media. More than just a semantic shift, this approach offers three advantages for the scholarly discussion about the politics of intellectual production. The first advantage is to lay the groundwork for a fuller description of think tanks than that typically found in scholarly and journalistic accounts. Neither purely academic nor anti-academic—nor, for that matter, marked by any clear "essence"— think tanks are constitutively hybrid creatures that function by assembling mixed bundles of institutionalized resources from the settings listed above. Hybridity is neither a secondary nor an accidental feature of their existence, but rather the very key to their functioning. To locate themselves between more established institutions, think tanks perform a complex balancing act that requires them to cultivate network ties to politicians, bureaucrats, foundation officers, activists, journalists, and professors; to solicit donations; to generate publicity; and to hire staff members with political knowhow and media savvy. Crucially, it is not by accumulating any one of these resources that a think tank succeeds, but by establishing the proper mixture.

The second benefit of reconceptualizing think tanks in this way is to shed new light on the scholarly discussion about the overrepresentation of liberals within the professoriate. Here my discussion extends the *reputation-based self-selection model* developed by Gross and his collaborators. The central claim of this approach is that professors tend to hold more liberal political views than other Americans because a preformed occupational subculture renders the profession more attractive to those with compatible political sensibilities (Fosse and Gross 2012; Gross and Cheng 2011; see also chapters 2 and 4 of this volume). The professoriate, Fosse and Gross (2012, 155) write, "has been 'politically typed' as appropriate for and welcoming of" liberals "and as inappropriate for conservatives." The major contribution of these studies has been to refute numerous false claims and assumptions that once dominated the debate about the political attitudes of professors. Most notable among these are two opposing but equally politically charged arguments: first, that there is an intrinsic relationship between liberalism and the capacity for abstract thinking, or intelligence itself; and second, that left-leaning intellectuals seized control of the university, closed ranks professionally, and excluded conservatives through discriminatory hiring practices.

The reputation-based self-selection model suggests a more complex process whereby the academic profession developed its own subculture inflected with liberal values and commitments. In response to this claim, Peter Wood (2011a, 2011b) argues that the model fails to disprove the theory that the overrepresentation of liberals in the professoriate is a result of liberal bias. I argue here that the reputation-based self-selection model should be understood as much as a call for historical study into the process of occupational subculture formation in the United States as a positive explanation for the overrepresentation of liberals in the professoriate. With respect to the current political composition of the professoriate, my claim is that the formation of a liberal academic subculture was but one part of a double-sided process that also involved the development of a conservative intellectual network. If we wish to understand why professors are liberal, we cannot simply portray conservative intellectuals as passive bystanders in the process. Nor can we relegate their strategies and self-understanding to the sidelines of the discussion. Instead, we must consider their role in actively reinforcing their academic marginality. In fact, I will insist on this term, *marginality* (as opposed to, say, underrepresentation), for reasons indicated above. Put simply, the current locus of conservative intellectualism in the United States is a network of organizations that are "quasi-academic," inasmuch as their very survival depends on their ability to gather and assemble certain academic resources and institutional forms. Whether or not think tank–affiliated policy experts are employed as professors is less consequential than the presence of dozens of conservative organizations that have embraced what I will call the "merits of marginality" by positioning themselves as outposts at the university's edge.

The third benefit of my approach comes from questioning an assumption that has gone largely unchallenged in the debate about the political culture of American academia. This is the idea that marginality in the academic profession necessarily constitutes some kind of social or political disadvantage for the marginalized group. When writers speak of conservatives as underrepresented in the professoriate or relegated to the sidelines of academic debate, the suggestion is typically that this circumstance works to their overall detriment. Yet there are compelling reasons to question this assumption. In the first place, as feminist scholars have noted, the outskirts of scholarly debate can be a privileged position from which to speak: "Maintaining a vocal and visible marginality offers us the opportunity to critique the center or the status quo; to engage in positive, subversive commentary—much as medieval manuscript marginalia does; and to speak what cannot be spoken by those in positions of institutional authority who have their positions to protect" (Howes 1993, 4). Even more important, however, are the advantages that attach to positions of marginality when we widen our view beyond the academic sphere. Just as marginality within a given physical setting implies greater proximity to neighboring ones, so marginality in the academic world can afford greater access to other powerful institutions. In the case of conservative intellectuals, I argue that this is precisely what happened: think tanks strengthened the ties connecting conservative intellectuals to like-minded politicians, bureaucrats, *political specialists*, financial sponsors, media gatekeepers, and activists. In the process, they shielded intellectuals of the right from the dangers of "ivory tower" scholasticism.

To summarize, then, my argument is that conservative activists and intellectuals built a network of think tanks neither as "rivals" to the university system, in any simple sense, nor as part of a project to "invade" the academy or accumulate scholarly prestige in large amounts. Instead, they built organizational instruments for converting academic marginality into a *political advantage*. Think tanks play a crucial role in connecting conservatives to the formal institutions of politics, the media, and philanthropy. In the next section, I elaborate the historical background for these claims by sketching a brief history of think tanks in the United States, including the rapid growth of conservative think tanks after the 1960s. The final section then relates this narrative to the debate about why American professors have predominantly liberal attitudes and elaborates the claim that think tanks enabled conservative intellectuals to embrace the "merits of marginality."

The Ambiguous Birth of Think Tanks in the United States

The predecessors of the modern-day think tank formed in the United States through a series of complex partnerships among variously situated actors and groups, including philanthropists, political reformers, aspiring statesmen and civil servants, businessmen, scholars, and journalists (Medvetz 2012; J. Smith 1991b).[2] Central to this process, which began in the late nineteenth century, was the appearance of several waves of organizations that fit most contemporary descriptions of a think tank—albeit decades before any such category became codified in popular, political, or academic discourses. The first of these waves consisted of several dozen civic federations created in the 1890s to address the growing problems of industrialism, especially urban poverty, urban blight, and immigrant assimilation.[3] The civic federations were direct descendants of the settlement houses and reform institutions that preceded them, but their focus lay more squarely on public policy issues. Administrative reforms related to the tax structure and the provision of social services became their chief concerns.

The civic federations were followed by a set of municipal research agencies that sought to reform local administrative and accounting procedures. Among the dozens of such groups that formed in major cities around the country, the New York Bureau of Municipal Research quickly became the leading crusader against inefficiency, "graft," and municipal corruption (Dahlberg 1966). Another organization from this period notable for its focus on federal policy and its later prominence as a think tank was the Institute for Government Relations. Founded in 1916, the institute's original purpose was to push for federal budget reform, although its aims soon broadened beyond this issue. In 1927, it merged with two affiliated organizations to become the Brookings Institution (Critchlow 1985; Saunders 1966; J. Smith 1991a).

Another predecessor of the modern think tank began at Stanford University when future president Herbert Hoover established a repository of papers related to World War I. Inspired by his experiences as a humanitarian relief worker and by the example of Andrew White, the first president of Cornell University, who had amassed a vast archive on the French Revolution, Hoover became dedicated to "the systematic collecting of contemporary documents on the Great War before they were lost to history" (Nash 1988, 287). In 1919, the "lifelong bibliophile" donated his papers to his alma mater, and the bequest grew into "the world's largest private repository of documents on twentieth-century political history" (287–88). Hoover shifted the archive's purpose during the 1950s, however, as the Cold War intensified. In 1959, the ex-president rededicated the archive-cum-research center to the struggle against what he called "the evils of the doctrines of Karl Marx" (Patenaude 2006, 114).[4] Because of its pointed ideological stance, the Hoover Institution's formal affiliation with Stanford became a double-edged source of intellectual legitimacy and perennial friction.[5]

America's growing internationalism during the interwar years led to the creation of a new set of research and discussion groups dedicated to foreign policy. The most important among them was the Council on Foreign Relations, formed in 1920 through the merger of "The Inquiry," a loosely connected set of advisers to President Woodrow Wilson, and a private, unnamed club of New York lawyers and businessmen led by Nobel Peace Prize winner Elihu Root, a senator and former secretary of the Departments of War and State (Grose 1996; Schulzinger

1984). Another new foreign policy discussion group founded during this period was the Foreign Policy Association, a New York–based organization consisting of lawyers, bankers, journalists, and aspiring statesmen. While these two groups focused almost exclusively on America's relations with Europe—especially the League of Nations—a third new foreign policy group, the Institute of Pacific Relations, devoted itself to the study of relations among Pacific Rim countries. Formed in 1925, the institute maintained a reputation for relative disinterestedness until the 1930s, when the deterioration of U.S.-Japanese relations made even the appearance of neutrality difficult for any such organization (Akami 2002; Davidann 2001; Hooper 1994; Raucher 1978; Yamaoka 1999).

The Great Depression and World War II supplied the impetus for the creation of more civil society–based research groups. Several of these organizations sought to harness the budding tools of macroeconomic analysis to recommend policies that might restore or maintain economic stability. Most notable among them was the Committee for Economic Development (CED), a business-led consortium created in 1943 and dedicated to solving the problem of mass unemployment amid widespread forecasts of economic collapse. While CED did nothing to hide its aim of defending business interests, its leaders were drawn from a politically moderate segment of the capitalist class. Accordingly, CED's leadership generally concurred with the progressive credo that scientific research and planning were indispensable tools of modern political administration. In the words of Alfred P. Sloan Jr., a CED member and chairman of General Motors, the committee was "a big broad movement on the part of business to attempt, through the scientific approach, to develop a plan . . . [for] perpetuating free enterprise" (Schriftgiesser 1960, 28). CED's leaders wished to aid in the search for technical solutions to the challenges facing capitalism; most were also committed to the corporatist tenet that dialogue and cooperation between business, labor, and state representatives were vital to modern society's well-being.

The next phase in the extended "prehistory" of American think tanks involved the creation of numerous postwar research and development groups, including the RAND Corporation, the Hudson Institute, and the Center for Naval Analyses (Miller 1989; B. Smith 1966). RAND, in particular, became the prime beneficiary of a major shift in government spending toward tactical planning and engineering. Most influential for the development of "systems analysis," the preferred technique of Pentagon planning, RAND became a prominent symbol of Cold War strategizing (Amadae 2003).

Although most of the policy research organizations that had emerged by the 1940s remained committed to the progressive view that managers and technocrats could enhance economic efficiency, new organizations soon emerged to defend "the invisible hand" of the market. The key condition for this development was the formation of a transnational network of libertarian economists who generally felt alienated from the mainstream of their profession. As Bockman and Eyal (2002) note, "Being a minority within the American economics profession, libertarian economists sought refuge in international libertarian associations, most importantly the Mont Pèlerin Society, with the financial support of conservative foundations" (332). Mont Pèlerin was formed in 1947 through a collaboration between Friedrich Hayek, then a professor at the London School of Economics, and Milton Friedman, then in transition from the University of Minnesota to the University of Chicago (Bockman and Eyal 2002; Hartwell 1995; Mirowski and Plehwe 2009). Friedman explained the society's birth in these terms: "in 1947 the people who believed in the market economy were mostly isolated individuals, almost completely separated from their intellectual environment." He argued that the "real function of the Mount Pèlerin Society, which it served magnificently in the early years, . . . was that it provided an opportunity for isolated people from around the world to get together for a week in which they could let their hair down and talk to one another about the things that really concerned them without looking over their shoulders all the time" (quoted in Blumenthal 1986, 108; see also Kelley 1997).

Another locus of 1940s libertarian economic thinking was the American Enterprise Association (later renamed the American Enterprise Institute). Founded in 1938 by Lewis H. Brown, chairman of the Johns-Manville Corporation, the association had more direct ties to corporations than many of the research groups that preceded it. Its earliest work consisted of reports issued to members of Congress that were meant to demonstrate the harmful effects of Depression-era government price and production controls (Wiarda 2009).[6] The transnational network of libertarian economists solidified further with the creation of the Foundation for Economic Education in 1946 (Phillips-Fein 2009; Plehwe 2006) and the United Kingdom–based Institute of Economic Affairs in 1955 (Cockett 1995; Muller 1996).

In recent years, scholars of American conservatism have developed a new appreciation for the importance of intellectuals such as the libertarian economists in shaping the conservative movement. But if it is true that conservative intellectuals shaped their movement in decisive ways, then it is also necessary to ask which forces, in turn, shaped the intellectuals' priorities, aims, and political strategies. Doubtless it is true that a sense of exclusion from the university played a key role in directing their energies and self-understandings, especially during the 1950s and 1960s. William F. Buckley Jr.'s 1951 *God and Man at Yale* was the first systematic attempt to problematize the marginalization of conservatives from the academy. Buckley argued that Yale, having strayed far from its original purpose of training ministers, had become a bastion of liberal thought where professors could impose subversive ideas on impressionable students under the guise of academic freedom. Describing his alma mater as an "institution that derives its moral and financial support from Christian individualists and then addresses itself to the task of persuading the sons of these supporters to be atheistic socialists," he recommended that alumni use their power to limit professors' control over hiring decisions and curriculum design (xv–xvi). While Buckley's analysis focused only on Yale, his designs extended beyond New Haven. "Ideally," he wrote, "my observations would be based on an exhaustive study of the curricula and attitudes of a number of colleges and universities." Indeed, "what is amiss at Yale is more drastically amiss in other of our great institutions of learning" (xvi).

Yet even Buckley did not want conservatives to abandon academia altogether. His understanding of the importance of campus outreach was made clear by his involvement with numerous campus groups such as the Intercollegiate Society of Individualists (later known as the Intercollegiate Studies Institute). Frank Chodorov, a libertarian who served as editor of the Foundation for Economic Education's journal *The Freeman*, founded the campus organization for young conservatives in 1953. In 1960, Buckley also established the Young Americans for Freedom, a conservative youth organization whose founding principles were laid out by M. Stanton Evans in the Sharon Statement.[7]

With respect to academia, then, the strategies of conservative intellectuals were marked by double-sidedness. This much is evident in the history of the American Enterprise Institute (AEI), whose fortunes were closely connected to its changing relation to the academic world. Initially a small organization, AEI entered a period of temporary hibernation in 1951 after the death of its first president, Lewis Brown, only to be granted a second life in 1954 when Chamber of Commerce official Allen D. Marshall rebuilt the organization. AEI's revitalization was attributable mainly to the efforts of William Baroody Sr., a former Chamber of Commerce official and vocal champion of free enterprise, who joined the organization in 1954. His loyalties to the business world notwithstanding, Baroody's first impression of AEI was that it bore too close a resemblance to a business trade association. Accordingly, he focused much of his initial effort on increasing the organization's ties to academia, the better to enhance its intellectual reputation. He did so first by "dumping the business types," in his words, and hiring more scholars (Klaidman 1977). In 1956, Baroody recruited Milton Friedman to serve on the AEI Council of Academic Advisers, a post Friedman retained until 1979. Extolling the "free competition of ideas," Baroody also hired University of Illinois economist Paul McCracken, who later became chairman of Richard Nixon's Council of Economic Advisers. As AEI fellow Robert Pranger later explained, "We had by the late 1960s a certain academic reputation. Whatever we did was credible" (quoted in Blumenthal 1986, 41).

Another outpost of conservative thought located at the edge of the academy was the Center for Strategic and International Studies (CSIS), an institute founded as part of Georgetown University in 1962 by David Abshire and Arleigh Burke. Abshire was a Korean War veteran who earned a PhD in history from Georgetown, where he taught in the School of Foreign Service. A Navy admiral during World War II, Burke became chief of Naval Operations in 1955. If AEI was the conservative answer to Brookings, then CSIS could be considered a kind of rejoinder to the Council on Foreign Relations. Over the next two decades, CSIS attracted foreign policy luminaries such as Henry Kissinger and Zbigniew Brzezinski (J. Smith 1993). However, like the Hoover Institution's troubled relationship with Stanford, CSIS's affiliation with Georgetown University became a source of tension until 1986, when the Georgetown trustees voted to disaffiliate themselves from the organization.

The conservative think tank–building effort began in earnest in the early 1970s. During the previous decade, the notion that America's major cultural institutions—particularly the universities, the media, and the philanthropic sector—were dominated by the left had become more influential in conservatives circles. Buckley had foreshadowed this concern, but the idea received its most systematic treatment in the work of M. Stanton Evans, starting with his 1961 book *Revolt on the Campus*. This was followed in 1965 by his *The Liberal Establishment*, which argued that American universities were central to a network of liberal institutions that included philanthropic foundations, policy and discussion groups, and major media organs. Lewis Powell's now famous 1971 memorandum calling for American business to fund new institutions of public and political outreach expressed clearly the need for a new strategy. William Simon and Irving Kristol were similarly vocal in promoting the idea that businessmen had become recalcitrant in their support of conservative causes. They urged their entrepreneurial allies to fund new centers of conservative thought. Kristol was part of the small band of neoconservative intellectuals whose gradual migration away from the Democratic Party owed much to their growing disillusionment with the academic world (Diggins 1994 [1975]; Ehrman 1995; Steinfels

1979). Simon, in his book *A Time for Action* (1980), referred to liberal professors as members of "the secret system."

By the mid-1970s, conservatives had ramped up their business outreach efforts and built new organizations to disseminate their ideas. Some conservative donors bankrolled endowed professorships in the hope of making the academy a more congenial home for conservative scholars; others built legal foundations (Teles 2008), foreign policy groups, and political action committees. The centerpiece of the effort, however, was the creation of new think tanks and the refurbishment of older ones. Among them, the most important became the Heritage Foundation, cofounded by Paul Weyrich and Edwin Feulner in 1973 with seed money from Joseph Coors.[8] Coors also funded the Independence Institute, a Colorado think tank focused on state-level policy issues. As former congressional staff members, Weyrich and Feulner had seen the effectiveness of organizations like Brookings and the Council on Foreign Relations. Unlike these organizations, however, Weyrich and Feulner also understood the growing importance of attracting news media attention and developed a sophisticated marketing and public relations apparatus (Bjerre-Poulsen 1991; Edwards 1997).

Pleas for business support by conservative intellectuals continued to shape philanthropic giving patterns during the 1970s and 1980s. For example, in 1977, Libertarian Party chairman Ed Crane founded the Cato Institute in San Francisco with funding from Kansas-based industrialists David and Charles Koch. A year after Cato's birth, Hayek's student Antony Fisher established the Manhattan Institute in New York. Fisher had been involved in the creation of conservative research organizations since 1955, when he cofounded the Institute of Economic Affairs in the United Kingdom. During the 1970s and 1980s, in fact, Fisher founded or cofounded free-market research centers throughout the English-speaking world, including the Fraser Institute in Canada (founded in 1974), the Center for Independent Studies in Australia (1976), the Adam Smith Institute in the United Kingdom (1977), and the Atlas Economic Research Foundation in the United States (1980). Ronald Reagan's election to the presidency in 1980 marked the beginning of a new era of influence for conservative think tanks. In filling administration posts, Reagan drew extensively from think tanks, recruiting fifty staff members from the Hoover Institution, thirty-six from the Heritage Foundation, thirty-four from AEI, and eighteen from CSIS (Blumenthal 1986, 35–37). A characteristic example was Murray Weidenbaum, the former editor of AEI's *Regulation* magazine, who became chairman of Reagan's Council of Economic Advisers.

Even after gaining substantial political recognition with relatively little academic authority at their disposal, conservative think tanks continued to maintain loose ties to the academic world. Heritage, for example, created an "Academic Bank" to broker connections between conservative intellectuals, especially professors, and political institutions. Blumenthal (1986, 48) calls the Academic Bank "instrumental in transforming isolated conservative intellectuals into a network." The Academic Bank's significance lay also in its ability to convert academic materials into useful political tools. As the Academic Bank's former director Willa Johnson put it, "Dealing with the academic community can be frustrating. They're used to their own deadlines with no concept of how to plug it in here. We've . . . helped refine their product. This [academic] community lacks marketing. We do that" (quoted in Blumenthal 1986, 49). A representative of the Business Roundtable, a business trade association, made a similar observation about the American Enterprise Institute: "AEI knows what's going on. If I wanted an economist I'd call Bill Baroody to give me a list. I can remember the early days when chief executive officers didn't want to have anything to do with these goddamned professors. Now we understand more about the impact of ideas" (42).

In making these observations, my point is not to suggest that AEI or other organizations like it are "really" academic centers, any more than it is to suggest that they are not. Instead, it is to show that any attempt to affix a simple institutional classification to think tanks would be to miss their essential *hybridity*. More broadly, I would argue that there are no natural or immutable lines of separation between academia and neighboring spheres. To resolve the problem of the think tank's identity, we need only recognize that the stance adopted by conservative think tanks is dynamic and multifaceted. Far from simply retreating from the academic world or becoming the "rivals" of universities, they carry out a complex balancing act that requires maintaining certain ties to universities, which allow them to lay claim to a form of scholarly authority. At the same time, they must maintain a proper distance from academic production to ensure their political relevance. Put differently, conservative think tanks strategically overlap the worlds of academic scholarship and politics. But it would be an overstatement to describe them as focused on building scholarly reputations in any concerted fashion. Like their organizations, think tank–affiliated policy experts must be willing to deviate radically from academic norms and adopt a style of intellectual production notable for its responsiveness to political, economic, and media demand (Medvetz 2010).

As a summary note, I would point out that by the 1960s, several dozen organizations fitting the present-day definition of the term *think tank* existed in the United States. Even so, it would be misleading to use this term for any of the pre-1970s organizations described here. To do so would be historically anachronistic, inasmuch as the think tank category itself had not yet formed in everyday or specialized discourse, be it journalistic, scholarly, or political. To impose the current classification on these organizations, then, would be tantamount to viewing the past through the lens of the present. Worse yet, it would be to imply that they were always "destined" to become think tanks.[9] It was only in the 1970s that the discursive creation of the think tank truly occurred. This is when organizations such as the Council on Foreign Relations, the American Enterprise Institute, and the RAND Corporation widely came to be regarded as examples of the same "thing." This point has significant implications for the present discussion, inasmuch as the conservative mobilization of the 1970s played a critical role in *creating* the think tank category itself.

Think Tanks and the Contemporary American Conservative Movement

The preceding narrative illustrates three points about the proliferation of conservative think tanks and their relationship to the liberal professoriate. The first point can be posed in relation to what I have called the counter-establishment thesis, which holds that conservatives built think tanks as a direct challenge to the power of liberal institutions, including a university system dominated by left-leaning professors. By now it should be clear that my argument is not based on a wholesale rejection of this thesis. On the contrary, the counter-establishment argument captures some of the most important features of American conservatism in the immediate post-Goldwater era. Nevertheless, when used to explain the growth of conservative think tanks, the counter-establishment narrative has certain shortcomings. By overemphasizing the themes of separation and rivalry, it tends to portray conservative think tanks in essentialist terms as "anti-academic" organizations. Micklethwait and Wooldridge (2005, 49), for example, suggest that conservatives created think tanks to meet a growing need for "places to meet outside the dreaded 'liberal' universities." Without disagreeing entirely, I would argue that we must also consider the myriad connections that think tanks establish between conservative sectors of the academy and the sphere of formal politics.

Equally important is that all think tanks, irrespective of political affiliation, siphon authority from the academic sphere by imitating its products and practices and adorning themselves in its symbolic vestments. It would therefore be problematic to describe conservative think tanks as simply "non-academic" organizations. But neither have they been involved in any systematic effort to change the ideological balance of the professoriate or to "reform" scholarly debates by moving them in a more conservative direction. Accordingly, neither the image of the counter-establishment nor that of academic "infiltration" offers a useful metaphor for capturing what is most important about conservative think tanks. Instead, the historical record suggests that these organizations have gained significance by spanning the boundaries between institutional spheres, especially those of academics, politics, business, and the media. To capture this point, I have argued that think tanks are best thought of as constitutively hybrid connectors in a political-intellectual network.

Think Tanks and the Reputation-Based Self-Selection Model

What implications does this argument have for the ongoing debate about the political attitudes of American professors? The second purpose of this narrative is to extend the reputation-based self-selection model developed by Neil Gross and his collaborators, which emphasizes the formation of a liberal subculture in academia as the key factor in explaining the surfeit of liberal professors. According to this theory, liberals are more likely to gravitate toward the academic profession because of an institutionalized political reputation that matches their pre-held political tastes (Fosse and Gross 2012; Gross and Cheng 2011). Rather than elaborate this argument, let me turn immediately to what I believe is the most noteworthy critique of it. This is the argument that the self-selection model leaves open the possibility that discriminatory practices better explain the pattern in question. In a response to the model, for example, Wood (2011b) makes no objection, per se, to the idea of self-selection but argues that it is ultimately a tautological or "foreshortened" explanation—"not unlike explaining the line in front of the movie theater by hypothesizing that the people in line want to see the movie."

While I think this criticism is based on an uncharitable reading of the study in question, I would agree that when read as a positive explanation for the overrepresentation of liberals in academia, the reputation-based self-selection model cannot provide a full explanation. As Wood suggests, the main cause it identifies for the liberalism of professors is so proximate to the outcome it seeks to explain as to be nearly indistinguishable from the outcome itself. In other words, the idea that liberals are drawn to the academic profession because the academic profession itself has a liberal culture is nearly tautological. However, to focus exclusively on this point is to overlook the two major contributions of the self-selection studies. The first contribution is to refute many of the false propositions that have long dominated the conversation about the political attitudes of American professors. Among the hypotheses ruled out by Fosse, Freese, and Gross in chapter 2 of this volume, for example, are numerous seemingly plausible explanations concerning the cognitive characteristics, personalities, lifestyles, and cultural perspectives of liberals and conservatives. Even if the reputation-based self-selection model does not pinpoint a definitive reason for the overrepresentation of liberals in academia, then, it improves our understanding by ruling out false explanations.

To my mind, the second major contribution of the studies by Gross and his collaborators has been to shift the explanandum of the discussion in a more fruitful direction. What they suggest, in short, is that it makes little sense to ask simply why professors are liberal; instead, what is needed is a detailed *historical analysis* of the formation of academia's distinctive subculture—and by extension, the subcultures of other occupational spheres.[10] Put differently, I read the reputation-based self-selection model less as an explanation per se than as a persuasive call for a more highly developed historical sociology of occupational group formation. When it comes to explaining the professional culture of academia, the most important task is to account for the formative postwar period during which higher education expanded dramatically in the United States and professors acquired a stable reputation for being liberal. This chapter points to an important subsequent stage in this process, during which conservative intellectuals, having come to regard academic culture as hostile, closed off, or otherwise uncongenial, actively embraced the "merits of marginality" and focused their energies elsewhere. I have identified the creation of think tanks as the locus of a collective effort to exert social and political influence, but this effort was not limited to think tanks. The core point is that like their liberal counterparts, conservative intellectuals developed their own occupational subculture with its own institutions, practices, and norms.

Like the reputation-based self-selection studies, my analysis casts doubt on the notion that discriminatory practices can account for the overrepresentation of liberals in the academic profession. While the narrative sketched above does not fully refute the claim, it does show that conservative intellectuals were actively reinforcing their own academic marginality by the early 1970s. Their massive investment in think tanks, along with the invention of "policy research" as a distinctive mode of intellectual production, became the primary means through which conservatives fortified their position at the edge of the academy.

The Benefits of the Border

The third and final lesson of my account follows closely from the previous one. In short, whatever the drawbacks of their underrepresentation within the professoriate, conservative intellectuals derive major benefits from their command of quasi-academic institutions such as think tanks. What advantages accrue to those who sit at the borderland of the academic profession? The first is signaled by Laura L. Howes's (1993) comment quoted earlier, which suggests that marginality can afford the marginal figure a certain freedom to engage in "subversive commentary," or say what is generally unsayable in mainstream discussion. In the present case, academic marginality frees conservative intellectuals from the strictures of academic production—particularly peer review, the plinth of scholarly credibility—while allowing them to draw strategically on certain forms of academic authority. It also leaves them better equipped than their liberal counterparts to discard the guise of political neutrality and to engage with politicians and journalists in creative ways, including through new intellectual genres, such as "policy briefs," "talking points memos," and presidential transition manuals. To argue that these genres have little academic legitimacy—which is to say that many professors would not recognize them as "intellectual" products at all—would be to overlook their most important effects, which occur when politicians read and cite these materials, journalists report on their contents, and foundation officers provide funding to those who write them. By facilitating these forms of influence, academic marginality functions as a guard against the public and political isolation that marks the experiences of many professors.

At this point it should be clear that the term *marginality* must be understood in a relative rather than an absolute sense, since a position of marginality in one setting may be equivalent to centrality in another. Thus, at a wider level, the proliferation of conservative think tanks is significant for its role in the formation of a kind of institutional buffer zone between the worlds of academics and politics—a weakly bounded space with its own rules, resources, and criteria of hierarchy and judgment. From the standpoint of a liberal professor not acclimated to this space, centrality in the academic sphere increasingly comes at the price of marginalization from public and policy debates.

NOTES

I thank Nicholas Bloom, Neil Gross, and Solon Simmons for their helpful feedback on this chapter.

1. Young America's Foundation is quoted from its "Top Conservative Colleges" list (www.yaf.org/innerpagetemplate.aspx?id=3368).

2. This paragraph and the later passages on the foreign policy centers and the Committee for Economic Development are adapted from Medvetz 2012, 55–65, 68–70.

3. For case studies of two of the most notable such organizations, see Cyphers 2002 (on the National Civic Federation) and Small 1895 (on the Chicago Civic Federation); see also Trattner 2007.

4. This quote is sometimes misattributed to the Hoover Institution's founding purpose (see, e.g., Higgott and Stone 1994; Williams 2000, 115). In fact, the institution's mission evolved over time as Hoover grew more convinced that the opposition between communism and capitalism had become a conflict of epochal significance.

5. For profiles of the Hoover Institution, see Campbell 2000, Patenaude 2006, and Paul 1974.

6. The year 1943 is often given as the founding date of the American Enterprise Institute because the onset of World War II led the organization to disband and reconvene several years later.

7. The Sharon Statement is so named because it was formally adopted by YAF members at Buckley Jr.'s Sharon, Connecticut estate. For text of the statement, see www.yaf .org/sharon_statement.aspx.

8. Over the years, however, Heritage's most generous funder became Richard Mellon Scaife.

9. Even today, the boundary of the *think tank* category varies from country to country and, in most settings, lacks a firm legal basis (Stone and Denham 2004). On the fallacy of assuming that ostensibly similar practices count as cases of the same "thing," see Schorske 1998.

10. This formulation is inspired by John Levi Martin's *The Explanation of Social Action* (2011), which argues that certain "why" questions in the social sciences are ultimately unanswerable.

Conclusion

From one point of view, it is something of a surprise that we find ourselves today in a new phase of conflict over the form and direction of the American university. After all, seen as an industry, American higher education enjoys an advantage over its international competitors that is rare in this globalized era. In the most recent *Times Higher Education* World University Rankings, eleven of the top fifteen universities were American. And in the Shanghai Jiao Tong index, American universities claim the top eight spots out of ten. The degrees offered by these schools and their faculties are highly sought after worldwide, and overseas branches of American institutions of higher learning are among the most prestigious in the world. This is true in oil-rich Gulf nations like Dubai and Qatar but also in less obvious places like Malta and Morocco. Far from being in crisis, American higher education seems to lead the world, much as the U.S. auto industry once did. A wag might claim that what is good for the American university is good for America.

And yet, in the course of their ascent, American colleges and universities have picked up plenty of critics. Since Cambridge backed Cromwell, it has been a tradition in Anglo-American experience to criticize higher education from the right, but in the contemporary politics of higher education, one finds adversaries who are better organized and more energized than has been true for some time. A skeptic might retort that, again, things are much as they always have been. Conservative criticism of the university in the United States has been a constant, punctuated by episodes associated with William F. Buckley Jr.'s critique of Yale, the McCarthy scare, the Vietnam War rebellions, and the culture and canon wars of the 1990s. Few should be surprised that our era's version of conservative anxiety might spawn organizations and efforts like the National Association of Scholars, the Manhattan Institute's "Minding the Campus" initiative, and the American Council of Trustees and Alumni, each of which objects strongly to the political climate said to prevail on campus. Criticism might also be expected as tuition costs soar at public universities, at rates often double the declining rate of state support. In a period of economic malaise, public sector services can reasonably be expected to come under closer scrutiny of the kind directed at higher education from websites such as CollegeMeasures.org, which are resorting to the most direct strains of American pragmatism by publicizing "cash value" metrics of dollar-out-for-dollar-in scorecards for colleges and universities in Arkansas, Tennessee, Virginia, and elsewhere. But it may be something of a surprise— and perhaps even cause for alarm for those who like the university as it is—that no less a figure than Barack Obama, in his 2013 State of the Union address, made a reference to higher education that showed little by way of defense of the American academy in response to criticisms and even advocated the use of just such pragmatic metrics to allow parents and students to compare "where you can get the most bang for your educational buck."

If a Democratic president who was once an academic lecturer is willing to cross the academy even in the midst of what has been described as a combative liberal mood, the nation must not have much practical faith in business as usual in the university. Just as a majority of Americans should be expected to think that little would be lost in gathering information on what tenured professors are doing in their enclaves of seclusion from recession-era market forces, so, too, they might support more vigorous oversight of the uses and even abuses of the advantages that professors enjoy relative to their professional peers. Competitive pressures on the traditional college lecture are rising as online alternatives—the so-called massive open online courses (MOOCs)—present alluring opportunities for credentialing outside the traditional model, and all American colleges and universities will soon be facing more stringent oversight through program review and assessments of their capacity to meet learning outcomes. If the signals from on high carry any predictive meaning, we might expect new political initiatives to gain traction that would advocate limits on publicly supported pensions, academic freedom in the classroom, and the institution of tenure itself.

With respect to this last and, in many ways, defining feature of university life in the United States, tenured professors may find their natural allies less dependable than they would hope. In a nationally representative poll that we conducted for the American Association of University Professors in 2006, we found that Americans' confidence in higher education was quite high (other polls suggest a subsequent drop), but ignorance about the tenure system was widespread. Only half of the respondents had heard of tenure, and a fair number of those familiar with tenure were critical of the institution when pressed. It is not hard to imagine that volatile and undefended public opinion on higher education could leave the tenure system—and the institutions of higher education supported by it—open to new rhetorical attack, much as labor's closed shop was easily positioned as incompatible with a liberal system of private enterprise in the mid twentieth century. Busy professionals who, in previous eras, might have considered a career in the professoriate now find themselves in far more precarious relation to their employers than their faculty counterparts, and former faculty who have joined the administrative workforce are often critical of tenure on the grounds that it can protect less-than-compliant university employees when they fail to meet basic obligations such as getting grades in on time. More pointedly, as fewer higher education workers find themselves on the tenure track to first-class university citizenship—having been sorted into research or term faculty roles—they might join ranks with the congeries of critics of this uniquely successful industry, bringing with them embarrassingly reliable insider information on internal operations.

Ironically, these internal operations might offer up increasingly uncomfortable anecdotes under financial pressures abetted by forces associated with the very reform movements now confronting the university. As revenues stagnate amid soaring demand, corners will be cut—yet few seem to be telling the story of the real reasons why. Absent vocal allies, the public is unlikely to see the various sources of financial strain that press on university budgets: back-to-basics transfers of education budgets from higher education to K–12 and early childhood education, increased spending on new buildings and student services that were unknown in previous generations, and increases in administrative costs mimicking the trends in executive compensation that mark the U.S. business model more generally. With no obvious narrative to support them in the general public, American professors, especially those with tenure, are poised to find themselves on the front lines of the public service wars of the early twenty-first century. These are the unlikely conjunctural strains that inform the new politics of higher education and speak to the need for a renewed sociological look at American colleges and universities.

We see this volume as a step in this process of renewal. Although once common to study politics and the university from a social science perspective, it has become less so, leaving the field open to activists of various stripes to weigh in either in support or in criticism of American higher education. As important to the policy debate as this must be, it does little to promote what should be our goal in the field: to understand in social science terms what is happening in the institution and to discover what these developments imply for state and society. Like it or not, American colleges and universities have become a central part of peak-level political debate, and the people in a position to speak most clearly about the inner workings of the system have demonstrated less scientific interest in the subject than it deserves. When attention is directed to politics and the academy, as is done by the contributors to this volume, the salutary effects become apparent.

Among the issues raised here are the causes of the political imbalances long observed in higher education and what this means for students. We also see new narratives of origin, of how ideas that push to the left can be worked into the very fabric of the institution, thereby ensuring a kind of left-of-center typing. Getting into the finer texture of the discussion, our contributors present us with investigations of the rise of specialty disciplines with partisan preoccupations that sometimes sidestep the classic divisions between left and right, liberal and conservative. They also offer new ways of thinking about para-university organizations such as think tanks that have become highly effective channels for the articulation of abstract ideas to practical problems. Here, as elsewhere across the knowledge landscape, the boundaries between theory and practice are narrowing in some cases, widening in others, and the margins of academic life serve to allow innovation and productive reform as well as competitive threat. The question before students of American higher education today is how to maintain a focus on academic quality and institutional integrity in an environment where experimentation and advocacy threaten to undo an educational network unparalleled in global history.

Orbiting all of these debates about the future of higher education in the United States, and in other countries as well, is the issue of professorial liberalism and political "bias" in the academy. Many of the contributors to the volume address this issue in some form. Our view is that few questions of substance can be directed toward the future of the nation's colleges and universities that ignore the bias charge. True, many of the innovations confronting the delivery of higher education services have as little to do with party politics as does the decline of the newspaper or the rise of the digital cloud, but technological change is never innocent. It is helped along—or hindered—by those with political interests and agendas. As many critics of the university point out, professors are something less than ordained priests of a new secular order; they are people just like anyone else, which also implies that they, like their critics, are political animals. This in turn suggests that we must treat the institutions they create in pursuit of their ideals as we would any other, as a field of contest and struggle over power, resources, visions, and vices. Although its theoretical tenets have yet to be sketched, a new political sociology of higher education seems long overdue. We hope that *Professors and Their Politics* will be one of its starting points.

Sample Student Emails

Kevin Cook, Sociology, Control Condition

Dear Professor ——,

My name is Kevin Cook. I'm a senior at UC Irvine majoring in sociology, and I'm extremely interested in pursuing graduate work in the field. I'm writing to ask whether you think I'd be a good fit for the —— program, which I'm considering applying to later this fall. I also have a question I couldn't find the answer to online.

My main interest is the sociology of culture. Several of the papers I've written for my classes have been on the topic and I hope to keep working on it in graduate school. From looking at your department's website it seems there are a number of outstanding professors in the area. Am I right that I would fit in there given my interests?

I want to become a sociologist because I find sociology fascinating, and because, naive as it might sound, I hope to have an impact on the world. In addition to working hard academically, I've spent a fair amount of time over the last couple of years volunteering for various local organizations.

My other question: I've heard that it's very important to get involved in professors' research projects and coauthor papers with them. Are there opportunities to do that in your program?

Many thanks, Kevin

Jeff Allen, Sociology, McCain Treatment Condition

Professor ——,

Greetings from Santa Barbara. I'm Jeff Allen, and this spring I'll graduate from the sociology department at UCSB.

Over the last couple of years I've come to realize that I want to pursue a career as a sociologist. I'm now wrestling with the question of to which graduate programs I should apply. I've spent a lot of my time as an undergraduate studying the sociology of culture, a topic for which I have a real passion.

As my transcript will show, I'm an extremely serious student. But I've also tried to stay well-rounded during my time in college, doing volunteer work and getting involved with student organizations. When I was a sophomore I also spent a few intense months working for the McCain campaign, which was quite a learning experience.

As I consider various graduate programs, one of my biggest concerns is the availability of funding for research. Are there scholarships students can apply to at —— that will help fund original research? Also, could you give me some sense for whether the department would be a good home for someone with my interests?

Thank you for your time. I'm sure you must get a lot of emails. Best, Jeff

Introduction

Arum, Richard, and Joseph Roksa. 2011. *Academically Adrift: Limited Learning on College Campuses*. Chicago: University of Chicago Press.

Berman, Elizabeth Popp. 2011. *Creating the Market University: How Academic Science Became an Economic Engine*. Princeton, NJ: Princeton University Press.

Bourdieu, Pierre. 1988 [1984]. *Homo Academicus*. Translated by Peter Collier. Stanford, CA: Stanford University Press.

Brym, Robert J. 1980. *Intellectuals and Politics*. London: G. Allen and Unwin.

California Association of Scholars. 2012. *A Crisis of Competence: The Corrupting Effect of Political Activism in the University of California*. New York: National Association of Scholars.

Camic, Charles, Neil Gross, and Michele Lamont, eds. 2011. *Social Knowledge in the Making*. Chicago: University of Chicago Press.

Delbanaco, Andrew. 2012. *College: What It Was, Is, and Should Be*. Princeton, NJ: Princeton University Press.

Eyal, Gil, and Larissa Buchholz. 2010. "From the Sociology of Intellectuals to the Sociology of Interventions." *Annual Review of Sociology* 36: 117–37.

Fine, Gary Alan. 2012. *Tiny Publics: A Theory of Group Action and Culture*. New York: Russell Sage Foundation.

Frickel, Scott, and Kelly Moore, eds. 2006. *The New Political Sociology of Science: Institutions, Networks, and Power*. Madison: University of Wisconsin Press.

Friedman, Thomas L. 2013. "Revolution Hits the Universities." *New York Times*, January 26.

Gouldner, Alvin W. 1979. *The Future of Intellectuals and the Rise of the New Class*. New York: Seabury Press.

Gross, Neil. 2013. *Why Are Professors Liberal and Why Do Conservatives Care?* Cambridge, MA: Harvard University Press.

Hacker, Andrew, and Claudia Driefus. 2010. *Higher Education? How Colleges Are Wasting Our Money and Failing Our Kids—and What We Can Do about It*. New York: Times Books.

Hanson, Jana M., Dustin D. Weeden, Ernest T. Pascarella, and Charles Blaich. 2012. "Do Liberal Arts Colleges Make Students More Liberal? Some Initial Evidence." *Higher Education* 63: 1–15.

Jaher, Frederic C. 2002. *The Jews and the Nation: Revolution, Emancipation, State Forma-tion, and the Liberal Paradigm in America and France.* Princeton, NJ: Princeton University Press.

Jaschik, Scott. 2012. "Moving Further to the Left." *Inside Higher Ed,* October 12.

Kleinman, Daniel Lee, Noah Weeth Feinstein, and Greg Downey. 2013. "Beyond Commercialization: Science, Higher Education and the Culture of Neoliberalism." *Science and Education* 22: 2385–401.

Kleinman, Daniel Lee, and Steven P. Vallas. 2001. "Science, Capitalism, and the Rise of the 'Knowledge Worker': The Changing Structure of Knowledge Production in the United States." *Theory and Society* 30: 451–92.

Kurzman, Charles, and Lynn Owens. 2002. "The Sociology of Intellectuals." *Annual Review of Sociology* 28: 63–90.

Ladd, Everett Carll, Jr., and Seymour Martin Lipset. 1976. *The Divided Academy: Professors and Politics.* New York: Norton.

Lazarsfeld, Paul F., and Wagner Thielens Jr. 1958. *The Academic Mind: Social Scientists in a Time of Crisis.* Glencoe, IL: Free Press.

Loss, Christopher. 2011. *Between Citizens and the State: The Politics of American Higher Education in the 20th Century.* Princeton, NJ: Princeton University Press.

Newfield, Christopher. 2011. *Unmaking the Public University: The Forty Year Assault on the Middle Class.* Cambridge, MA: Harvard University Press.

Novick, Peter. 1988. *That Noble Dream: The "Objectivity Question" and the American Historical Profession.* Cambridge: Cambridge University Press.

Rhoten, Diana, and Craig Calhoun, eds. 2011. *Knowledge Matters: The Public Mission of the Research University.* New York: Columbia University Press.

Riley, Naomi Schaefer. 2011. *The Faculty Lounges: And Other Reasons You Won't Get the College Education You Pay For.* Lanham, MD: Ivan R. Dee.

Schorske, Carl. 1997. "The New Rigorism in the Human Sciences, 1940–1960." *Daedalus* 126: 289–309.

Schrecker, Ellen. 1986. *No Ivory Tower: McCarthyism and the Universities.* New York: Oxford University Press.

Shils, Edward. 1972. *The Intellectuals and the Powers, and Other Essays.* Chicago: University of Chicago Press.

Slaughter, Sheila, and Gary Rhoads. 2009. *Academic Capitalism and the New Economy: Markets, State, and Higher Education.* Baltimore: Johns Hopkins University Press.

Stevens, Mitchell, Elizabeth Armstrong, and Richard Arum. 2008. "Sieve, Incubator, Temple, Hub: Empirical and Theoretical Advances in the Sociology of Higher Education." *Annual Review of Sociology* 34: 127–51.

Taylor, Mark C. 2010. *Crisis on Campus: A Bold Plan for Reforming Our Colleges and Universities.* New York: Knopf.

Chapter 1 · The Social and Political Views of American College and University Professors

Alwin, Duane, Ronald Cohen, and Theodore Newcomb. 1991. *Political Attitudes over the Life Span: The Bennington Women after Fifty Years.* Madison: University of Wisconsin Press.

Chait, Richard, ed. 2002. *The Questions of Tenure.* Cambridge, MA: Harvard University Press.

Converse, Philip. 2006 [1964]. "The Nature of Belief Systems in Mass Publics." *Critical Review* 18: 1–74.

Doumani, Beshara. 2006. "Between Coercion and Privatization: Academic Freedom in the Twenty-First Century." In *Academic Freedom after September 11*, edited by B. Doumani, 11–57. Brooklyn, NY: Zone Books.

Faia, Michael A. 1974. "The Myth of the Liberal Professor." *Sociology of Education* 47: 171–202.

Finkelstein, Martin J. 1984. *The American Academic Profession: A Synthesis of Social Scientific Inquiry since World War II*. Columbus: Ohio State University Press.

Frickel, Scott. 2004. *Chemical Consequences: Environmental Mutagens, Scientist Activism, and the Rise of Genetic Toxicology*. New Brunswick, NJ: Rutgers University Press.

Frickel, Scott, and Neil Gross. 2005. "A General Theory of Scientific/Intellectual Movements." *American Sociological Review* 70: 204–32.

Garfinkel, Simson. 1987. "Radio Research, McCarthyism and Paul F. Lazarsfeld." Thesis. Department of Political Science, Massachusetts Institute of Technology, Cambridge, MA.

Gouldner, Alvin W. 1965. *Enter Plato: Classical Greece and the Origins of Social Theory*. New York: Basic Books.

Gross, Neil. 2002. "Becoming a Pragmatist Philosopher: Status, Self-Concept, and Intellectual Choice." *American Sociological Review* 67: 52–76.

Gross, Neil, and Solon Simmons. 2006. "Americans' Attitudes toward Academic Freedom and Liberal Bias in Higher Education." Working paper. Department of Sociology, Harvard University.

Hamilton, Richard F., and Lowell L. Hargens. 1993. "The Politics of the Professors: Self-Identifications, 1969–1984." *Social Forces* 71: 603–27.

Jaschik, Scott. 2012. "Moving Further to the Left." *Inside Higher Ed*, October 12.

Kazin, Michael, and Joseph McCartin, eds. 2006. *Americanism: New Perspectives on the History of an Ideal*. Chapel Hill: University of North Carolina Press.

Klein, Daniel, and Andrew Western. 2004–5. "Voter Registration of Berkeley and Stanford Faculty." *Academic Questions* 18: 53–65.

Knorr Cetina, Karin. 1999. *Epistemic Cultures: How the Sciences Make Knowledge*. Cambridge, MA: Harvard University Press.

Kurzman, Charles, and Lynn Owens. 2002. "The Sociology of Intellectuals." *Annual Review of Sociology* 28: 63–90.

Ladd, Everett Carll, Jr., and Seymour Martin Lipset. 1976. *The Divided Academy: Professors and Politics*. New York: Norton.

Lazarsfeld, Paul F., and Wagner Thielens. 1958. *The Academic Mind: Social Scientists in a Time of Crisis*. Glencoe, IL: Free Press.

Messer-Davidow, Ellen. 1993. "Manufacturing the Attack on Liberalized Higher Education." *Social Text* 36: 40–80.

Nakhaie, M. Reza, and Robert Brym. 1999. "The Political Attitudes of Canadian Professors." *Canadian Journal of Sociology* 24: 329–53.

Novick, Peter. 1988. *That Noble Dream: The "Objectivity Question" and the American Historical Profession*. Cambridge: Cambridge University Press.

Pascarella, Ernest, and Patrick Terenzini. 1991. *How College Affects Students: Findings and Insights from Twenty Years of Research*. San Francisco: Jossey-Bass.

Rojas, Fabio. 2007. *From Black Power to Black Studies: How a Radical Social Movement Became an Academic Discipline*. Baltimore: Johns Hopkins University Press.

Rorty, Richard. 1998. *Achieving Our Country: Leftist Thought in Twentieth-Century America*. Cambridge, MA: Harvard University Press.

Rothman, Stanley, S. Robert Lichter, and Neil Nevitte. 2005. "Politics and Professional Advancement among College Faculty." *Forum* 3: art. 2.

Sanderson, Allen, Voon Chin Phua, and David Herda. 2000. "The American Faculty Poll." Report. New York: TIAA-CREF.

Schnittker, Jason, Jeremy Freese, and Brian Powell. 2003. "Who Are Feminists and What Do They Believe? The Role of Generations." *American Sociological Review* 68: 607–22.

Schofer, Evan, and John Meyer. 2005. "The Worldwide Expansion of Higher Education in the Twentieth Century." *American Sociological Review* 70: 898–920.

Slaughter, Sheila. 1988. "Academic Freedom and the State: Reflections on the Uses of Knowledge." *Journal of Higher Education* 59: 241–62.

Tobin, Gary A., and Aryeh K. Weinberg. 2006. "A Profile of American College Faculty: Political Beliefs and Behavior." Report. San Francisco: Institute for Jewish and Community Research.

Trow, Martin. 1973. "Problems in the Transition from Elite to Mass Higher Education." Report. Berkeley, CA: Carnegie Commission on Higher Education.

Wilson, John. 1995. *The Myth of Political Correctness: The Conservative Attack on Higher Education*. Durham, NC: Duke University Press.

Chapter 2 · Political Liberalism and Graduate School Attendance

Baldassari, Delia, and Andrew Gelman. 2008. "Partisans without Constraint: Political Polarization and Trends in American Public Opinion." *American Journal of Sociology* 114: 408–46.

Bell, Daniel. 1976. *The Coming of Post-Industrial Society: A Venture in Social Forecasting*. New York: Basic Books.

Bell, Nathan. 2010. *Graduate Enrollment and Degrees: 1999 to 2009*. Washington, DC: Council of Graduate Schools.

Bourdieu, Pierre. 1988 [1984]. *Homo Academicus*. Translated by Peter Collier. Stanford, CA: Stanford University Press.

Bowen, William G., and Derek Bok. 2000. *The Shape of the River*. Princeton, NJ: Princeton University Press.

Brint, Steven. 1984. "'New Class' and Cumulative Trend Explanations of the Liberal Political Attitudes of Professionals." *American Journal of Sociology* 90: 30–71.

———. 1985. "The Political Attitudes of Professionals." *Annual Review of Sociology* 11: 389–414.

Brooks, Arthur. 2008. *Gross National Happiness: Why Happiness Matters for America and How We Can Get More of It*. New York: Basic Books.

Bruce-Briggs, Barry, ed. 1979. *The New Class?* New Brunswick, NJ: Transaction Publishers.

Buckley, William F., Jr. 1951. *God and Man at Yale: The Superstitions of Academic Freedom*. Chicago: Regnery.

Campbell, Angus, Philip Converse, Warren Miller, and Donald Stokes. 1960. *The American Voter.* New York: Wiley.

Carney, Dana, John Jost, Samuel Gosling, and Jeff Potter. 2008. "The Secret Lives of Liberals and Conservatives: Personality Profiles, Interaction Styles, and the Things They Leave Behind." *Political Psychology* 29: 807–40.

Cherry, Conrad, Betty DeBerg, and Amanda Porterfield. 2001. *Religion on Campus.* Chapel Hill: University of North Carolina Press.

Chickering, Arthur. 1970. "Civil Liberties and the Experience of College." *Journal of Higher Education* 41: 599–606.

Conley, Dalton, and Brian Gifford. 2006. "Home Ownership, Social Insurance, and the Welfare State." *Sociological Forum* 21: 55–82.

Correll, Shelley. 2001. "Gender and the Career Choice Process: The Role of Biased Self-Assessments." *American Journal of Sociology* 106: 1691–730.

———. 2004. "Constraints into Preferences: Gender, Status, and Emerging Career Aspirations." *American Sociological Review* 69: 93–113.

Davis, Gerald, and Natalie Cotton. 2007. "Political Consequences of Financial Market Expansion: Does Buying a Mutual Fund Turn You Republican?" Paper presented at the American Sociological Association meetings, New York, August.

Deary, Ian J., G. David Batty, and Catherine R. Gale. 2008. "Bright Children Become Enlightened Adults." *Psychological Science* 19: 1–6.

Di Tella, Rafael, and Robert MacCulloch. 2005. "Partisan Social Happiness." *Review of Economic Studies* 72: 367–93.

Evans, Geoffrey, ed. 1999. *The End of Class Politics? Class Voting in Comparative Context.* Oxford: Oxford University Press.

Fay, Margaret, and Jeff Weintraub. 1973. *Political Ideologies of Graduate Students: Crystallization, Consistency, and Contextual Effects.* Berkeley, CA: Carnegie Commission on Higher Education.

Feldman, Kenneth, and Theodore Newcomb. 1969. *The Impact of College on Students.* Vols. 1–2. San Francisco: Jossey-Bass.

Fosse, Ethan, and Neil Gross. 2012. "Why Are Professors Liberal?" *Theory and Society* 41: 127–68.

Fourcade, Marion. 2010. *Economists and Societies: Discipline and Profession in the United States, Britain, and France, 1890s–1990s.* Princeton, NJ: Princeton University Press.

Gerteis, Joseph. 1998. "Political Alignment and the American Middle Class, 1974–1994." *Sociological Forum* 13: 639–66.

Gouldner, Alvin. 1979. *The Future of the Intellectuals and the Rise of the New Class.* New York: Oxford University Press.

Greely, Andrew M., and Michael Hout. 2006. *The Truth about Conservative Christians: What They Think and What They Believe.* Chicago: University of Chicago Press.

Gross, Neil, and Catherine Cheng. 2011. "Explaining Professors' Politics: Is It a Matter of Self-Selection?" In *Diversity in American Higher Education: Toward a More Comprehensive Approach*, edited by Lisa Stulberg and Sharon Weinberg, 178–194. New York: Routledge.

Gross, Neil, Tom Medvetz, and Rupert Russell. 2011. "The Contemporary American Conservative Movement." *Annual Review of Sociology* 37: 325–54.

Gross, Neil, and Solon Simmons. 2006. "Americans' Views of Political Bias in the Academy and Academic Freedom." Working paper. Department of Sociology, Harvard University.

———. 2009. "The Religiosity of American College and University Professors." *Sociology of Religion* 70: 101–29.

Grusky, David, and Jesper Sorensen. 1998. "Can Class Analysis Be Salvaged?" *American Journal of Sociology* 103: 1187–234.

Hayek, Friedrich. 1949. "The Intellectuals and Socialism." In *The Intellectuals: A Controversial Portrait*, edited by George B. de Huszar, 371–84. Glencoe, IL: Free Press.

Holland, John. 1984. *Making Vocational Choices: A Theory of Vocational Personalities and Work Environments*. New York: Prentice Hall.

Inglehart, Ronald. 1990. *Culture Shift in Advanced Industrial Society*. Princeton, NJ: Princeton University Press.

Inkeles, Alex. 1974. *Becoming Modern: Individual Change in Six Developing Countries*. Cambridge, MA: Harvard University Press.

Jennings, M. Kent, and Laura Stoker. 2008. "Another and Longer Look at the Impact of Higher Education on Political Involvement and Attitudes." Paper presented at the Midwest Political Science Association meetings, Chicago.

Jost, John. 2006. "The End of the End of Ideology." *American Psychologist* 61: 651–70.

Jost, John, and Orsolya Hunyadi. 2005. "Antecedents and Consequences of System Justifying Ideologies." *Current Directions in Psychological Science* 14: 260–65.

Jost, John, Aaron Kay, and Hulda Thorisdottir, eds. 2009. *Social and Psychological Bases of Identity and System Justification*. New York: Oxford University Press.

Kam, Cindy, and Carl Palmer. 2008. "Reconsidering the Effects of Education on Political Participation." *Journal of Politics* 70: 612–31.

Kanazawa, Satoshi. 2010. "Why Liberals and Atheists Are More Intelligent." *Social Psychology Quarterly* 73: 33–57.

Klein, Daniel, and Charlotta Stern. 2009. "Groupthink in Academia: Majoritarian Departmental Politics and the Professional Pyramid." In *The Politically Correct University: Problems, Scope, and Reforms*, edited by Robert Maranto, Richard Redding, and Frederick Hess, 79–98. Washington, DC: AEI Press.

Konrád, George, and Iván Szelényi. 1979. *The Intellectuals on the Road to Class Power*. New York: Harcourt Brace Jovanovich.

Ladd, Everett Carll, Jr., and Seymour Martin Lipset. 1976. *The Divided Academy: Professors and Politics*. New York: Norton.

Lamont, Michèle. 1987. "Cultural Capital and the Liberal Political Attitudes of Professionals: Comment on Brint." *American Journal of Sociology* 92: 1501–6.

———. 1992. *Money, Morals, and Manners: The Culture of the French and the American Upper-Middle Class*. Chicago: University of Chicago Press.

Leone, Luigi, and Antonio Chirumbolo. 2007. "Conservatism as Motivated Avoidance of Affect: Need for Affect Scales Predict Conservatism Measures." *Journal of Research in Personality* 42: 755–62.

Malka, Ariel, and Yphtach Lelkes. 2010. "More Than Ideology: Conservative-Liberal Identity and Receptivity to Political Cues." *Social Justice Research* 23: 156–88.

Manza, Jeff, and Clem Brooks. 1997. "Class Politics and Political Change in the U.S., 1952–1992." *Social Forces* 76: 379–408.

Manza, Jeff, Michael Hout, and Clem Brooks. 1995. "Class Voting in Capitalist Democracies since World War II: Dealignment, Realignment, or Trendless Fluctuation?" *Annual Review of Sociology* 21: 137–62.

Marini, Margaret Mooney, and Mary Brinton. 1984. "Sex Typing in Occupational Socialization." In *Sex Segregation in the Workplace: Trends, Explanations, Remedies*, edited by Barbara Reskin, 191–232. Washington, DC: National Academy Press.

Marini, Margaret Mooney, Pi-Ling Fan, Erica Finley, and Ann Beutel. 1996. "Gender and Job Values." *Sociology of Education* 69: 49–65.

Marini, Margaret Mooney, and Ellen Greenberger. 1978. "Sex Differences in Occupational Aspirations and Expectations." *Work and Occupations* 5: 147–78.

McAdams, Dan, and Bradley Olson. 2010. "Personality Development: Continuity and Change over the Life Course." *Annual Review of Psychology* 61: 517–42.

Menand, Louis. 2010. *The Marketplace of Ideas: Reform and Resistance in the American University*. New York: Norton.

Meyer, John, Francisco Ramirez, David Frank, and Evan Schofer. 2007. "Higher Education as an Institution." In *Sociology of Higher Education: Contributions and Their Contexts*, edited by Patricia Gumport, 187–221. Baltimore: Johns Hopkins University Press.

Mullen, Ann, Kimberly Goyette, and Joseph Soares. 2003. "Who Goes to Graduate School? Social and Academic Determinants of Matriculation in Master's, First-Professional, and Ph.D. Programs." *Sociology of Education* 76: 143–69.

Müller, Walter. 1999. "Class Cleavages and Party Preferences in Germany—Old and New." In *The End of Class Politics? Class Voting in Comparative Context*, edited by Geoffrey Evans, 137–80. New York: Oxford University Press.

Napier, Jaime L., and John T. Jost. 2008. "Why Are Conservatives Happier Than Liberals?" *Psychological Science* 19: 565–72.

Newcomb, Theodore. 1943. *Personality and Social Change*. New York: Dryden Press.

Parsons, Talcott, and Gerald Platt. 1973. *The American University*. Cambridge, MA: Harvard University Press.

Pascarella, Ernest, and Patrick Terenzini. 1991. *How College Affects Students: Findings and Insights from Twenty Years of Research*. San Francisco: Jossey-Bass.

———. 2005. *How College Affects Students, Vol. 2: A Third Decade of Research*. San Francisco: Jossey-Bass.

Porter, Stephen, and Paul Umbach. 2006. "College Major Choice: An Analysis of Person-Environment Fit." *Research in Higher Education* 47: 429–49.

Powell, Walter, and Kaisa Snellman. 2004. "The Knowledge Economy." *Annual Review of Sociology* 30: 199–220.

Rothman, Stanley, S. Robert Lichter, and Neil Nevitte. 2005. "Politics and Professional Advancement among College Faculty." *Forum* 3: art. 2.

Saint-Paul, Gilles. 2009. "Occupational Choice, the Evolution of Beliefs, and the Political Economy of Reform." Institute for the Study of Labor (IZA) working paper 4468. Bonn, Germany: IZA.

Shapiro, Virginia. 2004. "Not Your Parents' Political Socialization: Introduction for a New Generation." *Annual Review of Political Science* 7: 1–23.

Sherkat, Darren, and T. Jean Blocker. 1997. "Explaining the Political and Personal Consequences of Protest." *Social Forces* 75: 1049–70.

Stouffer, Samuel. 1955. *Communism, Conformity, and Civil Liberties: A Cross-Section of the Nation Speaks Its Mind*. Garden City, NY: Doubleday.

Summers, Lawrence. 2007. "Comments." Presented at symposium on professors and their politics, Department of Sociology, Harvard University.

Weeden, Kim, and David Grusky. 2005. "The Case for a New Class Map." *American Journal of Sociology* 111: 141–212.

Wilkins, Amy C. 2008. "'Happier Than Non-Christians': Collective Emotions and Symbolic Boundaries among Evangelical Christians." *Social Psychology Quarterly* 71: 281–301.

Wilson, John. 2008. *Patriotic Correctness: Academic Freedom and Its Enemies*. Boulder, CO: Paradigm Publishers.

Woessner, Matthew, and April Kelly-Woessner. 2009. "Left Pipeline: Why Conservatives Don't Get Doctorates." In *The Politically Correct University: Problems, Scope, and Reforms*, edited by Robert Maranto, Richard Redding, and Frederick Hess, 38–59. Washington, DC: AEI Press.

Zagar, Robert, and John D. Mead. 1983. "Analysis of Short Test Battery for Children." *Journal of Clinical Psychology* 39: 590–97.

Chapter 3 • Nations, Classes, and the Politics of Professors

Alwin, Duane F., Ronald L. Cohen, and Theodore M. Newcomb. 1991. *Political Attitudes over the Life Span: The Bennington Women after Fifty Years*. Madison: University of Wisconsin Press.

Arts, Wil, and John Gelissen. 2002. "Three Worlds of Welfare Capitalism or More? A State-of-the-Art Report." *Journal of European Social Policy* 12: 137–58.

Berggren, Niclas, Henrik Jordahl, and Charlotta Stern. 2010. "A Left-Right Divide: The Political Opinions of Swedish Social Scientists." Unpublished manuscript. Ratio Institute, Stockholm.

Bolzendahl, Catherine, and Sigrún Ólafsdóttir. 2008. "Gender Group Interest or Gender Ideology? Understanding U.S. Support for Family Policy in a Comparative Perspective." *Sociological Perspectives* 51: 281–304.

Bourdieu, Pierre. *Homo Academicus*. 1988 [1984]. Translated by Peter Collier. Stanford, CA: Stanford University Press.

———. 1990. "The Intellectual Field: A World Apart." In *In Other Words: Essays towards a Reflexive Sociology*, 140–49. Stanford, CA: Stanford University Press.

Bourdieu, Pierre, and Jean-Claude Passeron. 1979 [1964]. *The Inheritors: French Students and Their Relation to Culture*. Chicago: University of Chicago Press.

Breen, Richard, and David Rottman. 1995. "Class Analysis and Class Theory." *Sociology* 29: 453–73.

Brint, Steven. 1984. "'New Class' and Cumulative Trend Explanations of the Liberal Political Attitudes of Professionals." *American Journal of Sociology* 90: 30–71.

———. 1985. "The Political Attitudes of Professionals." *Annual Review of Sociology* 11: 389–414.

Brooks, Clem, and Stefan Svallfors. 2010. "Why Does Class Matter? Policy Attitudes, Mechanisms, and the Case of the Nordic Countries." *Research in Social Stratification and Mobility* 28: 199–213.

Bruce-Briggs, Barry, ed. 1979. *The New Class?* New Brunswick, NJ: Transaction Publishers.

Brym, Robert. 1988. "Structural Location and Ideological Divergence: Jewish Marxist Intellectuals in Turn-of-the-Century Russia." In *Social Structures: A Network Approach*, edited by Barry Wellman and Stephen Berkowitz, 59–79. New York: Cambridge University Press.

Castles, Frances Geoffrey, and Deborah Mitchell. 1993. "Worlds of Welfare and Families of Nations." In *Families of Nations*, edited by Frances Geoffrey, 93–128. Aldershot, UK: Dartmouth.

D'Souza, Dinesh. 1991. *Illiberal Education: The Politics of Race and Sex on Campus*. New York: Free Press.

Erikson, Robert, and John Goldthorpe. 1992. *The Constant Flux: A Study of Class Mobility in Industrial Societies*. Oxford: Clarendon Press.

Esping-Andersen, Gosta. 1990. *The Three Worlds of Welfare Capitalism*. Princeton, NJ: Princeton University Press.

Fosse, Ethan, and Neil Gross. 2012. "Why Are Professors Liberal?" *Theory and Society* 41: 127–68.

Garrett, Geoffrey. 1998. *Partisan Politics in the Global Economy*. New York: Cambridge University Press.

Goldthorpe, John. 2000. "Social Class and the Differentiation of Employment Contracts." In *On Sociology: Numbers, Narratives, and the Integration of Research and Theory*, edited by John Goldthorpe, 206–29. New York: Clarendon Press.

Gouldner, Alvin. 1979. *The Future of Intellectuals and the Rise of the New Class*. New York: Continuum.

Gross, Neil, and Catherine Cheng. 2011. "Explaining Professors' Politics: Is It a Matter of Self-Selection?" In *Diversity in American Higher Education: Toward a More Comprehensive Approach*, edited by Lisa Stulberg and Sharon Weinberg, 178–94. New York: Routledge.

Gross, Neil, and Solon Simmons. 2009. "The Religiosity of American College and University Professors." *Sociology of Religion* 70: 101–29.

Hall, Peter, and David Soskice, eds. 2001. *Varieties of Capitalism: The Institutional Foundations of Comparative Advantage*. New York: Oxford University Press.

Hamilton, Richard, and Lowell Hargens. 1993. "The Politics of the Professors: Self-Identifications, 1969–1984." *Social Forces* 71: 603–27.

Hicks, Alexander. 1999. *Social Democracy and Welfare Capitalism: A Century of Income Security Politics*. Ithaca, NY: Cornell University Press.

Hofstadter, Richard. 1963. *Anti-intellectualism in American Life*. New York: Knopf.

Huber, Evelyne, and John Stephens. 2001. *Development and Crisis of the Welfare State: Parties and Policies in Global Markets*. Chicago: University of Chicago Press.

International Social Survey Program (ISSP). 1993. *Role of Government II, 1990*. Machine-readable data files and codebooks. Ann Arbor, MI: Inter-University Consortium for Political and Social Research.

———. 1994. *Religion I, 1991*. Machine-readable data files and codebooks. Ann Arbor, MI: Inter-University Consortium for Political and Social Research.

———. 1997. *Family and Changing Gender Roles II, 1994*. Machine-readable data files and codebooks. Ann Arbor, MI: Inter-University Consortium for Political and Social Research.

———. 1999. *Role of Government III, 1996*. Machine-readable data files and codebooks. Ann Arbor, MI: Inter-University Consortium for Political and Social Research.

———. 2001. *Religion II, 1998.* Machine-readable data files and codebooks. Ann Arbor, MI: Inter-University Consortium for Political and Social Research.

———. 2004. *Family and Changing Gender Roles III, 2002.* Machine-readable data files and codebooks. Ann Arbor, MI: Inter-University Consortium for Political and Social Research.

———. 2008. *Role of Government IV, 2006.* Machine-readable data files and codebooks. Ann Arbor, MI: Inter-University Consortium for Political and Social Research.

Iversen, Torben, and David Soskice. 2001. "An Asset Theory of Social Policy Preferences." *American Political Science Review* 95: 875–93.

Jost, John, Christopher Federico, and Jaime Napier. 2009. "Political Ideology: Its Structure, Functions, and Elective Affinities." *Annual Review of Psychology* 60: 307–33.

Karabel, Jerome. 1996. "Towards a Theory of Intellectuals and Politics." *Theory and Society* 25: 205–33.

Katzenstein, Peter. 1985. *Small States in World Markets.* Ithaca, NY: Cornell University Press.

Kimball, Roger. 1990. *Tenured Radicals: How Politics Has Corrupted Our Higher Education.* New York: Harper and Row.

Kinder, Donald, and Lynn Sanders. 1996. *Divided by Color.* Chicago: University of Chicago Press.

Konrad, George, and Ivan Szelenyi. 1979. *The Intellectuals on the Road to Class Power.* New York: Harcourt Brace Jovanovich.

Korpi, Walter, and Joakim Palme. 1998. "The Paradox of Redistribution and Strategies of Equality: Welfare State Institutions, Inequality, and Poverty in the Western Countries." *American Sociological Review* 63: 661–87.

Kristol, Irving. 19972. "About Equality." *Commentary* 54: 41–47.

Kurzman, Charles, and Lynn Owens. 2002. "The Sociology of Intellectuals." *Annual Review of Sociology* 28: 63–90.

Ladd, Everett Carll, Jr., and Seymour Martin Lipset. 1976. *The Divided Academy: Professors and Politics.* New York: Norton.

Lamont, Michèle. 2009. *How Professors Think: Inside the Curious World of Academic Judgment.* Cambridge, MA: Harvard University Press.

Lazarsfeld, Paul, and Wagner Thielens. 1958. *The Academic Mind.* Glencoe, IL: Free Press.

Lijphart, Arend. 1999. *Patterns of Democracy: Government Forms and Performance in Thirty-Six Countries.* New Haven, CT: Yale University Press.

Lipset, Seymour Martin. 1981 [1960]. *Political Man.* Expanded ed. Baltimore: Johns Hopkins University Press.

———. 1996. *American Exceptionalism: A Double-Edged Sword.* New York: Norton.

Lipset, Seymour Martin, and Everett Ladd. 1971. "The Divided Professoriate." *Change* 3: 54–60.

Mannheim, Karl. 1956. "The Problem of the Intelligentsia." In *Essays on the Sociology of Culture,* 91–170. London: Routledge & Kegan Paul.

McClosky, Herbert, and Alida Brill. 1983. *Dimensions of Tolerance: What Americans Believe about Civil Liberties.* New York: Russell Sage.

Nakhaie, Reza, and Robert Brym. 1999. "The Political Attitudes of Canadian Professors." *Canadian Journal of Sociology* 24: 329–53.

Rothman, Stanley, S. Robert Lichter, and Neil Nevitte. 2005. "Politics and Professional Advancement among College Faculty." *Forum* 3: art. 2.

Said, Edward. 1994. *Representations of the Intellectual*. London: Vintage.

Sherkat, Darren, and Christopher Ellison. 1999. "Recent Developments and Current Controversies in the Sociology of Religion." *Annual Review of Sociology* 25: 363–94.

Shils, Edward. 1968. "Intellectuals." In *International Encyclopedia of the Social Sciences*, 399–415. New York: Macmillan & Free Press.

Smith, Tom W. 1990. "Liberal and Conservative Trends in the United States since World War II." *Public Opinion Quarterly* 54: 479–507.

Stouffer, Samuel. 1992 [1955]. *Communism, Conformity, and Civil Liberties*. New Brunswick, NJ: Transaction Publishers.

Svallfors, Stefan. 2006. *The Moral Economy of Class*. Stanford, CA: Stanford University Press.

Woessner, Matthew, and April Kelly-Woessner. 2009. "Left Pipeline: Why Conservatives Don't Get Doctorates." In *The Politically Correct University: Problems, Scope, and Reforms*, edited by Robert Maranto, Richard Redding, and Frederick Hess, 38–59. Washington, DC: AEI Press.

Zipp, John, and Rudy Fenwick. 2006. "Is the Academy a Liberal Hegemony? The Political Orientations and Educational Values of Professors." *Public Opinion Quarterly* 70: 304–26.

Chapter 4 · Political Bias in the Graduate School Admissions Process

Abbott, Andrew. 1988. *The System of Professions: An Essay on the Division of Expert Labor*. Chicago: University of Chicago Press.

Bargh, John. 1999. "The Cognitive Monster: The Case against the Controllability of Automatic Stereotype Effects." In *Dual Process Theories in Social Psychology*, edited by Shelly Chaiken and Yaacov Trope, 361–82. New York: Guilford Press.

Bertrand, Marianne, and Sendhil Mullainathan. 2004. "Are Emily and Greg More Employable Than Lakisha and Jamal? A Field Experiment on Labor Market Discrimination." *American Economic Review* 94: 991–1013.

Bourdieu, Pierre. 1988 [1984]. *Homo Academicus*. Translated by Peter Collier. Stanford, CA: Stanford University Press.

Cardiff, Christopher F., and Daniel B. Klein. 2004. "Faculty Partisan Affiliations in All Disciplines: A Voter-Registration Study." *Critical Review* 17: 237–55.

Cohen, Jacob. 1988. *Statistical Power Analysis for the Behavioral Sciences*. 2nd ed. Hillsdale, NJ: Lawrence Erlbaum Associates.

Fosse, Ethan, and Neil Gross. 2012. "Why Are Professors Liberal?" *Theory and Society* 41: 127–68.

Freidson, Eliot. 1986. *Professional Powers: A Study of the Institutionalization of Formal Knowledge*. Chicago: University of Chicago Press.

Inbar, Yoel, and Joris Lammers. 2012. "Political Diversity in Social and Personality Psychology." *Perspectives on Psychological Science* 7: 496–503.

Janis, Irving L. 1982. *Groupthink: Psychological Studies of Policy Decisions and Fiascoes*. 2nd ed. New York: Houghton Mifflin.

Karabel, Jerome. 1996. "Towards a Theory of Intellectuals and Politics." *Theory and Society* 5: 205–33.

Klein, Daniel, and Charlotta Stern. 2004–5. "Political Diversity in Six Disciplines." *Academic Questions* 18: 40–52.

———. 2009. "Groupthink in Academia: Majoritarian Departmental Politics and the Professional Pyramid." In *The Politically Correct University: Problems, Scope, and Reforms*, edited by Robert Maranto, Richard Redding, and Frederick Hess, 79–98. Washington, DC: AEI Press.

Ladd, Everett Carll, Jr., and Seymour Martin Lipset. 1976. *The Divided Academy: Professors and Politics*. New York: Norton.

Lamont. Michèle. 2009. *How Professors Think: Inside the Curious World of Academic Judgment*. Cambridge, MA: Harvard University Press.

Larson, Magali Sarfatti. 1977. *The Rise of Professionalism: A Sociological Analysis*. Berkeley: University of California Press.

Lodge, Milton, and Charles Taber. 2005. "Implicit Affect for Political Candidates, Parties, and Issues: An Experimental Test of the Hot Cognition Hypothesis." *Political Psychology* 26: 455–82.

Maranto, Robert. 2009. "Why Political Science Is Left but Not Quite PC." In *The Politically Correct University: Problems, Scope, and Reforms*, edited by Robert Maranto, Richard Redding, and Frederick Hess, 209–24. Washington, DC: AEI Press.

Musselin, Christine. 2010. *The Market for Academics*. New York: Routledge.

Neumark, David, Roy Bank, and Kyle Van Nort. 1996. "Sex Discrimination in Restaurant Hiring: An Audit Study." *Quarterly Journal of Economics* 11: 915–42.

Pager, Devah. 2003. "The Mark of a Criminal Record." *American Journal of Sociology* 108: 937–75.

———. 2007a. *Marked: Race, Crime, and Finding Work in an Era of Mass Incarceration*. Chicago: University of Chicago Press.

———. 2007b. "The Use of Field Experiments for Studies of Employment Discrimination: Contributions, Critiques, and Directions for the Future." *Annals of the American Academy of Political and Social Sciences* 609: 104–33.

Pager, Devah, Bruce Western, and Bart Bonikowski. 2009. "Discrimination in a Low-Wage Labor Market: A Field Experiment." *American Sociological Review* 74: 777–99.

Petersen, Trond, and Ishak Saporta. 2004. "The Opportunity Structure for Discrimination." *American Journal of Sociology* 109: 852–901.

Rosenbaum, Paul. 1991. "Discussing Hidden Bias in Observational Studies." *Annals of Internal Medicine* 115: 901–5.

———. 2002. *Observational Studies*. 2nd ed. New York: Springer.

Rothman, Stanley, S. Robert Lichter, and Neil Nevitte. 2005. "Politics and Professional Advancement among College Faculty." *Forum* 3: art. 2.

Rothman, Stanley, Matthew Woessner, and April Kelly-Woessner. 2010. *The Still Divided Academy: How Competing Visions of Power, Politics, and Diversity Complicate the Mission of Higher Education*. Lanham, MD: Rowman & Littlefield.

Taber, Charles, and Milton Lodge. 2006. "Motivated Skepticism in the Evaluation of Political Beliefs." *American Journal of Political Science* 50: 755–69.

Tobin, Gary, and Aryeh K. Weinberg. 2007. *Profiles of the American University, Vol. 2: Religious Beliefs and Behavior of College Faculty*. San Francisco: Institute for Jewish and Community Research.

Vaughan, Diane. 1996. *The Challenger Launch Decision: Risky Technology, Culture, and Deviance at NASA.* Chicago: University of Chicago Press.

Woessner, Matthew, and April Kelly-Woessner. 2009. "Left Pipeline: Why Conservatives Don't Get Doctorates." In *The Politically Correct University: Problems, Scope, and Reforms,* edited by Robert Maranto, Richard Redding, and Frederick Hess, 38–59. Washington, DC: AEI Press.

Yancey, George. 2011. *Compromising Scholarship: Religious and Political Bias in American Higher Education.* Waco, TX: Baylor University Press.

Chapter 5 · The Effect of College on Social and Political Attitudes and Civic Participation

Adorno, Theodor W., Else Frenkel-Brunswik, Daniel J. Levinson, and R. Nevitt Sanford. 1950. *The Authoritarian Personality.* New York: Harper.

Allison, Paul D. 2009. *Fixed Effect Regression Models.* Thousand Oaks, CA: Sage.

Anderson, Robert, James Curtis, and Edward Grabb. 2006. "Trends in Civic Association Activity in Four Democracies: The Special Case of Women in the United States." *American Sociological Review* 71: 376–400.

Armstrong, Elizabeth A., and Laura Hamilton. 2013. *Paying for the Party: How College Maintains Inequality.* Cambridge, MA: Harvard University Press.

Arnett, Jeffrey Jensen. 2000. "Emerging Adulthood: A Theory of Development from the Late Teens through the Twenties." *American Psychologist* 55: 469–80.

Arum, Richard, and Josipa Roksa. 2011. *Academically Adrift: Limited Learning on College Campuses.* Chicago: University of Chicago Press.

Astin, Alexander W. 1993. *What Matters in College? Four Critical Years Revisited.* San Francisco: Jossey-Bass.

Binder, Amy, and Kate Wood. 2013. *Becoming Right: How Campuses Shape Young Conservatives.* Princeton, NJ: Princeton University Press.

Bobo, Lawrence, and Frederick C. Licari. 1989. "Education and Political Tolerance: Testing the Effects of Cognitive Sophistication and Target Group Affect." *Public Opinion Quarterly* 53: 285–308.

Bourdieu, Pierre, and Jean-Claude Passeron. 1990. *Reproduction in Education, Society, and Culture.* London: Sage.

Brand, Jennie E. 2010. "Civic Returns to Higher Education: A Note on Heterogeneous Effects." *Social Forces* 89: 417–34.

Brewster, Karen L., and Irene Padavic. 2000. "Change in Gender-Ideology, 1977–1996: The Contributions of Intracohort Change and Population Turnover." *Journal of Marriage and Family* 62: 477–87.

Buckley, William F., Jr. 1951. *God and Man at Yale: The Superstitions of Academic Freedom.* Chicago: Regnery.

Cameron, Stephen V., and James J. Heckman. 1999. "Can Tuition Policy Combat Rising Wage Inequality?" In *Financing College Tuition: Government Policies and Educational Priorities,* edited by Marvin H. Kosters, 76–124. Washington, DC: AEI Press.

Campbell, Angus, Philip E. Converse, Warren E. Miller, and Donald E. Stokes. 1960. *The American Voter.* New York: John Wiley & Sons.

Campbell, Ernest Q. 1969. "Adolescent Socialization." In *Handbook of Socialization Theory and Research,* edited by David A. Goslin, 821–60. Chicago: Rand-McNally.

Converse, Philip E. 1964. "The Nature of Belief Systems in Mass Publics." In *Ideology and Discontent*, edited by D. E. Apter, 206–61. New York: Free Press.

Dalton, Russell J. 2008. *Citizen Politics: Public Opinion and Political Parties in Advanced Industrial Societies*. Washington, DC: Congressional Quarterly Press.

DiPrete, Thomas A., and Gregory M. Eirich. 2006. "Cumulative Advantage as a Mechanism for Inequality: A Review of Theoretical and Empirical Developments." *Annual Review of Sociology* 32: 271–97.

Featherman, David L., and Robert M. Hauser. 1978. *Opportunity and Change*. New York: Academic Press.

Fiorina, Morris. 1981. *Retrospective Voting in American National Elections*. New Haven, CT: Yale University Press.

Fosse, Ethan, and Neil Gross. 2012. "Why Are Professors Liberal?" *Theory and Society* 41: 127–68.

Franke, Ray, Sylvia Ruiz, Jessica Sharkness, Linda DeAngelo, and John Pryor. 2010. "Findings from the 2009 Administration of the College Senior Survey (CSS): National Aggregates." Report. Los Angeles: Cooperative Institutional Research Program at the Higher Education Research Institute.

Frisco, Michelle, Chandra Muller, and Kyle Dodson. 2004. "Participation in Youth-Serving Associations and Early Adult Voting Behavior." *Social Science Quarterly* 85: 660–76.

Halaby, Charles N. 2004. "Panel Models in Sociological Research: Theory into Practice." *Annual Review of Sociology* 30: 507–44.

Horowitz, David. 2006. *The Professors: The 101 Most Dangerous Academics in America*. Washington, DC: Regnery.

Hout, Michael. 1988. "More Universalism and Less Structural Mobility: The American Occupational Structure in the 1980s." *American Journal of Sociology* 93: 1358–400.

Huckfeldt, Robert, and John Sprague. 1987. "Networks in Context: The Social Flow of Political Information." *American Political Science Review* 81: 1197–216.

———. 1995. *Citizens, Politics, and Social Communication: Information and Influence in an Election Campaign*. New York: Cambridge University Press.

Hyman, Herbert. 1959. *Political Socialization: A Study in the Psychology of Political Behavior*. Glencoe, IL: Free Press.

Inglehart, Ronald. 1997. *Modernization and Postmodernization: Cultural, Economic, and Political Change in 43 Societies*. Princeton, NJ: Princeton University Press.

Jacobs, Jerry A. 1996. "Gender Inequality and Higher Education." *Annual Review of Sociology* 22: 153–85.

Jencks, Christopher, Marshall Smith, Henry Acland, and Mary Jo Bane. 1972. *Inequality: A Reassessment of the Effect of Family and Schooling in America*. New York: Basic Books.

Jennings, M. Kent, and Richard Niemi. 1974. *The Political Character of Adolescence: The Influence of Families and Schools*. Princeton, NJ: Princeton University Press.

———. 1981. *Generations and Politics*. Princeton, NJ: Princeton University Press.

Jennings, M. Kent, and Laura Stoker. 2008. "Another and Longer Look at the Impact of Higher Education on Political Involvement and Attitudes." Paper presented at the Midwest Political Science Association meetings, Chicago.

Kam, Cindy D., and Carl L. Palmer. 2008. "Reconsidering the Effects of Education on Political Participation." *Journal of Politics* 70: 612–31.

Kingston, Paul W., Ryan Hubbard, Brent Lapp, Paul Schroeder, and Julia Wilson. 2003. "Why Education Matters." *Sociology of Education* 76: 53–70.

Knoke, David. 1990. "Networks of Political Action: Toward Theory Construction." *Social Forces* 68: 1041–63.

Ladd, Everett Carll, Jr., and Seymour Martin Lipset. 1976. *The Divided Academy: Professors and Politics.* New York: Norton.

Lamont, Michèle. 1992. *Money, Morals, and Manners: The Culture of the French and the American Upper-Middle Class.* Chicago: University of Chicago Press.

MacKuen, Michael B., Robert S. Erikson, and James A. Stimson. 1989. "Macropartisanship." *American Political Science Review* 83: 1125–42.

McAdam, Doug. 1982. *Political Process and the Development of Black Insurgency, 1930–1970.* Chicago: University of Chicago Press.

———. 1986. "Recruitment to High-Risk Activism: The Case of Freedom Summer." *American Journal of Sociology* 92: 64–90.

McClosky, Herbert, and John Zaller. 1984. *The American Ethos: Public Attitudes toward Capitalism and Democracy.* Cambridge, MA: Harvard University Press.

McFarland, Daniel A., and Reuben J. Thomas. 2006. "Bowling Young: How Youth Voluntary Associations Influence Adult Political Participation." *American Sociological Review* 71: 401–25.

Meyer, John W. 1977. "The Effects of Education as an Institution." *American Journal of Sociology* 83: 55–77.

Miller, Warren E., and J. Merrill Shanks. 1996. *The New American Voter.* Cambridge, MA: Harvard University Press.

Morgan, Stephen L., and Young-Mi Kim. 2006. "Inequality of Conditions and Intergenerational Mobility: Changing Patterns of Educational Attainment in the United States." In *Mobility and Inequality: Frontiers of Research in Sociology and Economics,* edited by Stephen L. Morgan, David B. Grusky, and Gary S. Fields, 165–94. Stanford, CA: Stanford University Press.

Mutz, Diana. 2002. "The Consequences of Cross-Cutting Networks for Political Participation." *American Journal of Political Science* 46: 838–55.

Nie, Norman H., Jane Junn, and Kenneth Stehlik-Barry. 1996. *Education and Democratic Citizenship in America.* Chicago: University of Chicago Press.

Niemi, Richard G., and Mary A. Hepburn. 1995. "The Rebirth of Political Socialization." *Perspectives on Political Science* 24: 7–16.

Pallas, Aaron. 2002. "Educational Participation across the Life Course: Do the Rich Get Richer?" In *New Frontiers in Socialization,* edited by Richard A. Settersten Jr. and Timothy J. Owens, 327–54. Oxford: Elsevier Science.

Pascarella, Ernest, and Patrick Terenzini. 1991. *How College Affects Students: Findings and Insights from Twenty Years of Research.* San Francisco: Jossey-Bass.

Powell, G. Bingham. 1986. "American Voter Turnout in Comparative Perspective." *American Political Science Review* 80: 17–43.

Rosenstone, Steven J., and John Mark Hansen. 1993. *Mobilization, Participation, and Democracy in America.* New York: Macmillan.

Schofer, Evan, and John W. Meyer. 2005. "The Worldwide Expansion of Higher Education in the Twentieth Century." *American Sociological Review* 70: 898–920.

Steelman, Lala Carr, and Brian Powell. 1993. "Sponsoring the Next Generation: Parental Support for Higher Education." *American Journal of Sociology* 96: 1505–21.

Stuber, Jenny. 2011. *Inside the College Gates: How Class and Culture Matter in Higher Education*. Plymouth, UK: Lexington Books.

Thornton, Arland, Duane F. Alwin, and Donald Camburn. 1983. "Causes and Consequences of Sex-Role Attitudes and Attitude Change." *American Sociological Review* 48: 211–27.

Van Dyke, Nella. 1998. "Hotbeds of Activism: Locations of Student Protest." *Social Problems* 45: 205–20.

Verba, Sidney, Kay Lehman Schlozman, and Henry E. Brady. 1995. *Voice and Equality: Civic Voluntarism in American Politics*. Cambridge, MA: Harvard University Press.

Walters, Pamela Barnhouse. 1986. "Sex and Institutional Differences in Labor Market Effects on the Expansion of Higher Education, 1952 to 1980." *Sociology of Education* 59: 199–211.

———. 1990. "Post–World War II Higher Educational Expansion, the Organization of Work, and Changes in Labor Productivity in the United States." *Research in Sociology of Education and Socialization* 9: 1–23.

Walters, Pamela Barnhouse, and Richard Rubinson. 1983. "Educational Expansion and Economic Output in the United States, 1890–1969." *American Sociological Review* 48: 480–93.

Chapter 6 · "Civil" or "Provocative"?

Armstrong, Elizabeth A., and Laura Hamilton. 2013. *Paying for the Party: How College Maintains Inequality*. Cambridge, MA: Harvard University Press.

Arum, Richard, and Josipa Roksa. 2011. *Academically Adrift: Limited Learning on College Campuses*. Chicago: University of Chicago Press.

Astin, Alexander W. 1993. *What Matters in College? Four Critical Years Revisited*. San Francisco: Jossey-Bass.

Binder, Amy. 2007. "For Love and Money: Organizations' Creative Responses to Multiple Environmental Logics." *Theory and Society* 36: 547–71.

Binder, Amy, and Kate Wood. 2011. "Conservative Students on College Campuses: Discourses of Exclusion." In *Diversity in American Education: Toward a More Comprehensive Approach*, edited by Lisa Stulberg and Sharon Weinberg, 165–77. London: Routledge.

———. 2013. *Becoming Right: How Campuses Shape Young Conservatives*. Princeton, NJ: Princeton University Press.

Blumenthal, Max. 2009. *Republican Gomorrah: Inside the Movement That Shattered the Party*. New York: Nation Books.

Bourdieu, Pierre, and Randal Johnson. 1993. *The Field of Cultural Production: Essays on Art and Literature*. New York: Columbia University Press.

Bowen, William G., and Derek Curtis Bok. 1998. *The Shape of the River: Long-Term Consequences of Considering Race in College and University Admissions*. Princeton, NJ: Princeton University Press.

Buckley, William F., Jr. 1951. *God and Man at Yale: The Superstitions of Academic Freedom*. Chicago: Regnery.

Clark, Burton R. 1970. *The Distinctive College*. Chicago: Aldine.

Clydesdale, Timothy T. 2007. *The First Year Out: Understanding American Teens after High School*. Chicago: University of Chicago Press.

Cookson, Peter W., and Caroline Hodges Persell. 1985. *Preparing for Power: America's Elite Boarding Schools*. New York: Basic Books.

DiMaggio, Paul, and Walter W. Powell. 1991. "Introduction." In *The New Institutionalism in Organizational Analysis*, edited by Walter W. Powell and Paul DiMaggio, 1–38. Chicago: University of Chicago Press.

Einwohner, Rachel L. and J. William Spencer. 2005. "That's How We Do Things Here: Local Culture and the Construction of Sweatshops and Anti-Sweatshop Activism in Two Campus Communities." *Sociological Inquiry* 75: 249–72.

Eliasoph, Nina. 1998. *Avoiding Politics: How Americans Produce Apathy in Everyday Life*. New York: Cambridge University Press.

Eliasoph, Nina, and Paul Lichterman. 2003. "Culture in Interaction." *American Journal of Sociology* 108: 735–94.

Espeland, Wendy Nelson, and Michael Sauder. 2007. "Rankings and Reactivity: How Public Measures Recreate Social Worlds." *American Journal of Sociology* 113: 1–40.

Feldman, Kenneth A., and Theodore Mead Newcomb. 1994. *The Impact of College on Students*. New Brunswick, NJ: Transaction Publishers.

Fine, Gary Alan. 1984. "Negotiated Orders and Organizational Cultures." *Annual Review of Sociology* 10: 239–62.

Fligstein, Neil, and Doug McAdam. 2011. "Toward a General Theory of Strategic Action Fields." *Sociological Theory* 29: 1–26.

Fosse, Ethan, and Neil Gross. 2012. "Why Are Professors Liberal?" *Theory and Society* 41: 127–68.

Gitlin, Todd. 1980. *The Whole World Is Watching: Mass Media in the Making and Unmaking of the New Left*. Berkeley: University of California Press.

Granfield, Robert, and Thomas Koenig. 1992. "Learning Collective Eminence: Harvard Law School and the Social Production of Elite Lawyers." *Sociological Quarterly* 33: 503–20.

Gross, Neil. 2010. "Charles Tilly and American Pragmatism." *American Sociologist* 41: 337–57.

Hallett, Tim, and Marc Ventresca. 2006. "Inhabited Institutions: Social Interactions and Organizational Forms in Gouldner's *Patterns of Industrial Bureaucracy*." *Theory and Society* 35: 213–36.

Highton, Benjamin. 2009. "Revisiting the Relationship between Educational Attainment and Political Sophistication." *Journal of Politics* 71: 1564–76.

Holland, Dorothy C., and Margaret A. Eisenhart. 1990. *Educated in Romance: Women, Achievement, and College Culture*. Chicago: University of Chicago Press.

Horowitz, David. 2007. *Indoctrination U.: The Left's War against Academic Freedom*. New York: Encounter Books.

Horwitz, Robert B. 2013. *America's Right: Anti-establishment Conservatism from Goldwater to the Tea Party*. London: Polity Press.

Jennings, M. Kent, and Laura Stoker. 2008. "Another and Longer Look at the Impact of Higher Education on Political Involvement and Attitudes." Paper presented at the Midwest Political Science Association meetings, Chicago.

Karabel, Jerome. 2005. *The Chosen: The Hidden History of Admission and Exclusion at Harvard, Yale, and Princeton*. Boston: Houghton Mifflin.

Kaufman, Peter, and Kenneth Feldman. 2004. "Forming Identities in College: A Sociological Approach." *Research in Higher Education* 45: 463–96.

Kelly-Woessner, April, and Matthew Woessner. 2006. "My Professor Is a Partisan Hack: How Perceptions of a Professor's Political Views Affect Student Course Evaluations." *PS: Political Science and Politics* 39: 495–501.

Khan, Shamus. 2011. *Privilege: The Making of an Adolescent Elite at St. Paul's School*. Princeton, NJ: Princeton University Press.

Knox, William E., Paul Lindsay, and Mary N. Kolb. 1993. *Does College Make a Difference? Long-Term Changes in Activities and Attitudes*. Westport, CT: Greenwood Press.

Kors, Alan Charles, and Harvey Silverglate. 1998. *The Shadow University: The Betrayal of Liberty on America's Campuses*. New York: Free Press.

Lareau, Annette. 2003. *Unequal Childhoods: Class, Race, and Family Life*. Berkeley: University of California Press.

Lichterman, Paul, and Daniel Cefai. 2006. "The Idea of Political Culture." In *The Oxford Handbook of Contextual Political Analysis*, edited by Robert E. Goodin and Charles Tilly, 392–416. Oxford: Oxford University Press.

Lilla, Mark. 2009. "Taking the Right Seriously: Conservatism Is a Tradition, Not a Pathology." *Chronicle of Higher Education*, September 11.

Maranto, Robert, Richard E. Redding, and Frederick M. Hess. 2009. "The PC Academy Debate: Questions Not Asked." In *The Politically Correct University: Problems, Scope, and Reforms*, edited by Robert Maranto, Richard Redding, and Frederick Hess, 3–14. Washington, DC: AEI Press.

Massey, Douglas S., Camille Z. Charles, Garvey Lundey, and Mary J. Fischer. 2003. *The Source of the River: The Social Origins of Freshmen at America's Selective Colleges and Universities*. Princeton, NJ: Princeton University Press.

McAdam, Doug, Sidney G. Tarrow, and Charles Tilly. 2001. *Dynamics of Contention*. New York: Cambridge University Press.

Meyer, John W. 1977. "The Effects of Education as an Institution." *American Journal of Sociology* 83: 55–77.

Mische, Ann. 2008. *Partisan Publics: Communication and Contention across Brazilian Youth Activist Networks*. Princeton, NJ: Princeton University Press.

Naidoo, Rajani. 2004. "Fields and Institutional Strategy: Bourdieu on the Relationship between Higher Education, Inequality, and Society." *British Journal of Sociology of Education* 25: 457–71.

Nathan, Rebekah. 2005. *My Freshman Year: What a Professor Learned by Becoming a Student*. Ithaca, NY: Cornell University Press.

Pascarella, Ernest, and Patrick Terenzini. 1991. *How College Affects Students: Findings and Insights from Twenty Years of Research*. San Francisco: Jossey-Bass.

———. 2005. *How College Affects Students, Vol. 2: A Third Decade of Research*. San Francisco: Jossey-Bass.

Sanford, Nevitt, and Joseph Axelrod, eds. 1979. *College and Character*. Berkeley, CA: Montaigne.

Stevens, Mitchell L. 2007. *Creating a Class: College Admissions and the Education of Elites*. Cambridge, MA: Harvard University Press.

Tanenhaus, Sam. 2009. *The Death of Conservatism*. New York: Random House.

Tilly, Charles. 1995. *Popular Contention in Great Britain, 1758–1834*. Cambridge, MA: Harvard University Press.

Wallace, Walter L. 1966. *Student Culture: Social Structure and Continuity in a Liberal Arts College*. Chicago: Aldine.

Woessner, Matthew, and April Kelly-Woessner. 2009. "Left Pipeline: Why Conservatives Don't Get Doctorates." In *The Politically Correct University: Problems, Scope, and Reforms*, edited by Robert Maranto, Richard Redding, and Frederick Hess, 38–59. Washington, DC: AEI Press.

Yesnowitz, Joshua. 2010. "Talking 'bout My Generation: Campus Politics, Student Social Movements, and Youth Political Engagement in Early Twenty-First Century America." Unpublished paper. Boston University, 2010.

Chapter 7 · Naturalizing Liberalism in the 1950s

Abbott, Andrew, and James T. Sparrow. 2007. "Hot War, Cold War: The Structures of Sociological Action, 1940–1955." In *Sociology in America: A History*, edited by C. Calhoun, 281–313. Chicago: University of Chicago Press.

Abrams, Irwin. 1958. "What's Missing on the Campus?" *Phi Delta Kappan* 39: 310–13.

Adcock, Robert. 2007. "Interpreting Behavioralism." In *Modern Political Science: Anglo-American Exchanges since 1880*, edited by R. Adcock, M. Bevir, and S. C. Stimson, 180–208. Princeton, NJ: Princeton University Press.

Adorno, Theodor W., Else Frenkel-Brunswik, Daniel J. Levinson, and Nevitt Sanford. 1950. *The Authoritarian Personality*. New York: Harper.

Allardyce, Gilbert. 1982. "The Rise and Fall of the Western Civilization Course." *American Historical Review* 87: 695–725.

Allee, W. C. 1951. *Cooperation among Animals, with Human Implications*. New York: Henry Schuman.

Barber, Bernard. 1957. *Social Stratification: A Comparative Analysis of Structure and Process*. New York: Harcourt, Brace.

Barton, Allen H. 1959. *Studying the Effects of College Education: A Methodological Examination of Changing Values in College*. New Haven, CT: Edward W. Hazen Foundation.

Barzun, Jacques. 1952a. "America's Romance with Practicality." *Harper's Magazine* 204: 70–78.

———. 1952b. "The Great Books." *Atlantic* 190: 79–84.

———. 1954a. "America's Passion for Culture." *Harper's Magazine* 208: 40–47.

———. 1954b. *God's Country and Mine: A Declaration of Love Spiced with a Few Harsh Words*. Boston: Little, Brown.

Baumer, Franklin Le Van. 1952. *Main Currents of Western Thought*. New York: Knopf.

Bell, Daniel, ed. 1955. *The New American Right*. New York: Criterion.

Bloom, Benjamin S., and Harold Webster. 1960. "The Outcomes of College." *Review of Educational Research* 30: 321–33.

Boorstin, Daniel J. 1953. *The Genius of American Politics*. Chicago: University of Chicago Press.

Brick, Howard. 1998. *Age of Contradiction: American Thought and Culture in the 1960s*. New York: Twayne.

———. 2006. *Transcending Capitalism: Visions of a New Society in Modern American Thought.* Ithaca, NY: Cornell University Press.

Brinkley, Alan. 2001. "The Illusion of Unity in Cold War Culture." In *Rethinking Cold War Culture*, edited by P. J. Kuznick and J. B. Gilbert, 61–73. Washington, DC: Smithsonian Institution Press.

Buchanan, Patrick J. 1993. "Liberals Use 'Psychopolitics' to Smear Conservatives." *Human Events* 53: 13.

Ciepley, David. 2006. *Liberalism in the Shadow of Totalitarianism.* Cambridge, MA: Harvard University Press.

Cohen-Cole, Jamie. 2005. "The Reflexivity of Cognitive Science: The Scientist as Model of Human Nature." *History of the Human Sciences* 18: 107–39.

———. 2009. "The Creative American: Cold War Salons, Social Science, and the Cure for Modern Society." *Isis* 100: 219–62.

Commager, Henry Steele. 1950. *The American Mind: An Interpretation of American Thought and Character since the 1880s.* New Haven, CT: Yale University Press.

———. 1951. *Living Ideas in America.* New York: Harper.

———. 1954. *Freedom, Loyalty, Dissent.* New York: Oxford University Press.

Cravens, Hamilton. 1978. *The Triumph of Evolution: American Scientists and the Heredity-Environment Controversy, 1900–1941.* Philadelphia: University of Pennsylvania Press.

Curti, Merle, Richard H. Shryock, Thomas C. Cochran, and Fred Harvey Harrington. 1953. *A History of American Civilization.* New York: Harper.

Degler, Carl N. 1991. *In Search of Human Nature: The Decline and Revival of Darwinism in American Social Thought.* New York: Oxford University Press.

Dobzhansky, Theodosius. 1956. *The Biological Basis of Human Freedom.* New York: Columbia University Press.

Eddy, Edward D., Jr. 1959. *The College Influence on Student Character: An Exploratory Study in Selected Colleges and Universities.* Washington, DC: American Council on Education.

Edelstein, Alex S. 1962. "Since Bennington: Evidence of Change in Student Political Behavior." *Public Opinion Quarterly* 26: 564–77.

Edman, Irwin. 1947. "Classical Origins." In *Foundations of Democracy: A Series of Addresses*, edited by F. E. Johnson, 18–26. New York: Institute for Religious and Social Studies.

Emerson, Alfred E. 1954. "Dynamic Homeostasis: A Unifying Principle in Organic, Social, and Ethical Evolution." *Scientific Monthly* 78: 67–85.

Erikson, Erik H. 1950. *Childhood and Society.* New York: Norton.

Fowler, Robert Booth. 1978. *Believing Skeptics: American Political Intellectuals, 1945–1964.* Westport, CT: Greenwood Press.

Fromm, Erich. 1955. *The Sane Society.* New York: Rinehart.

Gabriel, Ralph Henry. 1956. *The Course of American Democratic Thought.* 2nd ed. New York: Ronald Press.

Gilman, Nils. 2003. *Mandarins of the Future: Modernization Theory in Cold War America.* Baltimore: Johns Hopkins University Press.

Gleason, Philip. 1984. "World War II and the Development of American Studies." *American Quarterly* 36: 343–58.

————. 1992. *Speaking of Diversity: Language and Ethnicity in Twentieth-Century America.* Baltimore: Johns Hopkins University Press.

Goldsen, Rose K. 1960. *What College Students Think.* Princeton, NJ: Van Nostrand.

Gottlieb, David, and Benjamin Hodgkins. 1963. "College Student Subcultures: Their Structure and Characteristics in Relation to Student Attitude Change." *School Review* 71: 266–89.

Hackett, Edward J., Olga Amsterdamska, Michael Lynch, and Judy Wajcman, eds. 2008. *The Handbook of Science and Technology Studies.* 3rd ed. Cambridge, MA: MIT Press.

Haney, David Paul. 2008. *The Americanization of Social Science: Intellectuals and Public Responsibility in the Postwar United States.* Philadelphia: Temple University Press.

Hartz, Louis. 1955. *The Liberal Tradition in America: An Interpretation of American Political Thought since the Revolution.* New York: Harcourt, Brace.

Harvard University Committee on the Objectives of a General Education in a Free Society. 1945. *General Education in a Free Society.* Cambridge, MA: Harvard University Press.

Hauser, Philip M. 1946. "Are the Social Sciences Ready?" *American Sociological Review* 11: 379–84.

Herman, Ellen. 1995. *The Romance of American Psychology: Political Culture in the Age of Experts.* Berkeley: University of California Press.

Hofstadter, Richard. 1948. *The American Political Tradition and the Men Who Made It.* New York: Vintage.

————. 1955. "The Pseudo-Conservative Revolt." In *The New American Right,* edited by D. Bell, 33–55. New York: Criterion.

Isaac, Joel. 2007. "The Human Sciences in Cold War America." *Historical Journal* 50: 725–46.

Jacob, Philip E. 1957. *Changing Values in College: An Exploratory Study of the Impact of College Teaching.* New York: Harper.

Jewett, Andrew. 2012. *Science, Democracy, and the University: From the Civil War to the Cold War.* New York: Cambridge University Press.

Johnson, Alvin. 1949. "The Faith of a Skeptic." In *Years of the Modern: An American Appraisal,* edited by J. W. Chase. New York: Longmans, Green.

Kahl, Joseph A. 1953. "Educational and Occupational Aspirations of 'Common Man' Boys." *Harvard Educational Review* 23: 186–203.

————. 1957. *The American Class Structure.* New York: Rinehart.

Latham, Michael E. 2000. *Modernization as Ideology: American Social Science and "Nation Building" in the Kennedy Era.* Chapel Hill: University of North Carolina Press.

Marx, Leo. 2005. "On Recovering the 'Ur' Theory of American Studies." *American Literary History* 17: 118–34.

Mead, Margaret. 1942. *And Keep Your Powder Dry: An Anthropologist Looks at America.* New York: William Morrow.

Montagu, Ashley. 1950. *On Being Human.* New York: Henry Schuman.

Moss, Vera M. 1960. "Evaluating 'Values.'" *Journal of Higher Education* 31: 153–55.

Muller, H. J. 1958. "Human Values in Relation to Evolution." *Science* 127: 625–29.

Naftalin, Arthur, Benjamin N. Nelson, Milford Q. Sibley, Donald W. Calhoun, and Andreas G. Papandreau. 1953. *An Introduction to Social Science.* Philadelphia: Lippincott.

Nevins, Allan, and Henry Steele Commager. 1956. *A Short History of the United States.* 2nd ed. New York: Modern Library.

Newcomb, Theodore M. 1943. *Personality and Social Change: Attitude Formation in a Student Community.* New York: Wiley.

Overstreet, Harry A. 1949. *The Mature Mind.* New York: Norton.

Pace, C. Robert, and Anne McFee. 1960. "The College Environment." *Review of Educational Research* 30: 311–20.

Parsons, Talcott. 1955. "Social Strains in America." In *The New American Right*, edited by D. Bell, 117–40. New York: Criterion.

Pells, Richard H. 1985. *The Liberal Mind in a Conservative Age: American Intellectuals in the 1940s and 1950s.* New York: Harper & Row.

Penister, Allan O. 1958. "Review of Jacob, *Changing Values in College.*" *School Review* 66: 238–44.

Potter, David M. 1954. *People of Plenty: Economic Abundance and the American Character.* Chicago: University of Chicago Press.

Queen, Stuart A., William M. Chambers, and Charles M. Winston. 1956. *The American Social System: Social Control, Personal Choice, and Public Decision.* Boston: Houghton Mifflin.

Robertson, Priscilla. 1956. "On Getting Values out of Science." *Humanist* 16: 168–74.

Rogin, Michael P. 1967. *The Intellectuals and McCarthy: The Radical Specter.* Cambridge, MA: MIT Press.

Roiser, Martin. 2001. "The American Reception of *The Authoritarian Personality.*" In *In Practice: Adorno, Critical Theory, and Cultural Studies*, edited by H. M. Briel and A. Kramer, 129–42. Oxford: Peter Lang.

Ross, Ralph, and Ernest van den Haag. 1957. *The Fabric of Society: An Introduction to the Social Sciences.* New York: Harcourt, Brace.

Rubin, Joan Shelley. 2006. "The Scholar and the World: Academic Humanists and General Readers in Postwar America." In *The Humanities and the Dynamics of Inclusion since World War II*, edited by D. A. Hollinger, 73–103. Baltimore: Johns Hopkins University Press.

Sanford, Nevitt. 1956. "Personality Development during the College Years." *Journal of Social Issues* 12: 3–12.

———. 1962. *The American College: A Psychological and Social Interpretation of the Higher Learning.* New York: Wiley.

Schapiro, J. Salwyn. 1958. *Liberalism: Its Meaning and History.* Princeton, NJ: Van Nostrand.

Schlesinger, Arthur M., Jr. 1949. *The Vital Center: The Politics of Freedom.* Boston: Houghton Mifflin.

Segal, Daniel A. 2000. "'Western Civ' and the Staging of History in American Higher Education." *American Historical Review* 105: 770–805.

Shils, Edward. 1954. "Authoritarianism: 'Right' and 'Left.'" In *Studies in the Scope and Method of "The Authoritarian Personality,"* edited by R. Christie and M. Jahoda. Glencoe, IL: Free Press.

Simpson, George Gaylord. 1949. *The Meaning of Evolution.* New Haven, CT: Yale University Press.

Sinnott, Edmund W. 1945. "The Biological Basis of Democracy." *Yale Review* 35: 61–73.

————. 1950. *Cell and Psyche: The Biology of Purpose.* Chapel Hill: University of North Carolina Press.

————. 1952. *Science and Religion: A Necessary Partnership.* New Haven, CT: Edward W. Hazen Foundation.

————. 1953. *Two Roads to Truth: A Basis for Unity under the Great Tradition.* New York: Viking Press.

————. 1955. *The Biology of the Spirit.* New York: Viking Press.

————. 1956. *Life and Mind.* Yellow Springs, OH: Antioch Press.

————. 1957. *Matter, Mind, and Man: The Biology of Human Nature.* New York: Harper.

Solovey, Mark. 2001. "Project Camelot and the 1960s Epistemological Revolution: Rethinking the Politics–Patronage–Social Science Nexus." *Social Studies of Science* 31: 171–206.

Stanley, William O. 1961. "Educational and Social Policy." *Review of Educational Research* 31: 91–108.

Taylor, Carl C. 1946. "The Social Responsibilities of the Social Sciences—the National Level." *American Sociological Review* 11: 384–92.

Wall, Wendy. 2008. *Inventing the "American Way": The Politics of Consensus from the New Deal to the Civil Rights Movement.* New York: Oxford University Press.

Warner, W. Lloyd, Marchia Meeker, and Kenneth Eells. 1949. *Social Class in America: A Manual of Procedure for the Measurement of Social Status.* Chicago: Science Research Associates.

Young, Robert M. 1981. "The Naturalization of Value Systems in the Human Sciences." *Problems in the Biological and Human Sciences* 6: 63–110.

Chapter 8 · Challenging Neutrality

Allen, Susan Huek. 2011. *Classical Spies: American Archeologists with the OSS in World War II Greece.* Ann Arbor: University of Michigan Press.

American Association of University Professors (AAUP). 1915. "General Report of the Committee on Academic Freedom and Academic Tenure." *Bulletin of the American Association of University Professors* 1: 15–43.

American Political Science Association. 1968. "Final Report of the American Political Science Association Committee on Professional Standards and Responsibilities: Ethical Problems of Academic Political Scientists." *PS: Political Science and Politics* 3: 3–29.

Bird, Kai, and Martin J. Sherwin. 2005. *American Prometheus: The Triumph and Tragedy of J. Robert Oppenheimer.* New York: Knopf.

Blum, Jeffrey, and Ronald H. Janis. 1969. "Faculty Ponders Vietnam Position." *Harvard Crimson*, October 7.

Bok, Derek. 1982. *Beyond the Ivory Tower: Social Responsibilities of the Modern University.* Cambridge, MA: Harvard University Press.

Bundy, McGeorge. 1970. "Were Those the Days?" *Daedalus* 99: 531–67.

Cardozier, V. R. 1993. *Colleges and Universities in World War II.* Westport, CT: Praeger.

Carrington, Paul D. 1969. "The Lawyer's Role in the Design of a University." In *Student Protest and the Law*, edited by Grace W. Holmes, 13–17. Ann Arbor, MI: Institute of Continuing Legal Education.

Conant, James Bryant. 1970. *My Several Lives: Memoirs of a Social Inventor.* New York: Harper & Row, 1970.

Davidson, Carl. 1971 [1967]. "Toward Institutional Resistance." In *The University Crisis Reader, Vol. II: Confrontation and Counter Attack*, edited by Immanuel Wallerstein and Paul Starr, 129–38. New York: Random House.

Diner, Steven J. 1980. *A City and Its Universities: Public Policy in Chicago*. Chapel Hill: University of North Carolina Press.

Doel, Ronald E. 2003. "Constituting the Postwar Earth Sciences: The Military's Influence on the Environmental Sciences in the USA after 1945." *Social Studies of Science* 33: 635–66.

Engerman, David. 2009. *Know Your Enemy: The Rise and Fall of America's Soviet Experts*. New York: Oxford University Press.

Fallows, James M. 1969. "150 Faculty Oppose Formal Vote on Vietnam." *Harvard Crimson*, October 7.

Furner, Mary O. 1975. *Advocacy and Objectivity: A Crisis in the Professionalization of American Social Science, 1865–1905*. Lexington: University of Kentucky Press.

Gitlin, Todd. 1971 [1967]. "Resistance and the Movement." In *The University Crisis Reader, Vol. II: Confrontation and Counter Attack*, edited by Immanuel Wallerstein and Paul Starr, 127–28. New York: Random House.

Glassberg, Victor. 1969. "Faculty Petition." *Harvard Crimson*, October 9.

Gross, Neil. 2011. "American Academe and the Knowledge-Politics Problem." In *The American Academic Profession: Changing Forms and Functions*, edited by Joseph Hermanowicz, 111–44. Baltimore: Johns Hopkins University Press.

Gruber, Carol S. 1975. *Mars and Minerva: World War I and the Uses of Higher Education in America*. Baton Rouge: Louisiana State University Press.

Herman, Ellen. 1995. *The Romance of American Psychology: Political Culture in the Age of Experts*. Berkeley: University of California Press.

Horowitz, David. 2007. *Indoctrination U.: The Left's War against Academic Freedom*. New York: Encounter Books.

Hoult, Thomas Ford. 1970. "Further Comments on Institutional Neutrality." *AAUP Bulletin* 56: 123–29.

ja. [1965]. "Memo to dick." Records of the Office of the Chancellor, Box 66, University of California, Berkeley Archives, Bancroft Library, Berkeley, CA.

Keller, Morton, and Phyllis Keller. 2007. *Making Harvard Modern: The Rise of America's University*. New York: Oxford University Press.

Keniston, Kenneth. 1968. "Criticism and Social Change." In *Whose Goals for American Higher Education?*, edited by Charles G. Dobbins and Calving T. B. Lee, 145–61. Washington, DC: American Council on Education.

Kerr, Clark. 1995 [1963]. *The Uses of the University*. 4th ed. Cambridge, MA: Harvard University Press.

Kevles, Daniel. 1987. *The Physicists: The History of a Scientific Community in Modern America*. Cambridge, MA: Harvard University Press.

"Kilson on Resolution." 1969. *Harvard Crimson*, October 14.

Kleinman, Daniel. 1995. *Politics on the Endless Frontier: Postwar Research Policy in the United States*. Durham, NC: Duke University Press.

Koster, Donald, and Winton U. Solberg. 1970. "On Institutional Neutrality." *AAUP Bulletin* 56: 11–13.

Landauer, Carl. 1964. "Letter to the Executive Committee of the FSM," October 17. Free Speech Movement Collection, Bancroft Library, Berkeley, CA.

Leslie, Stuart. 1993. *The Cold War and American Science: The Military-Industrial-Academic Complex at MIT and Stanford*. New York: Columbia University Press.

Loss, Christopher. 2012. *Between Citizen and the State: The Politics of Higher Education in the Twentieth Century*. Princeton, NJ: Princeton University Press.

Lowen, Rebecca. 1997. *Creating the Cold War University: The Transformation of Stanford*. Berkeley: University of California Press.

Marcus, Alan. 1985. *Agricultural Science and the Quest for Legitimacy: Farmers, Agricultural Colleges, and Experiment Stations, 1870–1890*. Ames: Iowa State University Press.

McCaughey, Robert A. 1984. *International Study and Academic Enterprise: A Chapter in the Enclosure of American Learning*. New York: Columbia University Press.

"Members of Liberal Caucus Will Fight for Floor Vote on Withdrawal Resolution." 1969. *Harvard Crimson*, October 4.

"More Than 600 Campuses Participate in Nationwide Vietnam Moratorium." 1969. *New York Times*, October 20.

Ness, Frederick. 1968. "Response to Kenniston." In *Whose Goals for American Higher Education?*, edited by Charles G. Dobbins and Calving T. B. Lee, 164–66. Washington, DC: American Council on Education.

New University Conference. 1969. "The Student Rebellion." New University Conference Papers, Box 11, Wisconsin Historical Society, Madison, WI.

Nisbet, Robert. 1971. *The Degradation of the Academic Dogma: The University in America, 1945–1970*. New York: Basic Books.

Perkins, James. 1966. *The University in Transition*. Princeton, NJ: Princeton University Press.

Reinhold, Robert. 1969. "A Harvard Faculty Urges War Pullout." *New York Times*, October 8.

Reuben, Julie. 1996a "Defining 'True' Knowledge: Consensus and the Growing Distrust of Faculty Activism, 1880s–1920s." In *Advocacy in the Classroom*, edited by Patricia Meyer Spacks, 127–34. New York: St. Martin's Press.

———. 1996b. *Making of the Modern University: Intellectual Transformation and the Marginalization of Morality*. Chicago: University of Chicago Press.

Rorabaugh, W. J. 1989. *Berkeley at War: The 1960s*. New York: Oxford University Press.

Rudy, Willis. 1991. *Total War and Twentieth Century Higher Learning: Universities of the Western World in the First and Second World Wars*. Rutherford, NJ: Fairleigh Dickinson University Press.

Schrecker, Ellen. 1986. *No Ivory Tower: McCarthyism and the Universities*. New York: Oxford University Press.

Shoben, Edward J., Jr. 1970. "Cultural Criticism and the American College." *Daedalus* 99: 676–99.

Simon, John G., Charles W. Powers, and John P. Gunnemann. 1972. *The Ethical Investor: Universities and Corporate Responsibility*. New Haven, CT: Yale University Press.

Simpson, Christopher. 1998. *Universities and Empire: Money and Politics in the Social Sciences during the Cold War*. New York: New Press.

Slaughter, Sheila. 1980. "The Danger Zone: Academic Freedom and Civil Liberties." *Annals of the American Academy of Political and Social Science* 448: 46–61.

Solovey, Mark. 2013. *Shaky Foundations: The Politics–Patronage–Social Science Nexus in Cold War America*. New Brunswick, NJ: Rutgers University Press.

Solovey, Mark, and Hamilton Cravens, eds. 2012. *Cold War Social Science: Knowledge Production, Liberal Democracy, and Human Nature*. New York: Palgrave Macmillan.

Townsely, Eleanor. 2000. "A History of Intellectuals and the Demise of the New Class: Academics and the U.S. Government in the 1960s." *Theory and Society* 29: 739–84.

Tugwell, Rexford. 1968. *Brains Trust*. New York: Viking Press.

Wallenstein, Peter, ed. 2008. *Higher Education and the Civil Rights Movement: White Supremacy, Black Southerners, and College Campuses*. Gainesville: University Press of Florida.

Wallerstein, Immanuel. 1969. *The University in Turmoil: The Politics of Change*. New York: Atheneum.

Williamson, Joy Ann. 2008. *Radicalizing the Ebony Tower: Black Colleges and the Black Freedom Struggle in Mississippi*. New York: Teachers College Press.

Wolff, Robert Paul. 1992 [1969]. *The Ideal of the University*. New Brunswick, NJ: Transaction Publishers.

Chapter 9 · Activism and the Academy

Aldridge, Dolores, and Carlene Young. 2000. "Introduction." In *Out of the Revolution: The Development of Africana Studies*. Lanham, MD: Lexington Books.

Alkalimat, Abdul. 2009. *Introduction to Afro-American Studies: A Peoples College Primer*. Chicago: Twenty-First Century Books.

Appiah, Anthony. 1993. *In My Father's House: Africa in the Philosophy of Culture*. New York: Oxford University Press.

Asante, Molefi. 2006. "A Discourse on Black Studies: Liberating the Study of African People in the Western Academy." *Journal of Black Studies* 36: 636–62.

Asante, Molefi, and Diane Ravitch. 1991. "Multiculturalism: An Exchange." *American Scholar* 60: 267–76.

Astin, Alexander. 1975. *The Power of Protest*. San Francisco: Jossey-Bass.

Bankole, Katherine O. 2006. "A Preliminary Report and Commentary on the Structure of Graduate Afrocentric Research and Implications for the Advancement of the Discipline of Africalogy, 1980–2004." *Journal of Black Studies* 36: 663–97.

Bayer, Alan E., and Alexander W. Astin. 1969. *Campus Disruption during 1968–1969*. ACE Research Reports. Washington DC: American Council on Education.

Belvin, Brent. 2004. "Malcolm X Liberation University: An Experiment in Independent Black Education." Master's thesis. Department of History, North Carolina State University, Raleigh, NC.

Blake, Elias, and Henry Cobb. 1976. *Black Studies: Issues in Their Institutional Survival*. Washington, DC: U.S. Department of Health, Education, and Welfare, Office of Education.

Brint, Steven, Lori Turk-Bicakci, Kristopher Proctor, and Scott Patrick Murphy. 2009. "Expanding the Social Frame of Knowledge: The Growth and Distribution of Interdisciplinary, Degree-Granting Programs in American Colleges and Universities, 1975–2000." *Review of Higher Education* 32: 155–83.

Bryson, Bethany. 2005. *Making Multiculturalism: Boundaries and Meaning in U.S. English Departments*. Palo Alto, CA: Stanford University Press.

Buchanan, Garth, and Joan Brackett. 1970. *Summary Results of the Survey for the President's Commission on Campus Unrest*. Washington, DC: Urban Institute.

Chang, Mitchell. 2002. "The Impact of an Undergraduate Diversity Course Requirement on Students' Racial Views and Attitudes." *Journal of General Education* 51: 21–42.

Chiang, Mark. 2009. *The Cultural Capital of Asian American Studies*. New York: New York University Press.

Churchill, Ward. 2007. *Pacifism as Pathology: Reflections on the Role of Armed Struggle in North America*. Oakland, CA: AK Press.

Clark, Terry N. 1968. "Institutionalization of Innovations in Higher Education: Four Models." *Administrative Science Quarterly* 13: 1–25.

Cole, Wade. 2006. "Accrediting Culture: An Analysis of Tribal and Historically Black College Curricula." *Sociology of Education* 79: 355–87.

Cowie, Jefferson. 2005. "Portrait of the Working Class in a Convex Mirror: Toward a History of the Seventies." *Labor: Studies in Working-Class History of the Americas* 2(3): 93–102.

Cunningham, Jo Ann. 1991. "Black Studies Programs: Reasons for Their Success and Non-success from Inception to the Present." *National Journal of Sociology* 5: 19–41.

Daniel, Phillip. 1980. "Black Studies: Discipline or Field of Study?" *Western Journal of Black Studies* 3: 195–200.

Dawson, Michael C. 2001. *Black Visions: The Roots of Contemporary African-American Political Ideologies*. Chicago: University of Chicago Press.

DiMaggio, Paul J., and Walter W. Powell. 1983. "The Iron Cage Revisited: Institutional Isomorphism and Collective Rationality in Organizational Fields." *American Sociological Review* 48: 147–60.

Ford, Nicholas Aaron. 1973. *Black Studies: Threat or Challenge*. Port Washington, NY: Kennikat Press.

Frank, David John, and Jay Gabler. 2006. *Reconstructing the University: Worldwide Shifts in Academia in the 20th Century*. Stanford, CA: Stanford University Press.

Frye, C. 1979. *The Impact of Black Studies on the Curricula of Three Universities*. Washington, DC: University Press of America.

Gilroy, Paul. 1993. *The Black Atlantic: Modernity and Double-Consciousness*. Cambridge, MA: Harvard University Press.

Glasker, Wayne. 2002. *Black Students in the Ivory Tower: African American Activism at the University of Pennsylvania, 1967–1990*. Amherst: University of Massachusetts Press.

Harris, Robert L., Darlene Clark Hine, and Nellie McKay. 1990. *Three Essays: Black Studies in the United States*. New York: Ford Foundation.

Hogan, David E., and Michael Mallott. 2005. "Changing Racial Prejudice through Diversity Education." *Journal of College Student Development* 46: 115–25.

Hoover, Mary Eleanor Rhodes. 1992. "The Nairobi Day School: An African American Independent School, 1966–1984." *Journal of Negro Education* 61: 201–10.

Jeffries, Leonard. 2011. "Reclaiming Nile Valley Civilization." National Black United Front. www.nbufront.org/MastersMuseums/LenJeffries/ReclaimingNileValley.html.

Kalu, Anthonia. 1991. "Multiculturalism as a Text: The Battle over the Canon." *Issue: A Journal of Opinion* 20: 61–64.

Kamoche, Jidlaph G. 1980. "The Interdepartmental and Autonomous Types of Afro-American Studies Program: A Comparative Perspective on Personnel Strengths and Weaknesses." *UMOJA* 4(4): 21–39.

Ladner, Joyce. 1998. *The Death of White Sociology*. Baltimore: Black Classic Press.

Lipset, Seymour Martin. 1976. *Rebellion in the University*. Chicago: University of Chicago Press.

McAdam, Doug. 1988. *Freedom Summer*. New York: Oxford University Press.

McWhorter, Gerald. 1968. "The Nature and Needs of the Black University." *Negro Digest* 17: 8–12.

Meyer, John W., and Brian Rowan. 1977. "Institutionalized Organizations: Formal Structure as Myth and Ceremony." *American Journal of Sociology* 83: 340–63.

Nelson, William E. 2000. "Black Studies, Student Activism, and the Academy." In *Out of the Revolution: The Development of Africana Studies*, edited by Dolores Aldridge and Carlene Young, 79–91. Lanham, MD: Lexington Books.

Powell, Walter W., Jason Owen-Smith, and Jeannette Colyvas. 2007. "Innovation and Emulation: Lessons from American Universities in Selling Private Rights to Public Knowledge." *Minerva* 45: 121–42.

Rojas, Fabio. 2006. "Social Movement Tactics, Organizational Change and the Spread of African-American Studies." *Social Forces* 84: 2147–66.

———. 2007a. "Faculty Development Problems in a Department of African-American Studies." In *Unleashing Suppressed Voices on College Campuses: Diversity Issues in Higher Education and Student Affairs*, edited by Mary Howard-Hamilton and O. Gilbert Brown, 81–89. New York: Peter Lang.

———. 2007b. *From Black Power to Black Studies: How a Radical Social Movement Became an Academic Discipline*. Baltimore: Johns Hopkins University Press.

———. 2008. "One Discipline, Two Tracks: An Analysis of the Journal Publication Records of Professors in Africana Studies Doctoral Programs." *Journal of Black Studies* 39: 57–68.

———. 2010. "Power through Institutional Work: Building Academic Authority in the 1968 Third World Strike." *Academy of Management Journal* 53: 1263–80.

———. 2011. "Institutions and Disciplinary Beliefs about Africana Studies." *Western Journal of Black Studies* 35: 92–106.

Rojas, Fabio, and Carson Byrd. 2012. "Intellectual Change in Africana Studies: Evidence from a Cohort Analysis." *Journal of African American Studies* 16: 550–73.

Rojas, Fabio, and Donald Shaffer. 2009. "What Have We Learned from the Black Studies Experience?" *Souls: A Critical Journal of Black Politics, Culture, and Society* 10: 442–47.

Rooks, Noliwe. 2006. *White Money/Black Power: The History of African American Studies and the Crisis in Higher Education*. Boston: Beacon Press.

Scott, Joseph, and Mohamed El-Assal. 1969. "Multiversity, University Size, University Quality and Student Protest: An Empirical Study." *American Sociological Review* 34: 702–9.

Seale, Bobby. 1970. *Seize the Time: The Story of the Black Panther Party and Huey P. Newton*. Baltimore: Black Classic Press.

Shelby, Tommie. 2007. *We Who Are Dark: The Philosophical Foundation of Black Solidarity*. Cambridge, MA: Harvard University Press.

Small, Mario L. 1999. "Departmental Conditions and the Emergence of New Disciplines: Two Cases in the Legitimation of African-American Studies." *Theory and Society* 28: 659–707.

Soule, Sarah A. 1997. "The Student Divestment Movement in the United States and Tactical Diffusion: The Shantytown Protest." *Social Forces* 75: 855–82.

Strub, Whitney. 2008. "Further into the Right: The Ever-Expanding Historiography of the U.S. New Right." *Journal of Social History* 42: 183–94.

Tarrow, Sidney. 1994. *Power in Movement: Social Movements, Collective Action, and Politics*. Cambridge: Cambridge University Press.

Thelwell, Michael. 1969. "Black Studies: A Political Perspective." *Massachusetts Review*, autumn, 703–12.

University of Washington, Department of American Ethnic Studies. 2011. "American Ethnic Studies." http://depts.washington.edu/aes

Van Deburg, William. 1992. *New Day in Babylon: The Black Power Movement and American Culture, 1965–1975*. Chicago: University of Chicago Press.

van Dyke, Nella. 1998. "Hotbeds of Activism: Locations of Student Protest." *Social Problems* 45: 205–20.

Vesey, Laurence. 1970. *The Emergence of the American University*. Chicago: University of Chicago Press.

Watkins, William. 2001. *The White Architects of Black Education: Ideology and Power in America, 1865–1954*. New York: Teachers College Press.

White, Derrick. 2004. "'New Concepts for the New Man': The Institute of the Black World and the Incomplete Victory of the Second Reconstruction." PhD dissertation. Department of History, Ohio State University, Columbus, OH.

Willie, C., and Cunnigen, D. 1981. "Black Students in Higher Education: A Review of Studies, 1965–1980." *Annual Review of Sociology* 7: 177–98.

Wong, Sau-ling. 1993. *Reading Asian American Literature*. Princeton, NJ: Princeton University Press.

Yamane, David. 2001. *Student Movements for Multiculturalism: Challenging the Curricular Color Line*. Baltimore: Johns Hopkins University Press.

Zanini, Adelino. 2010. "On the 'Philosophical Foundations' of Italian Workerism: A Conceptual Approach." *Historical Materialism* 18: 39–63.

Zhao, Dingxin. 2001. *The Power of Tiananmen: State-Society Relations and the 1989 Beijing Student Movement*. Chicago: University of Chicago Press.

Chapter 10 · *Rationalizing Realpolitik*

Abbott, Andrew. 2001. *Chaos of Disciplines*. Chicago: University of Chicago Press.

Abella, Alex. 2008. *Soldiers of Reason: The RAND Corporation and the Rise of the American Empire*. New York: Houghton Mifflin Harcourt.

Adcock, Robert, and Mark Bevir. 2010. "Political Science." In *The History of Postwar Political Science*, edited by Roger E. Backhouse and Philippe Fontaine, 71–101. Cambridge: Cambridge University Press.

Ashley, Richard K. 1986. "The Poverty of Neorealism." In *Neorealism and Its Critics*, edited by Robert O. Keohane, 255–300. New York: Columbia University Press.

Barry, Brian. 1970. *Sociologists, Economists, and Democracy.* London: Collier-Macmillan.

Boucoyannis, Deborah. 2007. "The International Wanderings of a Liberal Idea, or Why Liberals Can Learn to Stop Worrying and Love the Balance of Power." *Perspectives on Politics* 5: 703–27.

Bourdieu, Pierre. 2004. *Science of Science and Reflexivity.* Chicago: University of Chicago Press.

Deutsch, Karl Wolfgang. 1957. *Political Community and the North Atlantic Area: International Organization in the Light of Historical Experience.* Princeton, NJ: Princeton University Press.

———. 1963. *The Nerves of Government: Models of Political Communication and Control.* New York: Free Press.

Elman, Colin. 1996. "Horses for Courses: Why Not Neorealist Theories of Foreign Policy?" *Security Studies* 6: 7–53.

Frei, Christoph. 2001. *Hans Morgenthau: An Intellectual Biography.* Baton Rouge: Louisiana State University Press.

Gaus, John. 1946. "A Job Analysis of Political Science." *American Political Science Review* 40: 217–30.

Geertz, Clifford. 2000. *Local Knowledge: Further Essays in Interpretive Anthropology.* New York: Basic Books.

George, Alexander L. 1993. *Bridging the Gap: Theory and Practice in Foreign Policy.* Washington, DC: United States Institute of Peace Press, 1993.

Goddard, Stacey E., and Daniel H. Nexon. 2005. "Paradigm Lost? Reassessing Theory of International Politics." *European Journal of International Relations* 11: 9–61.

Goffman, Erving. 1959. *The Presentation of Self in Everyday Life.* New York: Anchor.

Guilhot, Nicolas. 2008. "The Realist Gambit: Postwar American Political Science and the Birth of IR Theory." *International Political Sociology* 2: 281–304.

Gunnell, John G. 1993. *The Descent of Political Theory: The Genealogy of an American Vocation.* Chicago: University of Chicago Press.

Hartz, Louis. 1991. *The Liberal Tradition in America.* 2nd ed. New York: Mariner Books.

Hauptmann, Emily. 2006. "From Opposition to Accommodation: How Rockefeller Foundation Grants Redefined Relations between Political Theory and Social Science in the 1950s." *American Political Science Review* 100: 643–49.

Jackson, Patrick Thaddeus. 2006. *Civilizing the Enemy: German Reconstruction and the Invention of the West.* Ann Arbor: University of Michigan Press.

———. 2010. "What Is Theory?" In *The International Studies Encyclopedia*, edited by Robert A. Denemark. Wiley-Blackwell. www.isacompendium.com/public

———. 2011. *The Conduct of Inquiry in International Relations.* London: Routledge.

Joas, Hans. 1997. *The Creativity of Action.* Chicago: University of Chicago Press.

Jordan, Richard, Daniel Maliniak, Amy Oakes, Susan Peterson, and Michael Tierney. 2009. "One Discipline or Many? 2008 TRIP Survey of International Relations Faculty in Ten Countries." www.wm.edu/offices/itpir/_documents/trip/2008-trip-survey-report.pdf

Katznelson, Ira. 2004. *Desolation and Enlightenment: Political Knowledge after Total War, Totalitarianism, and the Holocaust.* New ed. New York: Columbia University Press.

Keohane, Robert O., ed. 1986. *Neorealism and Its Critics.* New York: Columbia University Press.

Keohane, Robert O., and Joseph S. Nye. 1977. *Power and Interdependence: World Politics in Transition.* New York: Little, Brown.

Kratochwil, Friedrich. 2006. "History, Action and Identity: Revisiting the 'Second' Great Debate and Assessing Its Importance for Social Theory." *European Journal of International Relations* 12: 5–29.

Krebs, Ronald R., and Patrick Thaddeus Jackson. 2007. "Twisting Tongues and Twisting Arms: The Power of Political Rhetoric." *European Journal of International Relations* 13: 35–66.

Kruzel, Joseph, and James N. Rosenau, eds. 1989. *Journeys through World Politics: Autobiographical Reflections of Thirty-Four Academic Travelers.* Lanham, MD: Lexington Books.

Legro, Jeffrey W., and Andrew Moravcsik. 1999. "Is Anybody Still a Realist?" *International Security* 24: 5–55.

Levy, Marion J. 1969. "'Does It Matter If He's Naked?' Bawled the Child." In *Contending Approaches to International Politics,* edited by Klaus Knorr and James N. Rosenau, 87–109. Princeton, NJ: Princeton University Press.

Macy, Jesse. 1917. "The Scientific Spirit in Politics." *American Political Science Review* 11: 1–11.

Merriam, Charles E. 1921. "The Present State of the Study of Politics." *American Political Science Review* 15: 173–85.

Morgenthau, Hans J. 1946. *Scientific Man versus Power Politics.* Chicago: University of Chicago Press.

———. 1948. *Politics among Nations: The Struggle for Power and Peace.* New York: Knopf.

———. 1955. "Reflections on the State of Political Science." *Review of Politics* 17: 431–60.

———. 1965. "We Are Deluding Ourselves in Vietnam." *New York Times Magazine,* April 18. Reprinted in *The Viet-Nam Reader,* edited by M. Raskin and B. Fall, 37–45. New York: Vintage Books, 1967.

Niebuhr, Reinhold. 1932. *Moral Man and Immoral Society: A Study of Ethics and Politics.* Louisville, KY: John Knox Press.

Ninkovich, Frank. 1994. *Modernity and Power: A History of the Domino Theory in the Twentieth Century.* Chicago: University of Chicago Press.

Olson, Mancur. 1965. *The Logic of Collective Action: Public Goods and the Theory of Groups.* Cambridge, MA: Harvard University Press.

Oren, Ido. 2002. *Our Enemies and US: America's Rivalries and the Making of Political Science.* Ithaca, NY: Cornell University Press.

Pickering, Andrew. 1995. *The Mangle of Practice: Time, Agency, and Science.* Chicago: University of Chicago Press.

Porter, Theodore M. 1994. "The Death of the Object: Fin de Siècle Philosophy of Physics." In *Modernist Impulses in the Human Sciences, 1870–1930,* edited by Dorothy Ross, 128–51. Baltimore: Johns Hopkins University Press.

Price, Richard. 2008. "Moral Limit and Possibility in World Politics." *International Organization* 62: 191–220.

Ross, Dorothy. 1994. "Modernist Social Science in the Land of the New/Old." In *Modernist Impulses in the Human Sciences, 1870–1930,* 171–89. Baltimore: Johns Hopkins University Press.

Schmidt, Brian C. 1998. *The Political Discourse of Anarchy: A Disciplinary History of International Relations.* Albany: State University of New York Press.

Shaw, Albert. 1907. "Presidential Address: Third Annual Meeting of the American Political Science Association." *American Political Science Review* 1: 177–86.

Shimko, Keith I. 1992. "Realism, Neorealism, and American Liberalism." *Review of Politics* 54: 281–301.

Shotter, John. 1993. *Cultural Politics of Everyday Life.* Toronto: University of Toronto Press.

Singer, J. David. 1969. "The Incompleat Theorist: Insight without Evidence." In *Contending Approaches to International Politics,* 62–86. Princeton, NJ: Princeton University Press.

Thompson, Kenneth W. 1955. "Toward a Theory of International Politics." *American Political Science Review* 49: 733–46.

Wæver, Ole. 1996. "The Rise and Fall of the Inter-paradigm Debate." In *International Theory: Positivism and Beyond,* edited by Steve Smith, Ken Booth, and Marysia Zalewski, 149–85. Cambridge: Cambridge University Press.

Walker, Rob B. J. 1993. *Inside/Outside: International Relations as Political Theory.* Cambridge: Cambridge University Press.

Walt, Stephen M. 1987. *The Origins of Alliances.* Ithaca, NY: Cornell University Press.

Waltz, Kenneth N. 1979. *Theory of International Politics.* New York: McGraw-Hill.

———. 1997. "Evaluating Theories." *American Political Science Review* 91: 913–17.

Weber, Max. 1992 [1917/1919]. *Wissenschaft als Beruf / Politik als Beruf.* Edited by Wolfgang J. Mommsen and Wolfgang Schluchter. Tübingen: J. C. B. Mohr (Paul Siebeck).

Wight, Martin. 1960. "Why Is There No International Theory?" *International Relations* 2: 35–48.

Williams, Michael C. 2013. "In the Beginning: The International Relations Enlightenment and the Ends of International Relations Theory." *European Journal of International Relations* 19: 647–65.

Wilson, Woodrow. 1911. "The Law and the Facts: Presidential Address, Seventh Annual Meeting of the American Political Science Association." *American Political Science Review* 5: 1–11.

Chapter 11 · The Merits of Marginality

Akami, Tomoko. 2002. *Internationalization of the Pacific: The United States, Japan, and the Institute of Pacific Relations in War and Peace, 1919–45.* London: Routledge.

Amadae, S. M. 2003. *Rationalizing Capitalist Democracy: The Cold War Origins of Rational Choice Liberalism.* Chicago: University of Chicago Press.

Binder, Amy J., and Kate Wood. 2012. *Becoming Right: How Campuses Shape Young Conservatives.* Princeton, NJ: Princeton University Press.

Bjerre-Poulsen, Niels. 1991. "The Heritage Foundation: A Second Generation Think Tank." *Journal of Policy History* 3: 152–72.

Blumenthal, Sidney. 1986. *The Rise of the Counter-Establishment: From Conservative Ideology to Political Power.* New York: Crown.

Bockman, Johanna, and Gil Eyal. 2002. "Eastern Europe as a Laboratory for Economic Knowledge: The Transnational Roots of Neoliberalism." *American Journal of Sociology* 108: 310–52.

Bruce-Briggs, Barry, ed. 1979. *The New Class?* New Brunswick, NJ: Transaction Publishers.

Buckley, William F., Jr. 1951. *God and Man at Yale: The Superstitions of Academic Freedom.* Chicago: Regnery.

Callahan, David. 1999a. "$1 Billion for Conservative Ideas." *Nation*, April 26.

———. 1999b. *$1 Billion for Ideas: Conservative Think Tanks in the 1990s.* Washington, DC: National Committee for Responsive Philanthropy.

Campbell, Wesley G. 2000. *The Competition of Ideas: How My Colleagues and I Built the Hoover Institution.* Ottawa, IL: Jameson Books.

Cockett, Richard. 1995. *Thinking the Unthinkable: Think-Tanks and the Economic Counter-Revolution, 1931–1983.* Waukegan, IL: Fontana Press.

Covington, Sally. 1997. *Moving a Public Policy Agenda: The Strategic Philanthropy of Conservative Foundations.* Washington, DC: National Committee for Responsive Philanthropy.

Critchlow, Donald T. 1985. *The Brookings Institution, 1916–1952: Expertise and the Public Interest in a Democratic Society.* DeKalb: Northern Illinois University Press.

Cyphers, Christopher J. 2002. *The National Civic Federation and the Making of a New Liberalism, 1900–1915.* Westport, CT: Praeger.

Dahlberg, Jane. 1966. *The New York Bureau of Municipal Research, Pioneer in Government Administration.* New York: New York University Press.

Davidann, Jon Thares. 2001. "'Colossal Illusions': U.S.-Japanese Relations in the Institute of Pacific Relations, 1919–1938." *Journal of World History* 12: 155–82.

Diamond, Sara. 1995. *Roads to Dominion: Right-Wing Movements and Political Power in the United States.* New York: Guilford Press.

Diggins, John P. 1994 [1975]. *Up from Communism.* New York: Columbia University Press.

Dolny, Michael. 2000. "Think Tanks: The Rich Get Richer." *Extra!*, May 1. Fairness and Accuracy in Reporting. www.fair.org/index.php?page=12

Edwards, Lee. 1997. *The Power of Ideas: The Heritage Foundation at 25 Years.* Ottawa, IL: Jameson Books.

Ehrman, John. 1995. *The Rise of Neoconservatism: Intellectuals and Foreign Affairs, 1945–1994.* New Haven, CT: Yale University Press.

Evans, M. Stanton. 1961. *Revolt on the Campus.* Chicago: Regnery.

———. 1965. *The Liberal Establishment.* New York: Devin-Adair.

Fosse, Ethan, and Neil Gross. 2012. "Why Are Professors Liberal?" *Theory and Society* 41: 127–68.

Garnett, Mark, and Diane Stone. 1998. *Think Tanks of the World: Global Perspectives on Ideas, Policy, and Governance.* New York: St. Martin's Press.

Grose, Peter. 1996. *Continuing the Inquiry: The Council on Foreign Relations from 1921 to 1996.* New York: Council on Foreign Relations.

Gross, Neil, and Catherine Cheng. 2011. "Explaining Professors' Politics: Is It a Matter of Self-Selection?" In *Diversity in American Higher Education: Toward a More Comprehensive Approach,* edited by Lisa Stulberg and Sharon Weinberg, 178–94. New York: Routledge.

Hartwell, R. M. 1995. *History of the Mont Pèlerin Society.* Indianapolis, IN: Liberty Fund.

Higgott, Richard, and Diane Stone. 1994. "The Limits of Influence: Foreign Policy Think Tanks in Britain and the USA." *Review of International Studies* 20: 15–34.

Himmelstein, Jerome. 1990. *To the Right: The Transformation of American Conservatism.* Berkeley: University of California Press.

Hooper, Paul, ed. 1994. *Rediscovering the IPR: Proceedings of the First International Research Conference on the Institute of Pacific Relations.* Honolulu: University of Hawaii Press.

Howes, Laura L. 1993. "Are There Benefits to Marginality?" *Medieval Feminist Forum* 15: 3–4.

Jenkins, J. Craig, and Craig Eckert. 1989. "The Corporate Elite, the New Conservative Network, and Reaganomics." *Critical Sociology* 16: 121–44.

Kelley, John L. 1997. *Bringing the Market Back In: The Political Revitalization of Market Liberalism.* New York: New York University Press.

King, Lawrence P., and Ivan Szelenyi. 2004. *Theories of the New Class: Intellectuals and Power.* Minneapolis: University of Minnesota Press.

Klaidman, Stephen. 1977. "A Look at Former President Ford's Think Tank Institution." *Washington Post,* February 20.

Krehely, Jeff, Meaghan House, and Emily Kernan. 2004. *Axis of Ideology: Conservative Foundations and Public Policy.* Washington, DC: National Committee for Responsive Philanthropy.

Martin, John Levi. 2011. *The Explanation of Social Action.* New York: Oxford University Press.

McCright, Aaron M., and Riley E. Dunlap. 2003. "Defeating Kyoto: The Conservative Movement's Impact on U.S. Climate Change Policy." *Social Problems* 50(3): 348–73.

McGann, James G. 2012. "2011 Global Go To Think Tanks Report and Policy Advice." Report. Philadelphia: Think Tanks and Civil Societies Program, University of Pennsylvania.

McGann, James G., and R. Kent Weaver, eds. 2000. *Think Tanks and Civil Societies: Catalysts for Ideas and Action.* New Brunswick, NJ: Transaction Publishers.

Medvetz, Thomas. 2010. "'Public Policy Is Like a Having a Vaudeville Act': Languages of Duty and Difference among Think Tank–Affiliated Policy Experts." *Qualitative Sociology* 33: 549–62.

———. 2012. *Think Tanks in America.* Chicago: Chicago University Press.

Micklethwait, John, and Adrian Wooldridge. 2005. *The Right Nation: Conservative Power in America.* New York: Penguin.

Miller, Louis. 1989. *Operations Research and Policy Analysis at RAND, 1968–1988.* Santa Monica, CA: RAND Corporation.

Mirowski, Philip, and Dieter Plehwe, eds. 2009. *The Road from Mont Pèlerin: The Making of the Neoliberal Thought Collective.* Cambridge, MA: Harvard University Press.

Muller, Christopher. 1996. "The Institute of Economic Affairs: Undermining the Post-War Consensus." *Contemporary British History* 10: 88–110.

Nagy-Zekmi, Silvia, and Karyn Hollis, eds. 2010. *Truth to Power: Public Intellectuals In and Out of Academe.* Newcastle upon Tyne, UK: Cambridge Scholars Publishing.

Nash, George H. 1988. *The Life of Herbert Hoover: The Humanitarian, 1914–1917.* New York: Norton.

Patenaude, Bertrand M. 2006. *A Wealth of Ideas: Revelations from the Hoover Institution Archives.* Stanford, CA: Stanford University Press.

Paul, Gary N. 1974. "The Development of the Hoover Institution on War, Revolution, and Peace Library, 1919–1944." PhD dissertation. University of California, Berkeley. Ann Arbor: ProQuest/UMI.

Phillips-Fein, Kim. 2009. *Invisible Hands: The Making of the Conservative Movement from the New Deal to Reagan.* New York: Norton.

Pierson, Paul, and Jacob Hacker. 2011. "The Politics of Organized Combat." In *Winner-Take-All Politics: How Washington Made the Rich Richer—and Turned Its Back on the Middle Class*, 116–36. New York: Simon & Schuster.

Plehwe, Dieter. 2006. *Neoliberal Hegemony: A Global Critique*. London: Taylor & Francis.

Powell, Lewis F., Jr. 1971. "Attack on the American Free Enterprise System." Memorandum to Eugene B. Sydnor Jr., August 23.

Raucher, Alan. 1978. "The First Foreign Affairs Think Tanks." *American Quarterly* 30: 493–513.

Rich, Andrew. 2004. *Think Tanks, Public Policy, and the Politics of Expertise*. Cambridge: Cambridge University Press.

Rich, Andrew Owen, and R. Kent Weaver. 1998. "Advocates and Analysts: Think Tanks and the Politicization of Expertise." In *Interest Group Politics*, 5th ed., edited by Allan J. Cigler and Burdett A. Loomis, 235–54. Washington, DC: Congressional Quarterly Press.

Saunders, Charles B. 1966. *The Brookings Institution: A Fifty-Year History*. Washington, DC: Brookings Institution.

Schorske, Carl E. 1998. *Thinking with History: Explorations in the Passage to Modernism*. Princeton, NJ: Princeton University Press.

Schriftgiesser, Karl. 1960. *Business Comes of Age: The Story of the Committee for Economic Development and Its Impact upon the Economic Policies of the United States, 1942–1960*. New York: Harper.

Schulzinger, Robert D. 1984. *The Wise Men of Foreign Affairs: The History of the Council on Foreign Relations*. New York: Columbia University Press.

Simon, William E. 1980. *A Time for Action*. New York: Reader's Digest Press.

Small, Albion W. 1895. "The Civic Federation of Chicago: A Study in Social Dynamics." *American Journal of Sociology* 1: 79–103.

Smith, Bruce L. R. 1966. *The RAND Corporation: Case Study of a Nonprofit Advisory Corporation*. Cambridge, MA: Harvard University Press.

Smith, James A. 1991a. *Brookings at Seventy-Five*. Washington, DC: Brookings Institution Press.

———. 1991b. *The Idea Brokers: Think Tanks and the Rise of the New Policy Elite*. New York: Free Press.

———. 1993. *Strategic Calling: The Center for Strategic and International Studies, 1962–1992*. Washington, DC: Center for Strategic and International Studies.

Stefanic, Jean, and Richard Delgado. 1996. *No Mercy: How Conservative Think Tanks and Foundations Changed America's Social Agenda*. Philadelphia: Temple University Press.

Steinfels, Peter. 1979. *The Neoconservatives: The Men Who Are Changing America's Politics*. New York: Simon & Schuster.

Stone, Diane, and Andrew Denham, eds. 2004. *Think Tank Traditions: Policy Research and the Politics of Ideas*. Manchester: Manchester University Press.

Teles, Steven. 2008. *The Rise of the Conservative Legal Movement: The Battle for Control of the Law*. Princeton, NJ: Princeton University Press.

Trattner, Walter I. 2007. *From Poor Law to Welfare State: A History of Social Welfare in America*. 6th ed. New York: Simon & Schuster.

United Nations Development Program. 2003. *Thinking the Unthinkable: From Thought to Policy.* Bratislava, Slovakia: UNDP Regional Bureau for Europe and the Commonwealth of Independent States.

Weaver, R. Kent, and Paul B. Stares, eds. 2001. *Guidance for Governance: Comparing Alternative Sources of Public Policy Advice.* Tokyo: Japan Center for International Exchange.

Wiarda, Howard J. 2009. *Conservative Brain Trust: The Rise, Fall, and Rise Again of the American Enterprise Institute.* Plymouth, UK: Lexington Books.

Williams, Malcolm. 2000. *Science and Social Science: An Introduction.* London: Routledge.

Wood, Peter. 2011a. "Preferred Colleagues." *Chronicle of Higher Education* blog, April 6. http://chronicle.com/blogs/innovations/preferred-colleagues/29160

————. 2011b. "Unnatural Selection." *Chronicle of Higher Education* blog, March 22. http://chronicle.com/blogs/innovations/unnatural-selection/28946

Yamaoka, Michio, ed. 1999. *The Institute of Pacific Relations: Pioneer International Nongovernmental Organization in the Asia-Pacific Region.* Tokyo: Waseda University, Institute of Asia-Pacific Studies.

AMY J. BINDER is a professor of sociology at the University of California, San Diego. She is the author of *Contentious Curricula: Afrocentrism and Creationism in American Public Schools* (Princeton University Press, 2004) and *Becoming Right: How Campuses Shape Young Conservatives* (Princeton University Press, 2012, with Kate Wood).

CLEM BROOKS is Rudy Professor of Sociology at Indiana University. His interests are in the areas of political sociology, political psychology, and quantitative methods. With Jeff Manza, he is the author of *Social Cleavages and Political Change* (Oxford University Press, 1999), *Why Welfare States Persist* (University of Chicago Press, 2007), and *Whose Rights?* (Russell Sage Foundation, 2013). His current projects include research on the politics of the Great Recession and a study of ethnic and racial cues in the formation of policy attitudes.

KYLE DODSON is an assistant professor of sociology at the University of California, Merced. His current research focuses on the institutional factors that drive participation in both conventional and unconventional forms of political participation. Some of his recent studies include investigations into changes in social movement activities over time, the consequences of party polarization for voting behavior, and the relevance of foreign policy issues for national elections.

ETHAN FOSSE is a PhD candidate in the Department of Sociology at Harvard University. His research focuses on cultural sociology, statistics, and poverty, with a particular emphasis on the quantitative analysis of culture. He has written about culture and politics, social networks, and computational methods. Currently he is working on three interrelated projects: a cross-cultural analysis of political values, using millions of respondents around the world; a systematic study of the cultural aspects of severe poverty, especially among black youths; and a series of theoretical works setting a new agenda for cultural analysis in the social sciences. He is a junior fellow of the American Academy of Political and Social Science, a National Science Foundation Graduate Research Fellow, and a doctoral fellow in the Multidisciplinary Program in Inequality and Social Policy at the Harvard Kennedy School.

JEREMY FREESE is a professor of sociology and a faculty fellow in the Institute for Policy Research at Northwestern University. He has published numerous articles on the relationship between biology, psychological differences, and divergent social outcomes. He is also co-principal investigator of Time-sharing Experiments in Social Sciences, a project to promote survey experiments in social science.

NEIL GROSS is a professor of sociology at the University of British Columbia. He is the author of *Richard Rorty: The Making of an American Philosopher* (University of Chicago Press, 2008) and *Why Are Professors Liberal and Why Do Conservatives Care?* (Harvard University Press, 2013) and coeditor of *Durkheim's Philosophy Lectures: Notes from the Lycée de Sens Course, 1883–4* (Cambridge University Press, 2004, with Robert Alun Jones) and *Social Knowledge in the Making* (University of Chicago Press, 2011, with Charles Camic and Michèle Lamont).

PATRICK THADDEUS JACKSON is a professor of international relations and associate dean for undergraduate education in the School of International Service at American University. His most recent book, *The Conduct of Inquiry in International Relations* (Routledge, 2010), received the 2012 Yale H. Ferguson award for the book that most advances the vibrancy of international relations as a pluralist field.

ANDREW JEWETT is an associate professor in the History Department and the Social Studies program at Harvard University and the author of *Science, Democracy, and the American University: From the Civil War to the Cold War* (Cambridge University Press, 2012). Other recent writings include "Academic Freedom and Political Change: American Lessons"; "Canonizing Dewey: Columbia Naturalism, Logical Empiricism, and the Idea of American Philosophy"; "The Politics of Knowledge in 1960s America"; "The Social Sciences, Philosophy, and the Cultural Turn in the 1930s USDA"; and "Science and Religion in American Thought." He is currently a fellow at the National Humanities Center.

JOSEPH MA is an undergraduate student at the University of British Columbia, majoring in economics and sociology. He has special interests in social network analysis and computational social science.

THOMAS MEDVETZ is an assistant professor of sociology at the University of California, San Diego. His book *Think Tanks in America* was published in 2012 by the University of Chicago Press.

JULIE A. REUBEN is Charles Warren Professor of the History of American Education at the Harvard Graduate School of Education. She is interested in the intersection between American thought and culture and educational institutions and practice. She is the author of *Making of the Modern University: Intellectual Transformation and the Marginalization of Morality* (University of Chicago Press, 1996), as well as articles related to campus activism in the 1960s and the history of civics in public schools. Reuben is currently researching social science instruction in post–World War II America.

FABIO ROJAS is an associate professor of sociology at Indiana University. He is the author of *From Black Power to Black Studies: How a Radical Social Movement Became an Academic Discipline* (Johns Hopkins University Press, 2007). In addition to his work on black studies, Rojas works on the anti–Iraq War movement, social media and politics, and organizational behavior in medical settings.

SOLON SIMMONS is an associate professor in the School for Conflict Analysis and Resolution at George Mason University. He is a sociologist with interests spanning the range of disciplinary knowledge, with special focus on political ideas, social stratification, cultural sociology, collective memory, and the symbolic history of political dysfunction. His first book, *The Eclipse of Equality: Arguing America on Meet the Press* (Stanford University Press, 2013), tells the story of the atrophy in post–World War II America of one of the canonical categories of the moral imagination: equality.

KATE WOOD is a doctoral candidate in the Department of Sociology at the University of California, San Diego. Her dissertation research focuses on culture and education, with an emphasis on the role played by specific facets of the campus in students' perceptions of themselves and others and the impact of these perceptions on their interactions, aspirations, and understandings of their education.